BY THE EDITORS OF CONSUMER GUIDE®

WHOLE SEWING CATALOG

Simon and Schuster

New York

Published by Simon and Schuster
A Division of Gulf + Western Corporation
New York, New York 10020

LIBRARY OF CONGRESS CATALOGING IN
PUBLICATION DATA

Main entry under title:
Whole Sewing Catalog.
    (A Fireside book)
    Includes index.
    1. Sewing — Equipment and supplies — Catalogs.
    2. Sewing

I. Consumer guide.
TT715.W53   646.2'1   78-15439

Contents

Cover Design: Frank E. Peiler

Cover Photograph: Mel Weiner

Illustrations: Sandy Zimnicki

Sewing Machine Test Reports: Betty Silverman

Acknowledgements: The Editors of CONSUMER GUIDE® would like to thank Vogue Fabric Shop, Evanston, Ilinois, for permitting us to use some of their merchandise for photography. Our thanks also go to Sears, Roebuck and Co., Northbrook, Illinois, for their cooperation for purposes of photography.

The Editors of CONSUMER GUIDE® have made every effort to ensure the accuracy of the approximate retail prices given in this publication. Please note that prices may vary from coast to coast within the United States. Additionally, many of the items covered are imported and their prices could change with fluctuations in the value of the American dollar.

Before You Begin

Perhaps you dread picking up a needle, so you spend a fortune on dressmakers and ready-to-wear clothes (often shoddily made). Then again, maybe you learned to sew at your mother's knee but aren't quite up-to-date on the latest sewing techniques or sewing aids. Maybe you feel competent with most sewing methods but always have trouble with those pesky zippers or set-in sleeves. If so, the WHOLE SEWING CATALOG is for you. CONSUMER GUIDE®'s sewing experts provide something useful for everyone from the novice to the experienced sewer.

Step-by-step, the WHOLE SEWING CATALOG describes and clarifies the fundamentals of sewing, each point illustrated with large, easy to understand drawings. Professional tips on shortcuts and gadgets that simplify a sewing technique appear in boldface type right next to the relevant step. Nothing has been overlooked in making sewing as pleasureable and uncomplicated as possible. The WHOLE SEWING CATALOG also guides you through the marketplace of patterns, fabrics, sewing aids and sewing machines — brand by brand — offering sound purchasing advice.

The WHOLE SEWING CATALOG is divided in such a way that you can turn to the section that interests you at the moment without missing vital information given elsewhere. For example, if you are interested in buying a new sewing machine right now, turn to that section first. Keep this book next to your machine as a handy sewing reference when constructing your garment. Each project is complete unto itself, with the appropriate tips and helpful hints.

Note: In accordance with the current changeover to metric measurements in this country, all measurements in the WHOLE SEWING CATALOG are given in inches with their metric equivalents in parentheses. These are the metric equivalents standardized and approved by the Pattern Fashion Industry.

Setting Up

Since very few of us can afford the luxury of spending a whole day at the sewing machine, it becomes very important that the time spent sewing is used efficiently. The arrangement of the sewing area, whether it is in a room by itself or just a temporary setup in the kitchen, should be done so everything is within reach when seated at the sewing machine.

Make yourself as comfortable as possible. A secretary's chair is a good investment if you do a lot of sewing. Use an adjustable ironing board that is set at table height and positioned at right angles to the sewing machine on either the left or right. Swivel around on your secretary's chair whenever you need to iron and see how much time and effort you save.

A well lighted working area is a must. A clamp-on desk lamp with a jointed arm can be affixed to your sewing machine cabinet or sewing table. It allows you to direct light precisely where needed. A bulletin board placed above and in front of the sewing machine gives you a place to tack up your pattern instructions and keeps them off the floor. Sewing can be messy so place a wastebasket by your sewing area and use it.

Time-Saving Tips

Organize each project so you complete as many steps as possible at a time before going on to the next sewing activity. For example, cut out all garment, interfacing and lining pieces at one time so you don't have to do small cutting jobs during the garment construction.

If you don't have a large table for cutting, use a cardboard cutting board spread out on a small table, twin size bed or the floor.

If you have more than one sewing project scheduled, do all the cutting at once. Stack the pieces of each project in a neat pile and store them in a plastic bag until they are to be used.

Pin garment pieces right sides together at seamlines as you remove the pattern pieces from the fashion fabric. This can be done for most garment pieces unless darts, trim or other special sewing techniques are first required.

If you are using fusible interfacing, apply all the interfacing pieces to their corresponding garment pieces at one time.

Sew as many seams as you can and all darts at one sitting before pressing. Go back to the machine, sew more seams and follow by another pressing session. This is much faster than sewing and pressing each seam individually.

Choosing A Pattern

The beginning of the sewing process starts with a series of decisions. What type of garment, what kind of fabric — the size and figure type of the pattern. How you handle these decisions will determine the success of your project. The following information will help you make wise choices.

The first decision for any sewing project is what pattern to use and the second is what fabric to buy. To make these two important decisions we suggest you sit down with all the newspapers, magazines and mail order catalogs you can find. Especially collect retail store, mail order catalogs because they show ready-to-wear fashions very clearly.

Why look at ready-to-wear fashions if you plan to make them yourself? Because you probably want the items you make to look professional. The "loving hands at home" look tends to be amateurish. Choosing the right pattern and finding the right fabric have as much to do with a professional look as the quality of your workmanship. If you make the right decisions, you will be happy with the results even if every stitch isn't perfect. If your choice of pattern and fabric is wrong you will not be happy with the garment no matter how good the workmanship. It's possible to learn these things from looking carefully at ready-to-wear fashions.

Take a good look at advertised fashions and designs in the editorial sections of all fashion publications. Cut out designs you like and start a file of ideas. When you cut out pictures be sure to include a description of the garment, fabric, sizes and price. Include the price because it is always nice to know how much money you are saving. The size range should be included because not every garment is good in every size. The fabric and garment description will help you choose the correct pattern and fabric combination.

Look carefully at the picture you like best and ask yourself why you like it. Is it the loose or fitted silhouette, that particular collar, or sleeve? You should be able to say to yourself, "this dress is right for me because. . . ."

The next step is to look carefully at the ready-to-wear garment fabric. Is it a print or a solid, big print or a small one, a soft clingy fabric or firm crisp one? Will the fabric flatter your figure? Is there more than one fabric in the garment? What colors does it come in? Will your accessories match the color?

Trust the fabric choice of the manufacturer because he can't afford to make mistakes. When manufacturers show their seasonal lines to store buyers, buyers won't order if they don't think the fabric is right for the style. Every season many samples never go into production or stores because buyers didn't like them.

Figure Flattering Selections

We suggest following three ground rules that are not difficult to remember or apply when selecting a pattern to flatter your figure.

The first is to *divide and conquer*. Divide bust, waist and hips into small parts with vertical seams and the parts will add up to less than the whole. For example, a princess dress is usually made with three panels in front and three in back. The vertical seams divide bust, waist and hips making them seem smaller.

The second rule is to *consider proportion*. Very often circumference measurements are not large but they are not in good proportion. For example, if your waist is 24 inches (61cm) and your hips measure 38 inches (96.5cm), you don't have huge hips, but they are slightly out of proportion to your waist. Make your waistlines and waistbands slightly loose because tight waistlines and waistbands will make hips appear to balloon, emphasizing the difference between waist and hips. Then apply the *divide and conquer* rule by wearing gored skirts which divide hips into small vertical parts. This same rule works for a busty woman with a small waist and hips. Don't wear clothes that are tight through the bust and waist. Bring bust and waist into better proportion by wearing princess seams, V-necklines or a bow-tied top. A woman with this type of figure should also wear a waistline that is a bit loose.

The third rule is to *accentuate the positive*. In other words, emphasize your best features. An empire dress accentuates a small, pretty bustline. A wide neckline shows off a good neck and shoulders. A pretty collar draws attention to a pretty face.

How To Use Counter Catalogs

Your next step is to go to the stores. Check windows and interior displays for the kind of clothes you wish to make. This may prompt you into buying a garment instead of making it, especially if you are in a hurry. But, we also think when you see the prices, fit and quality of workmanship, you will run, not walk, to the nearest pattern counter.

By now you should have some

pretty firm ideas about the garment you want. Can you find a pattern that will come as close as possible to duplicating your picture? We think you can. Home sewing fashions used to be six to nine months behind ready-to-wear garments in design. Today pattern companies are just as anxious to get the newest hot fashions into stores as are ready-to-wear manufacturers. The four largest suppliers — Vogue, Butterick, McCalls, and Simplicity — send representatives to Europe. They also see all the important ready-to-wear lines in New York. Consequently, looking through the catalogs of these companies is like looking at a "who's who" of contemporary designers. This is not to say you must make a designer pattern to have good design. The name is nice, but you are looking for a design that is as close as possible to your idea.

How do you find what you're looking for in the big catalogs? After all, catalogs are divided into so many sections it can be puzzling. There are easy sections, designer sections, sportswear, dress shop, separates and several other categories. Obviously, if you're after a dress you'll look in the dress section, but don't overlook evening or sportswear, which also have dress designs. Some catalogs have subdivisions according to figure type, such as Half-Size, Petite, Junior and more. We'll talk about these figure types later.

If you're a beginner, it would be wise to look for an easy pattern. All pattern companies offer them under their own special names, but there are details easy patterns have in common no matter which company produces them. They all have few main pattern pieces, usually from one to four. There are no complicated sewing details and no big fitting problems. The pattern instruction sheets are as simple as possible with extra clear diagrams and instructions. We suggest trying some from each company to see which ones you like best.

The art work in the counter

catalog is meant to convey information as well as attractiveness. Often there are photographs to show how the garment will look on a real person. Always there are drawings to show not only how the garment will look front and back but where the seams and darts are placed.

There will be several different views of the pattern on the catalog page. You may be able to make a dress with or without sleeves or in a long and short length. In some sportswear patterns you will find pants and a skirt, perhaps a jacket and vest as well. Such wardrobe patterns are usually a good buy because you pay only slightly more for four or five items than you would for a single skirt or pants pattern. There is no need to make all the pieces at once. Take care of your pattern and use the same one to make the pants in wool for winter and the skirt in cotton for summer.

There is even more to be learned from the catalog art work such as suggested fabrics. If the garment is suitable for plaid, one of the drawings will show it in plaid and you know the plaid can be matched at the seamlines. If plaid is not shown, that does not rule it out completely, but it does mean you may not be able to match plaids perfectly. Of course, if the pattern says, "Not suitable for plaids" do not try a plaid fabric.

If the pattern is shown in a print fabric, lines are usually simple and the fashion message is in the silhouette and print itself. Using a print fabric for a complicated design is not a good idea because print obscures and loses detail. For instance, making tiny tucks on a blouse with small print is probably a waste of time because they won't be seen.

In the back of every counter catalog is an index. If you have seen a picture of a pattern in a magazine and made a note of the number, there is no need to go through the whole catalog. The index will give you the page.

The counter catalogs have yardage charts and back views. However, other information varies with each company. Vogue includes suggested fabrics; Butterick doesn't. Vogue prints the pattern description from the back of the envelope unlike other companies. Bust or waist size is usually on the catalog page, but the full measurement chart is in back of the book. All companies tell you if the pattern is designed for knits and print a gauge in back of the book and on the pattern envelope so you can check for the proper amount of stretch. The information on the catalog page is designed to sell the pattern in the right figure type and size.

Additional information will be on the pattern envelope.

One more word about your original idea — the ready-to-wear design you really like. When you study the catalog, if you find something close to your picture, but not exactly like it, remember you are after *the look* of the original. You may find a pattern that has raglan sleeves but the picture has set-in sleeves. If the look is the same in all other respects, go with the pattern. Remember, you can combine two patterns from the same company or make adjustments in one

pattern. For example, if the dress is right but the pattern doesn't have pockets, buy a little extra fabric and add pockets. If there is a pointed collar, but your design shows a rounded collar, round the points on the collar pattern piece.

If this is your first project you'll probably want to follow the pattern exactly, but the more you sew, the more you will realize the pattern is a starting point. Our aim is to help you be happy and successful in your sewing endeavors and help you choose the right pattern and fabric combination.

Multi-Size Patterns

Multi-size patterns are a concept that have been around for many years but have only recently been adopted by big pattern companies. European pattern companies such as Burda, printed in Germany, now available in the U.S.A., have used multi-size patterns for years. The idea behind multi-size patterns in this country first started in the late 1960s when sewing with knit fabrics became popular. Small pattern companies printed specialty knit patterns and put all sizes for each style on one heavy white pattern sheet. This was done originally for economy but women soon realized it made simple alterations much easier. These master patterns, as they were called, were designed to be traced rather than cut out and used like regular patterns.

Now large pattern companies have all jumped on the bandwagon and offer some designs with more than one size in the envelope. This is a great help to the woman who is a combination of two sizes — perhaps a size 10 bust and size 12 hips. On a two-piece dress or pants/blouse combination you simply use the size 10 top and the

size 12 bottom. On a one-piece dress with a waistline seam, take your curved ruler and draw a new cutting line connecting the waist

and hips. These patterns save an enormous amount of adjusting and measuring and will give you a good fit the easy way.

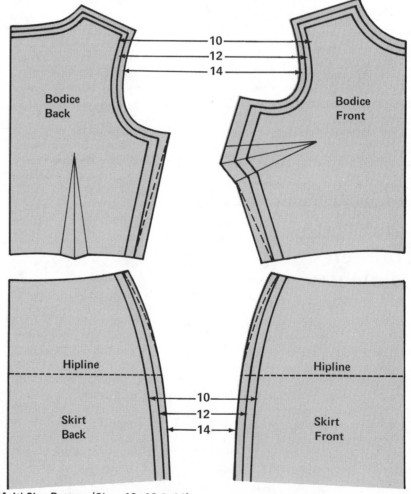

Multi-Size Pattern (Sizes 10, 12 & 14)

8

Today, many small pattern companies specialize in "knits only" patterns but most of them offer patterns that can also be used with woven fabrics. All offer patterns for every member of the family and some specialize in unique designs such as ethnic styles, western wear, equestrian attire and outer or ski wear. A list of these companies and their specialities can be found in the *Buyer's Guide to Patterns* section.

Tip

Pellon's new product Perma-Trace can be used with "master" patterns. It is a tracing tissue and pattern maker in one and can also be used for making test garments. It comes pre-packaged and measures 13.1 feet by 25 inches (4m by 63.5 cm). Manufactured by Pellon Corp.

Tip

The curved, plastic Fashion Ruler is a valuable aid for making adjustments. It is also good to use for armhole and waistline alterations. Manufactured by Fashionetics Inc.

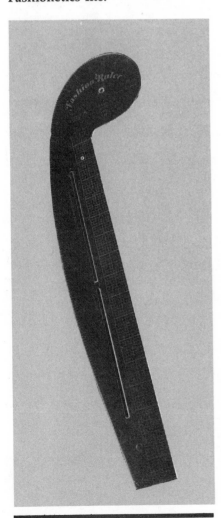

Selecting The Right Figure Type

It's easy to notice, looking through various catalogs, that patterns are classified according to figure type as well as styles and size ranges. For women the figure types are Misses', Junior, Half-Size, Women's, Miss Petite, and Junior Petite. For children there are Infants, Toddlers, Child, Girls, and Boys. Teenagers are divided into Young Junior/Teen and Teenage Boy. Some pattern companies offer Chubbie Girls and, of course, all companies have Men's patterns. The following chart will show the difference between various figure types.

Many years ago the pattern industry started with Misses' patterns. Other figure types were developed as variations of the Misses' measurements. When we talk about bust position, we compare it to the Misses' by saying a Junior has a high bust position and a Half-Size has a low bust position. What we mean is higher or lower than the Misses'.

If you have a Junior build you will have fewer pattern adjustments to make if you buy a Junior pattern. The only difficulty is that pattern companies feature more styles in the Misses' figure type. Our advice is to buy a

pattern in your figure type if possible. Otherwise, be prepared to make a few adjustments in order to obtain a perfect fit.

Adjustments are not difficult. The circumference measurements on patterns of similar size but different figure types are very close. For example, there is only ½ inch (13 mm) difference between a Misses' size 10 and a Junior size 9 at the bust, waist and hips. Such a small difference is easily adjusted during the construction process as is the 1 inch (25 mm) in height. Where fit is concerned, the important difference is the higher bust position of the Junior and square rather than slanted shoulders. Half-Size figures have the same problems in reverse with bust position lower and shoulders slanted more than a Misses'.

How do you decide on your figure type? Read the descriptions of different types on the figure type chart. Consider your height, bust position and back neck to waist measurement. If you've been buying Junior or Half-Size clothes buy the same type pattern. Also, if you've been using Misses' patterns which don't fit properly, try a different figure type.

YOUNG JUNIOR/ TEEN

About 5'1" to 5'3" (1.55 to 1.60 m) tall— larger waist in proportion to small, high bust

JUNIOR PETITE

About 5' to 5'1" (1.53 to 1.55 m) tall—well- developed figure— shorter waist length than Junior

JUNIOR

About 5'4" to 5'5" (1.63 to 1.65 m) tall— higher bust and shorter waist length than Miss

MISS PETITE

About 5'2" to 5'4" (1.57 to 1.63 m) tall— shorter waist length, larger waist than Miss

MISS

About 5'5" to 5'6" (1.65 to 1.68 m) tall—well- proportioned, well- developed— the "average" figure

HALF-SIZE

About 5'2" to 5'3" (1.58 to 1.60 m) tall—fully developed figure

WOMAN

About 5'5" to 5'6" (1.65 to 1.68 m) tall— larger overall proportions than Miss

Figure Types

TODDLER

Taller than a baby, shorter than a Child

CHILD

Taller with wider shoulders and back than Toddler

GIRL

About 4'2" to 5'1" (1.27 to 1.55 m) tall—no bust develop- ment

CHUBBIE

Same height as Girl but weighs more than average

BOY

About 4' to 4'10" (1.22 to 1.47 m) tall

TEEN BOY

About 5'1" to 5'8" (1.55 to 1.73 m) tall

MAN

About 5'10" (1.78 m) tall —average adult male

Deciding Your Right Size

Size and figure type aren't the same. To find your correct size you need to know your body measurements. Start by filling in Your Personal Measurement Chart. Ask a friend to help you measure — it's difficult to measure yourself accurately. Using a non-stretch, plastic coated tape measure, take measurements over your usual undergarments but never over dresses, blouses, slips or pants. Tie a string snugly around your waist; the string will settle at the smallest part of your body indicating your natural waistline.

Have your helper measure you as shown in the following illustrations and record each measurement in the second column of the chart.

Height: Measure against the wall without shoes.

(A) High Bust: Measure around the chest, under the arms, directly above the bust.

(B) Full Bust or Chest: Measure around the fullest part of the bust or chest keeping the tape measure level around the back.

(C) Waist: Measure around the waist over the string.

(D) Hips: Measure at the fullest part of the hips.

(E) Hip Drop: Measure the distance from the waist to the fullest part of the hips.

(F) Back Waist Length: Measure from the prominent vertebrae at the base of the neck to the waist string.

(G) Bust Position: Measure from the center of the shoulder to the high point of the bust.

(H) Front Waist Length: Measure from the center of the shoulder, down over the bust, to the waist string.

(I) Shoulder Width: Measure from the base of the neck to the tip of the shoulder bone.

(J) Back Width: Measure across the back 5 inches (12.5cm) below the neck bone.

(K) Sleeve Length: Measure from the point of the shoulder to the wrist bone with a slightly bent elbow.

(L) Shoulder to Elbow: Measure from the point of the shoulder to the point of the bent elbow.

(M) Upper Arm: Measure around the fullest part of the upper arm.

(N) Back Skirt Length: Measure from the center back at the waist to the desired length.

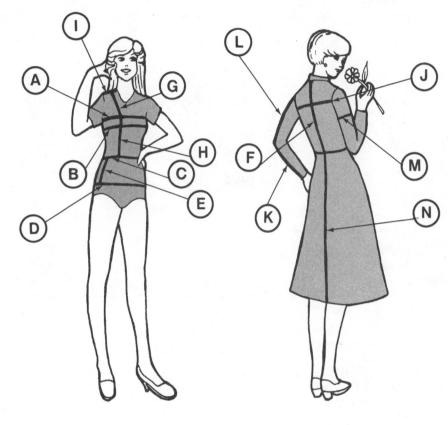

Tip

Take your measurements using the Dritz Lifetime Tape Measure. It has a replacement guarantee against stretching or tearing during normal use and the centimeters on one side will help you make metric conversions. Manufactured by Scovill, Sewing Notions Divisions.

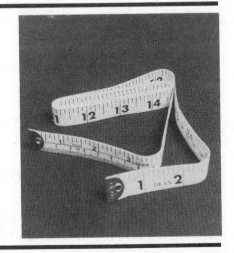

YOUR PERSONAL MEASUREMENT CHART

Where To Measure	Your Body Measurements	Standard Body or Pattern Measurements	Amount of Adjustment
Height			
High Bust*			
Full Bust* or Chest			
Waist*			
Hips*			
Hip Drop			
Back Waist Length*			
Bust Position			
Front Waist Length			
Shoulder Width			
Back Width			
Sleeve Length			
Shoulder to Elbow			
Upper Arm			
Back Skirt Length			

* Measurements marked with an asterisk determine pattern size.

Fill in the third column of the chart with body measurements given in the Standard Body Measurement Chart if using a Vogue, Butterick, Simplicity or McCalls pattern. If you are using a pattern from another company it will give you a body measurement chart or tell you it uses the same standard chart as other companies.

Finished garment lengths are not on the chart since they change with current fashion.

Circumference of the upper arm, bust position, shoulder and back width should be measured from actual pattern pieces. *(continued)*

STANDARD BODY MEASUREMENTS
Centimeters

MISSES'

Size	6	8	10	12	14	16	18	20
Bust	78	80	83	87	92	97	102	107
Waist	58	61	64	67	71	76	81	87
Hip	83	85	88	92	97	102	107	112
Back Waist Length	39.5	40	40.5	41.5	42	42.5	43	44

MISS PETITE

Size	6mp	8mp	10mp	12mp	14mp	16mp
Bust	78	80	83	87	92	97
Waist	60	62	65	69	73	78
Hip	83	85	88	92	97	102
Back Waist Length	37	37.5	38	39	39.5	40

STANDARD BODY MEASUREMENTS
Centimeters

HALF-SIZE

Size	10½	12½	14½	16½	18½	20½	22½	24½
Bust	84	89	94	99	104	109	114	119
Waist	69	74	79	84	89	96	102	108
Hip	89	94	99	104	109	116	122	128
Back Waist Length	38	39	39.5	40	40.5	40.5	41	41.5

YOUNG JUNIOR/TEEN

Size	5/6	7/8	9/10	11/12	13/14	15/16
Bust	71	74	78	81	85	89
Waist	56	58	61	64	66	69
Hip	79	81	85	89	93	97
Back Waist Length	34.5	35.5	37	38	39	40

JUNIOR

Size	5	7	9	11	13	15
Bust	76	79	81	85	89	94
Waist	57	60	62	65	69	74
Hip	81	84	87	90	94	99
Back Waist Length	38	39	39.5	40	40.5	41.5

JUNIOR PETITE

Size	3jp	5jp	7jp	9jp	11jp	13jp
Bust	76	79	81	84	87	89
Waist	56	58	61	64	66	69
Hip	79	81	84	87	89	92
Back Waist Length	35.5	36	37	37.5	38	39

WOMEN'S

Size	38	40	42	44	46	48	50
Bust	107	112	117	122	127	132	137
Waist	89	94	99	105	112	118	124
Hip	112	117	122	127	132	137	142
Back Waist Length	44	44	44.5	45	45	45.5	46

GIRLS'

Size	7	8	10	12	14
Breast	66	69	73	76	81
Waist	58	60	62	65	67
Hip	69	71	76	81	87
Back Waist Length	29.5	31	32.5	34.5	36
Approx. Height	127	132	142	149	155

STANDARD BODY MEASUREMENTS
Inches

MISSES'

Size	6	8	10	12	14	16	18	20
Bust	30½	31½	32½	34	36	38	40	42
Waist	23	24	25	26½	28	30	32	34
Hip	32½	33½	34½	36	38	40	42	44
Back Waist Length	15½	15¾	16	16¼	16½	16¾	17	17¼

MISS PETITE

Size	6mp	8mp	10mp	12mp	14mp	16mp
Bust	30½	31½	32½	34	36	38
Waist	23½	24½	25½	27	28½	30½
Hip	32½	33½	34½	36	38	40
Back Waist Length	14½	14¾	15	15¼	15½	15¾

HALF-SIZE

Size	10½	12½	14½	16½	18½	20½	22½	24½
Bust	33	35	37	39	41	43	45	47
Waist	27	29	31	33	35	37½	40	42½
Hip	35	37	39	41	43	45½	48	50½
Back Waist Length	15	15¼	15½	15¾	15⅞	16	16⅛	16¼

YOUNG JUNIOR/TEEN

Size	5/6	7/8	9/10	11/12	13/14	15/16
Bust	28	29	30½	32	33½	35
Waist	22	23	24	25	26	27
Hip	31	32	33½	35	36½	38
Back Waist Length	13½	14	14½	15	15⅜	15¾

JUNIOR

Size	5	7	9	11	13	15
Bust	30	31	32	33½	35	37
Waist	22½	23½	24½	25½	27	29
Hip	32	33	34	35½	37	39
Back Waist Length	15	15¼	15½	15¾	16	16¼

JUNIOR PETITE

Size	3jp	5jp	7jp	9jp	11jp	13jp
Bust	30	31	32	33	34	35
Waist	22	23	24	25	26	27
Hip	31	32	33	34	35	36
Back Waist Length	14	14¼	14½	14¾	15	15¼

STANDARD BODY MEASUREMENTS
Inches

WOMEN'S

Size	38	40	42	44	46	48	50
Bust	42	44	46	48	50	52	54
Waist	35	37	39	41½	44	46½	49
Hip	44	46	48	50	52	54	56
Back Waist Length	17¼	17⅜	17½	17⅝	17¾	17⅞	18

GIRLS'

Size		7	8	10	12	14
Breast		26	27	28½	30	32
Waist		23	23½	24½	25½	26½
Hip		27	28	30	32	34
Back Waist Length		11½	12	12¾	13½	14¼
Approx. Height		50"	52"	56"	58½"	61"

With the first two columns of your chart filled you have all the measurements needed to determine your pattern size. Measurements marked with an asterisk (*) are the ones used to determine pattern size. Other measurements are used to help you adjust proper fit of the pattern.

Dresses, blouses and tops are bought by bust measurement. Use the high bust measurement to determine the correct size if the difference between the high and full bust is 2 inches (5cm) or more. This might require a slight alteration in the bust area but you will get a much better fit throughout the upper bodice and armhole than selecting a size according to the full bust measurement. Coat and jacket patterns should be selected using the same measurements. Sufficient ease has been allowed so they will fit comfortably over other garments.

Pants and skirts are bought by hip measurement. Find the pattern size closest to your body measure. The waist can be adjusted if there is a 2 inch (5cm) or less difference between your waist and Standard Body Measurements. Buy the next size larger or smaller if the difference is greater than 2 inches (5cm). A

few alterations will then be required.

You are now ready to fill in the fourth column of Your Personal Measurement Chart. Compare measurements in the first two columns. Write down differences, if any, in the fourth column and place a plus or minus in front of that number. For example, if your

waist measures 27 inches (68.5cm) and the pattern allows for 28 inches (71cm) you would put minus 1 inch (25mm) in the fourth column — meaning it is necessary to take in the waistline or waistband 1 inch (25mm). These figures will be used to help you make the right pattern alterations.

Reading The Pattern Envelope

Once you have chosen your pattern and given the store clerk the right number and size, you will be handed a pattern envelope containing useful information. Let's explore both sides of the envelope and see what everything means.

The front of the envelope will give the following information:

(A) The pattern brand, number and size will be printed on the envelope front. Some patterns are available in Multi-Sizes — all printed on the envelope.

(B) The pattern art work on the envelope is the same as the catalog page. It shows the different views, or ways of making

the various pattern items.

Now turn the envelope over and look at the back.

(C) Find the pattern description which will give information such as lined yokes, pockets in side seams, extensions of the shoulder or a lowering of the back neckline, etc.

(D) The measurement chart will give measurements for each size. Use this information for reference and when altering the pattern.

(E) Looking at the yardage chart, find your size at the top. Read down to your view for yardage requirements. Also check

16

6341

MISSES' UNLINED JACKET OR VEST, SKIRT AND PANTS: Buttoned jacket or vest has shawl collar and welts. Pants have soft front pleats, front zipper and side seam pockets. Skirt in two lengths has inverted front pleat with underlay, soft side front pleats and side seam pockets.

BODY MEASUREMENTS							BODY MEASUREMENTS					
Size	6	8	10½	12	14	Ins.		6	8	10	12	14
								78	80	83	87	92 cm
Bust	30½	31½	32½	34	36	"		58	61	64	67	71 cm
Waist	23	24	25	26½	28	"		83	85	88	92	97 cm
Hip	32½	33½	34½	36	38	"		39.5	40	40.5	41.5	42 cm
Back waist length	15½	15¾	16	16¼	16½	"						

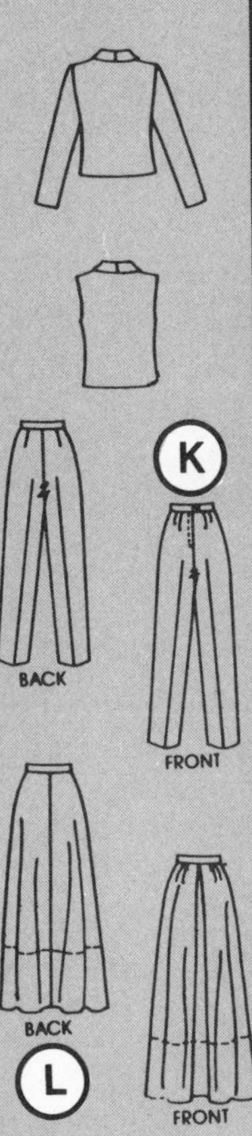

SIZES	6	8	10	12	14			6	8	10	12	14
Jacket							**Jacket**					
44/45"*	1⅝	1⅝	1⅝	1¾	1⅞	Yds.	115cm*	1.50	1.50	1.50	1.60	1.70 m
58/60"*	1⅜	1⅜	1⅜	1⅜	1½	"	150cm*	1.30	1.30	1.30	1.30	1.30 m
Vest							**Vest**					
44/45"*	1⅜	1⅜	1¾	1½	1½	Yds.	115cm*	1.30	1.30	1.30	1.30	1.30 m
58/60"*	1	1	1	1⅛	1⅛	"	150cm*	0.90	0.90	0.90	1.00	1.00 m

Jacket or Vest – Interfacing, 21" thru 25", woven or non-woven, fusible or non-fusible, ⅞ yd.

Jacket or Vest – Interfacing, 53cm thru 64cm, woven or non-woven, fusible or non-fusible, 0.80m

Pants							**Pants**					
44/45"*	2⅜	2⅜	2½	2⅝	2⅝	Yds.	115cm*	2.10	2.20	2.30	2.40	2.40 m
58/60"*	1⅝	1⅝	1⅝	1⅝	1⅝	"	150cm*	1.50	1.50	1.50	1.50	1.50 m
Width, each leg	17¼	17¾	18¼	18¾	19¼	Ins.	Width, each leg	44	45	46	48	49 cm

Short Skirt							**Short Skirt**					
44/45"*	2¼	2⅜	2⅜	2¾	2¾	Yds.	115cm*	2.10	2.40	2.40	2.50	2.50 m
58/60"*	2	2	2	2	2	"	150cm*	1.80	1.80	1.80	1.80	1.80 m
Bottom width	81½	82½	83½	85	87	Ins.	Bottom width	207	210	212	216	221 cm

Long Skirt							**Long Skirt**					
44/45"*	3¾	3¾	3⅞	3⅞	4¼	Yds.	115cm*	3.40	3.50	3.50	3.60	3.80 m
58/60"*	2⅝	2⅝	2⅝	2⅝	2¾	"	150cm*	2.40	2.40	2.40	2.40	2.50 m
Bottom width	98	99	100	101½	103½	Ins.	Bottom width	249	251	254	258	263 cm

Pants or Skirt – Waistband Interfacing – 21" thru 25", woven or non-woven, fusible or non-fusible, 1 yd.

Pants or Skirt – Waistband Interfacing – 53cm thru 64cm, woven or non-woven, fusible or non-fusible, 0.90m

	6	8	10	12	14			6	8	10	12	14
Finished length from back of regular neckline												
Jacket or Vest	18½	18¾	19	19¼	19½	Ins.		47	48	48	49	50 cm
Finished side length from natural waistline												
Pants	42¼	42½	42¾	43	43¼	"		107	108	109	109	110 cm
Finished length at center back from natural waistline												
Short Skirt	29½	29¾	30	30¼	30½	"		75	76	76	77	77 cm
Long Skirt	41½	41¾	42	42¼	42½	"		105	106	107	107	108 cm

*With Nap   **Without Nap   ***With or Without Nap

Use *With Nap yardages and layouts for pile, shaded or one-way design fabrics. Additional fabric may be needed to match stripes, plaids, one-way designs.

SUGGESTED FABRICS: All Views - Lightweight Wool, Wool Blends, Lightweight Corduroy, Lightweight Wool or Synthetic Gabardine, Velveteen, Chino, Poplin; Skirt - also Challis, Cotton Blends; Jacket, Vest, Skirt Suitable for Small Checks.

NOTIONS: Thread; Jacket or Vest - Three ¾" (2cm) Buttons; Pants - 7" (18cm) Skirt Zipper, One ⅝" (1.5cm) Button; Skirt - 2 Waistband Hooks and Eyes; Pants or Skirt - Optional Seam Binding or Stretch Lace.

BACK   FRONT   BACK   FRONT

K   L

19 PATTERN PIECES

C   D   E   G   F   I   J   H

Pattern #6341 copyright 1978, The McCall Pattern Company

---

this chart for necessary lining and interfacing fabric.

(F) This * next to a fabric width means "for napped fabric." Buy this amount if the fabric shades in one direction, has a pile like velvet or a one-way print. This ** means the yardage requirement for fabric without nap.

(G) The finished width and length chart indicates how wide the bottom of a garment will be . The finished length of the garment

will also be given.

(H) Notions for each view are given including the size and number of buttons, zippers, hooks and/or snaps, seam binding, thread and other items.

(I) Fabric notations are sometimes listed indicating if certain fabrics, such as plaids, stripes, or diagonals are suitable. This will also tell if yardage has been allowed for matching plaids or one-way designs.

(J) Suggested fabric information is usually very general but will always tell you if knits are suitable for the pattern.

(K) Back views are given of each garment piece included in the pattern. These line drawings show design details.

(L) Some pattern companies show silhouettes of each pattern piece with shape indications that may not be apparent on the art work.

Pattern Storage And Care

Anyone who sews at home is familiar with problems of pattern storage and care. A bit of thought and planning can easily solve the problem of a bulging collection of tattered envelopes.

Choose a drawer in the family file cabinet or buy a small one just for the sewing room. Make dividers according to your pattern styles and file accurately after each use. Special pattern-size, cardboard boxes are available at many notions counters but if you want to save money, look around for a discarded box at home large and strong enough to serve as a pattern file. Don't forget the divider cards which can be made from different colored poster board.

Now about those tattered envelopes. Who says you have to put hundreds of pattern pieces back in the small envelope? Why not use a large (9"x12") kraft paper envelope instead? These can be purchased at any stationary or drug store or better yet, save the envelopes you receive in the mail for use in the sewing room. Cut the pattern envelope along two sides and paste it on the large envelope. Now you have the pattern information at a glance and a conveniently sized envelope for storing all those pattern pieces.

Ziploc storage bags can also be used for pattern storage. They are a little more expensive than paper envelopes but last longer and allow you to see through the envelope. One pattern company is currently offering their extra easy patterns in a small Ziploc storage bag.

Patterns can wear out after repeated use and this is unfortunate if it happens to be a favorite that has been discontinued in the catalog. Once you have established the fact that a particular pattern is going to be used many times, preserve it with

Tip

Preserve your favorite pattern and patch up an old one with Pattern Saver. This new product irons on to the back of your tissue pattern making it like new. It is pre-packaged, with full instructions, and measures 8.2 feet by 22 inches (2.5m by 55.5cm). It is also handy for home decorating and craft projects. Manufactured by Pellon Corp.

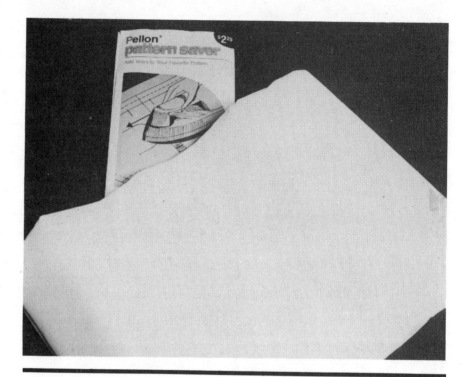

some kind of backing. Two excellent items can be used — one available at the fabric store and one at the grocery store.

Fabric stores sell a special non-woven, fusible material that can be fused to the backs of pattern pieces to preserve them. Or you can use non-woven fusible interfacing. Buy the least expensive and apply with a dry iron.

Plastic coated freezer wrap is available at most grocery stores. Place your pattern piece wrong side down on the plastic surface and press with a dry iron.

Caution should be used with these materials. Don't let the hot iron touch the fusible surface of the pattern backing material, interfacing or plastic surface of the freezer wrap. These surfaces will coat the bottom of your iron with a sticky substance that is difficult to remove. Position pattern pieces wrong side down on the fusing surface of the materials and keep the iron well within the pattern margins. Cut away excess pattern backing, interfacing or freezer paper around the pattern piece and finish pressing the edges together.

Once a pattern has been reinforced, you may find folding it for storage less than satisfactory. Try rolling all pattern pieces together and placing them plus the instruction sheet in a cardboard tube saved from paper towels or gift wrap. Label each tube and keep them standing in a separate box in the sewing room. Rolling rather than folding makes patterns last longer.

Fitting A Pattern

This chapter is about fitting your garment and we hope you will read it carefully before shopping. Good fit begins with the right figure type and right size pattern selection. You will then have a minimum of adjustments to make and can begin your project knowing it will fit.

What Is Good Fit?

How do you know when the fit is good? A garment that fits well is comfortable to wear. It's comfortable not only when you're standing in front of a mirror but when you walk, move and sit. It doesn't need constant adjusting because it follows body contours.

The muslin fitting shell in our illustration little resembles current fashion but it is ideal for explaining good basic fit. (fig. 1) Styles change frequently and each time a different part of the body is emphasized. When skirts are straight, waist and hips are emphasized. When clothes are loose and soft, the neck and shoulders must fit. There is always some area of the fashion silhouette emphasized requiring good fit. If you know how it should look transfer the look of these areas from the muslin shell.

fig. 1

Tips

Starting at the top, the neckline should fit comfortably at the neck base. It shouldn't gap, stand away, or be tight enough to rub the skin. A shirt collar should fit this way even if you wear it open.

The shoulder seam should fall straight across the shoulder center. It should not angle off toward the front or back and it should meet the sleeve seam at the shoulder bone tip.

The sleeve should allow easy movement when you move or bend your arm. A long straight sleeve should end slightly below the wrist bone. Too long sleeves appear dowdy. The armhole seam should follow body contours.

Bust and waist darts should point to the high point of the bust and end 1 inch (25mm) short of the apex. Hip darts should stop 1 inch (25mm) short of the fullest part of hips and buttocks. When darts are used correctly they release fabric where the body is biggest and remove unnecessary fabric at the waist and side seams.

Waistline seams should fall at the natural waistline and fit comfortably. A too tight waistline will pull side seams out of line. A too loose waistline will drop below the correct position. This also applies to skirt waistbands.

The center front, center back and side seams of a garment should hang at right angles to the floor. For example, if the bust area is too tight, the center front seam in that area will pull to one side. If you were to make a button front blouse with those measurements it would be difficult to keep buttoned. If the garment is too tight through the hips, the side seams will pull to the front or back instead of skimming the body.

The length of your garment should be flattering to your figure, meaning the proportion should be pleasing to the eye. Perhaps the best way to explain this is by recalling mini-skirts. It was difficult to find good proportion with them because the garment's total length was hardly more than the width. It gave everyone except the very thin and young an unflattering square boxy look. Longer skirts elongate the body and are generally more pleasing to the eye. Even though fashion decrees mid-calf or below the knee you can still find your best length in that area and have the current style.

Pattern Ease

If you measure pattern pieces from seamline to seamline at bust, waist and hips you will find the pieces are from ½ inch (13mm) to 2 inches (5cm) bigger than your body measurements. This necessary difference is known as basic ease. Basic ease makes it possible to move comfortably when you wear your clothes. Otherwise, your clothes would fit like a second skin.

Patterns designed for a stretchable knit depend on the fabric stretch for basic ease. If you measure those pattern pieces they will be close to your body measurement. That's why it is so important to check knit fabrics against the gauge printed on the pattern envelope. Without enough stretch, clothes will be too tight.

The amount of basic ease differs with pattern companies and the type of garment. A dress with sleeves needs more bust ease than one without sleeves. The variation in basic ease may be the reason you will find patterns from one company fit better than another even though the Big Four pattern companies all use the same body measurements.

In addition to basic ease, patterns also have designer ease. Full skirts have more designer ease than straight skirts. Blouson tops have more designer ease than empire tops. This type of ease gives the style its characteristic look. When you are adjusting a pattern or altering a garment, do not take out the designer ease or you will lose the look that attracted you to the pattern in the first place.

Adjusting The Pattern

With pattern, fabric and notions in hand, you are ready to begin your sewing project. First decide whether you need to make any adjustments in your pattern.

Pattern adjustments in THE WHOLE SEWING CATALOG are divided into two groups. Group I covers adjustments you know must be made because column four of your Personal Measurement Chart shows a difference between your measurements and the Standard Body Measurements. The Group II adjustments cannot be shown on the chart and only your past experience with sewing or ready-to-wear clothes will indicate if those adjustments are necessary. The slanting shoulder is a good example. If past experience has taught you that your shoulders slant more than the average, you know you should make that adjustment. If you don't know what, if any, Group II adjustments you should make, don't worry about it. In the future you may decide that one or two are indicated.

Tip

Mend-a-Pattern is a good product to use for pattern adjustments. Lengthen pattern pieces by joining the two cut edges with a strip of the pattern tissue held in place by the glue stick. The 1-inch markings help make the adjustment even and accurate. From Fantastic Fit Products.

We recommend adjusting the pattern before cutting it out because some things cannot be changed once the garment is cut. If you are taller than the standard Misses' 5'5" to 5'6" (1.65m to 1.68m), you cannot add length after cutting. If you are much shorter than a Misses' you will get a better line and save fabric if you shorten the pattern pieces before cutting.

Additional Adjustment Hints

Press wrinkled pattern pieces with a warm, dry iron to avoid distorting pattern size.

When you adjust length, respace buttonholes evenly. It may also be necessary to raise or lower pocket locations.

The procedure for length adjustments is always the same whether you are adjusting back neck to waist or skirt length.

Make the same length adjustments on all connecting pattern pieces. That is, if you shorten one skirt piece all joining skirt pieces must be equally shortened.

When notches are affected by adjustment, redraw them. You will need them when constructing the garment.

If the pattern grainline is affected by adjustments, it should be straightened.

Use lined pad paper to add to patterns. It saves drawing lines. Otherwise use extra pattern tissue or plain tissue paper.

Group I Adjustments

Length

Pattern pieces that might need to be lengthened or shortened are the bodice, sleeve and skirt. Your Personal Measurement Chart will

Tip

Respacing buttonholes is a snap when you use the Simflex Gauge. This expandable measuring device automatically and accurately measures spaces between up to eight buttons. This is much quicker than using a conventional ruler. Available from Brewer Sewing Supplies Co.

tell you where and how much adjustment is necessary. Most pattern companies print an alteration line on these pattern pieces so you will know just where to make these changes.

To lengthen cut along the pattern alteration line. Tape the

edge of one pattern piece to a wide piece of paper. Spread pattern pieces apart the necessary amount, making sure the grainline matches exactly across the gap. Tape in place. (fig. 2) Trim away excess paper at the pattern edges blending the cutting lines where necessary. *(continued on next page)*

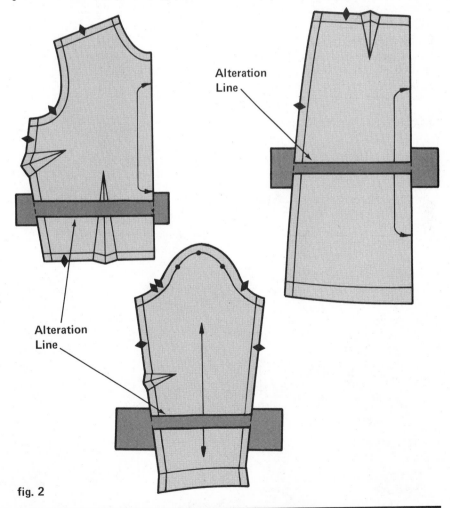

Alteration Line

Alteration Line

fig. 2

To shorten, draw a line on the pattern piece parallel to the alteration line with the distance between the two lines the amount of adjustment. (fig. 3)

Fold the bottom line up to meet the top line and tape the fold in place. (fig. 4) Correct the cutting line, blending where necessary.

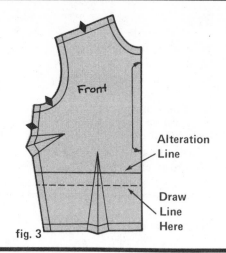

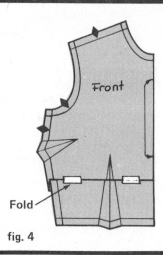

fig. 3

fig. 4

Tip

Some patterns tell you to adjust the skirt length at the hemline. Don't do it unless the skirt is very straight. It's better to draw an alteration line 5 inches (12.5cm) above the hemline, at right angles to the lengthwise grain, and adjust as above. It is a nuisance to draw a new hemline, especially on a full skirt.

Tip

The 2 inch wide, 18 inch long C-Thru Plastic Ruler will help you draw this new line. Just lay the ruler over the existing alteration line and adjust it so the top edge of the ruler now marks the needed difference. The red ⅛ inch grid on the ruler makes this adjustment easy. Manufactured by C-Thru Ruler Co.

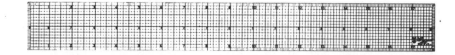

Special Length Adjustment — Empire Top

A Misses' pattern is designed for a B cup. If you have a larger or smaller cup size you may find the empire seamline falling in the wrong place. (fig. 5)

This can usually be determined by holding the pattern up against the body. Lengthen the empire bodice as shown in the illustration, (fig. 6) using the preceding techniques. Shorten the bodice as shown above. Remember to correct the cutting lines and redraw the dart as necessary.

fig. 5

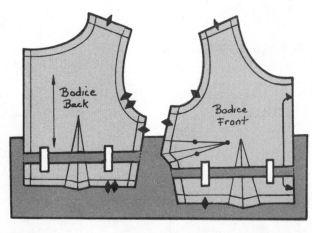

fig. 6

Bust Position

Darts should release fabric at the fullest part of the figure. If bust darts are too low or high the fabric will not be released where necessary. Adjust the bust dart location if there is a difference between your body measure and pattern measurement.

To locate the bust apex, on the front pattern piece extend the center line of the bust dart to the center front line. Draw a second line from the center of the shoulder seamline down and through the first line. The intersecting point indicates the bust apex of the pattern. (fig. 7)

Measure the distance from the center of the shoulder seamline to the apex point and compare this

number with your body measurement. If there is a difference mark your bust point on

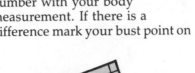
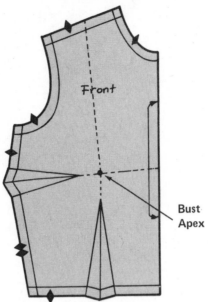

fig. 7

the vertical line, measuring down from the center of the shoulder seam. (fig. 8)

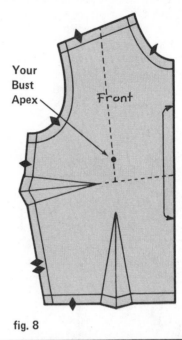

fig. 8

Now determine the bust separation. This varies with individuals and is important since darts are only sewn to within 1 inch (25mm) of the apex. Measure the distance from apex to apex and divide this number in half. (fig. 9)

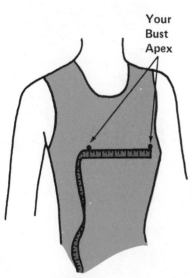

fig. 9

Measure in from the center front of the pattern piece, at the level of your relocated bust point and shift the dot to the left or right so it reflects one half the bust separation measurement. (fig. 10)

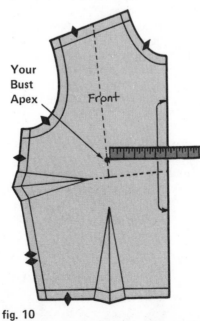

fig. 10

To adjust the dart position, draw a box around the bust dart that is square with the center front line. Keep the box front edge close to the point of the dart. (fig. 11) Cut around the dart along the box lines. *(continued on next page)*

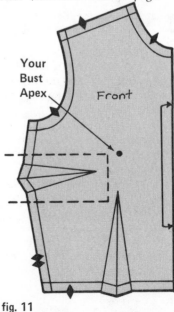

fig. 11

Move the box up or down, keeping the front edge parallel to the center front, until the dart points to the new apex point. Tape the dart box in place. Fill in any gap with a piece of paper and connect the cutting lines, blending where necessary. (fig. 12)

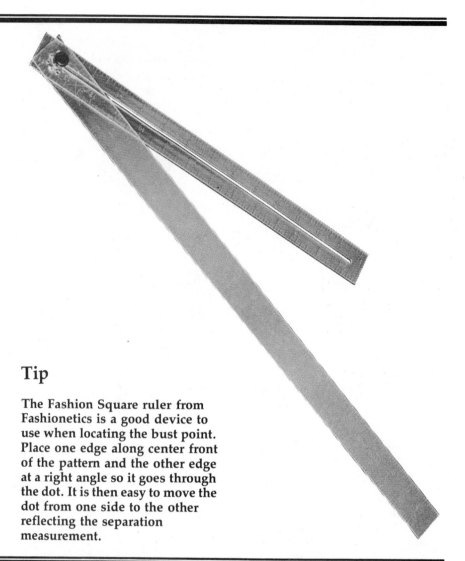

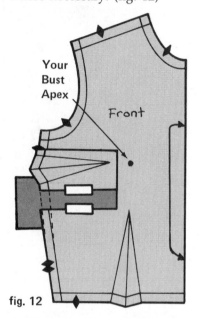

fig. 12

Check the dart length. It should end 1 inch (25mm) behind the apex dot. Draw the dart longer or shorter if necessary.

Tip

The Fashion Square ruler from Fashionetics is a good device to use when locating the bust point. Place one edge along center front of the pattern and the other edge at a right angle so it goes through the dot. It is then easy to move the dot from one side to the other reflecting the separation measurement.

Shoulder Width

Shoulder width varies with fashion, type of garment and pattern company. You must know the pattern shoulder length just as you know the bust and hip measurements to make adjustments. Unfortunately most pattern companies do not publish this information. The best way to find it is to measure a pattern front with a basic shoulder seam, that is one without gathers or dart. Measure from neckline seamline to shoulder seamline. Enter this measurement in column three and the measurement of your own shoulder difference, if any, in column four of Your Personal Measurement Chart. This must be done once for each pattern brand. You will then know how much to alter each pattern so the shoulder will fit and fashion will not be lost.

To increase width tape a piece of paper under the front and back shoulder/armhole area and measure out the required amount along the shoulder seamline. (fig. 13) *(continued on next page)*

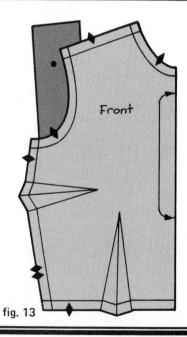

fig. 13

Using a curved ruler, place the curve at the armhole bottom and match the upper edge to the new mark at the shoulder seamline. Draw a new armhole cutting line following the curve of the ruler. Redraw any notches or dots affected by the alteration. (fig. 14)

To decrease width, place a dot on the shoulder seamline that reflects the desired decrease in width. (fig. 15)

Using a curved ruler, place the curve at the bottom of the armhole and match the upper edge with the new dot at the shoulder seamline. Draw a new armhole cutting line following the curve of the ruler. Redraw any notches or dots affected by the alteration. (fig. 16)

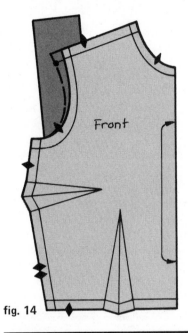

fig. 14

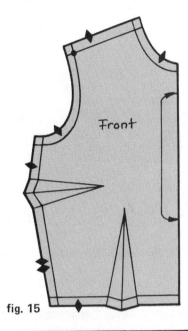

fig. 15

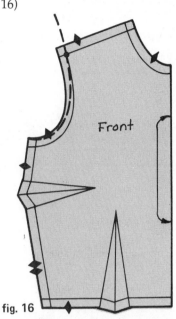

fig. 16

Width Adjustments For Pattern With Separate Front And Back Yokes

Pin the yoke patterns to the lower front and back pattern pieces matching seamlines. Increase or decrease the shoulder width as described above. (fig. 17 & 18). Unpin the yokes and lower pattern pieces, cutting through any added paper if necessary.

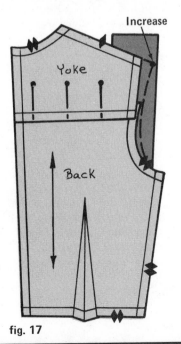

fig. 17

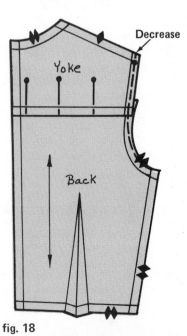

fig. 18

Width Adjustments For Pattern With Combined Front And Back Yoke

Pin the yoke pattern to the front and back pattern pieces matching seamlines. Tape extra paper in the armhole area if the shoulder width is to be increased. Increase or decrease the shoulder width at the dot marking the true shoulder line. (fig. 19). Using a curved ruler blend the armhole edges as instructed. Unpin the yoke from the front and back pattern pieces, cutting through any added paper.

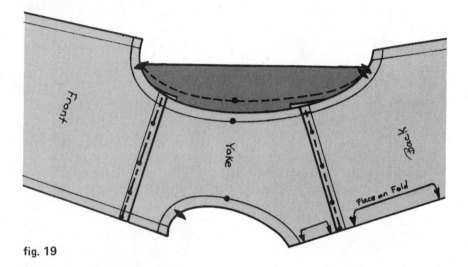

fig. 19

Tip

The Fashion Ruler from Fashionetics, Inc. is easy to use for armhole alterations. Not only efficient for armhole adjustments, it is useful for any pattern adjustment involving curved and straight lines. See-through plastic helps you position the ruler accurately.

Circumference Adjustments

Circumference adjustments are done to the bustline, waistline and hipline if your body measure differs from the Standard Pattern Measurements. Multi-size patterns make these types of alterations easy because you can blend from one size to another wherever adjustments are necessary.

Bust Circumference

Since you bought your pattern according to the bust size there shouldn't be a need for large (more than 1 inch (25mm) alterations in the bust circumference. An alteration that might be necessary is an increase or decrease in the dart width determining the bust cup size. This alteration will be covered in the Group II section. If a circumference alteration is necessary, decide how much change is needed and divide that number by two. The result will be added to or removed from the bodice front.

To increase the bust tape a strip of paper to the side of the bodice front. Extend the dart center line out onto the paper and place a dot on the extended line, away from the pattern edge, that reflects the needed change. (fig. 20)
(continued on next page)

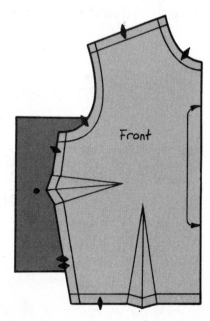

fig. 20

Redraw the sides of the pattern above and below the dot, blending into the pattern at the underarm and waist. (fig. 21)

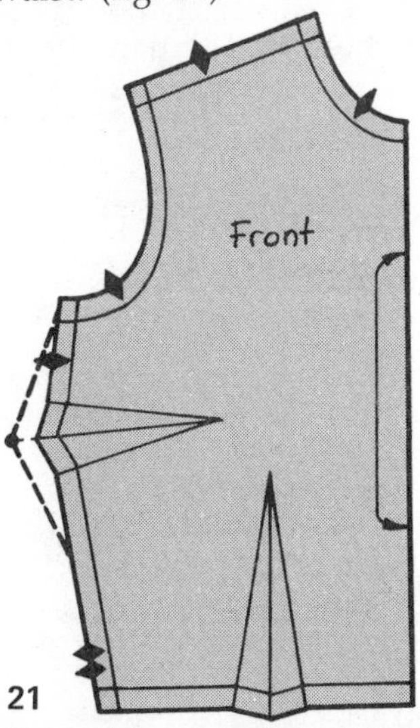

To decrease the bust place a dot on the dart center line that reflects the needed change. (fig. 22)

Redraw the sides of the pattern, above and below the dot, blending into the pattern at the underarm and waist. (fig. 23)

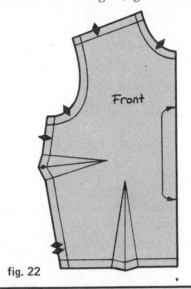

fig. 21

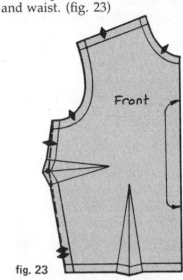

fig. 22

fig. 23

Waistline And Hipline Circumference

As in lengthening or shortening a pattern, there is a standard procedure for increasing or decreasing the waistline and hipline. Using a Multi-size pattern purchased by bust measurement is certainly the easiest way to make these alterations. Barring that solution, select a single size pattern to fit you.

First we should say pattern pieces are only given for half the garment. If you pin pattern pieces together and try them on you will have only half a garment. Each pattern piece is to be cut from two layers of fabric or cut twice from a single layer. Since the pattern involves just half a garment you must take the total amount of adjustment from column four of Your Personal Measurement Chart and divide in half. Then divide this figure equally among the number of cutting lines in the involved area.

Example

Waist must be increased a total of 2 inches (5cm). Divide by two for a result of 1 inch (25mm).

Diagram shows four cutting lines. (fig. 24). Therefore ¼ inch (6mm) should be added to or subtracted from each cutting line at the waistline. (*continued on next page*)

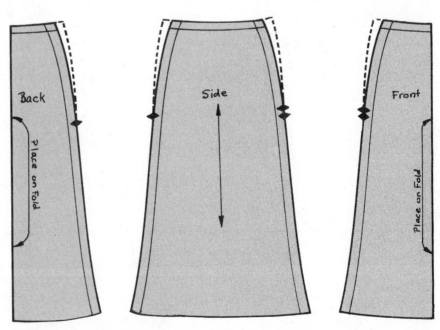

fig. 24

To increase or decrease the waistline, divide the amount of change by two and again by the number of cutting lines involved in the alteration. Tape extra paper to the alteration area if you are increasing the circumference. Measure in (fig. 25) or out (fig. 26) the divided amount and make a mark at the waist cutting line. Using a curved ruler for the skirt and a straight ruler for the bodice, draw a new cutting line from the mark blending back into the original cutting line as shown. Dresses with waistline seams must have both the skirt and bodice changed an equal amount.

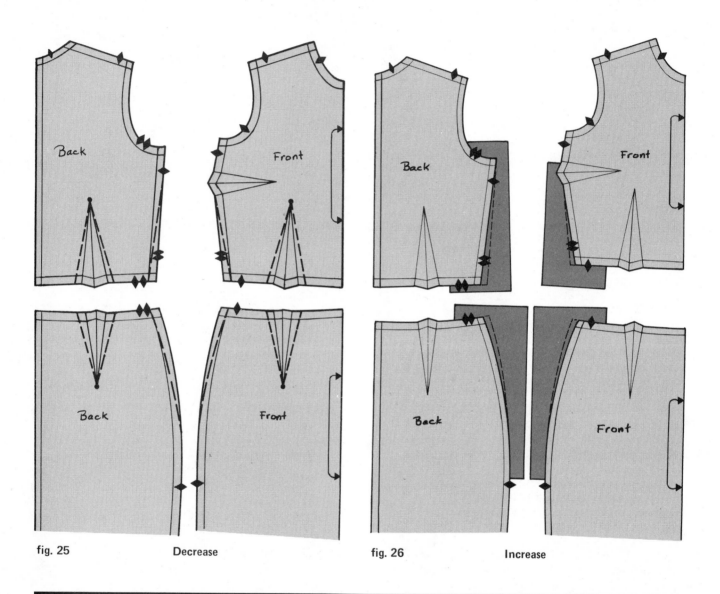

fig. 25   Decrease   fig. 26   Increase

On the skirt, adjust the waistband the total amount of change. (fig. 27). (continued on next page)

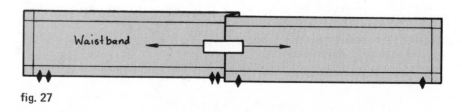

fig. 27

To increase or decrease the hipline, divide the changed amount by two and then again by the number of cutting lines involved in the alteration. Tape extra paper to the alteration area if you are increasing the circumference. Measure in (fig. 28) or out (fig. 29) the divided amount at the hipline as determined by the hip drop measurement in column two. Using a curved ruler, draw a new cutting line up from the mark blending into the original cutting line at the waist. Using a straight ruler, draw a line from the mark to the hem adding or taking away an even amount the entire length of the skirt.

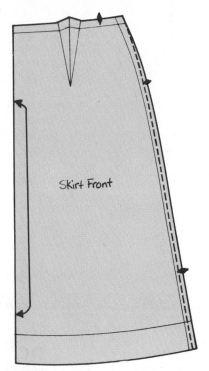

fig. 28   Decrease

Tip

Make hip and waist adjustments where you need them. If the abdomen or buttocks are large, adjustment may be made just to the front or back seams.

Tip

Do not depend on designer ease to correct adjustments. A skirt might be full enough to go around your hips but you will lose the appearance that attracted you to the design if you do not make adjustments.

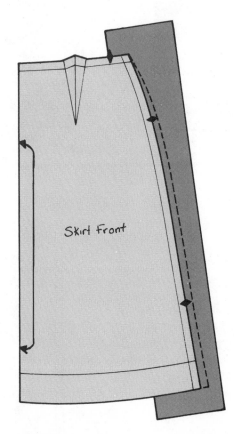

fig. 29   Increase

Sleeve Circumference

Woven fabric garments with straight sleeves need a 2 to 2½ inch (5cm to 6.3cm) basic ease in the upper arm while knit fabric garments require a 1 to 2 inch (25mm to 5cm) ease. The need for alteration in the sleeve width is determined by measuring the width of the upper sleeve of a basic pattern between the seamlines. (fig. 30) Compare this measurement with your body measure plus the recommended ease. Any difference between these two measurements will indicate the total amount of alteration necessary.

To increase or decrease sleeve width, draw a line down the center of the sleeve parallel with the grainline. Increase the sleeve width by cutting along this line and spreading the two sleeve pieces apart the total changed amount. Tape a strip of paper in the gap. (fig. 31)

Decrease the sleeve width by overlapping cut edges the total amount of change. Tape or pin in place. (fig. 32)

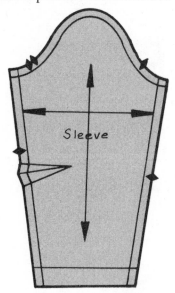

fig. 30

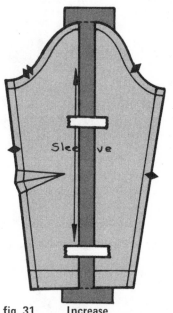

fig. 31   Increase

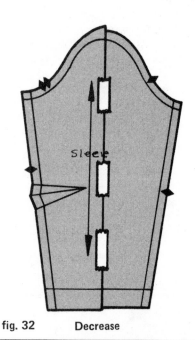

fig. 32   Decrease

Add one half the total amount of change to the back and one half to the front bodice, at the underarm, if you are increasing the sleeve width. (fig. 33)
(continued on next page)

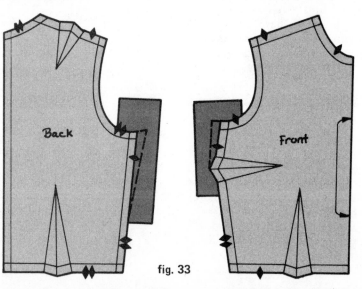

fig. 33

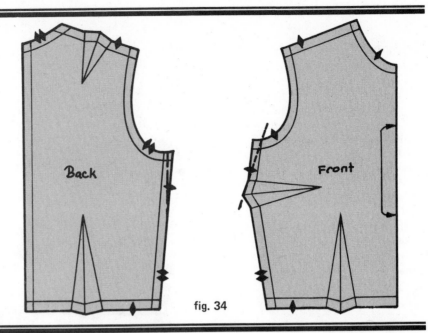

Remove one half the total amount of change from the back and front bodice, at the underarm if you are decreasing the sleeve width. (fig. 34)

fig. 34

Group II Adjustments

Group I and II adjustments are separated because Group II adjustments are problems difficult to measure and solve from a chart. Nor does pinning the pattern together and trying it on solve problems since tissue does not drape like fabric. Group II adjustments are the result of past experience. If you haven't had

enough sewing experience to be aware of problems, don't worry about it. Come back to this section at a later time.

The most practical way to explain Group II adjustments is to assume you have made a muslin fitting shell and don't mind cutting it up in order to find some solutions. The Big Four pattern companies each have basic patterns just for making such a shell. It is simple and time saving and has only to be done once. You then will know what the problems are and how to solve them. You

will also know the kinds of fitting problems that can't be measured without a muslin shell. Any adjustment is transferred to each pattern piece and you can proceed feeling reasonably sure of good fit. Making these adjustments will become second nature.

Follow pattern instructions when making the muslin shell. You will notice that the zipper is not required but all seams and darts are to be plainly marked with tracing paper so you can accurately measure and transfer alterations to the paper pattern.

Tip

An alternative to the muslin shell is use of the Fashionetics, Inc. product called Fash-On. This is a fusible backing material that reinforces pattern pieces enough to fit like fabric. A real time saver, Fash-On eliminates the need for transferring shell adjustments back to a paper pattern.

Sloping Shoulders

Because your shoulders slope more than average, the garment wrinkles diagonally from the base of the neck to the armhole. (fig. 35)

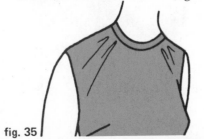

fig. 35

Pin the shoulders of the muslin shell as illustrated, taking the greatest amount at the armhole edge until wrinkles disappear. (fig. 36) *(continued on next page)*

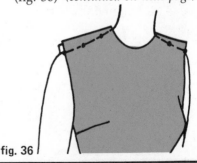

fig. 36

Take the garment off and measure the amount of adjustment made at the shoulder/armhole point from the original seamline to the pins. Enter this amount in column four of Your Personal Measurement Chart. On the pattern front and back measure down from the shoulder/armhole cutting line the amount of adjustment and mark. Draw a new cutting line from the mark to the neck point. Measure down at the armhole/side seam point the same amount of the adjustment and lower the armhole using a curved ruler. (fig. 37)

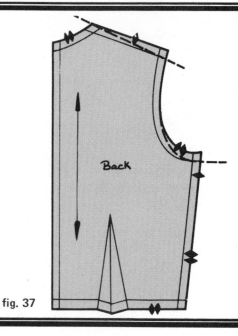
fig. 37

Square Shoulders

Because your shoulders are square and do not slope, the garment pulls diagonally from the tip of the shoulder to the center front and back. (fig. 38)

fig. 38

Open the shoulder seam of the muslin shell almost to the base of the neck. Re-pin the seam until the bodice fits smoothly. Add scrap fabric to the shoulder front and back if needed. (fig. 39). Determine the amount of change by measuring between the original seamline and pins. Enter this amount in column four of Your Personal Measurement Chart.

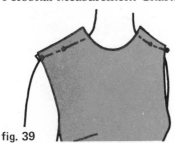
fig. 39

Tape extra paper to the front and back pattern pieces at the shoulder area and measure up from the shoulder/armhole point the necessary amount. Draw a new cutting line from the mark to the neck point. Raise the armhole on both the front and back pattern piece the same amount using a curved ruler to help you get the correct curve. (fig. 40)

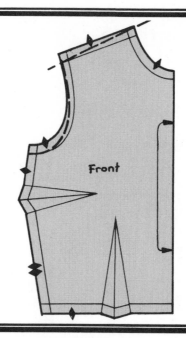

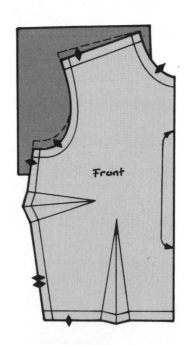
fig. 40

Tip

If the shoulder seam of the muslin seems to curve slightly, draw the new cutting line with a curved rather than a straight ruler for a better fit.

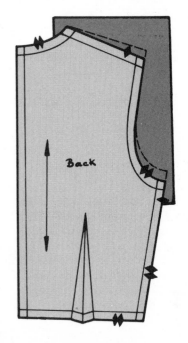

Round Shoulders

The garment pulls across the shoulders and sleeve top and rides up at the waistline because you have round shoulders. (fig. 41)

fig. 41

Try on the muslin shell and slash across the back as shown in the diagram. Allow the garment to spread until the waistline is in the right position. Measure the width of the spread and enter this amount in column four of Your Personal Measurement Chart. (fig. 42)

fig. 42

Draw a line across the pattern back at the same position you made the slash. Cut the pattern apart along this line to, but not through, the armhole edge. Spread the edges of the pattern the required amount and tape in an extra piece of paper. True the center back line with a straight ruler. (fig. 43) Increase the width of the neckline dart, or add one, to make up for the increased width at the center back neck edge.

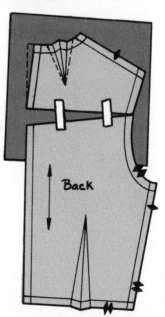

fig. 43

Erect Back

Horizontal wrinkles form between the neck and shoulder blade area because you have very erect posture. (fig. 44)

Try on the muslin shell and pin a horizontal tuck across the back from armhole to armhole, taking up the excess fabric. (fig. 45)

fig. 44   fig. 45

Measure the width of fabric contained in the tuck. This is the amount that must be removed from center back of the pattern. Draw a line across the pattern back at the same position you made the tuck. Slash the pattern apart along this line to, but not through, the armhole edge. (fig. 46)

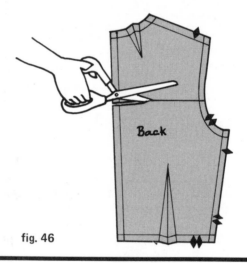

fig. 46

Overlap the pattern the required amount and tape in place. Straighten the center back line using a straight ruler. (fig. 47). Decrease width of the neckline dart, or eliminate it entirely to make up for the amount of pattern trimmed away at the center back.

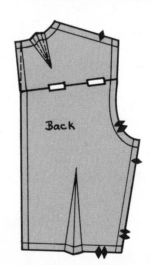

fig. 47

Wide Back

The garment pulls across the shoulder blade area because of a wide back. (fig. 48)

fig. 48

Release the armhole seams of the muslin shell where you feel the pull is greatest. Measure the gap necessary for a comfortable fit. Enter this measurement in column four of Your Personal Measurement Chart and note this is one half the total width adjustment. (fig. 49)

fig. 49

Slash the pattern back as indicated, from the center of the shoulder or shoulder dart, if there is one, to the level of the underarm seam. Spread the two pattern pieces apart the amount determined in the muslin adjustment. Tape the pattern pieces together with extra paper. True the underarm and shoulder cutting line with a straight ruler. Increase the shoulder dart width or create a shoulder dart to take care of the spread at shoulder edge. (fig. 50)

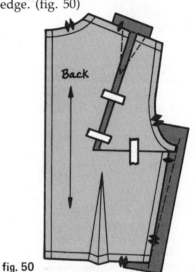

fig. 50

Narrow Back

Your garment has vertical wrinkles in the shoulder blade area because you have a narrow back. (fig. 51)

Pin a vertical tuck down each side of the back on the muslin shell so the wrinkles disappear. Measure the entire width of one tuck (tucks should be equal width) and enter this measurement in column four of Your Personal Measurement Chart. Note that this is just one half the total width adjustment necessary. (fig. 52)
(continued on next page)

fig. 51

fig. 52

Slash the pattern back as indicated, from the center of the shoulder or shoulder dart, if there is one, to the level of the underarm seam. Overlap the two pattern pieces the amount determined in the muslin adjustment and tape in place. True the underarm and shoulder cutting line with a straight ruler. (fig. 53) Decrease or totally eliminate the width of the shoulder dart to take care of the pattern overlap. **Note:** The width of the back shoulder should always equal or be a little wider than the front shoulder. The extra width is taken care of with a dart or easing. If you have to add some width to the back shoulder, do so at the shoulder/armhole point as described in *Wide Shoulder* instructions.

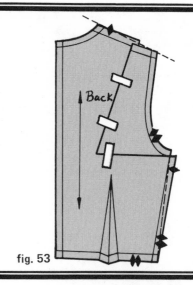

fig. 53

Tight Neckline

The neckline feels tight and uncomfortable with wrinkles forming at the neck base because the neckline is too small or is positioned wrongly for your posture. (fig. 54)

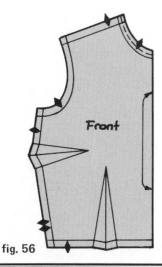

fig. 54

Try on the muslin shell and clip the neckline seam allowance until the neckline feels comfortable and lies flat at the neck base — front and back. The clips should be evenly spaced and the same depth. Mark the new neckline seam at the ends of the clips. Measure the distance between the new and original neckline seam. (fig. 55)

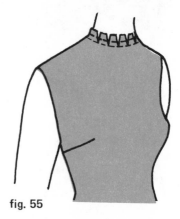

fig. 55

Lower the cutting of the front and back neckline the amount measured above. Lower the facing cutting lines the same amount. (fig. 56)

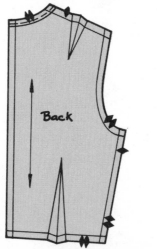

fig. 56

If the pattern calls for a collar, measure the difference between the total original and new neck seamline. Divide the measurement in half and add to the center back of the collar. (fig. 57)

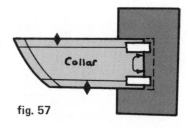

fig. 57

Loose Neckline

When a neckline looks too large and reveals bones at the neck base, the neckline is too big. (fig. 58)

On the muslin shell mark a new neckline seam above the given one so it properly fits the body. (fig. 59)

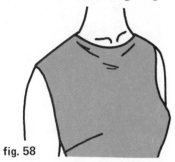

fig. 58

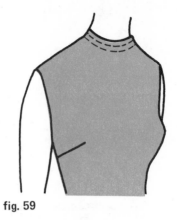

fig. 59

Measure the distance between the original and new seamline using this measurement to add to the cutting line of the front and back pattern pieces. Add the same amount to the cutting line of the neckline facing pieces. (fig. 60)

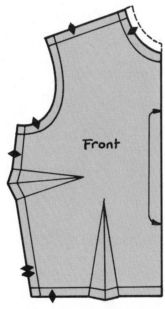

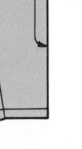

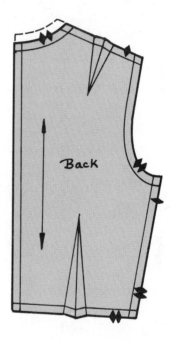

fig. 60

If the pattern calls for a collar, measure the difference between the total original and new neck seamline. Divide this measurement in half and remove the result from the collar at the center back. (fig. 61)

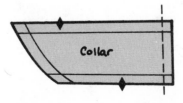

fig. 61

Gaping Neckline

When scoop, V, or square necklines gape away from your body make the alterations on the actual garment pieces rather than the muslin shell.

Baste side seams and pin shoulder seams wrong sides together. Wearing the garment, un-pin the shoulders at the neck edge. Raise the front shoulder only until the gaping disappears. Re-pin, making sure the pins go through the original seamline on the garment back and at the front and back shoulder/armhole edges. (fig. 62). Mark the new seamline on the wrong side of the front garment piece and stitch.

fig. 62

Neckline Too Low

The depth of a neckline depends on your comfort. If you wish to make alterations, they must be done on the pattern before the fashion fabric is cut.

Pin front and back pattern pieces together and carefully try them on to see if the neckline is a comfortable depth. Remember the seam allowance will not be there in the finished garment. Decide how much you want the neckline raised and draw a new cutting line after taping extra paper in place. Use a straight or curved ruler. (fig. 63)

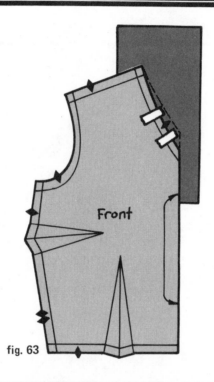

Front

fig. 63

Alter the front facing the same way. (fig. 64)

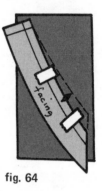

facing

fig. 64

Bust Cup Adjustment

Even though the pattern was purchased by your closest measurement, you might still need to increase or decrease the bust area because Misses' patterns are made for a B-cup and Half-Size patterns for a C-cup. If you wear a larger or smaller cup size than your figure type a change might be indicated. This alteration must first be done on the muslin shell.

To increase the cup, try on the muslin shell and slash as indicated through the high points of the bust from shoulder seamline to waist seamline, from left underarm seamline to right underarm seamline right through the bust dart. Allow muslin to spread the necessary amount for a good fit and pin fabric strips under the openings. (fig. 65) (continued)

fig. 65

Slash and spread the pattern front the same way. Tape extra paper under the openings to hold them in position. The darts will become wider giving you more fullness in the bust area. Redraw the dart points as shown. (fig. 66)

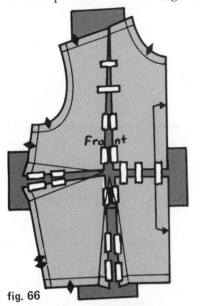

fig. 66

To decrease the cup, wearing the muslin, pin equal vertical tucks down over the bust, tapering from the edge of the pattern at the shoulder seamline to the edge at the waist seamline. Pin a horizontal tuck over the fullest part of the bust, tapering at the side seam until the excess fullness is removed. (fig. 67)

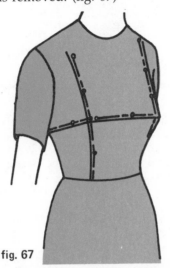

fig. 67

Transfer these same tucks to the front pattern piece by slashing and overlapping the full width of the tucks as indicated on the diagram. (fig. 68). The darts will now become narrower, removing excess fullness from the garment front. Redraw the dart points if necessary.

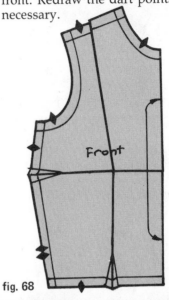

fig. 68

Sleeveless Armholes

It is very important that the armhole be the right size on a sleeveless garment. Sleeveless armholes can be too small, large or gaping. Any of these conditions is uncomfortable and unattractive. A correctly fitted armhole will not bind, pull or gape and the underarm portion will fall ½ inch (13mm) below the armpit. If you have problems with sleeveless armholes test the fit of the garment in muslin first. Stitch along the armhole seam, clip, turn under and stitch the seam allowance in place. Try on the muslin and assess the fitting problem.

For too small armholes, clip the armhole until it is comfortable. The clips should be evenly spaced having the same depth. Draw a new seamline at the ends of the clips (fig. 69)

Measure distance between the original and new seamlines and mark this change on the pattern front and back and facing pieces. (fig. 70) *(continued on next page)*

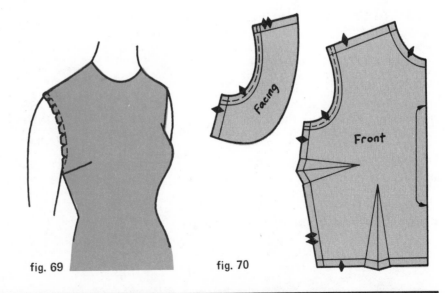

fig. 69   fig. 70

For too large armholes, try on the muslin and decide how much you need to raise the armhole (fig. 71)

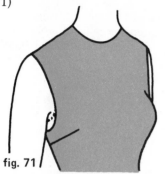

fig. 71

Add this amount to the underarm area of the front and back pattern pieces. Change the facing pieces the same amount. (fig. 72)

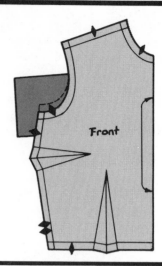

fig. 72

For gaping armholes, release the shoulder seam and re-pin until the armhole lies properly and the gaping disappears. (fig. 73)

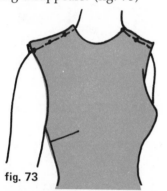

fig. 73

Measure the difference between the original and new armhole seam and transfer it to the pattern front and back. Adjust the facing pieces also. (fig. 74)

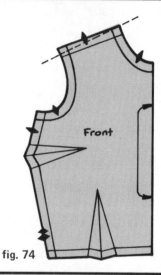

fig. 74

Armholes With Sleeves

Armholes that are too small or large can also occur on garments with sleeves. These problems will cause binding and pulling in the upper sleeve area restricting arm movement and making the garment feel uncomfortable.

For small armholes, follow the instructions given for the small sleeveless armhole, except have the armhole finish 1 inch (25mm) below the armpit. (fig. 75)

Lower the underarm area front and back of the sleeve pattern the same amount. (fig. 76)
(continued on next page)

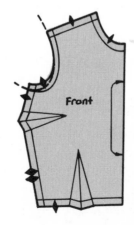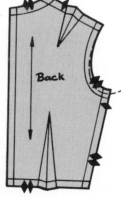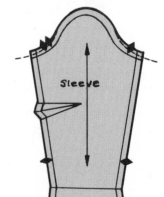

fig. 75

fig. 76

For large armholes, follow instructions given for the large sleeveless armhole except with the armhole finish placed 1 inch (25mm) below the armpit. Raise the underarm area of the front and back of the sleeve pattern the same amount. (fig. 77 & fig. 78)

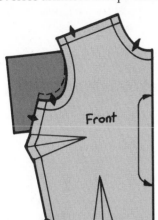

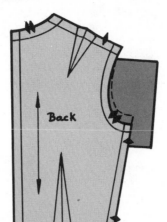

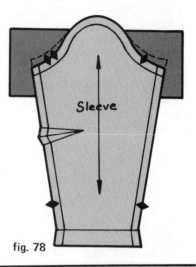

fig. 77

fig. 78

Skirt Adjustments

Skirt adjustments are easier to make than top adjustments, and also less complicated. The most important skirt adjustment is restoring grain lines so the center front, center back and side seams hang at right angles to the floor and horizontal grain lines of the skirt are parallel to the floor.

Flat Buttocks

Too much fullness in the skirt back because of flat buttocks causes vertical wrinkles and sagging at the hem. (fig. 79)

Pin a horizontal tuck on the skirt back across the fullest part of the buttocks so the skirt hangs correctly. The tuck will be wide at the center back and taper to nothing at the side seams. Pin equal vertical tucks on each side of the skirt, as indicated, until fullness is removed and side seams hang at right angles to the floor. The tucks should taper to nothing at the waistline with the widest part over the full part of the buttocks. Be sure to allow ease for comfortable sitting. (fig. 80)

Measure the full width of the horizontal tuck at the center back. Next, measure the full width of one vertical tuck at the fullest part of buttocks. Slash the pattern back as shown and overlap the cut edge the full width of the horizontal tuck; tape in place. Redraw the waistline, as shown, using a curved ruler. (fig. 81)

Decrease side seams the width of one vertical tuck. Decrease the width of back darts if necessary in order to retain the original waist measurement. (fig. 82)

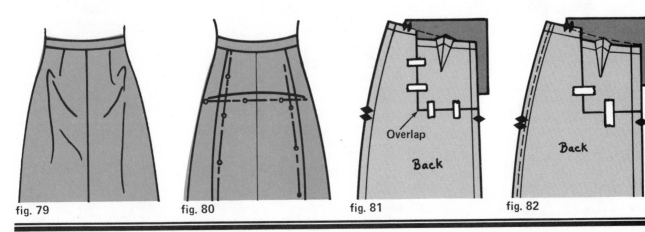

fig. 79

fig. 80

Overlap

Back

fig. 81

Back

fig. 82

Full Buttocks

Skirts pulling across full buttocks cause horizontal wrinkles and the garment to ride up at the waist and hemline. (fig. 83)

Release the center back and side seams from the waist to just below the hipline. Release the waist seam from left to right side seams. Adjust the skirt back until it hangs straight, spreading the vertical seams and waistline seam as necessary. Pin extra strips of fabric in seam openings to secure the adjustment. Measure the total amount added across the fullest part of the buttocks and distance from the original waistline to where it now lies. (fig. 84)

Slash the pattern as indicated and spread it the amount of the difference between the new and original waist seam. Tape the pieces together with extra paper and redraw the waistline with a curved ruler. (fig. 85)

Divide the total spread measurement by two and slash and spread pattern that amount. Increase the back dart width, if necessary, to retain the original waist measurement. (fig. 86)

fig. 83

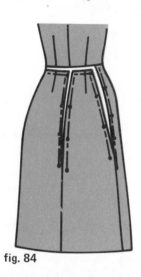

fig. 84

fig. 85

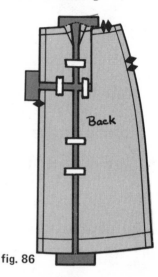

fig. 86

Sway Back

Wrinkles form just below the waistline because of a sway back. (fig. 87)

Take a tuck across the skirt back a few inches below the waistline so the skirt back hangs smoothly. The tuck should be wide at the center back and taper to nothing at each side seam. Measure the entire width of the tuck at the center back. (fig. 88)

Slash the pattern as indicated and overlap lower cut edge the total width of the tuck; tape in place. (fig. 89) Redraw the waistline with a curved ruler. **Note:** Make sure the skirt is large enough through the hips before making this alteration. Wrinkles below the waistline can also be caused by a skirt too tight across the buttocks (see *Full Buttocks* alteration).

fig. 87

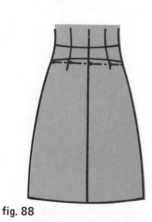

fig. 88

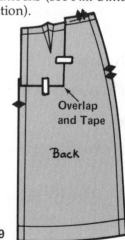

Overlap and Tape

Back

fig. 89

Full Tummy

The skirt pulls across the tummy causing the waist and hemline to ride up. (fig. 90)

Release the center front and side seams from waist to just below the hipline. Release the waist seam from right to left side seams.

Adjust the skirt front until it hangs straight, spreading the vertical seams and waistline seam as necessary. Pin extra strips of fabric in seam openings to secure the adjustment. (fig. 91) Measure the total amount added across the fullest part of the tummy and the distance from the original waistline to where it now lies.

Slash the pattern as indicated and spread it the amount of difference between the new and original waist seam. Tape the pieces together with extra paper and re-draw the waistline with a curved ruler. (fig. 92)

Divide the total spread measurement by two and slash and spread pattern that amount. Increase the front dart width, if necessary, to retain the original waist measurement. (fig. 93)

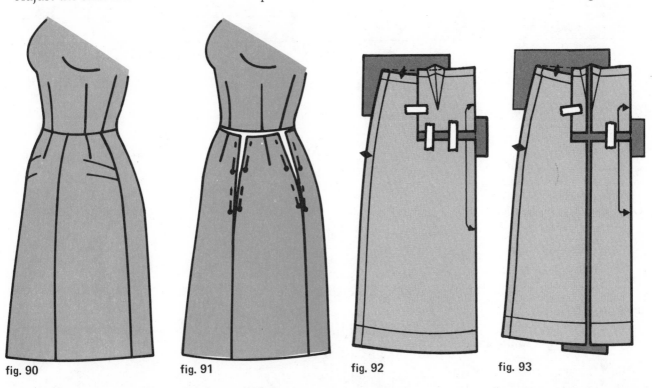

fig. 90   fig. 91   fig. 92   fig. 93

Pants Adjustments

Pants are part of everyone's wardrobe — quick and easy to make. The trick is to get a good fit. The best method to follow for a perfect fit is to first buy the pattern according to your hip measurement, take all your measurements accurately, compare them with the Standard Body Measurement and make up a muslin shell.

Ask a friend to help take your pants measurements which can be difficult to do accurately by yourself. Wear your regular undergarments and the shoes you will wear with the pants because heel height determines the finished pants length. Tie a string snugly around your waist and let it settle at the smallest part of your body indicating your natural waistline. Fill in your body measurements in column two of Your Pants Measurement Chart.

YOUR PANTS MEASUREMENT CHART

Where To Measure	Your Body Measurements	Standard Pattern or Body Measurements	Amount of Adjustment
Waist			
Hips			
Hip Drop			
Finished Length			
Thigh			
Crotch Depth			

(A) Waist: Measure around waist over the string.

(B) Hips: Measure at the fullest part of the hips.

(C) Hip Drop: Measure the distance from waist to the fullest part of the hips.

(D) Finished Length: Measure over hip to desired finished length.

(E) Thigh: Measure the thigh at the fullest part while seated. Add 2 inches (5cm) for basic ease.

(F) Crotch Depth: While sitting on a flat chair, measure from the waist string to the chair surface with a ruler. Add ½ inch (13mm) for sitting ease.

Measurements for the third column of Your Pants Measurement Chart will come from several sources. Waist and hip measurements are on the Standard Body Measurement Chart. The finished length is given on the back of the pattern envelope. The thigh and crotch depth measurements are taken from the actual pattern.

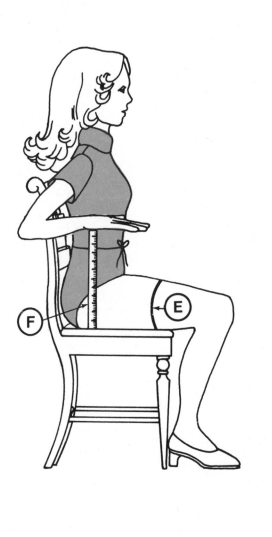
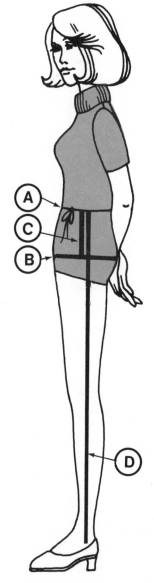

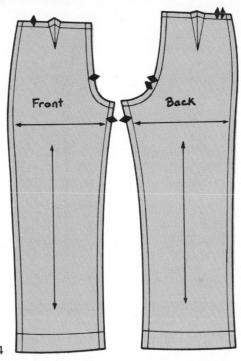

fig. 94

Thigh: Measure the pattern front and back, from seamline to seamline, at the point you took your thigh measurement. (fig. 94). Add these two numbers together and enter this amount in column three of Your Pants Measurement Chart.

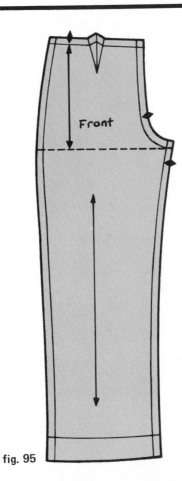

fig. 95

Crotch Depth: Working with the front pattern piece, draw a horizontal line from the crotch and inseam intersection to the side cutting line. This line must be at right angles to the grainline. Measure the distance from the drawn line to the waistline seam and add ½ inch (13mm) sitting ease. (fig. 95)

Pants adjustments will be divided into Group I and Group II Adjustments. Group I adjustments are done when your body measurements differ from the Standard Body or pattern measurements. Group II adjustments are done to take care of individual shape problems that cannot be measured with a tape. The only way to accurately define and correct these problems is with a muslin pants shell. Most pattern companies offer basic pants patterns that can be used for this shell. It is possible to use other pants patterns but the pattern should fit up to the natural waistline rather than ride low on the hips.

Gingham fabric is a good choice for a pants shell since the woven checks act as horizontal and vertical grainlines while you fit the garment. One of the key features of good fitting pants, as well as any other garment, is straight grainlines which gingham will help you achieve easily.

Mark all darts and seamlines of the shell with tracing paper before you stitch it up. This allows you to accurately measure alterations and transfer them to the paper pattern. The zipper does not have to be sewn in; just pin the opening closed for fitting.

Front and back crease lines should fall on the straight grainline and hang at right angles to the floor. (fig. 96) Make sure you are on grain when you lay out the pattern pieces on the fabric. Before you stitch the shell together, press the front and back creases so they will act as guidelines for the alterations.

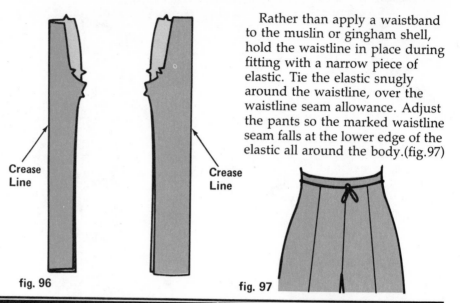

Crease Line

Crease Line

Rather than apply a waistband to the muslin or gingham shell, hold the waistline in place during fitting with a narrow piece of elastic. Tie the elastic snugly around the waistline, over the waistline seam allowance. Adjust the pants so the marked waistline seam falls at the lower edge of the elastic all around the body.(fig.97)

fig. 96

fig. 97

Group I Adjustments

Pants Length

The finished pants length might need to be increased or decreased according to your height or shoe height. Make these changes at the alteration line given on the lower pants front and back, not at the lower edge of the pants. Alter front and back pattern pieces the same amount.

To lengthen, cut along the alteration line. Tape edge of pattern piece to a wide piece of paper. Spread pattern pieces apart the needed amount, making sure the grainline matches exactly across the gap. Tape in place. (fig. 98) Trim away excess paper at the pattern edges, blending the cutting lines where necessary.

To shorten, draw a line on the pattern piece parallel to the alteration line with the distance between the two lines equal to the adjustment amount. (fig. 99)

Fold the bottom line up to meet the top line and tape the fold in place. (fig. 100) Correct the cutting line, blending where necessary.

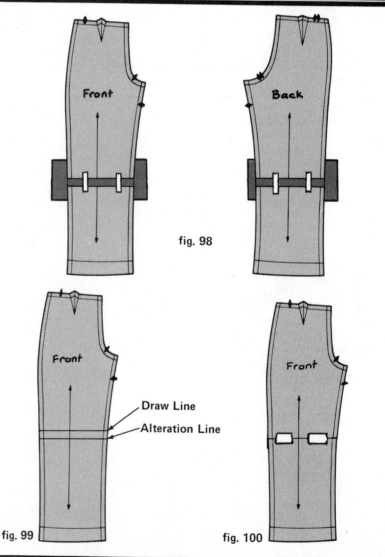

Front

Back

fig. 98

Front

Front

Draw Line

Alteration Line

fig. 99

fig. 100

46

Crotch Depth

Lengthen or shorten the crotch depth if your body measurement plus the recommended ease differs from the pattern measurement. Alter front and back pattern pieces the same amount.

To lengthen, cut along the pattern alteration line. If the pattern doesn't have one, draw your own half way between the crotch and waistline. Tape the edge of the pattern piece to a wide piece of paper. Spread the pattern pieces apart the needed amount, making sure the grainline matches exactly across the gap. Tape in place. (fig. 101) Trim away excess paper at the pattern edges blending the cutting lines where necessary.

To shorten, draw a line on the pattern piece parallel to the alteration line with the distance between the two lines equal to the amount of adjustment. Fold the bottom line up to meet the top line and tape the fold in place. (fig. 102) Correct the cutting line, blending where necessary.

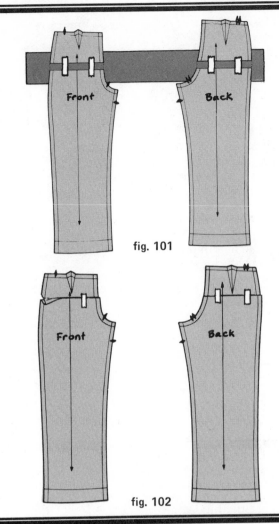

fig. 101

fig. 102

Waist Adjustments

Increase or decrease the waist measurement if your body measurement differs from the pattern measurement. Divide the difference by four and add or subtract results from the side of the front and back pattern pieces. Do not alter the center front or center back.

To increase waist, tape extra paper to the alteration area and measure out the needed amount at the waistline. Using a curved ruler, redraw the side cutting line blending it into the hip area. (fig. 103) Increase the length of the waistband or waist facings (if the pattern calls for a faced waist finish) to correspond with the above change. *(continued)*

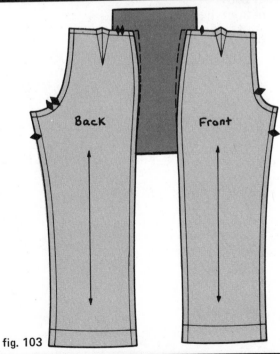

fig. 103

To decrease waist, measure in at the waist edge the desired amount and mark with a dot. Using a curved ruler, redraw the side cutting line from the dot, down to and blending with the hipline. (fig. 104) Decrease the length of the waistband and waist facings to correspond with the above change.

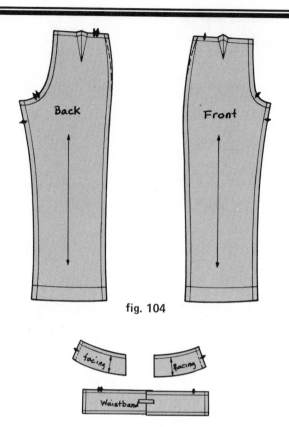

fig. 104

Hip Adjustments

Increase or decrease the hip measurement if your body measurement differs from the pattern measurement. Divide the difference by four and add or subtract the result from the side of front and back pattern pieces.

To increase hip, tape extra paper to the alteration area and measure out the needed amount at the hipline, as determined by the hip drop measurement in column two. Using a curved ruler, draw a new cutting line blending into the waist as shown. Add the increased width to the entire length of the pants leg. (fig. 105)   (continued)

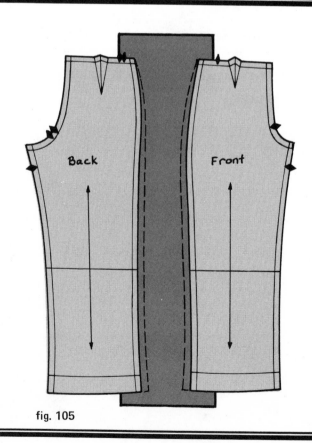

fig. 105

To decrease hip, measure in the needed amount at the hipline, as determined by the hip drop measurement in column two. Using a curved ruler, draw a new cutting line blending into the waist as shown. Remove the decreased width the entire length of the leg. (fig. 106)

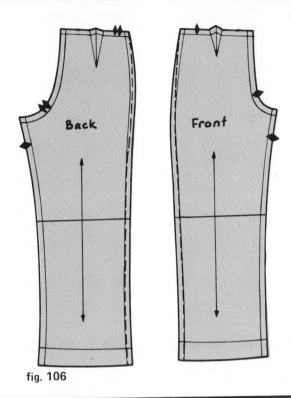

fig. 106

Thigh Adjustments

Heavy or thin thighs will require an alteration. Divide the difference between your body plus basic ease measurement and the pattern measurement by four. Add or subtract the result from each side of the pattern at the thigh measurement point. Remember, some pants styles call for fuller legs so don't decrease the thigh measurement until you have made up and tried on the pants or gingham shell.

To increase thigh, tape extra strips of paper to both sides of the pattern pieces. Measure out at the thigh measurement point one fourth the amount of increase. Redraw the side cutting line, blending into the crotch and hipline and add the increased width to the entire length of the leg. (fig. 107)

(continued on next page)

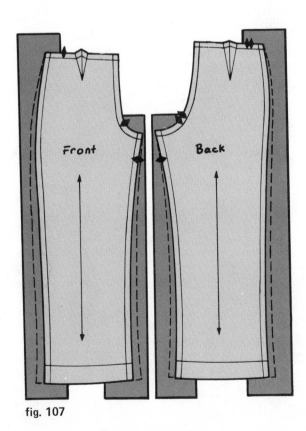

fig. 107

To decrease thigh measure in on both sides of the front and back pattern pieces at the thigh measurement point one fourth the amount of decrease. Redraw the side cutting lines, blending into the crotch and hipline; remove decreased width the entire length of the leg. (fig. 108)

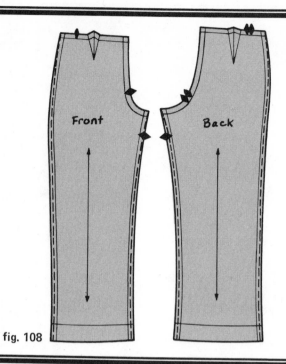

fig. 108

Group II Adjustments

Group II adjustments are made after any Group I adjustments are completed. They are the result of fitting problems that show up in the fitting shell. Remember, as you fit your shell, don't over fit. Allow enough room so you can comfortably sit and move.

Large Tummy

A large tummy will create diagonal wrinkles that point toward the abdomen causing your pants to feel short in the front crotch. (fig. 109)

Allow center front of the pants to drop at the waistline seam until wrinkles disappear and the crotch feels comfortable. Measure the distance between the lowered waist seamline and the bottom edge of the elastic. This is the amount of adjustment. (fig. 110)

Slash the pattern as indicated and spread the amount of the adjustment. Tape in an extra piece of paper to hold the alteration in place. Using a curved ruler, redraw the waist edge. Check the dart length and shorten if necessary for a good fit. (fig. 111)

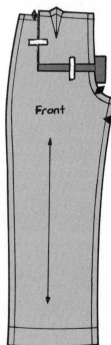

fig. 109

fig. 110

fig. 111

Front "Smile" Wrinkles

These wrinkles are caused by a short front crotch curve. This problem can occur as part of the full tummy problem or because the whole figure is very deep. (fig. 112)

fig. 112

Release the inseam below the crotch about 6 inches (15cm). Allow the seam to spread open until the "smile" wrinkles disappear. Pin in a fabric scrap to hold the alteration in place. Measure the distance of the spread at the crotch seamline. Tape an extra piece of paper to the front crotch area and measure out from the crotch seamline the amount of spread; mark with a dot. Using a curved ruler, redraw the crotch and inseam cutting line, blending into the original line as shown. (fig. 113)

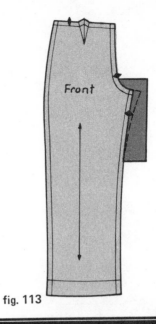

fig. 113

Front Crotch Fullness

Fullness in the front crotch area can be caused by two problems — flat tummy or a crotch curve of the wrong shape. You will have to decide which alteration solves your problem by analyzing your figure and/or perhaps trying each suggested alteration to see which one works best. The solution could also be a combination of the two. (fig. 114)

fig. 114

For flat tummy, release the inseam below the crotch about 6 inches (15cm). Re-pin taking in the front seam allowance only. Measure the amount of difference between the original and new inseam for the amount of adjustment. Measure in and mark along the crotch seamline the adjustment amount. Using a curved ruler, redraw the crotch and inseam cutting line blending into the original line as shown. (fig. 115)

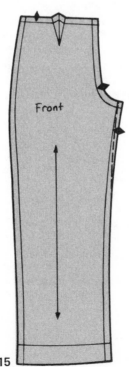

fig. 115

For wrong crotch curve, try on the fitting shell inside out and pin the front crotch curve deeper until wrinkles disappear. Using a curved ruler, redraw the front crotch curve seamline and cutting line to correspond to the changed shape. (fig. 116)

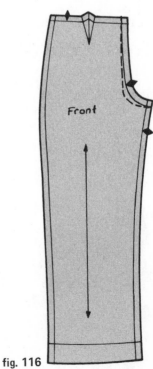

fig. 116

Sway Back

Wrinkles just below the back waistline indicate a sway back. (fig. 117)

Pull up the back waistline at the center back until wrinkles disappear. Measure the difference between the marked seamline and bottom edge of the elastic. This is the amount of adjustment. (fig. 118)

Slash the pattern back as shown and overlap the horizontal cut edges the amount of adjustment and tape in place. Using a curved ruler, redraw the waist cutting line. (fig. 119)

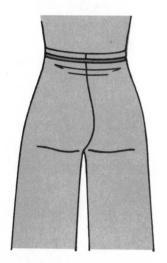

fig. 117

fig. 118

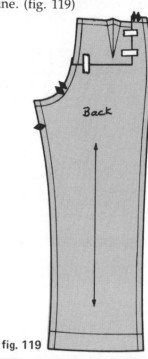

fig. 119

Back Crotch Fullness

Back crotch fullness can be caused by thin thighs and/or flat buttocks that don't quite fill the crotch curve. The problem can be solved by using one or both of the following pattern adjustments. (fig. 120)

For thin thighs, release the inseam about 6 inches (15cm) below the crotch seam. Re-pin, taking in the back seam allowance only. Measure the difference between the original and new back inseam. This is the amount of adjustment. Measure in and mark along the crotch seamline on the pattern the amount of adjustment. Using a curved ruler, redraw the crotch and inseam cutting edge blending into the original edge as shown. (fig. 121)
(continued on next page)

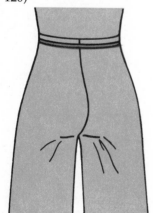

fig. 120

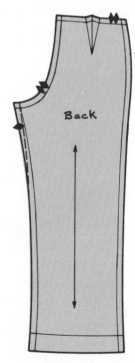

fig. 121

For flat buttocks, pull the waistline up at the center back until wrinkles disappear. Measure the difference between the marked waistline seam and bottom edge of the elastic for the amount of adjustment. (fig. 122)

Slash the pattern as shown and overlap the amount of adjustment taping in place. Using a curved ruler, redraw the waist cutting line. (fig. 123)

fig. 122

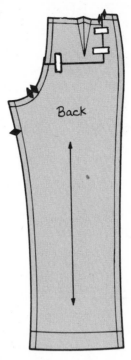

fig. 123

Back "Smile" Wrinkles

Buying your pattern by the hip measurement will take care of your hip circumference but you may find some pulling in the back crotch area caused by full buttocks or full thighs. The problem is indicated by "smile" wrinkles at the back crotch curve. (fig. 124)

Release the inseam about 6 inches (15cm) below the crotch and allow the seam to spread until wrinkles disappear. Pin in a fabric scrap to hold the alteration in place. Measure the distance of the spread at the crotch seamline. Tape an extra piece of paper to the back crotch area on the pattern piece and measure spread amount along the crotch seamline. Using a curved ruler, redraw the crotch and inseam cutting line. (fig. 125)

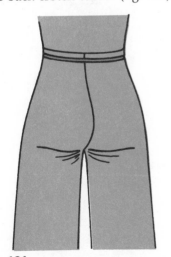

fig. 124

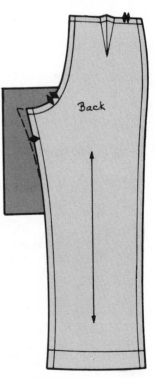

fig. 125

"Sit Down" Problems

Sometimes pants will "sit down" more than you do, pulling the waistband down at the center back. This is caused by low buttocks and the change must be made in the shape of the back crotch curve. (fig. 126)

Stitch the back crotch seam lower, ¼ inch (6mm) at a time, until the pants back hangs straight and doesn't pull when you sit down. Transfer this change in the shape of the crotch curve to the paper pattern. (fig. 127)

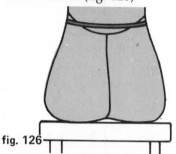

fig. 126

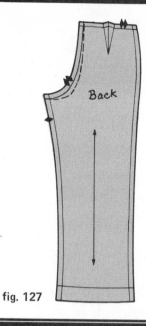

fig. 127

Seat Wrinkles

Wrinkles just below the crotch seam can be caused by flat buttocks or a crotch curve of the wrong shape. (fig. 128)

Pin a horizontal tuck across pants back at the fullest part of the buttocks so wrinkles disappear. The tuck should taper to nothing at the side seam. (fig. 129)

Measure full width of the tuck at the center back for the adjustment amount. Measure the distance of the tuck to the waist seam. Draw a horizontal line across the pattern back at the level of the tuck. Slash the pattern to but not through the side edge. Overlap slash the full width of the tuck and tape in place. Using a curved ruler, redraw the center back cutting line. (fig. 130)

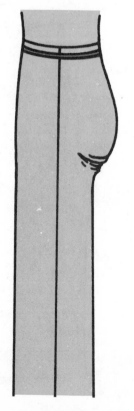

fig. 128

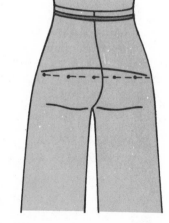

fig. 129

fig. 130

Pattern Layout, Cutting and Marking

Now that you have your pattern, fabric, interfacing and notions, you'll need to become acquainted with pattern pieces and the guide sheet. They provide useful information. Learning the vocabulary is easy and will make you feel like a pro.

Reading The Pattern

Every pattern piece is identified by name, number and sometimes the view. Identify and sort pattern pieces you need to make your view. Sorting is necessary because you might waste fabric cutting a piece you don't need.

The alteration line shows where to shorten or lengthen the pattern. It is located where there will be least disruption of garment lines.

The grainline, shown as a heavy black line with arrows on each end, is essential when laying out the pattern. It must always be parallel to lengthwise or crosswise threads of the fabric. (fig. 1)
(continued on next page)

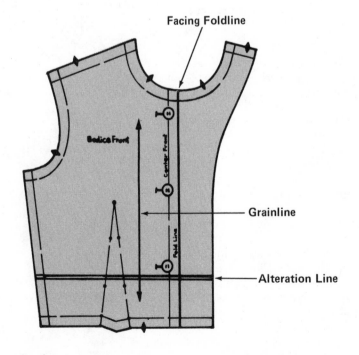

Facing Foldline

Bodice Front

Center Front

Fold Line

Grainline

Alteration Line

fig. 1

The "Place on Fold" bracket in this illustration (fig. 2) means the black line must be perfectly placed on the fold of the fabric.

The cutting line is usually a heavy black line around the outside edge of the pattern piece. (fig. 2) Some might be different colors or types of broken lines. A cutting line will occur in the middle of a pattern piece if a sleeve skirt or dress comes in two lengths. (fig. 3)

fig. 2

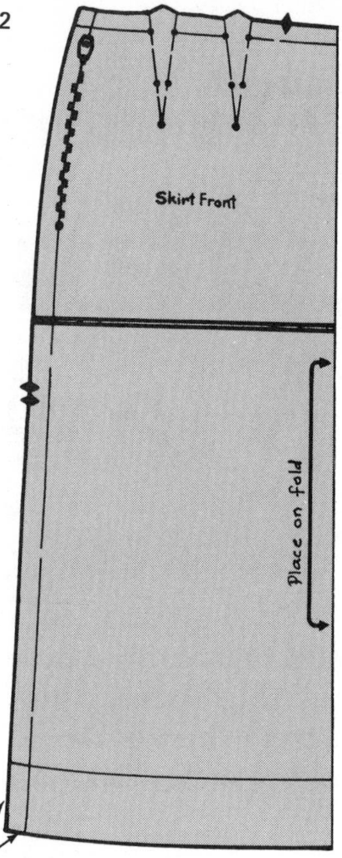

Skirt Front

Place on fold

Cutting Line

Construction Symbols

Construction symbols such as these — ● ▲ ■ — are important matching points on the pattern or they mark the beginning and end of a seam. Be sure to transfer them to your fabric when marking. (fig. 3)

The seamline is indicated by a long broken line that usually parallels the cutting line. (fig. 3). The space between the cutting line and seamline is the seam allowance, usually ⅝ inch (15mm). If the allowance is not the standard ⅝ inch (15mm) it will be called to your attention on the pattern piece or guide sheet.

(continued on next page)

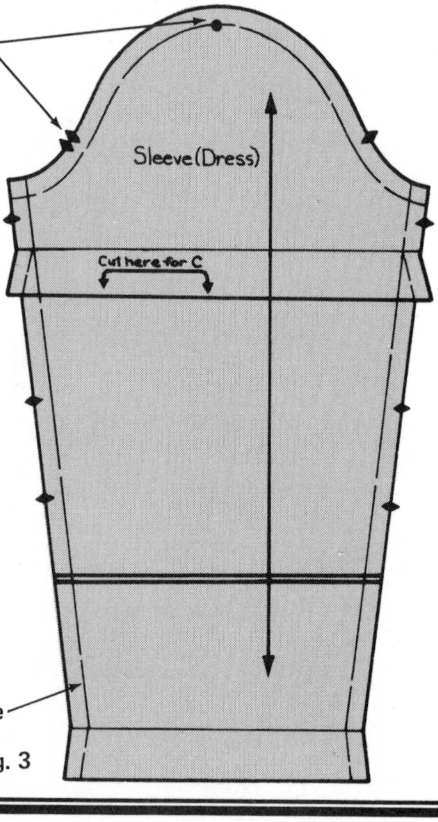

Sleeve (Dress)

Cut here for C

Seamline

fig. 3

Tip

EZ Buckle's cardboard cutting board makes an ideal surface for laying out fabric and patterns. Spread it out on a large table or on the floor so you can use its large 36 x 60 inch (91.44 x 152.40cm) surface. The basic pattern sizes on the board can help you make minor pattern adjustments and the bias markings will assist you in cutting bias strips.

Tip

Cutting lines on some patterns are very wide. The width of the seam allowance will be affected depending on which side of the line you cut. Measure the distance from the marked seamline to the cutting line and see just where the ⅝ inch (15mm) falls so you can cut accurately.

Darts are used to shape two dimensional fabric to a three dimensional figure. They look like this (fig. 4) but can also come to a point at both ends.

Notches show correct edges to join for a seam; single notches always match singles, double notches always match doubles, etc. Notches are numbered in the order they will be used in construction.

Buttons and buttonholes have distinct, clear markings. Be sure to respace them if you adjust the length of the pattern.

Center front and center back should never be changed except for length. Collars, buttons and buttonholes are closely related to the center front and/or center back. Mark them carefully and accurately.

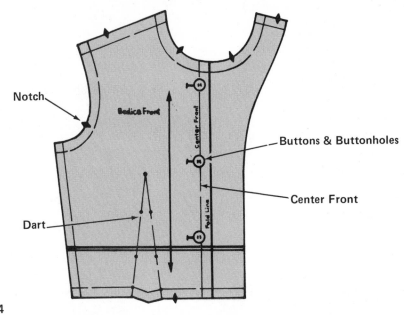

fig. 4

The Guide Sheet

The guide sheet gives useful information in addition to layout and construction directions. Look for the key to symbols and explanation of sewing terms.

The pattern may have different views of one garment or several garments in one envelope. Draw a circle around the view or items you will make.

Find the layout diagram for your view, fabric width and size and circle it. Be sure it is the "with nap" or "without nap" layout you need.

Pattern Layout

Several pattern pieces are printed on one big sheet of tissue. Cut and separate the pieces you need. If your measurement chart shows any pieces need to be increased, leave as much blank tissue as possible around the edges. This will save adding tissue later.

Separate the pattern pieces you will not use and keep them in the envelope. Compare the remaining pattern pieces to the guide sheet.

Press pattern pieces with a warm, dry iron before using.

Make any pattern adjustments now while the pieces are separated, before doing the layout.

Press wrinkled fabric lightly, removing the center crease. If the crease cannot be removed, do not use that area of fabric. Dabbing colorfast fabric with white vinegar sometimes helps when pressing out creases.

Work on a large, flat surface protected with a cutting board, if necessary. All fabric should lie on the work surface. Do not let it hang over the edge; some fabrics stretch when not supported.

Fold fabrics right sides together for the layout. If the selvage edge is puckered clip it every couple of inches until it lies flat.

Pin all pattern pieces to the fabric with the printed side up except when a piece is shaded in the layout diagram. In that case place the pattern piece printed side down on the fabric. (fig. 5)

(continued on next page)

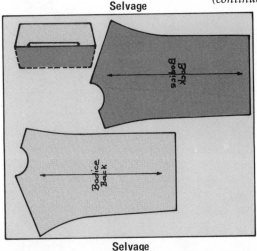

fig. 5

The layout diagram shows the location of all pattern pieces. Remember to place each piece precisely on a fold or the straight grain of the fabric.

Pattern pieces with a black Place on Fold bracket should be pinned exactly on a fabric fold. (fig. 6)

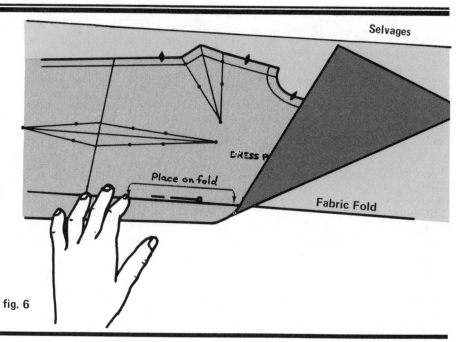

Selvages

Place on fold

DRESS P

Fabric Fold

fig. 6

Locate the placement of the other pieces on the layout diagram and pin one end of the marked grainline to the straight grain of the fabric. Move the other end of the grainline mark until it measures exactly the same distance from the selvage or fabric fold. Don't cheat to save fabric. Garments must be on grain so they will hang properly. (fig. 7)

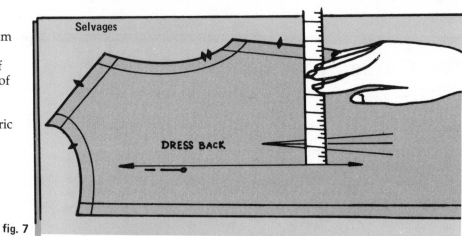

Selvages

DRESS BACK

fig. 7

If the grainline is too short to be useful, extend it the full length of the pattern piece. (fig. 8)
(continued on next page)

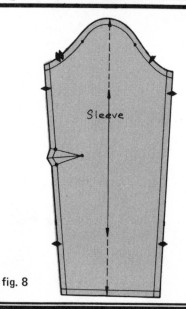

Sleeve

fig. 8

Tip

The 18 inch C-Thru Plastic Ruler is a good ruler to use when laying out your pattern. Measure from the fabric fold to both ends of the grainline markings for accurate placement of all pattern pieces. Manufactured by the C-Thru Ruler Co.

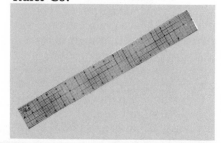

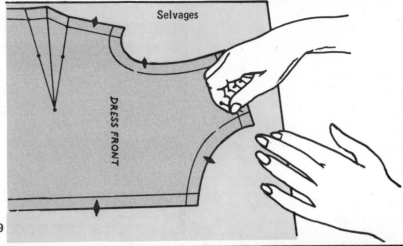

Once you have pinned all pattern pieces to the grainline or fold with two pins you will know if you have enough fabric and can finish the pinning process. Keep the pins well inside the cutting line, place a pin at each pattern corner smoothing the tissue as you go. Do not overpin; it distorts the pattern and the fabric. (fig. 9)

fig. 9

Tip

On heavy fabrics, such as quilts or coatings, pin through only one layer of fabric to make the cutting process more accurate.

Tip

A Magnetic Pin Dispenser is a handy pin holder when doing a pattern layout. The magnet around the large top opening keeps pins handy all the time and prevents them from spilling if you accidently tip it over. Also great for picking up stray pins. Manufactured by Risdon Mfg. Co.

When a pattern piece extends beyond the fabric fold on the layout diagram, pin as shown. Cut it out after all the other pieces have been cut. You will then be able to open up the fabric fold so you can cut the whole piece. (fig. 10) *(continued on next page)*

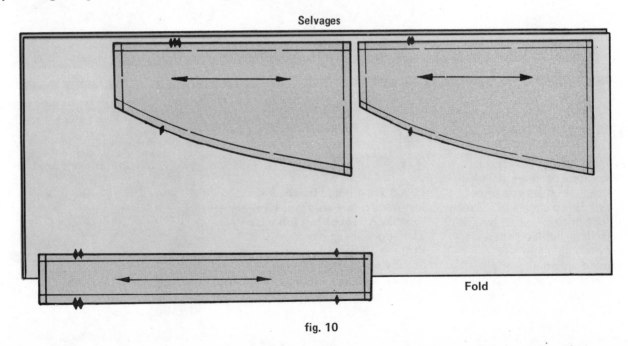

fig. 10

Lay out the interfacing pattern pieces according to the given diagram. (fig. 11) Follow the fabric grainline if the interfacing is woven. Consider the direction of stretch if the interfacing is a stretch, non-woven fabric. Stretch interfacing should be cut with the greatest stretch going around the body. Interfacing for garment areas that have buttonholes should be cut so the lengthwise grain or non-stretch direction follows the length of the buttonholes.

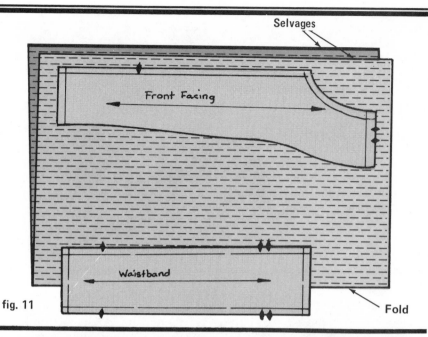

fig. 11

Tip

Pattern Weights from Bo Sew Accents can speed up the pinning and cutting process. Just lay the weights where needed to hold the pattern pieces to the fabric and cut.

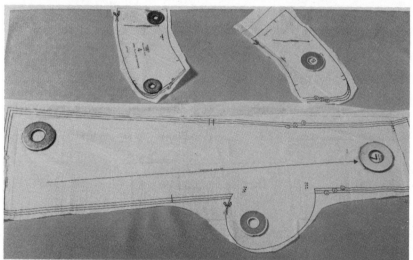

Cutting

Accurate cutting is very important for a professional touch. Make sure cut edges are smooth and even. Sharp shears of a 7 inch (18cm) or 8 inch (20.5cm) length are best. Bent handled shears are most comfortable and use left-handed shears if you are a lefty. Never use pinking shears to cut out a pattern. They do not cut accurately and are meant for seam finishing only.
(continued on next page)

Tip

If you are a lefty, try the left-handed shears from Gingher to make your cutting job easier. The super sharp shears cut through all types and many layers of fabric with no problem. Available from Gingher, Inc.

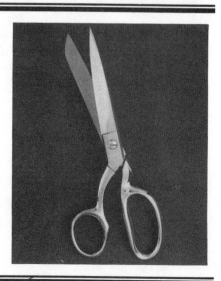

Cut precisely on the cutting line and around notches. Accuracy is important. Cut two or three notches together as shown. (fig. 12)

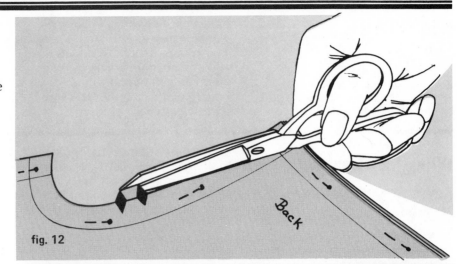

fig. 12

On thick fabrics, slip the shears between fabric layers. Cut the top layer and then the bottom layer. Cutting thick layers together distorts the edges.

Keep one hand on the pattern and fabric as you cut with the other hand. (fig. 13)

Don't move fabric and pattern pieces when cutting out. If a cutting angle is difficult, move around the table rather than move the fabric. Distorted fabric pieces can result if the fabric is moved.

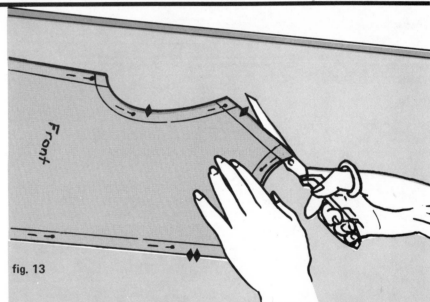

fig. 13

Tip

Lightweight shears make cutting easy. You will appreciate Talon's bent-handled lightweights when you have lots of cutting to do or if you have hand problems. From Donahue Sales, Talon Division of Textron, Inc.

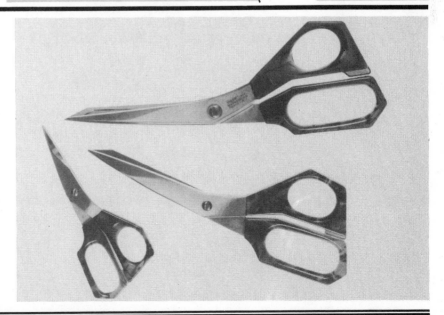

Marking

In order to put the garment together, darts, construction symbols and placement lines must be transferred from the pattern pieces to the wrong side of the garment pieces. This step, known as marking, is done after cutting while the pattern is still in place. First you must know what and how to mark. The symbols vary slightly with each pattern company but they are all explained on the guide sheet. If you have any doubts about whether or not to mark something, go ahead and mark it. It will take the guess work out of constructing the garment and save time as you sew.

What To Mark

Darts shape the garment to the body. (fig. 14)

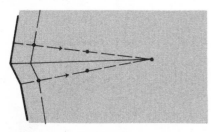

fig. 14

Tucks are similar but do not come to a point. (fig. 15)

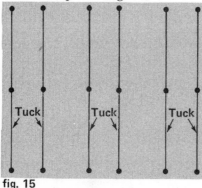

fig. 15

Construction marks indicate points that must be matched when sewing or they show the beginning or ending of a seam. (fig. 16)

fig. 16

Placement lines for pockets are marked on the right side of the fabric.

Pleats use a combination of solid and broken lines. The instructions will tell you to fold on the solid line and bring to the dotted line. Mark the two different types of lines with two different threads or tracing paper colors. (fig. 17)

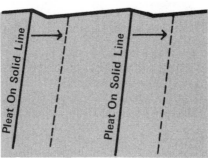

fig. 17

Hem is shown with a solid line. This is important on long sleeves and pants. (fig. 18)

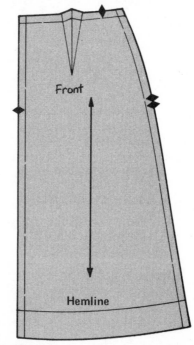

fig. 18

Center front and foldlines for the facing are crucial. Use a ruler to be accurate. Where there is interfacing, mark the center front on that too before attaching it to the garment. (fig. 19)

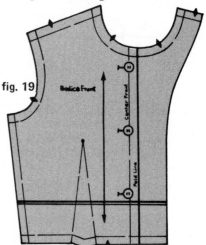

fig. 19 Bodice Front

Draw 1 inch (25mm) lines on either side of the clip mark. Do not clip until you start sewing. Instructions will tell you to stitch and then clip. (fig. 20)

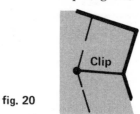

fig. 20

Seamlines should be marked only at places where it would be difficult to follow the seam guide, such as curved seams or pockets set in a side seam. (fig. 21)

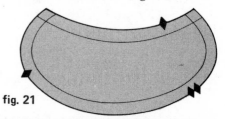

fig. 21

How To Mark

There are several acceptable ways of marking fabric. It is useful to know more than one since one method cannot be used in all situations.

Tracing Paper and Tracing Wheel

Tracing paper and a tracing wheel provide the easiest, quickest and most accurate method of marking fabric. However it does have one disadvantage; tracing paper is not always 100 percent removable. If you are marking on the wrong side of a heavy fabric you'll have no problem. But on a sheer cotton, the marks will show through to the right side and another method is advisable.

Place one sheet of tracing paper underneath the fabric and pattern with the colored side against the wrong side of the fabric. Slip a second sheet of tracing paper between the pattern and fabric on top so the colored side is against the wrong side of the fabric. Mark with the tracing wheel using a ruler for all straight lines. (fig. 22)

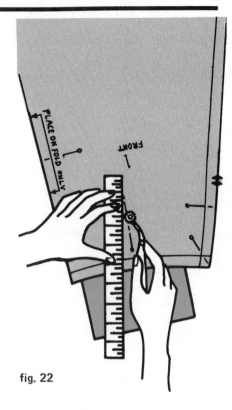

fig. 22

Mark dart ends with a short line. Run the wheel over all symbols and lines using an X as a good way to mark dots. (fig. 23)
(continued on next page)

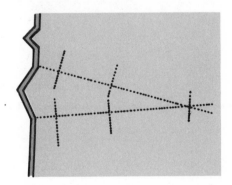

fig. 23

Tip

Use the E-Z Buckle Double Faced Tracing Paper and Tracing Wheel to transfer construction marks to your fabric. Five colors come in the package of tracing paper and the chubby plastic handle of the tracing wheel is easy to hold. Available from E-Z Buckle Co.

Pins And Chalk Pencil

When tracing paper is not suitable, pins and chalk pencil provide a good method of marking. Test the chalk pencil on a fabric scrap to see if it will show up and brush off.

With the pattern up, push pins straight down through the pattern and both layers of fabric at the points to be marked. (fig. 24)

Turn the fabric over and make a chalk mark at each pin. Remove the pins that hold the pattern to the fabric. Pull the pattern gently over the other pin heads and set aside. (fig. 25) Make chalk marks at every pin head, removing the pins as you go.

On both layers, connect the chalk marks for darts or any place where a continuous line is needed. (fig. 26) Keep the pattern and marked pieces together until ready to sew.

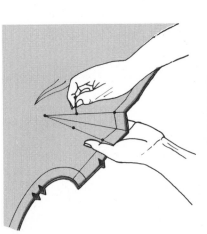

fig. 24

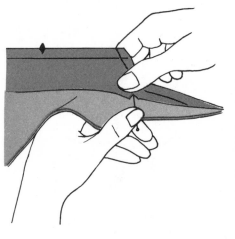

fig. 25

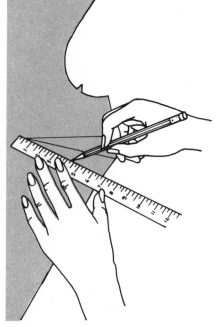

fig. 26

Tip

The yellow chalk Dressmaker's Pencil from Fashionetics will show up on most any fabric and has a handy brush on the end to remove the chalk marks from the fabric afterward. Available from Fashionetics, Inc.

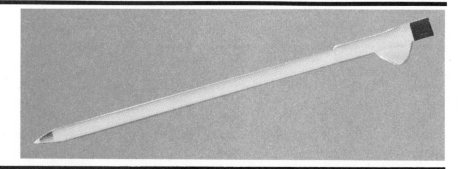

Tip

Use the washable Marking Pen to mark construction marks instead of chalk. Make a dot where the pin comes through each layer of fabric as described above. Remove the marks with a damp cloth or drop of clear water immediately after using. Available from Risdon Mfg. Co.

Tailor Tacks

The best method of marking for delicate fabrics or nubby fabrics is the use of tailor tacks.

Use a double thread with no knot and take two loose stitches through the pattern and fabric at the point to be marked while the pattern is still pinned to the fabric. Leave large thread loops at each mark. If the marks are close together carry the thread over between marks. Otherwise, cut the threads, leaving long tails, and move to the next mark. (fig. 27)

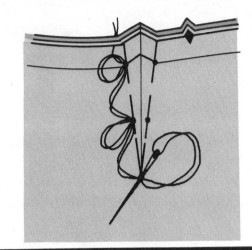

fig. 27

When all marks on one piece are stitched, gently pull the pattern away from the threads. Separate the two layers of fabric, snipping the threads of each tack between the fabric layers, leaving some thread in each garment piece. (fig. 28)

Tip

When making tailor tacks in delicate fabrics always use a fine needle and silk thread so the tack won't leave marks.

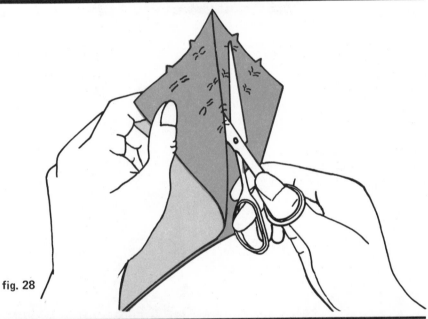

fig. 28

Thread Tracing

Thread tracing is used with all three methods of marking. When a continuous line of marking needs to be seen on the right side of the fabric, it is thread traced.

Using a single thread, no knot, baste along lines marked on the wrong side of the fabric. Silk thread is best because it leaves no mark even when pressed. Use thread tracing for marking center front, buttonholes, foldlines, pocket placement, etc. This method can also be done by machine with a long basting stitch. (fig. 29)

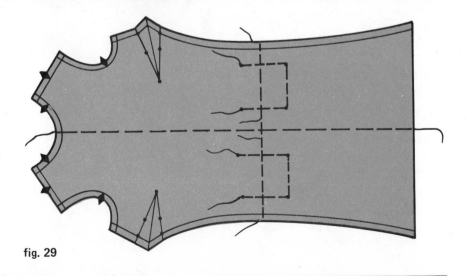

fig. 29

Pressing

Good pressing techniques are just as important to the look of the finished garment as being able to sew a straight seam. Seams should be pressed as they are sewn and body shape should be built into the garment by use of proper pressing tools.

Pressing Tools

Using the correct pressing tool will speed along the garment construction and guarantee a professionally pressed look. All the following tools are available at notions or houseware counters. However, some of them can be replaced by homemade substitutes at a fraction of the cost.

The steam iron is your most important pressing tool. Select one that is comfortable in your hand and not too heavy. Some of the most useful features on new steam irons are big water reservoirs with a water level gauge, a shot of steam or spray device to apply more moisture to the fabric and self-cleaning ability. Just as important as the features is the

care. Make sure you read and follow the manufacturer's instructions and your iron should give you years of good service.

A well covered, adjustable ironing board will make your pressing tasks much easier. Make sure the board is padded adequately and wash or replace

the cover whenever it becomes soiled.

Spring clips, available at most housewares counters, will keep the ironing board cover taut.

A collapsible, clamp-on cord holder will keep the iron cord out of your way and up off the fabric while pressing.

Tip

If your iron gets dirty or begins to form a build-up of fusible residue or starch, clean the soleplate with Dritz Iron-Off. It can be used on the soleplate of a hot iron so there is no need to wait for your iron to cool when you are in the middle of a project. From Scovill, Sewing Notions Division.

Spring Clips *(Travco)*

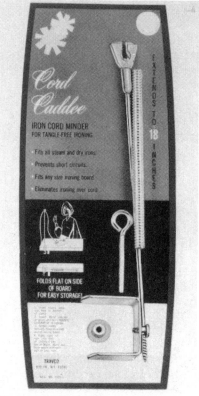

Clamp-On Cord Holder *(Travco)*

Tip

The Steamstress iron, which comes in two different sizes, is a lightweight, non-metal iron which does not become hot but produces a large amount of steam. It is a must when working with napped fabrics such as velvet since steam does the pressing rather than pressure. It is also a handy travel iron because of size and weight.

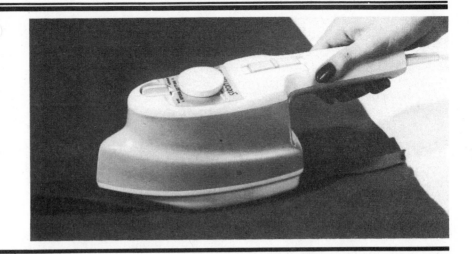

A seam roll should be used whenever pressing seams open. It prevents the seam edges from leaving impressions on the right side of the fabric. Ready-made seam rolls are approximately 13 inches (32.5cm) long. Longer seam rolls, which are handy when pressing open long seams, can be made from heavy cardboard tubes covered with a sleeve of cotton knit. These tubes are usually available at no cost at most fabric stores.

The tailor's ham is a ham shaped cushion used to build in garment shape. It should be used when pressing open curved seams or darts. It is also useful when steaming and shaping collars. *(continued on next page)*

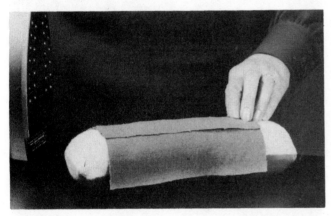

Seam Roll *(June Tailor, Inc.)*

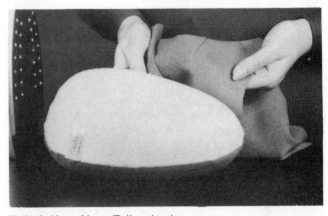

Tailor's Ham *(June Tailor, Inc.)*

A hamholder is a plastic or wooden cradle with multiple curved sides. The angles help position the ham in various ways to make pressing jobs easier.

Hamholder *(June Tailor, Inc.)*

A point presser is a wooden tool used when pressing open seam allowances in points and corners and along lapel and collar edges. One end of the tool is narrow and pointed for fitting into points or corners.

A clapper or pounding block is used to flatten garment edges and set creases. It can be purchased from a notions counter or you can use a large wooden block as a substitute.

A needle board is used when pressing pile fabrics such as velvet. The needles support the fabric but prevent the pile from being crushed. A folded terry towel can also serve as a needle board in a pinch.

The sleeve board is used to press sleeves after they are sewn. It slips inside the sleeve fitting the shape.

A pressing cloth is used to protect the right side of the fabric. Pressing cloths can also be dampened if more moisture is needed for specific areas. Various types of pressing cloths are available at notions counters. However, a piece of lightweight muslin or batiste fabric can be used. Handi-Wipes towels also make good pressing cloths.

Brown paper strips are available in pad form to be used when pressing open seams and hems to prevent impressions from appearing on the right side of the garment. These can be purchased at notions counters or you can cut your own from brown paper bags or discarded legal size envelopes.

Point Presser *(June Tailor, Inc.)*

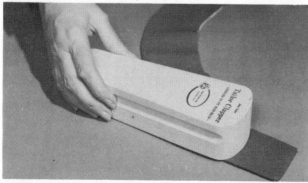

Clapper *(June Tailor, Inc.)*

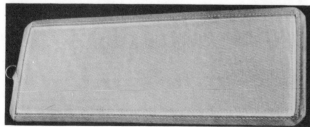

Needle Board *(Scovill-Dritz)*

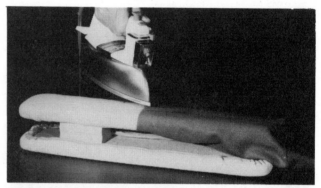

Sleeve Board *(June Tailor, Inc.)*

Pressing Cloths *(June Tailor, Inc.)*

Brown Paper Strips *(June Tailor, Inc.)*

Tip

Two sole plate attachments are available which control the iron heat. They also allow you to press on the right side of the fabric without a pressing cloth. Iron All, available from Stacy Fabrics Corp., and Iron Safe, available from Jacobson Products Co., Inc., are the names of these attachments. The Iron All is made from a space-age material while the Iron Safe is made from metal covered with a thick coat of Teflon. The advantage of using the Teflon coated attachment is that nothing will stick to it. Bits of fusible material will stick to the Iron All eventually causing it to be discarded.

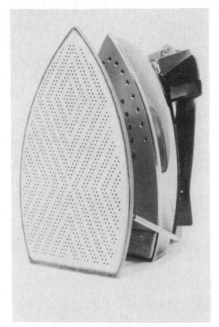

Iron All

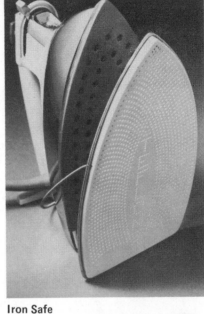

Iron Safe

Pressing Techniques

There are six basic rules to follow when pressing a garment during and after construction for a custom look.

Use the proper heat setting on the iron for the fabric you are pressing. Most irons have recommended temperature information on the iron top. Too hot an iron might scorch or melt the fabric. Too low a setting won't press effectively.

Press rather than iron to prevent wrinkles and distortion of the fabric. This means use an up and down motion rather than a back and forth motion. (fig. 1)

(continued on next page)

fig. 1

Press in order of construction. Never cross one seam with another unless the seam has been pressed. First, press seam in the flat position (fig. 2) to set the stitches and then press seam open or to one side as pattern indicates. (fig. 3)

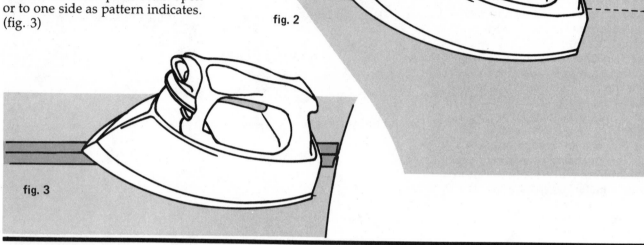

fig. 2

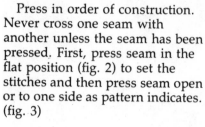

fig. 3

Pressing on the right side of the fabric with a bare iron will always leave a mark. Use either a pressing cloth or a sole plate attachment to protect the fabric and prevent iron marks.

Prevent seam impressions from showing on the right side of your fabric by using a seam roll (fig. 4) or paper strips (fig. 5) placed under seam allowances. Also use these paper guards whenever you press up hems or mitered corners.

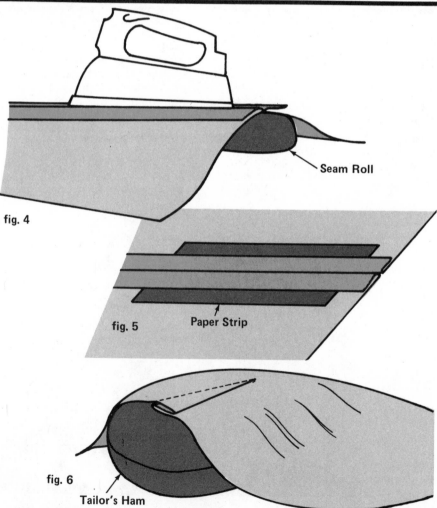

Seam Roll

fig. 4

Paper Strip

fig. 5

Use a tailor's ham to build in garment shape whenever you press darts or curved areas of the garment. (fig. 6)

fig. 6

Tailor's Ham

Interfacings

Interfacing is an important part of well-made clothes. It adds support and firmness to garment edges, collars, cuffs and other small design details. It also helps keep the garment crisp and fresh looking through repeated wearings.

Interfacing Types

There are two main types of interfacing available on the market today; nonfusible and fusible interfacing. Each basic type is made in woven and non-woven fabrics, some with stretch in one or more directions and some stable in all directions. Each interfacing type comes in various weights or thicknesses.

Both types of interfacing can be used on most any type of fabric so the choice is up to you. However, fusible interfacings have some advantages over nonfusible interfacings which should be considered when buying.

Fusible interfacing is fused to the fashion fabric so the two layers can be handled as one.

Seam allowances can be removed from the interfacing before fusing to reduce thickness and bulk in the finished seam area.

Small detail pieces, such as pocket flaps or welts are easier to work with if the interfacing is first fused in place.

Selecting Interfacings

Have your fashion fabric with you when selecting interfacing. Drape the two fabrics together to see which interfacing gives the desired finished look. Some heavy fabrics may need just a light touch of interfacing while a thin fabric may need the support of a medium to heavy-weight interfacing.

Sometimes a combination of interfacing weights is required in one garment. For example, you might use a firm, medium-weight interfacing for the cuffs and pocket details, but a supple, lighter-weight interfacing for the soft, roll collar.

Interfacings with all-bias or crosswise stretch are ideal for knit garments. They add needed support but retain the "give" of knit. Be sure to cut interfacing pieces so stretch goes around the body. This will provide the most wearing comfort.

Non-stretch, woven interfacings can also be used for knits. However, they must be cut on the bias when covering large areas of

Tip

Protect your iron when bonding fusible interfacing by using the Dritz Vue-thru Pressing Cloth. It will allow you to see what you are doing but will prevent fusible residue from collecting on the soleplate. From Scovill, Sewing Notions Division

Tip

Fusible interfacing, after application, stiffens the fashion fabric. Keep this in mind when selecting interfacing.

the garment so the interfacing "gives" with the fabric.

Fusible interfacings can be used for nearly all interfacing requirements. Nonfusibles can be used anywhere too, but might require hand work. They are not quite as easy to handle as a fusible interfacing bonded to the fashion fabric. Some delicate, lightweight, synthetic fabrics cannot stand the heat needed to apply a fusible interfacing. A nonfusible one should be used in this situation.

Interfacings are made in various colors. Most common is white, but you will see some cream, grey and black interfacings. Use the darker colors only on dark or heavy fabrics where the color will not show through.

Machine buttonhole areas should always be supported by some type of interfacing. If you use lining or underlining fabric color-matched to the fashion fabric, you will avoid a line of white showing along the edge of the buttonhole. If you have to use white interfacing, camouflage the white line with a matching colored pencil or pen.

Interfacing Application

Some interfacings, wovens more than non-wovens, tend to shrink. Unless the hang-tag or bolt end states differently it is advisable to pre-shrink all interfacing fabrics. Nonfusibles can be pre-shrunk in the washing machine and dryer. Fusible interfacings should be placed in a bowl of warm water and allowed to drip-dry. Do not pre-shrink fusible interfacings in the washer; it will cause the fusing material to come off.

Cut all interfacing pieces accurately. Cut on the same grain line as the garment piece when using a woven interfacing. Exceptions are bias cuts for knit garments and collars. Stretch interfacings should be cut with the stretch going around the body.

Apply interfacing to the wrong side of the visible garment piece. For example: interface the upper pieces of collars, cuffs and pocket flaps; apply the interfacing to the wrong side of the facing when the garment has a turn-back lapel. Doing this will prevent "shadowing through" of the seam allowances. This is especially important on lightweight or sheer fabrics.

Nonfusible Interfacing

Trim away interfacing at corners and points before applying to the fashion fabric. This will eliminate bulk and allow them to turn smoothly. (fig. 1)

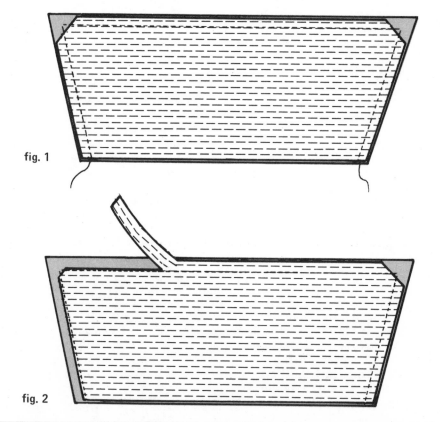

fig. 1

fig. 2

Nonfusible interfacing is held in place by being included in the garment seam allowances or by being stitched to the garment piece ⅛ inch (3mm) away from the given seamline. The interfacing seam allowance is then trimmed as close to the stitching as possible. (fig. 2)

Fusible Interfacing

Make sure you get bonding instructions when purchasing fusible interfacing. Each interfacing requires a slightly different technique, and what works with one doesn't necessarily work with another.

Follow the manufacturer's instructions precisely when bonding fusible interfacing to the fashion fabric. If bonded imperfectly, the interfacing will blister and pull away from the fabric in the first washing or cleaning. It is very difficult, if not impossible, to re-bond the interfacing after this happens.

Trim away seam allowances and the corners of fusible interfacing before applying to the garment. (fig. 3) *(continued on next page)*

Tip

If your iron soleplate happens to pick up fusible interfacing residue remove it with Dritz iron-off. This product removes fabric deposits, melted synthetics and starch build up and can be used on a hot iron. Made by Scovill, Sewing Notions Division.

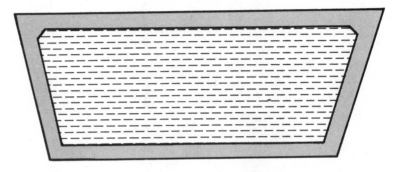

fig. 3

Tip

A new product on the market saves time when interfacing waistbands, cuffs, front bands and plackets. It is a pre-cut strip of non-woven, fusible interfacing in two weights and four widths. It also has pre-marked stitching lines so it is very easy to get even edges on the finished garment. The product is called Fuse'N Fold and is made by the Pellon Corporation. It is available at most notions counters.

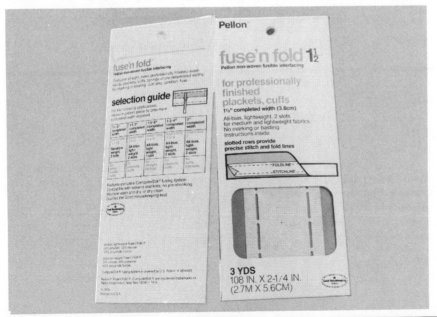

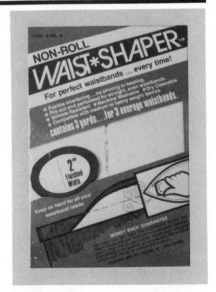

Tip

Waist Shaper is also a new fusible waistband product that makes non-roll waistbands. Available in two widths, 1¼ inch and 2 inch (31cm and 50cm) the package contains enough for three average waistbands. Available from Stacy Fabrics Corp.

Fuse-baste large pieces of interfacing to the garment. This is done by positioning interfacing over the garment piece and then touching the tip of the iron to the interfacing at various key points to hold the interfacing in place. This prevents the interfacing from slipping while fusing smaller sections.

Fusible interfacing should completely cover the garment piece to which it is being applied, except for the seam allowances. Otherwise it will leave a visible line on the right side of the garment, where the interfacing ends. (fig. 4)

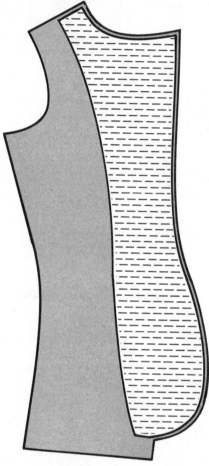

Wrong Application

fig. 4

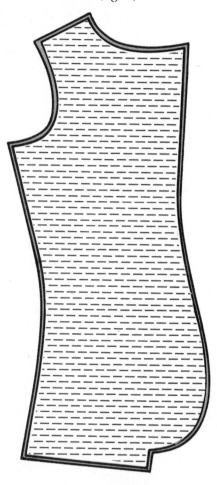

Correct Application

Tip

A thin web of fusing material is available in narrow, pre-packaged strips or wider widths by the yard. It is used to bond two layers of fabric together, and can be used to put up hems, hold appliques in place and secure patches before stitching. Because the fused web adds some firmness to fabrics, it can also be used across the top of pockets and at hem and sleeve edges to add a bit of firmness.

Tip

Occasionally small pieces of fusing material will stick to the ironing-board cover. This can be prevented by covering the ironing board with a piece of sheeting or an old pillow case.

Tip

Nonfusible interfacing pieces can be held temporarily in place with glue from a glue stick. This eliminates the need to stitch interfacing to the garment piece and makes sewing faster.

Seams

Seams get your sewing project all together. The type of seam you use will depend on the fabric, style and use of the garment. Commercial patterns generally use a ⅝ inch (15mm) seam width. However, that is not always the case and some speciality patterns call for ¼ (6mm), ⅜ (10mm) and ½ (13mm) inch seams. Check your pattern carefully for the given seam width before you start to sew.

Directional Stitching

Seams should be stitched in the direction of the grain in order to prevent distortion of the fabric edge. This is especially important on angled or curved areas. The grain direction can be determined by running your finger along the cut edge. You are going against the grain if the fabric threads tend to spread apart. (fig. 1)

You are going with the grain if the fabric threads lie smoothly along the cut edge. (fig. 2)

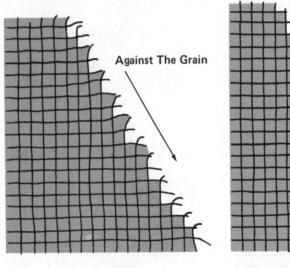

Against The Grain

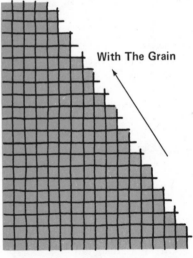

With The Grain

fig. 1

fig. 2

A rule to follow for directional stitching is to stitch from the widest portion of the garment toward the narrowest. (fig. 3)
(continued on next page)

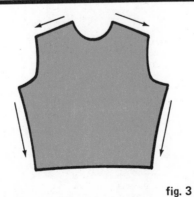
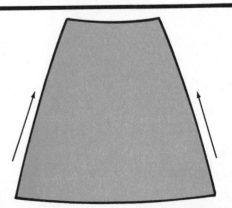

fig. 3

Curved areas should be stitched in two directions because the grain direction changes so often along the curve. (fig. 4)

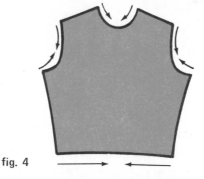

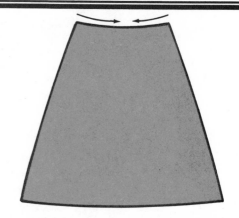

fig. 4

Staystitching

Staystitching is a technique used to stabilize certain seam areas so they retain their proper size and shape during handling of the garment. Staystitching should be done directionally, a scant ⅛ inch (3mm) to the right of the seamline. Staystitch immediately after removing the pattern from the fabric using a regular stitch length and a matching thread. Change directions of the staystitching as often as necessary in order to conform to directional stitching rules. (fig. 5)

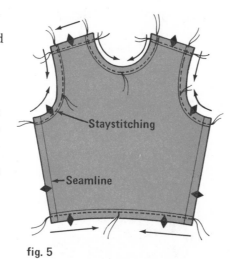

Staystitching

Seamline

fig. 5

Tip

Knit fabrics handle differently than woven fabrics since they have no pronounced lengthwise or crosswise grain. Directional stitching is not necessary. However, staystitching is sometimes required to stabilize certain seams so they retain the proper size and shape in the finished garment. Examples of the seam areas are: necklines which require collars, waistline seams, shoulder seams and armhole seams.

The Basic Seam

Pin the fabric layers right sides together matching construction marks. The pins should enter the fabric at the seamline for best control. (fig. 6)

Insert the machine needle in the fabric ½ inch (13mm) from the edge at the given seam width. Backstitch to the edge, then stitch forward and complete the seam. Backstitch again for approximately ½ inch (13mm) at the end of the seam. Remove each pin before the needle stitches over it to prevent needle damage. (fig. 7)

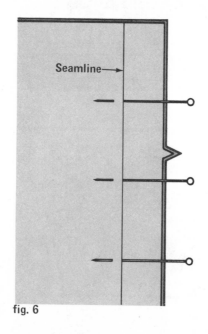

Seamline

fig. 6

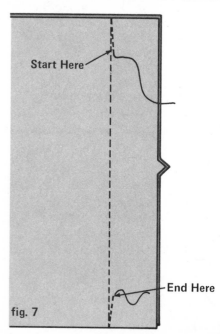

Start Here

End Here

fig. 7

Seams that will be crossed with other seams and then trimmed should have backstitching done where seamlines cross rather than at the end of the fabric. This keeps the seam secure after seam allowances have been trimmed. (fig. 8)

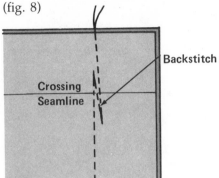

Crossing Seamline

Backstitch

fig. 8

Seams crossed by other seams should also have ends of the seam allowances trimmed as indicated in order to reduce bulk in the crossed seam area. (fig. 9)

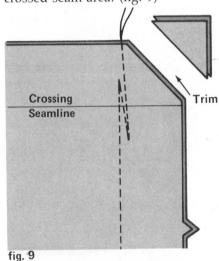

Crossing Seamline

Trim

fig. 9

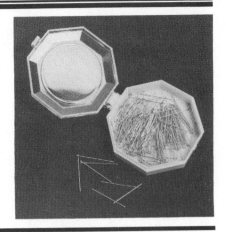

Press seam in the flat position to relax the thread and set the stitches. (fig. 10)

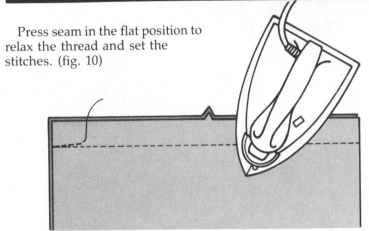

fig. 10

Then press seam allowances open. (fig. 11)

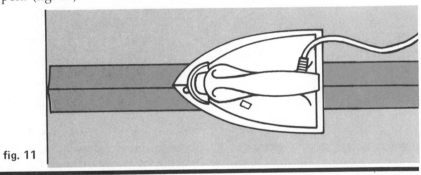

fig. 11

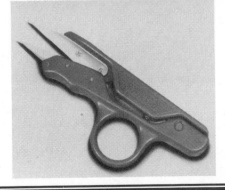

Tip

Some fabrics tend to pucker slightly when sewn. This can usually be prevented if the fabric layers are held taut as they go under the presser foot. Hold the fabric in front of and behind the presser foot, keeping it taut but not stretching it or pulling it through the machine.

Seam Guides

Use a seam guide to help keep seams an even width. Many machines have seam width guidelines etched on the throat plate. Guide the edge of the fabric along the line marking the desired seam width. (fig. 12)

Make your own seam guide with a strip of tape placed on the throat plate, if your machine is not marked. Measure the desired width from the machine needle. Reposition the tape for each different seam width. (fig. 13)

A mechanical seam guide attachment is available for some machines which is adjustable for different seam widths. It is especially useful for curved seams. (fig. 14)

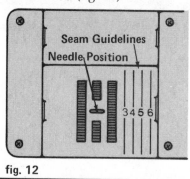

fig. 12

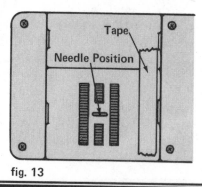

fig. 13

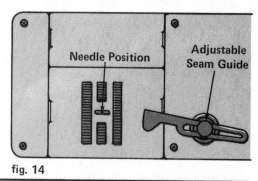

fig. 14

Seam Finishes

Many fabrics need the edges of seam allowances finished in some way to prevent fraying or to give a more finished look to the inside of unlined jackets. The type of fabric, the garment's use and whether it is lined or unlined will determine the choice of seam finish.

Overcast Finish

Overcast the seam edges by hand or with a machine zigzag stitch. This technique is suitable for most woven fabrics and can be used on knits when a more finished look than a raw edge is desired. (fig. 15)

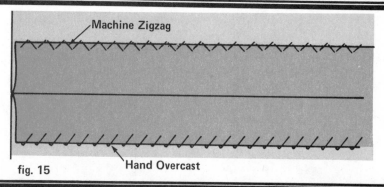

fig. 15

Stitched and/or Pinked Finish

Pink the edges of firmly woven fabrics after the seam has been stitched and pressed open. Combine the pinked edge with a row of straight stitching about ¼ inch (6mm) in from the seam edge for fabrics which tend to ravel. (fig. 16)

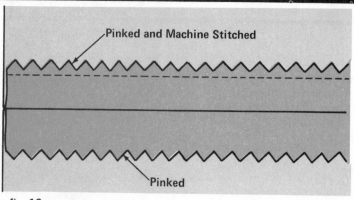

fig. 16

Clean Finish

Straight stitch along the edge of each pressed open seam allowance a generous ⅛ inch (3mm) from the edge. Turn under the seam edge along the stitching and edgestitch. Use this method on light to medium weight woven fabrics. Do not use on knits. (fig. 17)

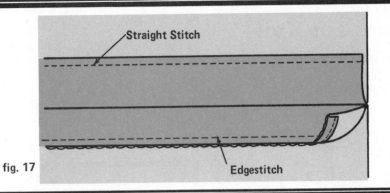

fig. 17

Bound Finish

Tailored jackets to be partially lined or left completely unlined should have a more attractive and durable seam finish. Binding edges of the seam allowance with either double fold bias tape or bias strips of lining fabric gives the desired finish. These seam finishes can also be used to finish the edges of vents and hems of an unlined garment. They work equally well with woven or knit fabric.

Enclose the seam edge in matching double fold bias tape with the narrow folded section up. Edgestitch, catching both layers of bias tape in the stitching. (fig. 18)

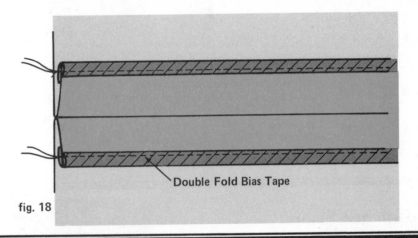

fig. 18

Hong Kong Seam Finish

Cut 1 inch (25mm) wide bias strips of matching or contrasting lining fabric. Seam the strips together where necessary when binding long seam edges. Stitch the bias strip to the seam edge, right sides together, with a scant ¼ inch (6mm) seam. (fig. 19)

Wrap the strip around the seam edge to the wrong side. Secure by stitching-in-the-ditch on the right side. Use a short stitch length — 18-20 stitches per inch — and the stitches will be invisible. (fig. 20)

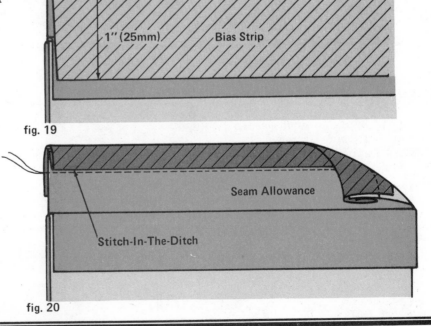

fig. 19

fig. 20

Seams For Knits

Knit fabrics need seams that give with the fabric. This can be done manually, by stretching the fabric slightly as it goes under the presser foot. Use a stitch length of 9-10 stitches per inch. (fig. 21)

Seams with give can also be made using a very small zigzag or an automatic straight stretch stitch found on many modern sewing machines. (fig. 22) The fabric does not have to be stretched when either of these stitches is used.

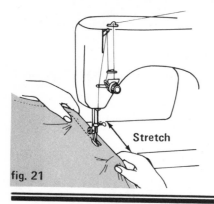

Stretch

fig. 21

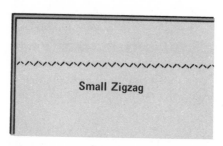

Small Zigzag

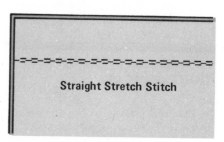

Straight Stretch Stitch

fig. 22

Knit Seam Finishes

Knit fabrics sometimes need special seam treatments — not because the fabric frays but because some knits will not hold a press, making the conventional pressed-open seam allowance unsuitable. Test the pressing ability of your knit fabric on a seam sample made from scrap fabric before you start to sew. If the seam refuses to stay pressed open use one of the following knit seam finishes.

Topstitched Seam

Press both seam allowances to one side and topstitch through all layers from the right side of the garment about ¼ inch (6mm) from the seamline. (fig. 23)

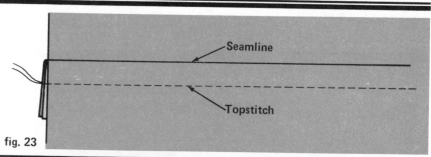

Seamline

Topstitch

fig. 23

Narrow Knit Seam

Using a wide zigzag, stitch close to the straight seam. Trim away the excess seam allowance and press to one side. (fig. 24)

Use the stretch overlock stitch which is available on many newer sewing machines. Trim the seam allowances close to the edge of stitching and press to one side. (fig. 25)

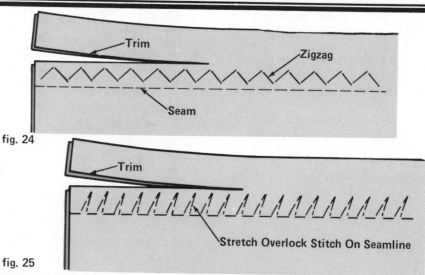

Trim

Zigzag

Seam

fig. 24

Trim

Stretch Overlock Stitch On Seamline

fig. 25

Special Seam Techniques

Many patterns call for seam techniques other than the basic seam. These different seam techniques add durability and style to the garment. Special fabrics, such as fake suedes and felt, can use special seam techniques not suitable to more conventional fabrics.

Welt Seam

Make a basic seam and press both seam allowances to one side. Trim the under seam allowance to slightly less than ¼ inch (6mm). Working on the right side, topstitch ¼ inch (6mm) from the seam, catching the untrimmed seam allowance in place. (fig. 26) This type of welt seam is especially useful on white or pastel colored pants which tend to show through a bit. It is more attractive than a conventional pressed-open seam. It is suitable for both knits and woven fabrics.

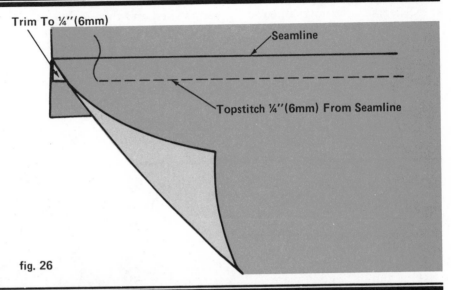

fig. 26

Double Welt Seam

Construct as for the welt seam except trim the underseam to slightly less than ⅜ inch (10mm). Topstitch at ⅜ inch (10mm) and again close to the seamline. This seam technique can take the place of a flat felled seam on fabric that doesn't ravel. (fig. 27)

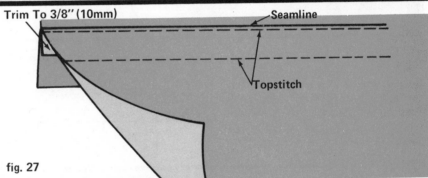

fig. 27

Flat Felled Seam

Use this seam on tailored shirts and reversible garments. Stitch a basic seam, with the wrong sides together. Press both seam allowances to one side and trim the under seam allowance to approximately ⅛ inch (3mm). (fig. 28)

Turn under the raw edge of the upper seam allowance. Baste in place over the trimmed seam allowance. Topstitch close to the fold. Remove the basting stitches and press. (fig. 29)

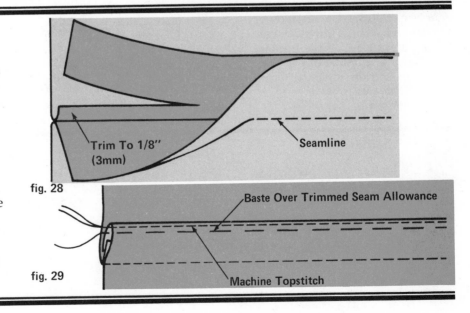

fig. 28

fig. 29

French Seam

This seam is used on sheer fabrics for a neat look, and is suitable for underarm seams on blouses and tailored shirts when a flat felled seam is not wanted. Since the seam is stitched twice and all raw edges are completely enclosed it is great for sportswear too.

With wrong sides together, stitch a basic seam ¼ inch (6mm) in from the given seamline. Press as stitched and then to one side. Trim the seam allowance to ⅛ inch (3mm). (fig. 30)

Position the garment pieces right sides together and press the seam edge. Stitch at ¼ inch (6mm), which will be the original seamline, and enclose the seam edges. (fig. 31)

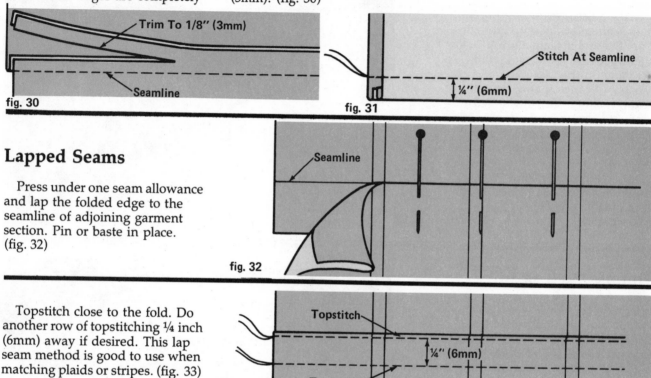

Trim To 1/8" (3mm)

Seamline

fig. 30

Stitch At Seamline

¼" (6mm)

fig. 31

Lapped Seams

Press under one seam allowance and lap the folded edge to the seamline of adjoining garment section. Pin or baste in place. (fig. 32)

Seamline

fig. 32

Topstitch close to the fold. Do another row of topstitching ¼ inch (6mm) away if desired. This lap seam method is good to use when matching plaids or stripes. (fig. 33)

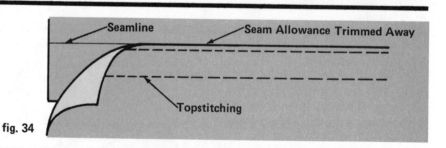

Topstitch

¼" (6mm)

Topstitch

fig. 33

Leather, fake suedes and matted fabrics can also use a variation of the lapped seam. Trim away one seam allowance. Lap the trimmed seam to the seamline of the adjoining section. Pin or baste and secure with two rows of topstitching. (fig. 34)

Seamline

Seam Allowance Trimmed Away

Topstitching

fig. 34

Tip

A glue stick can be used in place of pins and/or basting when making lapped seams. Apply the glue to the underside of the overlapping section. Press in place, allow to dry a minute or two, and topstitch.

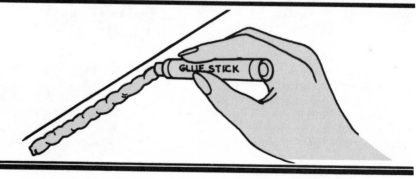

GLUE STICK

Machine Basting

Machine basting is done with the longest stitch length on the machine. It holds fabric layers together for fitting or permanent stitching and is much faster and stronger than hand basting. (fig. 35)

Some sewing machines have special cams or built-in mechanisms which will allow an extremely long basting stitch. (fig. 36) Always test your machine basting on a scrap of your fashion fabric to make sure it won't leave needle marks after it has been removed.

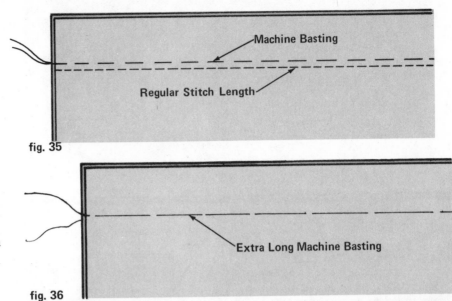

fig. 35

fig. 36

Topstitching

Topstitching adds a decorative touch to many garments. It is also functional because it keeps edges flat, facings in position and hems secured.

Topstitching is always done with a long stitch length and can be one row of stitching or multiple rows.

Use a matching or contrasting thread depending on the desired look. Although regular thread can be used for topstitching, a special polyester topstitching thread is now available which is a heavier weight and gives a bold look to the finished topstitching. Topstitching thread requires a larger than regular machine needle; use either a size 14 (90) or 16 (100). Use regular thread in the bobbin when using topstitching thread.

Tip

A topstitching needle, designed specifically for heavy topstitching thread is now available. It is a size 14 (90) with a specially shaped tip for heavy thread. Try it if you have trouble using a regular needle. Made by Ferd. Schmetz Needle Corp.

Some machines have difficulty handling the heavy topstitching thread. Always test stitch a seam sample made of four to six layers of scrap fabric to see if the stitching is satisfactory.

If your machine can't handle the heavier thread you can still achieve the desired look by placing a bobbin wound with regular thread on top of the thread spool on the machine. Thread both the bobbin and spool thread through the machine and needle eye as though they were one and complete the topstitching.

Topstitching must be even in order to look good. Use the edge of your presser foot as a guide for the topstitching width. (fig. 37) Swinging the needle all the way to the right will give a ⅛ inch (3mm) width. The center needle position gives a ¼ inch (6mm) width and the left needle position gives a ⅜ inch (10mm) width.

The guidelines etched on the throat plate of the machine can also be used as guides for topstitching. (fig. 38)
(continued on next page)

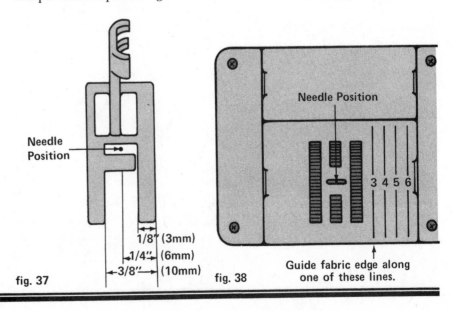

fig. 37

fig. 38

Special stitching tape can be used to help keep topstitching even. Cut tape the needed lengths and separate at the desired width. Position the tape along a seamline or fabric edge and use the other edge as a stitching guideline. Do not stitch through the tape and remove it immediately after stitching. (fig. 39)

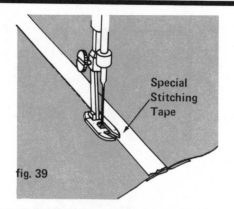

fig. 39

Special Stitching Tape

Tip

Regular drafting or magic transparent tape, in different widths, can also be used as a topstitching guide. Position along a seamline or fabric edge as you would the special stitching tape, and topstitch along the opposite edge. Again, remember not to stitch into the tape and remove it immediately after stitching.

Enclosed Seams

Seam allowances of enclosed seams need to be trimmed to different widths in order to reduce bulk along the finished edge after the seam is turned and pressed. The seam allowance which is directly under the visible part of the garment should be trimmed ¼ (6mm) to ⅜ (10mm) inch — allow the wider width for bulky fabrics. All other seam allowance layers should be trimmed slightly narrower. This procedure is known as grading. (fig. 40)

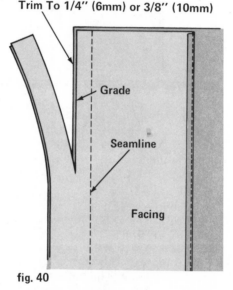

Trim To 1/4" (6mm) or 3/8" (10mm)

Grade

Seamline

Facing

fig. 40

Tip

All seam allowances can be trimmed in one cut if the scissors are held at an acute angle to the fabric.

Curved Seams

Curved seams should be trimmed and then clipped or notched so seam allowances can lie flat. Clip inside curved seams at regular intervals until the pressed-open seam allowance will lie flat or the turned seam edge makes a smooth curve. (fig. 41)

Notch outside curved seams for the same reasons. Be careful not to cut the stitching when clipping and notching. (fig. 42)

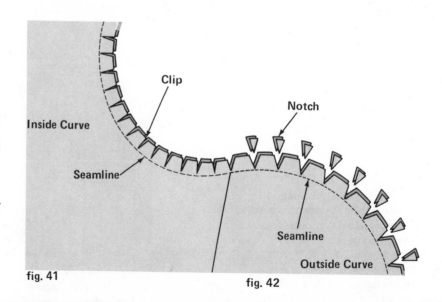

Inside Curve

Clip

Notch

Seamline

Seamline

Outside Curve

fig. 41

fig. 42

Pointed Seams

Seams which come to a point should be graded and trimmed as shown. Shorten the stitch length to 14-16 stitches per inch (25mm) for about ¾ inch (20mm) on each side of the point. This reinforces the seamline and keeps it from fraying after trimming. (fig. 43)

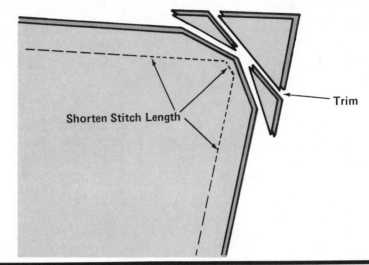

Shorten Stitch Length

Trim

fig. 43

Take one or more stitches across all corners and points to allow turning room for the seam allowances. Lightweight fabrics require one or two stitches, bulky fabrics may need four or more. (fig. 44)

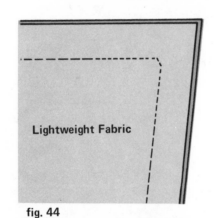
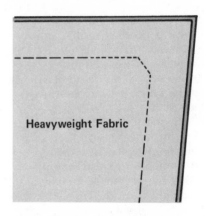

Lightweight Fabric

Heavyweight Fabric

fig. 44

Understitched Seams

Understitching is used on facing seams to give a firm turning edge. An understitched seam also keeps the facing in position and prevents it from rolling to the right side. Understitching is done after the seam allowances are trimmed, graded, clipped or notched.

With the garment right side up pull the facing and all seam allowances to one side. Using a regular stitch length, stitch close to the seamline through all layers. (fig. 45)

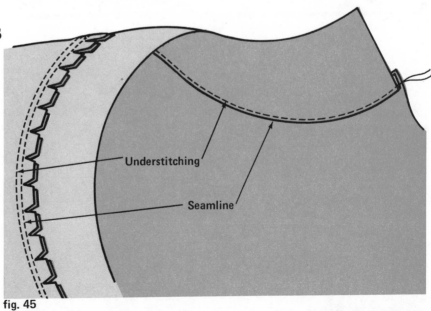

Understitching

Seamline

fig. 45

Eased Seams

An eased seam is required whenever two sections of fabric are of unequal length, such as front and back shoulders. The longest section is eased in to fit the shorter section. Fullness is controlled by pins or easestitching just inside the seamline of the longer garment section.

Pin together ends of the unequal garment sections matching up construction marks. Pin the fullness evenly along the seamline using as many pins as necessary. Stitch the seam with the eased section on the bottom and the shorter section on the top, removing pins along the way. (fig. 46)

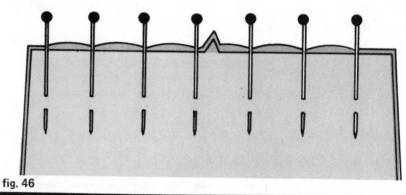

fig. 46

Seams needing more control than pins provide should be easestitched first. Hold your thumb or the eraser end of a pencil on the fabric behind the presser foot as you stitch with a regular stitch length. Let the fabric pile up for a bit, release, and then place your thumb or pencil back in position. Do this stitching just inside the normal seamline so it won't show on the finished garment. (fig. 47)

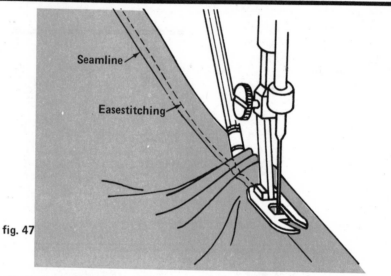

Seamline

Easestitching

fig. 47

Pin the fabric layers right sides together. Stitch along given seamline with the eased section underneath. (fig. 48)

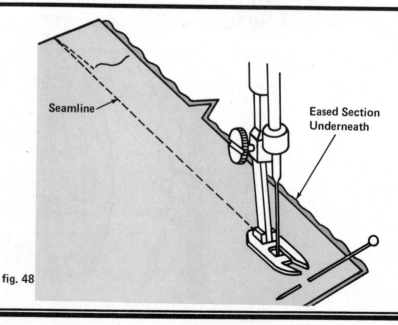

Seamline

Eased Section Underneath

fig. 48

Shaping The Garment

Darts, pleats, tucks and gathers are used to add shape to the finished garment. They control and release fullness where it is needed by the figure. They are also used as design and style lines on some patterns.

Types Of Darts

Single point darts originate at a seamline such as underarm bust or waistline darts. They can be straight, open or curved in shape. (fig. 1)

Double pointed darts are contained entirely within the garment piece as in front and back of jackets and one-piece dresses. They are usually straight but can be curved when used at the base of the neck. (fig. 2)

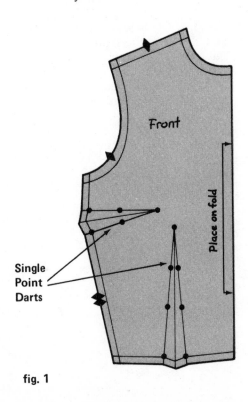

Front

Place on fold

Single Point Darts

fig. 1

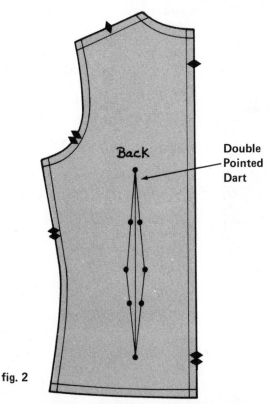

Back

Double Pointed Dart

fig. 2

Stitching Techniques

Fold the fabric right sides together matching up construction marks and pin securely. (fig. 3)

Stitch single point darts from the wide end to the point. Backstitch at the beginning, follow markings exactly and remove each pin just before you come to it. Taper the stitching line to the point, taking the last two or three stitches along the fabric fold. (fig. 4)

Double pointed darts should be stitched from the middle to each end. Gradually taper to each point taking the last two or three stitches along the fold. (fig. 5)

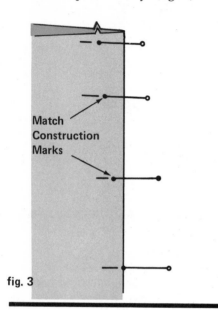

Match Construction Marks

fig. 3

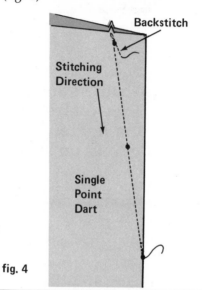

Backstitch

Stitching Direction

Single Point Dart

fig. 4

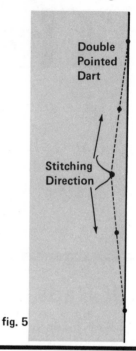

Double Pointed Dart

Stitching Direction

fig. 5

Secure the pointed ends of each dart with a square knot or carefully backstitch along the fabric fold about ¼ inch (6mm). (fig. 6)

Patterns which require extremely wide darts will use an open dart in order to reduce bulk in the finished dart area. The dart is stitched like a seam and then pressed open. (fig. 7)

Open darts are also used wherever a curved dart is required in the pattern design. Care must be taken when pinning these darts together so construction marks match exactly. Mismatched marks will result in a rippled dart line. (fig. 8)

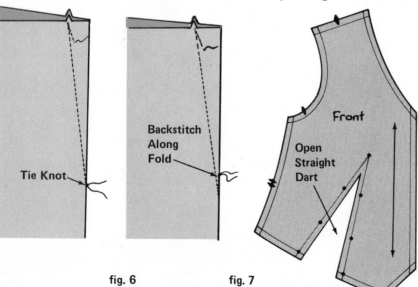

Tie Knot

Backstitch Along Fold

fig. 6

Front

Open Straight Dart

fig. 7

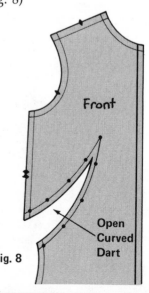

Front

Open Curved Dart

fig. 8

Tip

Clip the folded edge of double pointed and curved darts in three or four places after stitching. This will allow them to be pressed and shaped correctly.

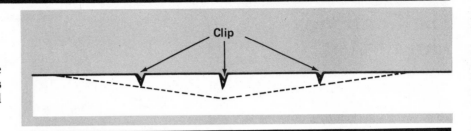

Clip

Press darts from the wrong side only over a tailor's ham to build shape in the dart area. Place a strip of paper or an envelope between the dart and garment fabric while pressing to prevent an impression showing on the right side of the garment. (fig. 9)

Press horizontal darts (underarm, elbow and armhole darts) down toward the waistline. Press vertical darts (waistline, neckline and double pointed darts) toward the center of the body. (fig. 10)

Darts in heavy fabrics should be trimmed to within ¾ inch (20mm) of the point, leaving no more than ½ inch (13mm) of the dart width. Press the dart open pressing the untrimmed point flat. (fig. 11)

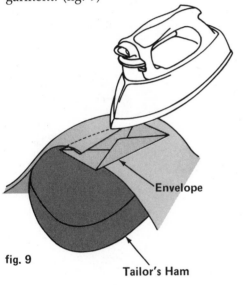

fig. 9

Envelope

Tailor's Ham

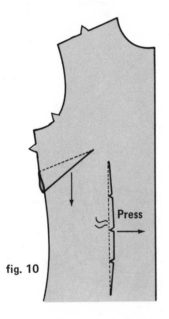

Press

fig. 10

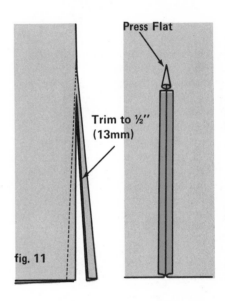

Press Flat

Trim to ½"
(13mm)

fig. 11

Darts in sheer fabrics should be trimmed to ¼ inch (6mm). Overcast the trimmed edges

together for a neat appearance from the right side of the garment. (fig. 12)

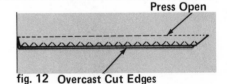

Press Open

fig. 12 Overcast Cut Edges

Tip

Set your Ham in a Ham Holder to get the right position when pressing darts. This multi-curved box allows you to position the ham in various ways for every pressing need. Both Ham and Holder are available from June Tailor, Inc.

Tip

Use a pair of small scissors for all clipping and trimming jobs. The 5 or 6 inch (125cm or 150cm) lengths work best and are much easier to handle than the large shears for small sewing tasks. Manufactured by Joy Scissors, Division of Cole National Corp.

The Continuous Thread Dart

The continuous thread dart should be used on sheer fabrics when thread ends at the point of the dart would show through to the right side of the garment. It should also be used whenever darts are stitched on the right side of the garment for design purposes. (fig. 13)

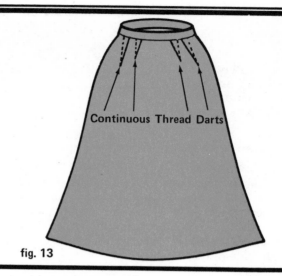

fig. 13

Unthread the machine needle. Pull a long thread out of the bobbin and insert it through the eye of the needle opposite the direction in which it is usually threaded. Tie the bobbin thread to the spool thread and pull the bobbin thread up through the thread and tension guides. Wind enough bobbin thread on the spool to stitch the dart (about three times the length of the dart). The sewing machine must be rethreaded in this manner for each continuous stitched dart. (fig. 14 & 15)

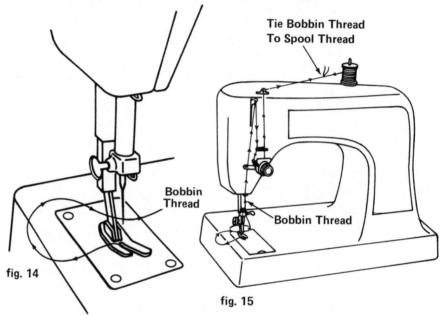

fig. 14

fig. 15

Start the dart stitching at the pointed end of the dart. Make sure the needle goes into the fabric exactly on the fold. Stitch the dart to the wide end, backstitch for strength and cut the threads. (fig. 16)

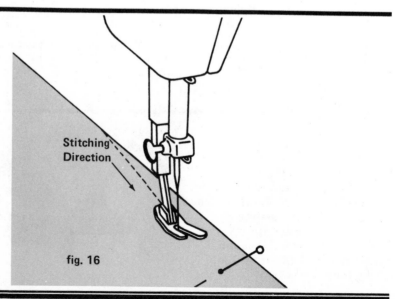

fig. 16

Pleats

Pleats are folds of fabric which give fullness to a garment. Pressed pleats are used for fabrics which will hold a sharp crease. Unpressed pleats are used for fabrics which will not hold a crease or where a soft look is desired. Various pleat styles illustrated are Knife (fig. 17), Inverted (fig. 18), and Box (fig. 19).

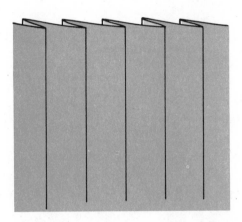

fig. 17　　　　**Knife Pleat**

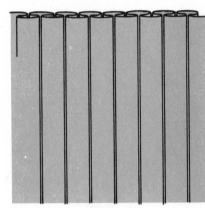

fig. 18　　　　**Inverted Pleat**

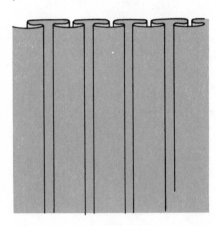

fig. 19　　　　**Box Pleat**

Carefully transfer pattern construction marks for pleats to the right or wrong side of the fabric, as indicated on your pattern. Place pattern over proper side of the cut-out garment piece to be marked. Mark the ends of each pleat with a pin. (fig. 20)

Pull the pattern away from the fabric leaving the pins in place. Using a ruler and chalk pencil, mark the pleat lines using the pins as a guide. (fig. 21)　　*(continued)*

Tip

The two-color chalk pencil from Talon is handy to use when marking pleat lines. With a blue and white side you can mark any color fabric. The marks brush away with a separate brush. Available from Donahue Sales, Talon Division of Textron.

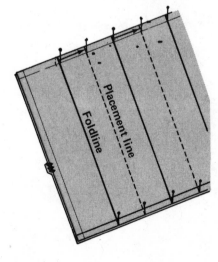

fig. 20

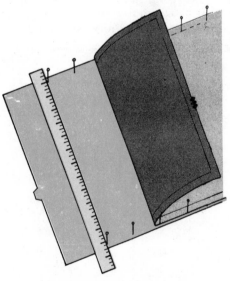

fig. 21

Pleat construction marks will be accompanied by arrows showing which way the fabric is to be folded. Indicate these on the fabric in the seam allowance. (fig. 22)

Working on a large, flat surface

form each pleat by folding the fabric along each foldline bringing the fold over to meet the placement line. Pin and baste each pleat the length of the fold. Baste across the top of the pleated section to hold pleats in place for

the joining seam. (fig. 23)

Press pleats from the right side using a pressing cloth. Press lightly for a soft look. Use more pressure for a sharp finish. Turn over and press again. (fig. 24)

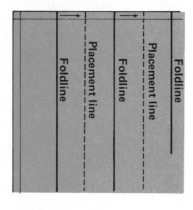

fig. 22

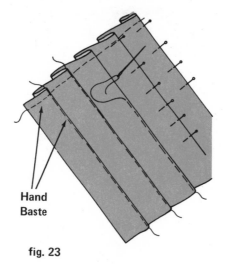

Hand Baste

fig. 23

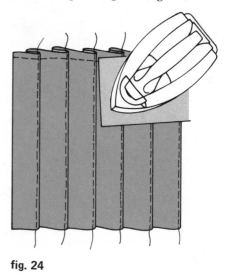

fig. 24

Tip

Use the Dritz Vue-Thru Pressing Cloth to protect your fabric when pressing on the right side of pleats. It allows you to see what you are doing but prevents fabric damage. From Scovill, Sewing Notions Division.

Tip

If the underpleat fold leaves marks on the right side of the garment after pressing lift up each pleat and steam out the mark from the wrong side. Place long strips of paper underneath each pleat and press the entire area again.

Pin and stitch the pleated section of the garment to the adjoining garment piece with the pleated section on top. Make sure the under pleats stay flat and neat too. Remove the vertical pleat basting after the garment has been completed. (fig. 25)

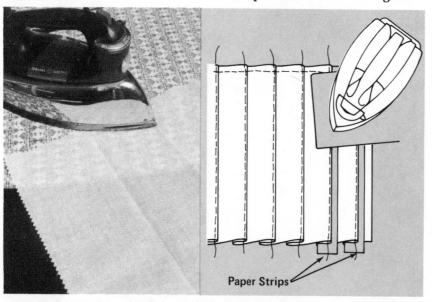

Paper Strips

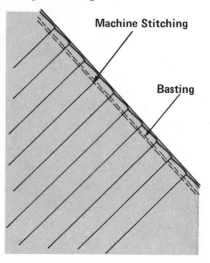

Machine Stitching

Basting

fig. 25

Tip

Hem lower edge of the multiple pleated garment before the pleats are formed. This makes the hemming process much easier. However, the finished length of the garment must be accurately known if this technique is used.

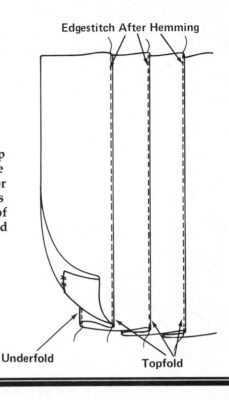

Edgestitch After Hemming

Underfold   Topfold

Tip

Pleats can be edgestitched to keep the creases sharp. Do this before attaching the skirt to the bodice or waistband and after the hem has been completed. The underfold of the pleats can also be edgestitched for a sharp finish.

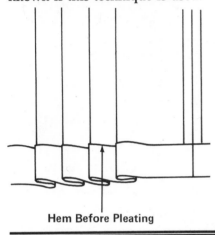

Hem Before Pleating

Tucks

Tucks are permanently stitched folds of fabric used to hold fullness in place and add design interest. They can run the full length of a garment piece or end at various points. Tucks can be stitched in different widths and with varying width between each tuck. Different tuck styles are Blind, Spaced, and Pin. (fig. 26 - 27 - 28)
(continued on next page)

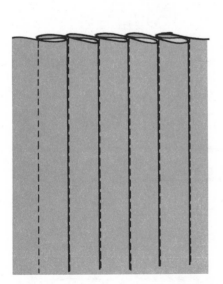

fig. 26   Blind Tucks

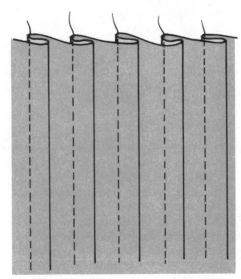

fig. 27   Spaced Tucks

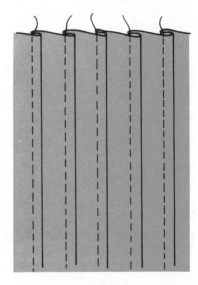

fig. 28   Pin Tucks

Transfer tuck construction marks to the right side of the cutout garment section. Place pattern over the right side of the fabric and mark the ends of each tuck line with a pin. (fig. 29)

----- Stitching Line
——— Foldline

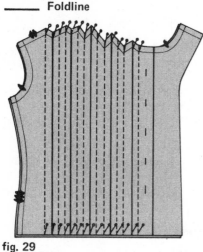

fig. 29

Carefully pull pattern away from the fabric leaving pins in place. Using a ruler and chalk pencil, mark each tuck line using pins as a guide. The tuck foldline should be marked as a solid line and the stitching line should be marked as a broken line. (fig. 30)

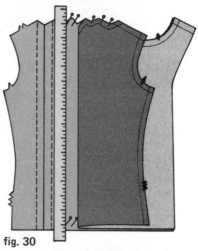

fig. 30

Working on the right side of the garment, form each tuck by folding on a solid line and stitching on a broken line.(fig. 31)

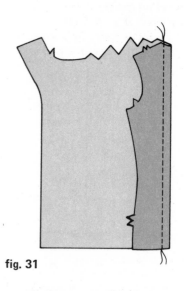

fig. 31

Press the resulting folds in one direction, as the pattern indicates. Work from the right side of the garment and use a pressing cloth to protect the fabric. (fig. 32)

Machine baste across both ends of a tucked section to hold the tucks in the proper direction while completing the garment. (fig. 33)

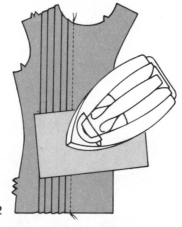

fig. 32

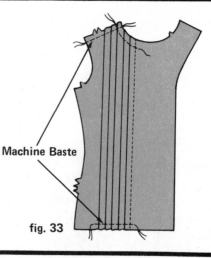

Machine Baste

fig. 33

Tip

A cardboard tucking gauge can be made, eliminating the need for transferring all the tuck marking to the cutout garment piece. Transfer the first tuck stitching and folding lines to the garment. Stitch the first tuck as directed and fold and stitch the other tucks using the tucking gauge as a guide.

Make the tucking gauge from a piece of cardboard taken from a seam tape package. Mark each tuck width with a notch in the edge of the gauge. Mark the width between tuck folds with another notch. The lower notch is placed along the foldline of a completed tuck. The top of the gauge marks the next foldline while the upper notch marks the next stitching line.

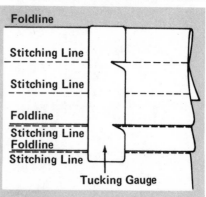

Foldline

Stitching Line

Stitching Line

Foldline
Stitching Line
Foldline
Stitching Line

Tucking Gauge

Gathers

Gathers are used to gently control fullness in a garment. They can be soft and draped or full and billowy depending on the type of fashion fabric used and the amount of fullness allowed. Some fabrics do not gather well. Non-supple fabrics such as fake suedes, vinyls or heavy woolens become very bulky when gathered. Choose patterns without gathers when working with fabrics of this type.

With the garment right side up run two rows of stitching along the fabric edge to be gathered — one row right along the given seamline and the other row ¼ inch (6mm) above. Loosen the upper thread tension and lengthen the stitch length when doing gathering stitching. This makes the gathers easier to form. (fig. 34)

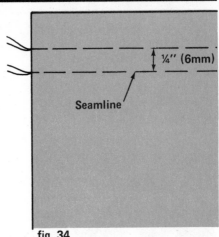

fig. 34

Large sections of garments that have gathers running across joining seams should be stitched together before the gather stitching is done. However, the gathering threads should be broken and started again at each seamline. (fig. 35)

Pin the garment pieces right sides together matching up construction marks. With the gathered section up, pull the bobbin thread with one hand while you slide and adjust the gathers with the other hand. (fig. 36)
(continued on next page)

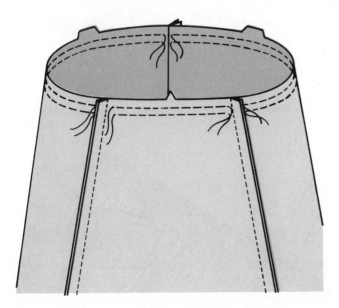

fig. 35

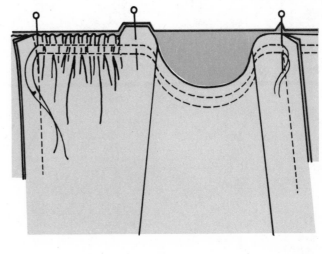

fig. 36

Tip

Test gather a scrap of your fabric to see if you are getting the desired look. A long, stitch length should be used with heavyweight fabrics while a shorter stitch length is more suitable for fine fabrics. Adjust the stitch length for your type of fabric.

Use a heavy duty thread on the bobbin when making gathering stitching if you have problems with the bobbin thread breaking when pulling up the gathers.

Reset the upper thread tension and stitching length of the machine. Stitch the garment sections together with the gathered section up so you can prevent tucks and pleats from forming. (fig. 37). Finish the seam with another row of stitching, straight or zigzag, and press the seam allowances together with the tip of the iron.

Open up the garment and working on the wrong side, press the joining seam into the ungathered section. Make sure the tip of the iron doesn't go beyond the seamline. Remove any gathering threads that may show on the right side of the garment. (fig. 38)

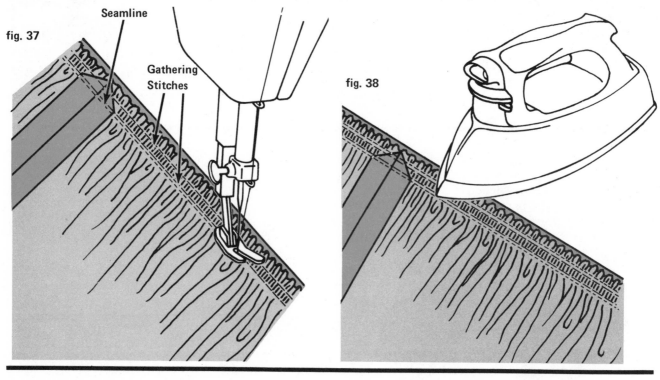

fig. 37

Seamline

Gathering Stitches

fig. 38

Tip

Carefully press finished gathers from the wrong side. Slide the tip of the iron up into the gathers without moving it from side to side. This technique will keep the gathers full and soft.

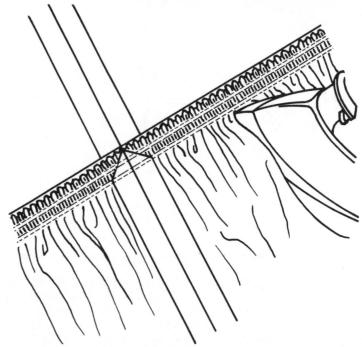

Facings

Facings are pieces of fabric used to smoothly finish edges of garments. They are placed around necklines, armholes, front and back openings of garments and at waistlines of skirts and pants. Facings are also used to finish collars, cuffs and pocket flaps. Facings are cut the same shape as the garment section being faced with the exception of bias facings. Shaped facings can be cut as separate pieces or as extensions of the garment section being faced. Fashion fabric is usually used for facings, however, matching lightweight fabric can also be used to reduce bulk at the faced edge.

Faced edges usually have some kind of interfacing included in order to support and smooth the finished edge. A fusible or nonfusible type of interfacing can be used of either woven or non-woven fabric. Fusible interfacing should have the seam allowances trimmed away before applying. (fig. 1). Nonfusible interfacing should first be stitched to the wrong side of the garment piece within the seam allowance, close to the seamline and then trimmed as close to the stitching as possible. (fig. 2)
(continued on next page)

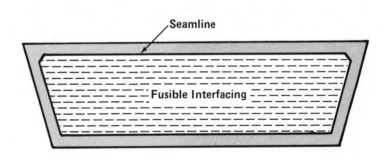

fig. 1

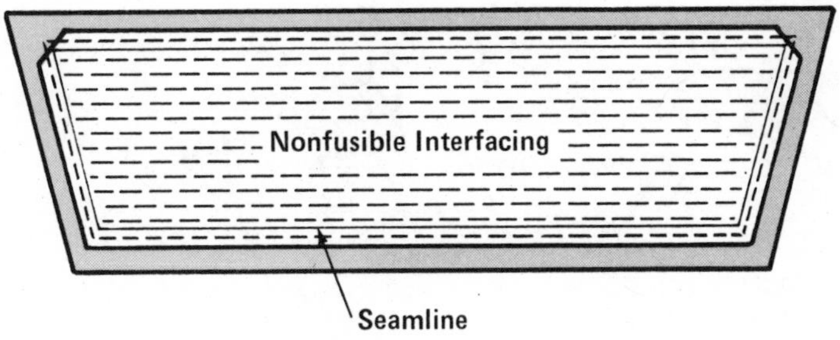

fig. 2

Tip

All facings should be finished before attachment to the garment.

Interfacing should always be applied to the wrong side of the fabric layer which will be visible on the finished garment. This means the upper collar and cuff piece rather than the under collar and cuff piece, and the wrong side of the garment neckline, armhole and waistline. (fig. 3). This technique pads the graded seam allowances and prevents them from shadowing through to the right side of the garment.

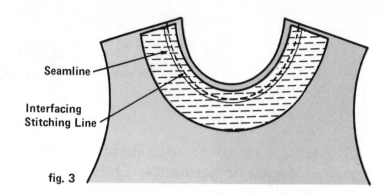

fig. 3

The exception to this rule applies to application of a fusible interfacing to garment edges. Fusing the interfacing to the wrong side of the garment will cause a line to show through on the right side where the interfacing ends. (fig. 4)

The interfacing should be applied to the wrong side of the facing pieces in this case. (fig. 5)

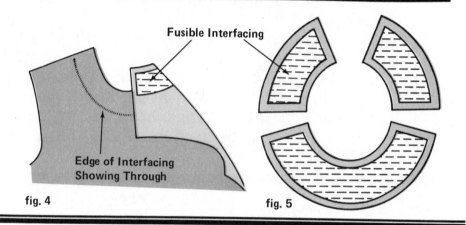

fig. 4

fig. 5

Shaped Facings

Shaped facings should have the free edge finished in some manner. The method used will be determined by the fashion fabric.

Stitch and press open all facing seams. Trim the seam allowances to ¼ inch (6mm). (fig. 6)

Turned and Stitched Finish

Stitch ¼ inch (6mm) away from the edge, turn on the stitching line and edgestitch. Use on light to medium weight woven fabrics only. (fig. 7)

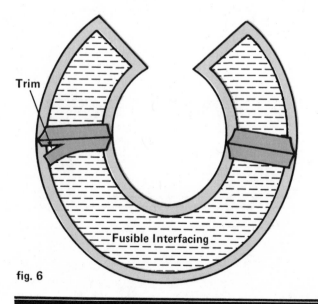

fig. 6

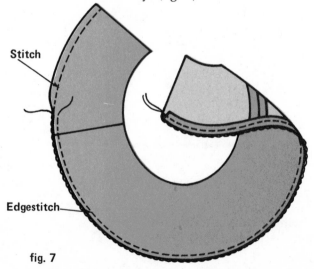

fig. 7

Pinked Finish

Trim the edge with pinking shears. Do a row of straight stitching next to the pinked edge on woven fabrics. Use on knits or woven fabrics. (fig. 8)

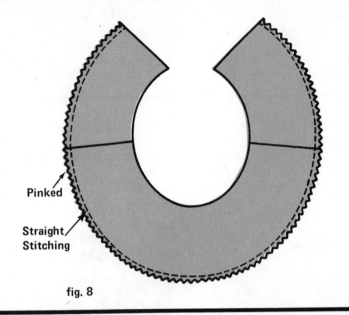

Pinked

Straight Stitching

fig. 8

Tip

Wiss Pinking Shears have a larger bite than most other brands of pinking shears, which is better to stop raveling on loosely woven fabrics. They are also available with a scalloped design for an extra decorative touch. From Wiss-The Cooper Group.

Overcast Finish

Machine zigzag or hand overcast the facing edge. This method is suitable for knits or woven fabrics. (fig. 9)

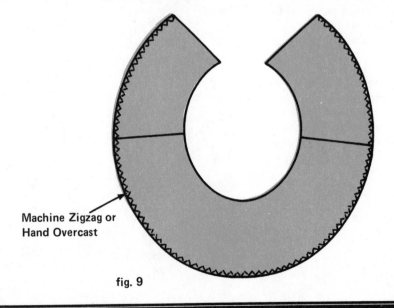

Machine Zigzag or Hand Overcast

fig. 9

Bound Edge Finish

A bound edge finish is used on heavy weight woven fabrics or double knit fabrics, wherever a flat finished look is desired. The edge can be bound with a commercially prepared double fold, bias tape or 1 inch (25mm) wide bias strips cut from matching lining fabric. This type of edge finish is recommended for unlined jackets. Apply it to the hem and seam edges as well for a custom look.

Enclose the facing edge with the double fold bias tape, positioning the widest section on the bottom and the narrowest section on top. Hand baste in position and then machine stitch along the edge catching all layers. (fig. 10)

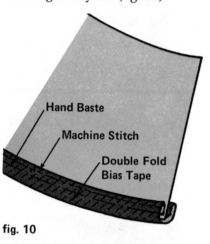

Hand Baste

Machine Stitch

Double Fold Bias Tape

fig. 10

Apply bias strips of lining to the facing edge with a scant ¼ inch (6mm) seam, right sides together. (fig. 11)

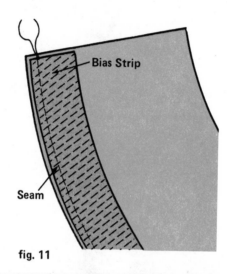

Bias Strip

Seam

fig. 11

Wrap the bias strip around the facing edge to the wrong side. Baste in place and secure by stitching-in-the-ditch from the right side. (fig. 12)

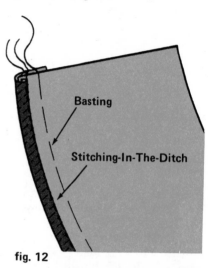

Basting

Stitching-In-The-Ditch

fig. 12

Facing Application

Pin the prepared facing to the garment edge, right sides together, matching all seams and construction marks. Stitch together with the given seam width. Shorten the stitch length when stitching curves or around corners in order to reinforce these areas. Shortening the stitching length around curves also helps make a smoother stitching line.

Press, trim, grade, clip and/or notch the seam allowances as necessary. (fig. 13)
(continued on next page)

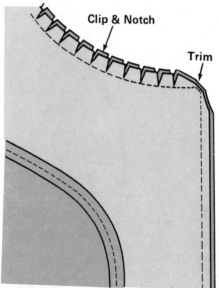

Clip & Notch

Trim

fig. 13

Tip

Take one or more stitches across the diagonal when stitching around corners to provide turning room for the seam allowances. Heavyweight fabrics will require more diagonal stitching length than lightweight fabrics, sometimes up to ¼ inch (6mm) or ⅜ inch (10mm).

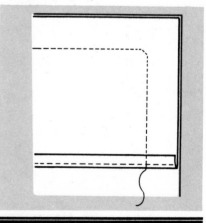

Understitch the facing seam and turn the facing to the finished position, rolling the seam to the facing side. Press only from the wrong side. (fig. 14)

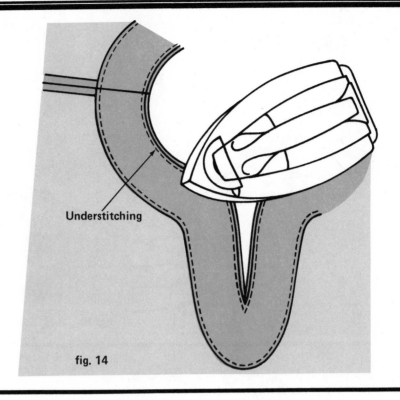

Understitching

fig. 14

Secure facing at the garment seams using one of the following methods.

Pin the facing in place at the garment seamlines. Working on the right side, stitch-in-the-ditch through all layers. (fig. 15)

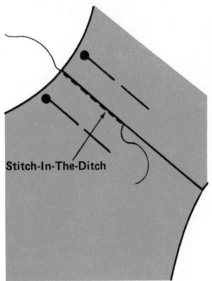

Stitch-In-The-Ditch

fig. 15

Using a hand needle and thread, catch the edge of the facing to the garment seam allowance. (fig. 16)

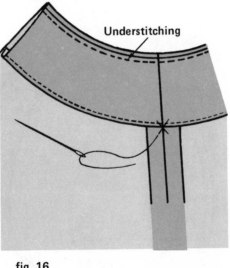

Understitching

fig. 16

Using a small piece of fusible web fuse the garment and facing seam allowances together. Do not let the fusible web get on the wrong side of the fashion fabric. (fig. 17)

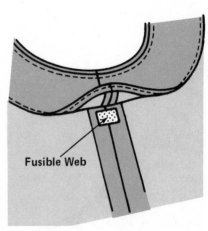

Fusible Web

fig. 17

Tip

Never secure a facing to the garment by stitching all around the outside edge. This always shows through to the right side of the garment and is not necessary.

Bias Facings

Bias facings are sometimes used around necklines and armholes instead of shaped facings. Cut a bias strip of fashion or lining fabric 1 inch (25mm) wide. Fold over ¼ inch (6mm) of one edge and press. (fig. 18) Shape the bias strip with the iron to follow the garment curve.

Trim the garment seam allowances to ¼ inch (6mm). Pin the bias strip to the garment, right sides together. Stitch with a ¼ inch (6mm) seam. (fig. 19)

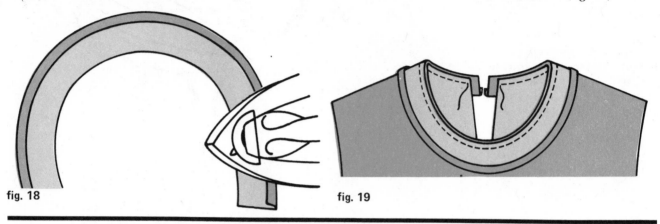

fig. 18

fig. 19

Fold over the ends of the bias at each end of the facing strip. (fig. 20). Overlap the ends of the bias when facing a closed circle such as an armhole. (fig. 21)

Clip the seam allowance. Understitch if desired and turn the bias strip to the inside. Roll the seam to the inside and press from the wrong side only. Catch the facing edge to the garment with machine or hand stitching. (fig. 22)

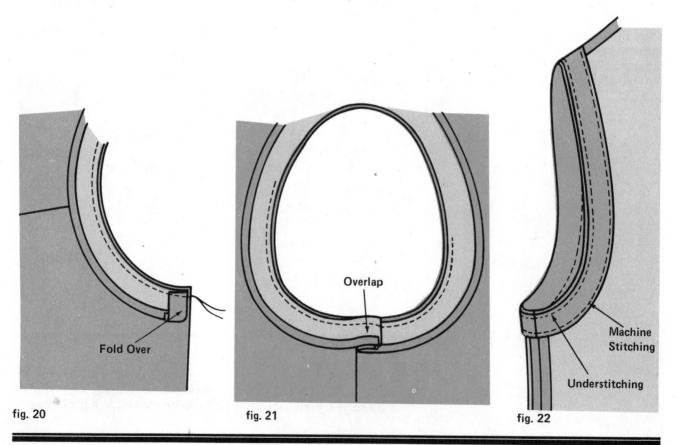

Fold Over

Overlap

Machine Stitching

Understitching

fig. 20

fig. 21

fig. 22

Combined Facings

Combine facing pattern pieces wherever possible in order to reduce bulk and eliminate seams.

Armhole Facings

Overlap the front and back armhole facing patterns at the shoulder so the seamlines meet. Pin or tape the pattern pieces together and use to cut the fabric. Use the grainline given on the front armhole pattern piece as a guide for positioning the pattern on the fabric. (fig. 23)

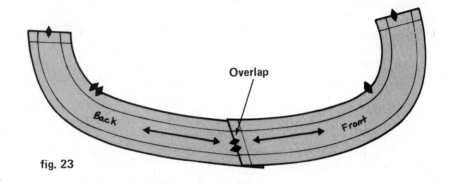

fig. 23

Neckline-Armhole Facings

Sleeveless, scoop-neck garments look nicer if the neckline and armhole facings are combined. If your pattern doesn't utilize this technique, combine the two facings yourself for a smooth finish.

Lay a piece of tracing paper over the bodice front pattern and draw around the neckline, shoulder and armhole plus 3 inches (7.5cm) down the underarm area. Making the facing 3 inches (7.5cm) wide at the armhole and center neckline, draw the lower edge of the facing as shown. Make sure the line curves up above the bust area so it won't bind across the front. The back facing should curve up over the shoulder blade area. (fig. 24 & 25)

Tip

Use Perma Trace whenever you make your own facing patterns. This new pattern tracing material is sheer, for transparency, and is durable. Available from Pellon Corp.

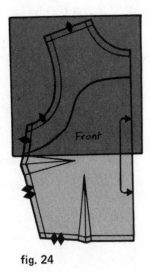

fig. 24

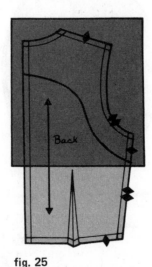

fig. 25

Front Facings

Many patterns having a front opening call for a separate pattern piece for the front facing. This pattern piece can be combined with the garment front if the front edge of the garment is a straight line, thus eliminating a seam along the front edge.

Overlap the front facing and garment front pattern pieces until the seamlines meet. Pin or tape together and use this combined pattern to cut the fabric. (fig. 26)

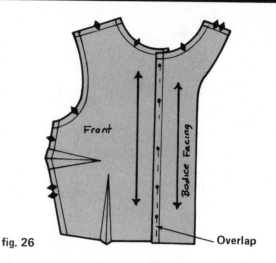

fig. 26

Overlap

Facing Sheer Fabrics

Sheer fabric presents some unique problems since the facing will always show through to the right side. One way of solving this problem is to completely underline the bodice of the garment and then proceed with regular facing techniques. However, this method is not applicable if you want to

retain the sheer look of the fabric. Using faced facings will successfully solve the show-through problem since the facings will have finished edges and look nice from the right side.

Cut one set of facings from the fashion fabric and one set of facings from lining fabric. Eliminate any interfacing at the edge to be faced. Assemble each set of facing pieces as the pattern indicates, leaving the outside edges unfinished. (fig. 27)

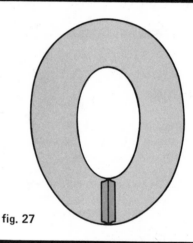

fig. 27

Pin two assembled facings right sides together, one from fashion fabric and one from lining fabric, and stitch the lower edge with a ¼ inch (6mm) seam. Clip to the stitching line on any inside curves and notch to the stitching line on any outside curves. (fig. 28). Understitch the facing seam and turn the two facing sections wrong sides together. Press the stitched edge, rolling the seam to the understitched side.

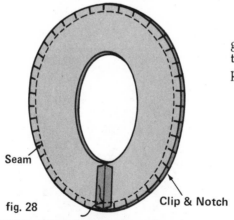

Seam

fig. 28

Clip & Notch

Pin the faced facing to the garment edge, right sides together. Stitch and finish as previously directed. (fig. 29)

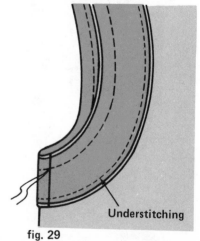

Understitching

fig. 29

Tip

Facing seams on sheer or loosely woven fabrics should be stitched with a short stitch length (14-16 stitches per inch (25mm) or a stitch length of 1.5mm). This enables you to trim and clip or notch the seam allowance without having it fray away.

Pockets

Pockets make sewing fun. Besides being functional, they add style and interest to all types of fashions. They can be made from matching or contrasting fabric and finished with or without topstitching. Use your imagination for pockets that add unique, decorative interest to your garment.

Patch Pocket Construction

The basic patch pocket consists of a pocket piece that has a round, square or angled bottom edge. The top can have either a wide or narrow, topstitched hem. The pocket is usually topstitched to the garment but can also be hand stitched if desired.

Patch pockets should be interfaced unless the fabric has sufficient body or is very heavy. Fusible interfacing is ideal for this purpose since the interfacing can be eliminated in the seam and hem allowances. Use a non-stretch interfacing fabric in order to stabilize the pocket. This is especially important when working with knit fabrics.

Cut the pocket interfacing using the pocket pattern, then trim away the hem and all seam allowances. Carefully fuse the interfacing piece to the wrong side of the pocket. (fig. 1) *(continued on next page)*

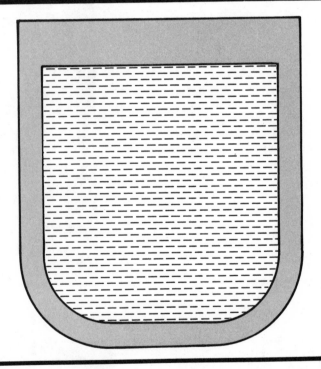

fig. 1

Tip

Pocket location information should be carefully transferred to cutout garment pieces before the pattern is removed from the fabric. This should be done accurately so matching pockets will be positioned identically on each side of the garment.

Tip

Use an Iron Safe soleplate attachment on your iron whenever you bond fusible interfacings. The slick surface will not pick up any fusible residue, eliminating the need to clean the iron soleplate afterwards. Manufactured by Jacobson Products Co., Inc.

Fold over and finish the top edge of the pocket as the pattern indicates. If you have a wide hem at the top of the pocket, fold the hem along the foldline, right sides together, pull the hem edge ⅛ inch (3mm) beyond the pocket edge as shown, and stitch sides of the hem with the given seam width. (fig. 2)

Clip to the end of the stitching, trim the corners and turn to the right side. (fig. 3)

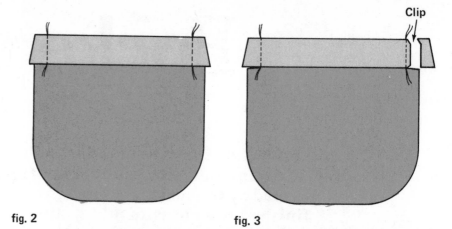

fig. 2   fig. 3

Tip

Use the Multipurpose Point and Tube Turner to get perfect points at the pocket corners. This handy tool makes turning and shaping the point a one-motion operation and is also good for turning belts and spaghetti straps. From Fashion Services, Inc.

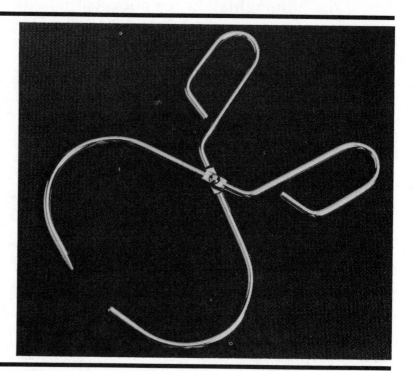

Easestitch just inside the seamline of round corner pockets to help make corners smooth and even. Begin and end the easestitching approximately 1 inch (25mm) on each side of the curved area. (fig. 4)

Trim the seam allowance to ¼ inch (6mm). Use pinking shears in the curved areas for notching. Press over the seam allowance, rolling the easestitching so it doesn't show on the right side of the pocket. (fig. 5)

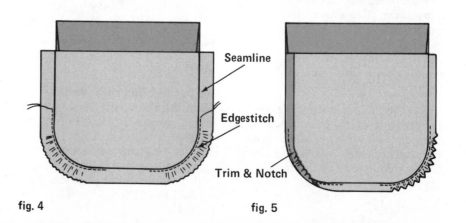

Seamline

Edgestitch

Trim & Notch

fig. 4   fig. 5

Pockets with square or angled corners should have each corner mitered for a flat finish. Press over all the seam allowances and mark the seam edges where they meet with a small clip. (fig. 6)

Refold the corner, right sides together, matching clip marks. Stitch from the clips to the point where creaselines meet on the folded edge. Trim the seam to a scant ¼ inch (6mm), press it open with your fingers and turn the corner to the right side. (fig. 7)

Repeat this process for each pocket corner. Trim seam allowances to ¼ inch (6mm) and press them over to the wrong side of the pocket. (fig. 8)

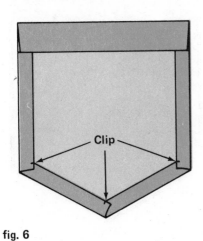

fig. 6

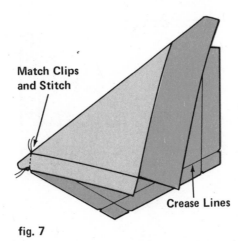

Match Clips and Stitch

Crease Lines

fig. 7

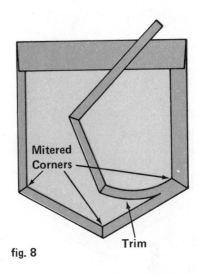

Mitered Corners

Trim

fig. 8

Tip

The lightweight trimming scissors from Scissors II make pocket trimming an easy job. Their small size makes them easier to use than regular shears and they are less tiring on the hands. Manufactured by Rex Cutlery, Division of Cole National Corp.

The Lined Patch Pocket

Some patch pockets will require a full lining. Your pattern will indicate if this is necessary. Interface the pocket piece as previously described unless the fabric is very heavy.

Use the pocket pattern to cut the pocket lining with these modifications. Fold the pattern along the pocket hemline and measure ½ inch (13mm) up from the lower edge of the hem. Fold the pattern down along this line and use this pattern piece to cut the pocket lining. (fig. 9)

(continued on next page)

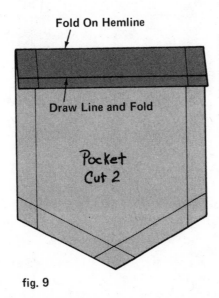

Fold On Hemline

Draw Line and Fold

Pocket Cut 2

fig. 9

Tip

If you have trouble threading the eye of a hand needle try the Self Threading Needles from Belding Lily. They have a small slot in the eye so you can slip the thread in easily. They're great for people with impaired eyesight.

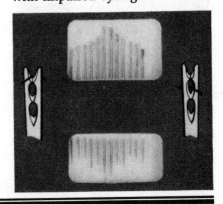

Stitch the lining and pocket along the top edge with a ¼ inch (6mm) seam, right sides together. Leave 1 inch (25mm) unstitched in the middle. Press open the seam allowance. (fig. 10)

Pin the lining and pocket as shown, pulling the lining out beyond the pocket edge about ⅛ inch (3mm). Stitch around the pocket, grade the seam allowances and trim corners or notch curves. Turn the pocket to the right side

through the opening in the seam. (fig. 11)

Press the pocket from the wrong side, rolling the seam to the lining side. Close the open seam with a few hand stitches. (fig. 12)

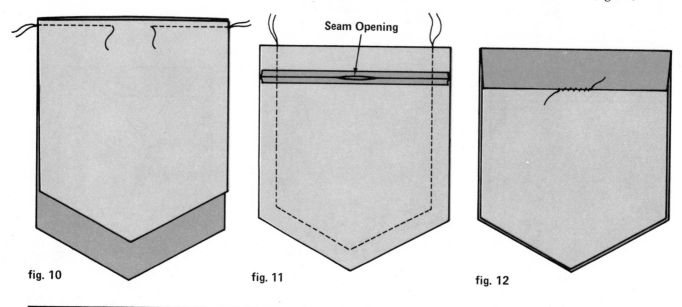

fig. 10   fig. 11   fig. 12

The Self-Lined Patch Pocket

The technique of self-lining a patch pocket can be used on light to medium weight fabrics, either knits or wovens.

Fold down the hem at the top of the pocket pattern. Place the pattern fold on a fabric fold and cut out a double pocket. (fig. 13)

Interface one half of the pocket with a fusible interfacing. Remember to trim away all seam allowance. (fig. 14)

(continued on next page)

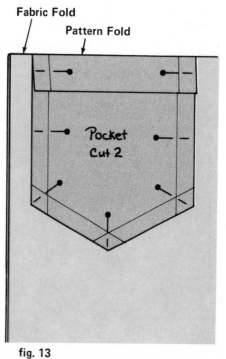

fig. 13

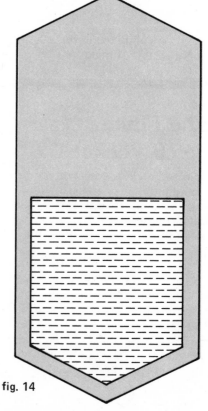

fig. 14

Fold the pocket right sides together and pin. Pull the non-interfaced layer out beyond the other layer ⅛ inch (3mm) all around. This layer will act as the pocket lining. Stitch with the given seam and grade, trim and notch the seam allowance as necessary. (fig. 15)

Cut a 1 inch (25mm) slit on the non-interfaced side of the pocket. Cut the slit on the bias if you are working with a woven fabric. Turn the pocket through the slit to the right side. (fig. 16)

With the slit side up, press the pocket edges, rolling the seam to the lining side. Close the slit with a few hand stitches or a patch of iron-on interfacing. (fig. 17)

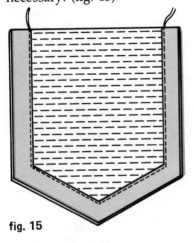

fig. 15

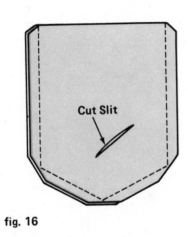

Cut Slit

fig. 16

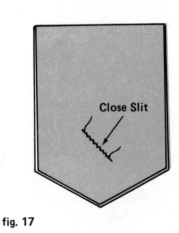

Close Slit

fig. 17

The self-lined pocket technique can also be used for novelty pocket shapes such as hearts, flowers, balloons, etc. Combine the novelty shapes with appliques for a different look.

Cut the pocket from a double layer of fabric. Interface one layer with a fusible interfacing, remembering to first trim away the seam allowance. Pin right sides together, off-setting the non-interfaced layer about ⅛ inch (3mm) all around. Stitch, grade, trim and clip or notch the seam allowance as necessary. (fig. 18)

Cut the slit in the non-interfaced layer and turn the pocket through to the right side. Press the pocket edges and close the slit as directed in figure 17. (fig. 19)

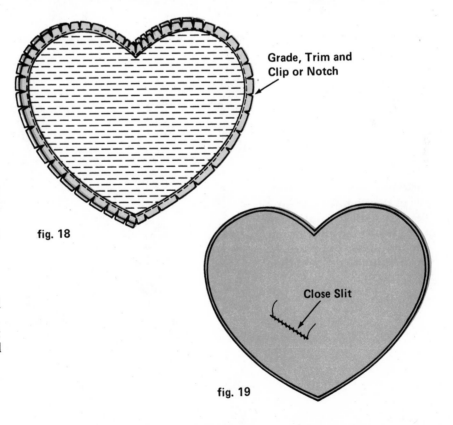

Grade, Trim and Clip or Notch

fig. 18

Close Slit

fig. 19

Pocket Application

Transfer the pocket location marks to the right side of the cutout garment pieces by sticking pins through each mark on the wrong side. Use the pins as placement marks for the pockets. (fig. 20)

Position the pocket on the garment using the pins as guides and hold it in place for the final stitching with pins or hand basting. (fig. 21)

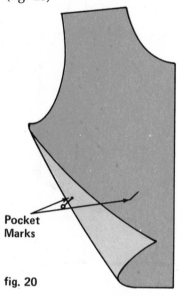

Pocket Marks

fig. 20

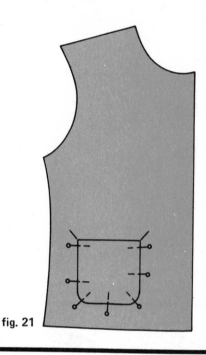

fig. 21

Tip

Pocket location marks can be made directly on the right side of the fabric with the Chacopa Marking Pen. The pen marks can be removed from the fabric with a drop of clear water. Use this pen whenever you need to see construction marks on the right side of the garment. Available from Risdon Mfg. Co.

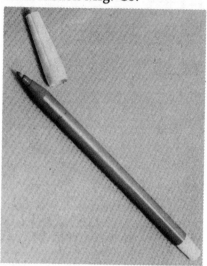

Tip

A quick and easy way to hold a pocket in position for stitching is to use a glue stick. Apply a thin strip of glue to the edge of the pocket and press it in place. Allow the glue to dry and then stitch in place.

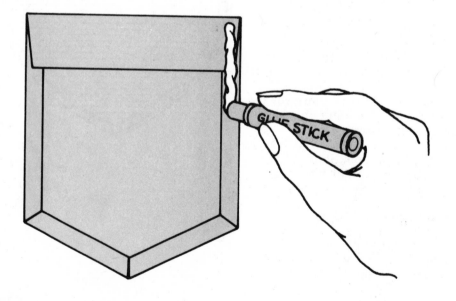

Machine Stitched Pockets

Stitch the pocket to the garment using either a matching or contrasting thread and a long stitch length. Start the stitching line ¼ inch (6mm) below the top edge of the pocket, backstitch to the top and then stitch around the pocket, backstitching for ¼ inch (6mm) at the other corner. (fig. 22)

Do another row of decorative stitching ¼ inch (6mm) inside the first row if desired. (fig. 23)

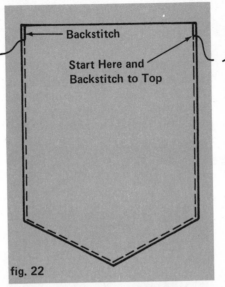

fig. 22

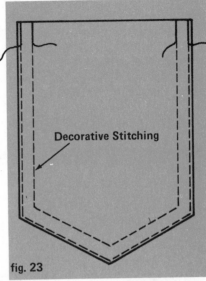

fig. 23

Hand Stitched Pockets

Pockets can be hand stitched to the garment if you don't want stitching visible on the right side of the finished pocket. Hand baste the pocket to the garment in the proper position. (fig. 24)

Working on the wrong side, hand stitch the pocket in place with small backstitches. Catch the underside of the finished pocket edge, leaving threads loose enough to eliminate puckers on the right side of the pocket. Reinforce the corners of the pocket with extra stitches. (fig. 25)

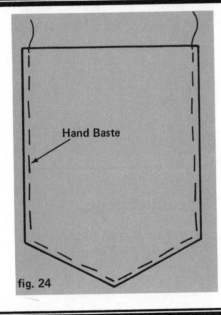

fig. 24

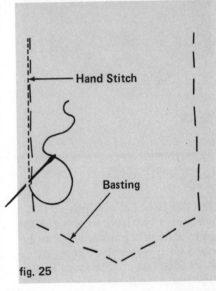

fig. 25

Pocket Flaps

Flaps add a tailored look to patch pockets. They are easy to make and apply. The most important thing to remember is to make the flap big enough so that it completely covers the pocket width with ⅛ inch (3mm) to spare on each side of the pocket.

Interface the upper flap piece with fusible interfacing.

Remember to trim away all seam allowances from the interfacing before fusing in place. (fig. 26)

Pin the flap and lining right sides together. Pull the lining out

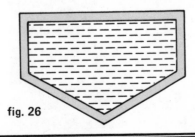

fig. 26

beyond the flap ⅛ inch (3mm) all around. Stitch with the given seam width. Grade, trim and clip or notch the seam allowance as necessary. (fig. 27) *(continued)*

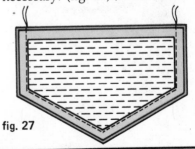

fig. 27

111

Turn the flap right side out. Press from the wrong side, rolling the seam to the lining side. Topstitch the edge of the flap if desired. (fig. 28)

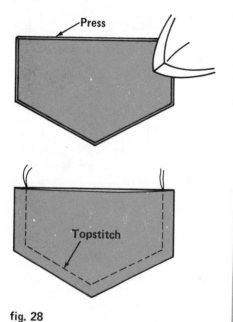

fig. 28

Position the flap above the pocket as the pattern indicates, right sides together. Make sure the flap extends ⅛ inch (3mm) beyond each side of the pocket so that the pocket edges will be covered when the flap is down. Pin in place and stitch with the given seam width, backstitching at each end. (fig. 29)

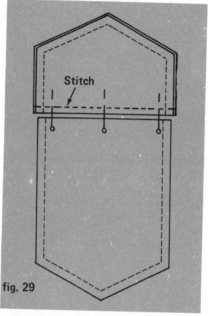

fig. 29

Trim the seam allowance to a scant ¼ inch (6mm), cutting the corners at an angle. (fig. 30)

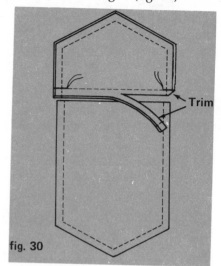

fig. 30

Fold the flap down in the finished position and press, using a press cloth to protect the right side of the garment.

The top edge of the flap should now be secured to the garment so the flap will stay down in position. This can be done by machine or hand.

Tip

Try the Jiffy Press Cloth whenever you have to press on the right side of a garment. It can be used with water if extra moisture is needed. Available from Staple Sewing Aids Corp.

Machine Finish

Topstitch ¼ inch (6mm) away from the flap fold using a long stitch length. Pull thread ends through to the wrong side and tie in square knots. (fig. 31)

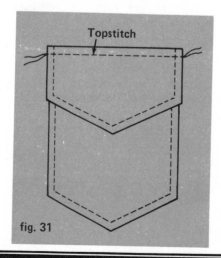

Topstitch

fig. 31

Hand Finish

Hand baste ¼ inch (6mm) below the flap fold. Lift up the flap and attach flap lining only to the garment fabric with small hand stitches. Reinforce the ends with a few extra stitches for strength. (fig. 32)

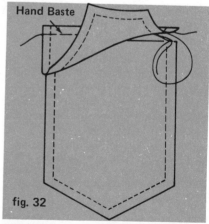

Hand Baste

fig. 32

Collars

A well-made collar will have the following characteristics: each side of the collar will be identical in size and shape; the collar will fit smoothly around the back of the neck, hiding the neckline seam; the undercollar will not show; and the collar will either hug the neck or stand away, as designed. These things are easy to achieve if care is used at each step of collar construction and application.

Types Of Collars

Three basic collar types are the flat, rolled and standing collars.

The flat collar lies flat against the garment rising only slightly above the garment neck edge. The most common type of flat collar is the Peter Pan style. (fig. 1)

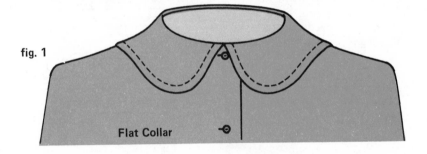
fig. 1 — Flat Collar

The rolled collar stands up around the neck in back and then falls down against the garment in front. Rolled collars are usually found on dresses, blouses, coats and men's sports shirts. (fig. 2)

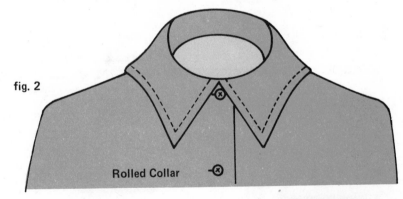
fig. 2 — Rolled Collar

The standing collar stands up all around the neck. A turtleneck and mandarin collar are considered standing collars. The tailored shirt collar with a band is also a type of standing collar. (fig. 3)

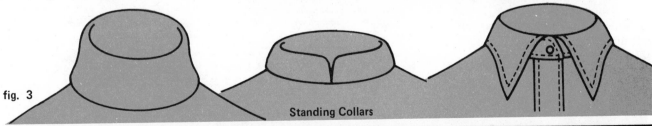
fig. 3 — Standing Collars

Collar Interfacing

Most collars should be interfaced. Interfacing adds the body and shape so necessary to perfect collars. Choose the type and weight of interfacing that compliments your fashion fabric.

Fusible interfacing is a good choice for collars because it allows you to eliminate interfacing in the seam allowances, thus reducing bulk in the finished edge of the collar. Nonfusible interfacing can also be used if desired.

Tip

The grainline or direction of stretch of the collar interfacing will affect the way the collar rolls. Woven interfacing should be cut on the lengthwise grain for a sharp crease along the collar roll line, and on the bias for a soft roll. Stretch, non-woven interfacing should be cut with the stretch running the length of the collar for a soft roll and across the width of the collar for a sharp crease.

Tip

Apply any type of interfacing to the wrong side of the upper collar piece. This will prevent the "shadowing through" of the seam allowances to the right side of the finished collar. This is especially important for knit and lightweight, woven fabrics.

Fusible Interfacing Application

Cut the interfacing using the collar pattern. Trim away all seam allowances and corners. Fuse in place to the wrong side of the upper collar piece. (fig. 4)

Fuse the interfacing just to the foldline of one-piece collars. (fig. 5)

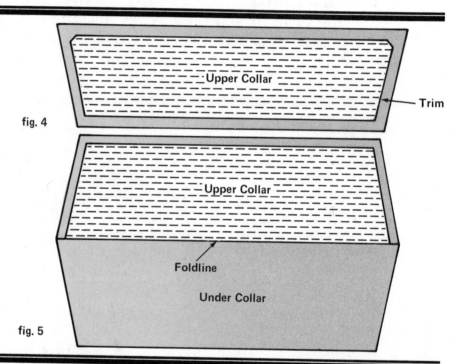

fig. 4

fig. 5

Nonfusible Interfacing Application

Cut the interfacing using the collar pattern. Trim only the corners and machine stitch the interfacing to the wrong side of the upper collar piece. Stitch just ⅛ inch (3mm) outside the given seamline. (fig. 6). Trim the interfacing close to the machine stitching. (fig. 7)

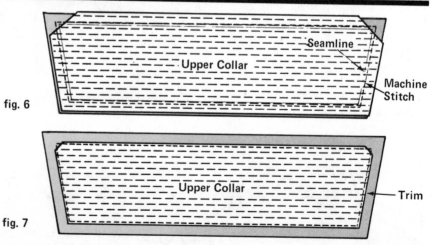

fig. 6

fig. 7

One-piece collars should have the interfacing applied just to or slightly beyond the foldline. Catch the free edge of the interfacing to the wrong side of the collar fabric with invisible hand stitches. (fig. 8)

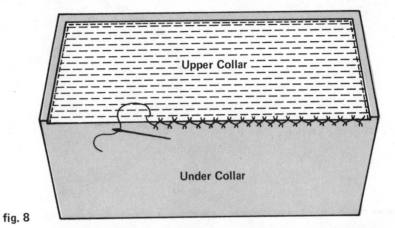

fig. 8

Tip

Ever have trouble threading your needle? The thin wire Needle Threader by Dritz makes needle threading a snap. Three come in one package so you can keep one at the machine, one in your mending box and one in your travel sewing kit. From Scovill, Sewing Notions Division

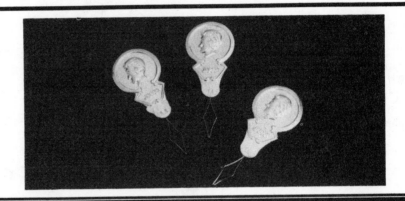

Flat Collar Construction

Pin the upper and under collar pieces right sides together. Pull the under collar out beyond the upper collar edges about ⅛ inch (3mm) so that the finished under collar will be slightly smaller than the upper collar. Stitch the two collar pieces together with the given seam width. (fig. 9)

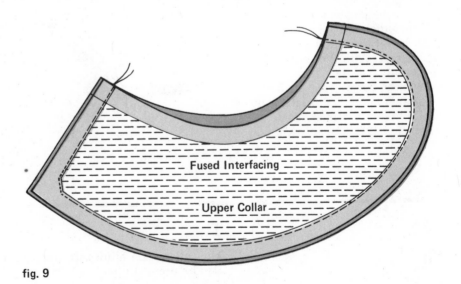

fig. 9

Tip

Shorten the stitch length when stitching around collar curves.

This will reinforce the seam and make the curves smoother. Shorten the stitch length and take one or more diagonal stitches across all corners. This also reinforces the corners and allows room for the seam allowances when the collar is turned.

Trim and grade the seam allowances. Trim close to the stitching at each corner. Notch any outside curves and clip any inside curves at regular intervals. (fig. 10)

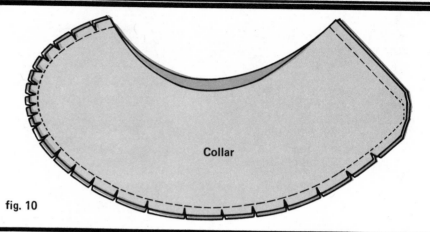

fig. 10

Collar

Press the collar in the flat position to set the stitches. Press open the seam allowances using the tip of the iron. Then press both seam allowances over to the under collar side. (fig. 11)

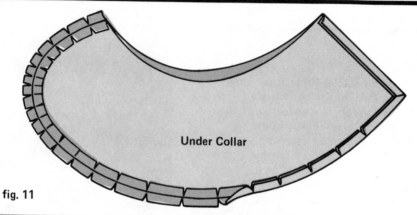

fig. 11

Under Collar

Understitch the collar edge if the collar is not going to be topstitched. With the collar still inside out, pull the seam allowances out into the under collar area and stitch on the right side of the under collar beside the seam. (fig. 12)

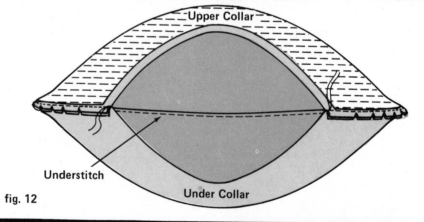

fig. 12

Upper Collar

Understitch

Under Collar

Tip

Notching can be done quickly if you use pinking shears. Trim as close to the seamline as possible without cutting the stitching around outside curves.

Tip

The collar seam allowance can also be pressed open on a Tailor Board. This curved pressing device can be used for pressing open any straight or curved seams in hard to reach places. Use as is or purchase padded covers to fit its many curves. Manufactured by June Tailor, Inc.

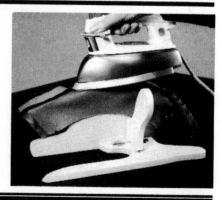

Turn the collar right side out. Carefully work out any corners using a point turner. (fig. 13)

Working on the wrong side only, press the collar edge rolling the seam to the under collar side. (fig. 14)

Add shape to the collar by rolling the neck edge over your fingers. Pin the two collar layers as they roll. The under collar will extend a bit beyond the upper collar. Trim the under collar neck edge even with the upper collar neck edge. Topstitch the collar edge if desired. (fig. 15)

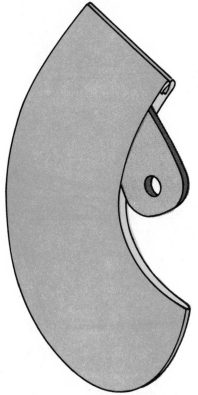

fig. 13

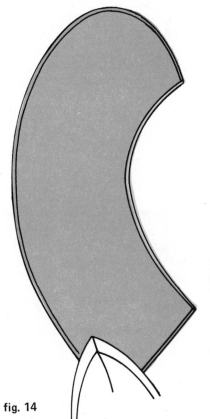

fig. 14

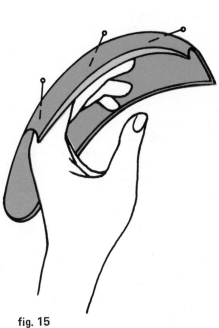

fig. 15

Tip

The Point and Tube Turner from Fashion Services, Inc. makes turning collar points a snap. Turn the collar and neatly shape the point in one quick operation. Use also for corners of pockets or pocket flaps and whenever turning spaghetti straps.

Tip

Setting your tailor's ham in a Ham Holder will make the shaping and steaming of the collar much easier since the ham will be held firmly in an upright position. A versatile Ham Holder is available from June Tailor, Inc.

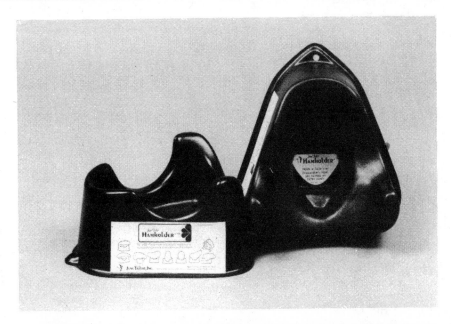

Rolled Collar Construction

Some rolled collars have the upper and under collar pieces cut from the same pattern while other rolled collars use different pattern pieces for the upper and under collar pieces. Collars that use different pattern pieces should be pinned together so that the edges of both collar pieces are even before they are stitched. The under collar will then be slightly smaller than the upper collar when finished.

Collars that use the same pattern piece for both the upper and under collar should be pinned with the under collar extending out beyond the upper collar about ⅛ inch (3mm). Stitch the two collar pieces together, holding them taut while stitching so the upper collar won't pucker. (fig. 16)

Trim and grade the seam allowances. Trim close to the stitching at each corner. Notch any outside curves and clip any inside curves at regular intervals. (fig. 17)

Press the collar in the flat position to set the stitches. Press open the seam allowances using the tip of the iron. Then press both seam allowances over to the under collar side. (fig. 18)

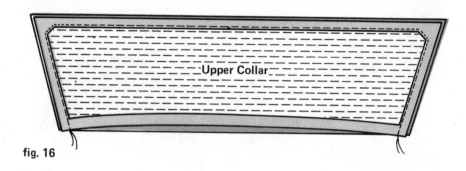

fig. 16

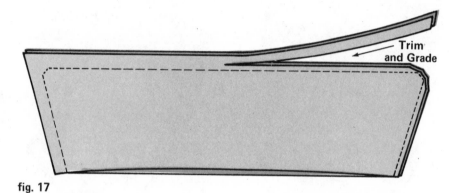

fig. 17

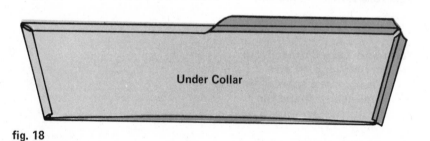

fig. 18

Tip

Shorten the stitch length when stitching around collar curves. This will reinforce the seam and make the curves smoother. Shorten the stitch length and take one or more diagonal stitches across all corners. This also reinforces the corners and allows room for the seam allowances when the collar is turned.

Tip

Notching can be done quickly if you use pinking shears. Trim as close to the seamline as possible without cutting the stitching around outside curves.

Understitch the collar edge if the collar is not going to be topstitched. With the collar still inside out, pull the seam allowances out into the under collar area and stitch on the right side of the under collar beside the seam. (fig. 19)

Turn the collar right side out. Carefully work out any corners using a point turner. (fig. 20)

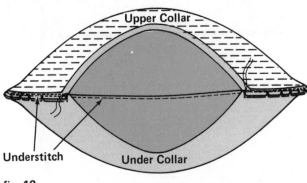

Understitch

fig. 19

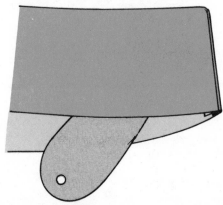

fig. 20

Working on the wrong side only, press the collar edge, rolling the seam to the under collar side. (fig. 21)

Under Collar

fig. 21

Add shape to the collar by wrapping it around the small end of a tailor's ham and securing the roll line with pins. Steam the roll line with the steam iron. (fig. 22)

Remove the collar from the ham and trim the under collar neck edge even with the upper collar neck edge. Do this while the collar is still in the shaped position. (fig. 23)

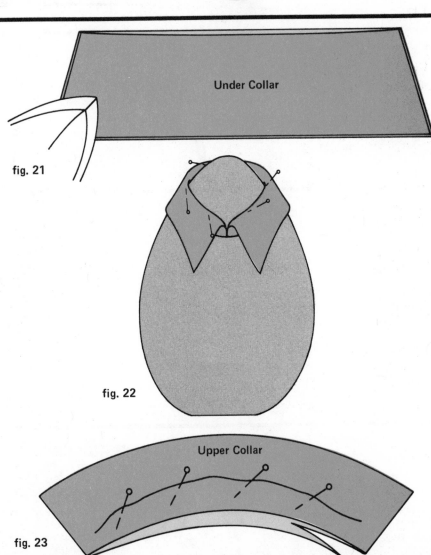

fig. 22

Upper Collar

fig. 23

One-Piece Rolled Collar Construction

Fold the collar along the foldline right sides together. Pull the edges of the under collar section about ⅛ inch (3mm) beyond the edges of the upper collar section. Stitch with the given seam width. (fig. 24)

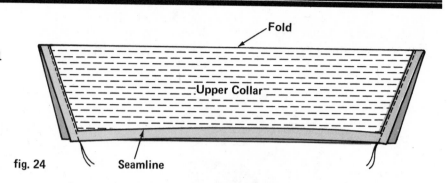

Fold

Upper Collar

Seamline

fig. 24

Trim and grade the seam allowances. Trim the seam allowances on the diagonal at each collar point. (fig. 25)

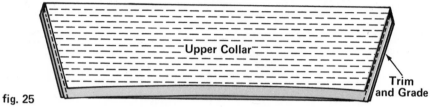

Upper Collar

Trim and Grade

fig. 25

Press the collar in the flat position to set the stitches. Press open the seam allowances using the tip of the iron. Then press both seam allowances over to the under collar side. (fig. 26)

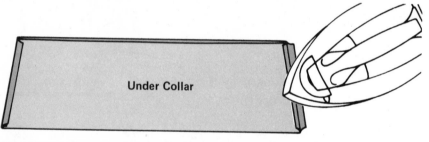

Under Collar

fig. 26

Turn the collar right side out. Carefully work out the corners with a point turner. (fig. 27)

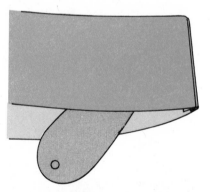

fig. 27

Working on the wrong side only, press the collar edges, rolling the seam to the under collar side. (fig. 28)

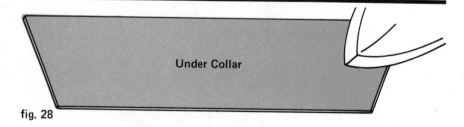

Under Collar

fig. 28

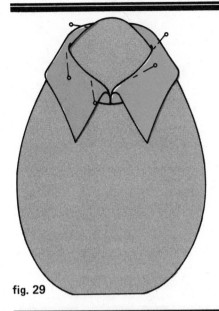

fig. 29

Add shape to the collar by wrapping it around the small end of a tailor's ham and securing the roll line with pins. Steam the collar roll line with a steam iron. (fig. 29)

Remove the collar from the ham and trim the under collar neck edge even with the upper collar neck edge. Do this while the collar is still in the rolled position. (fig. 30)

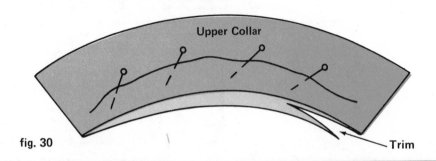

fig. 30

Standing Collar Construction

Standing collars can be made from one or two pieces. The turtleneck type of standing collar is always cut from one piece which is then folded, stitched and turned. Mandarin type collars usually have some curve and are made from two separate collar pieces. The tailored shirt collar, which is also a form of the standing collar, is made from four collar pieces; two collar pieces and two band pieces.

One-Piece Standing Collar

Fold over the seam allowance at the neckline edge of the facing section of the collar piece. Baste in place, press and trim to ¼ inch (6mm). (fig. 31)

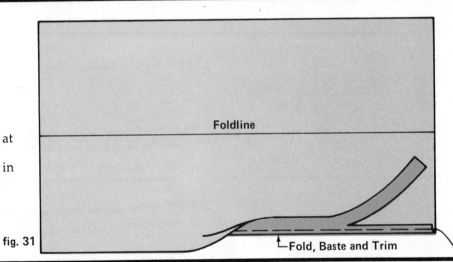

fig. 31

Fold the collar, right sides together, along the fold line. Offset the collar edges, pulling the facing section out beyond the collar portion about ⅛ inch (3mm). Pin and stitch with the given seam width. (fig. 32)

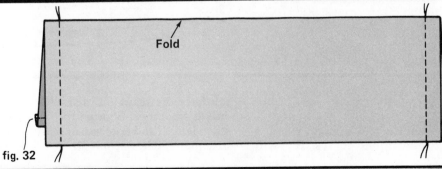

fig. 32

Trim the seam allowances and corners. Press the seam allowances open with the tip of the iron. (fig. 33)

fig. 33

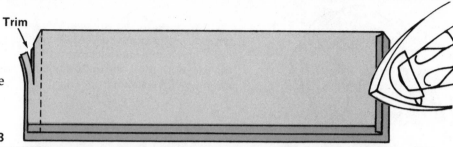
Trim

Turn the collar right side out. Carefully work out the corners with a point turner. Working on the wrong side only, press the collar edges, rolling the seam to the facing side. (fig. 34)

fig. 34

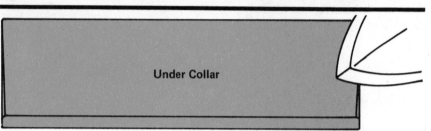
Under Collar

Two-Piece Standing Collar

Apply the interfacing to the wrong side of the collar piece. (fig. 35)

fig. 35

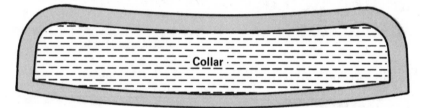
Collar

Fold up, baste and press the neck edge seam allowance of the collar facing. Trim this seam allowance to ¼ inch (6mm). (fig. 36)

fig. 36

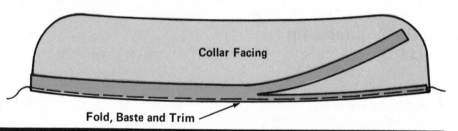
Collar Facing

Fold, Baste and Trim

Pin the two collar pieces right sides together. Offset the facing piece so it extends ⅛ inch (3mm) beyond the collar piece. Stitch with the given seam width. (fig. 37)

fig. 37

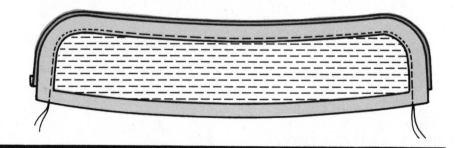

Tip

Shorten the stitch length when stitching around curves. This will reinforce the seam and make the curves smoother. Shorten the stitch length and take one or more diagonal stitches across all corners. This also reinforces the corners and allows room for seam allowances when the collar is turned.

Trim and grade the seam allowances. Trim close to the stitching at any corners. Notch any outside curves and clip any inside curves at regular intervals. (fig. 38)

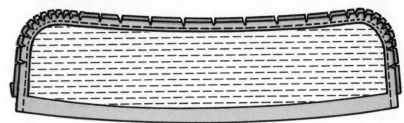

fig. 38

Tip

Notching can be done quickly if you use pinking shears. Trim as close to the seamline as possible without cutting the stitching around outside curves.

Press the collar in the flat position to set the stitches. Press open the seam allowance using the tip of the iron. Then press both seam allowances over to the collar facing. (fig. 39)

Collar Facing

fig. 39

Understitch the collar edge if the collar is not going to be topstitched. With the collar still inside out, pull the seam allowances out into the under collar area and stitch on the right side of the collar facing beside the seam. (fig. 40)

Turn the collar right side out. Carefully work out any corners or curves. Working on the wrong side only, press the collar edge rolling the seam to the under collar side.

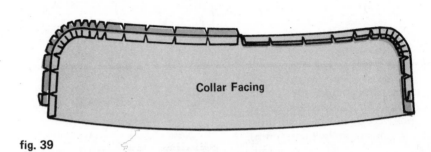

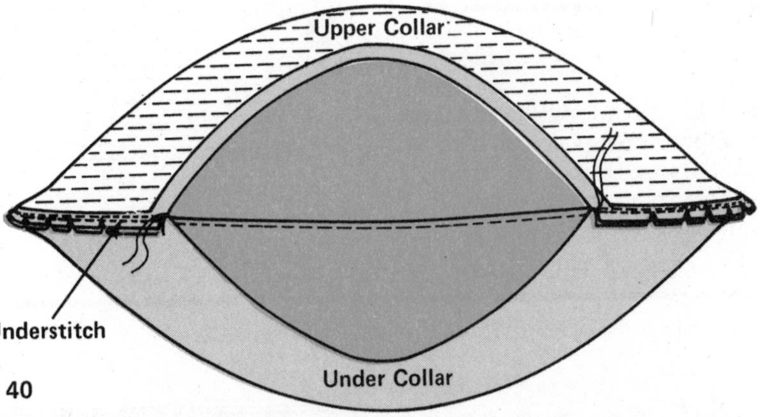

Upper Collar

Understitch

Under Collar

fig. 40

Tailored Shirt Collar

A tailored shirt collar usually has a separate neckband that is stitched to the collar before being applied to the neck edge of the garment. However, some shirt collars have the band cut as one with the collar portion. The finished effect is the same but the construction is much quicker. Follow instructions for the rolled collar if you are making a shirt collar with an attached band. (fig. 41). Use the following instructions if you are making the collar with a separate neckband. (fig. 42)

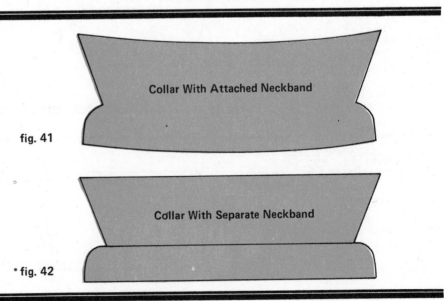

fig. 41

Collar With Attached Neckband

Collar With Separate Neckband

• fig. 42

Apply interfacing to the wrong side of the upper collar and to both neckband pieces, or just the inner neckband piece if a softer look is desired. Make sure the interfacing is eliminated from all seam allowances. (fig. 43)

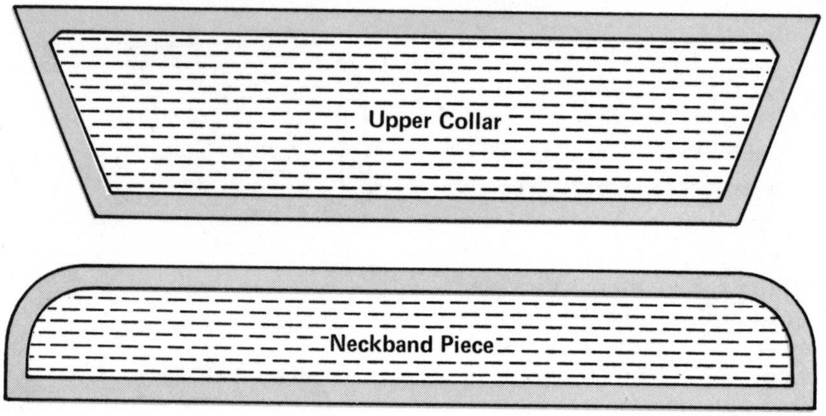

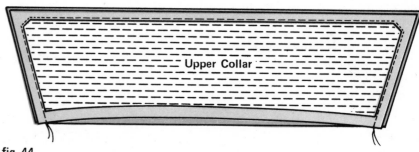

fig. 43

Pin the upper and under collar pieces right sides together. Pull the under collar out beyond the upper collar about ⅛ inch (3mm). Stitch with the given seam width. (fig. 44)

Tip

Shorten the stitch length and take one or more stitches across each corner. This reinforces the corner and allows room for seam allowances when the collar is turned.

fig. 44

Trim and grade the seam allowances and trim corners close to the stitching. (fig. 45)

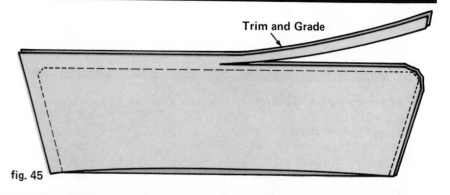

fig. 45

Press the collar in a flat position to set the stitches. Press open the seam allowances using the tip of the iron. Then press both seam allowances over to the under collar side. (fig. 46)

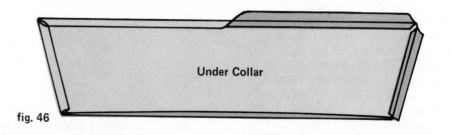

fig. 46

Understitch the collar edge if the collar is not going to be topstitched. With the collar still inside out, pull the seam allowances out into the under collar area and stitch on the right side of the under collar beside the seam. (fig. 47)

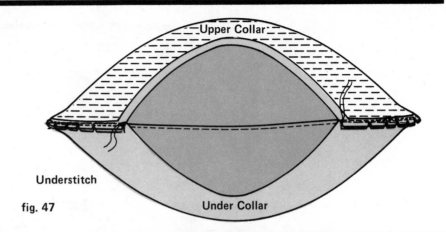

Understitch

fig. 47

Turn the collar right side out. Carefully work out the corners with a point turner. (fig. 48)

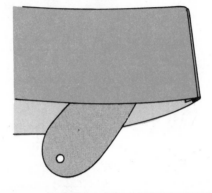

fig. 48

Working on the wrong side only, press the collar edge rolling the seam to the under collar side. Topstitch the collar if desired. (fig. 49)

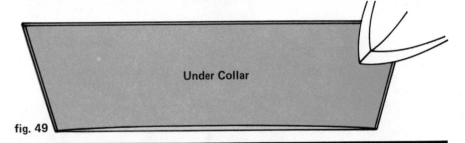

Under Collar

fig. 49

Fold up the neckline seam allowance of the inner neckband. Baste in place, press and trim to ¼ inch (6mm). (fig. 50)

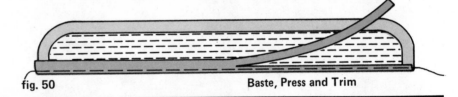

fig. 50   **Baste, Press and Trim**

Sandwich the finished collar between the two band pieces, right sides together. Match construction marks, making sure equal amounts of band extend beyond both sides of the collar. Stitch the bands to the collar with the given seam width. (fig. 51)

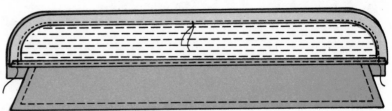

fig. 51

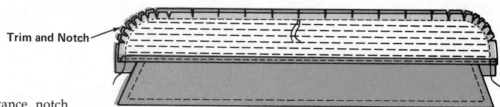

Trim and Notch

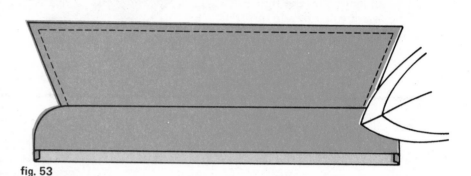

fig. 52

Trim the seam allowance, notch the band curves and turn the band to the right side and press. The seam on each end of the band should not be rolled to the underside; keep it right on the edge of the collar band.(fig.52-53)

fig. 53

Collar Application

Collars are applied to the neck edge of garments with or without facings. Sometimes just a front facing instead of a complete neckline facing is used and the inside back of the collar is finished by hand. Standing type collars are usually applied to the neck edge without any facing. The final stitching can be done by machine or hand.

Before any collar is applied the neck edge of the garment should be staystitched just to the right of the given neckline seam and then clipped at regular intervals so the neck edge can be straightened to meet the collar edge. (fig. 54)

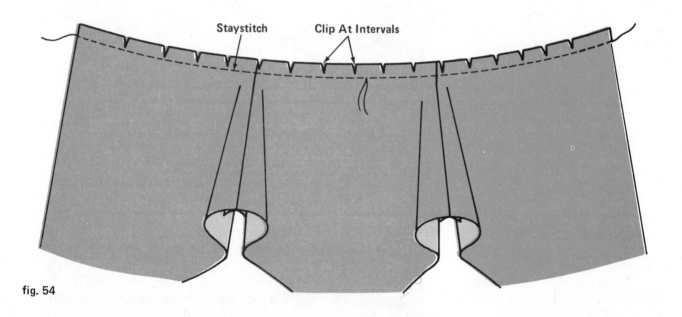

Staystitch   Clip At Intervals

fig. 54

Collar With A Facing

Stitch the facing pieces together, press open the seams, staystitch the neck edge and finish the lower edge of the facing as the pattern directs.

Pin the collar to the neckline matching construction marks. The under collar should be positioned against the right side of the garment. (fig. 55)

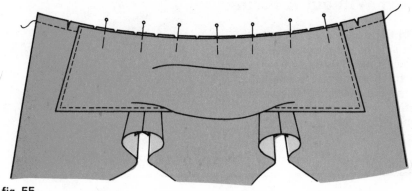
fig. 55

Tip

Patterns which have a small section of neck edge extending beyond the finished edge of the collar should be double checked after pinning to make sure the same amount of neck edge extends beyond each end of the collar. Adjust the pins holding the facing in place if necessary. Collars that are finished flush with the front edge of the garment should have the facing wrapped snugly around the collar ends so bumps don't form at the joining seam after the collar is stitched in place.

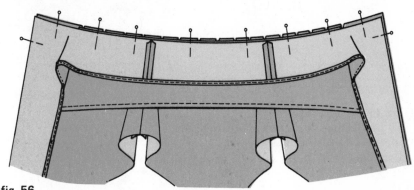
fig. 56

Position the facing over the collar so that all neckline edges are even and construction marks match, clipping the facing seam allowance if necessary. Pin securely. (fig. 56)

Stitch the collar to the garment, starting at each front edge and joining the stitching at the center back. Collars should always be stitched in this manner so that drag doesn't accumulate around the neckline and distort the collar appearance. (fig. 57)

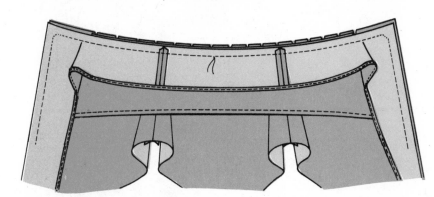
fig. 57

Trim, grade and understitch the neckline seam allowance. Turn the facing to the inside and catch in place at the garment shoulder seams only. (fig. 58)

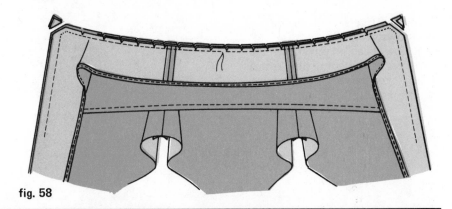
fig. 58

Collar Without A Facing

Pin the under collar only to the right side of the garment keeping the neck edges even and construction marks matched. Stitch with the given seam width starting the stitching at each end of the collar, joining it in back. (fig. 59)

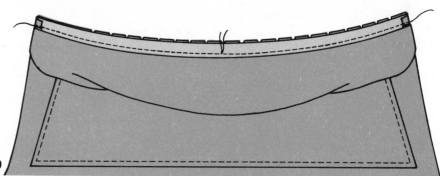

fig. 59

Trim, grade and clip the seam allowances. Using the tip of the iron, press the seam allowances up into the collar. (fig. 60)

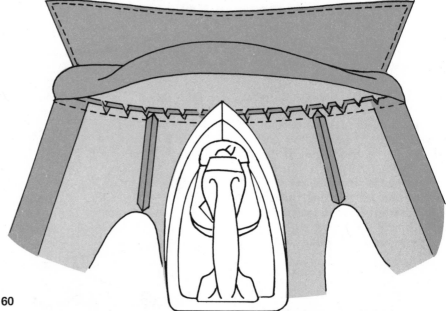

fig. 60

Bring the free section of the collar down over the neckline seam allowance and pin so the fold just covers the stitching line. Stitch the collar to the garment edge by machine or hand (fig. 61)

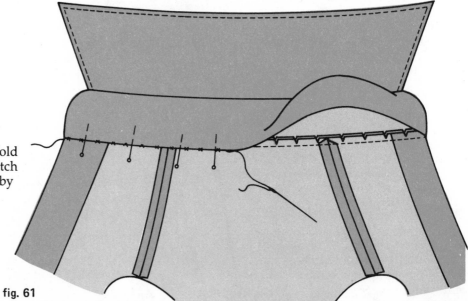

fig. 61

Collar With A Front Facing

Prepare and finish the front facing as the pattern directs. Pin the under collar only to the neck edge of the garment matching construction marks. Clip the upper collar to the seamline at each shoulder seam. (fig. 62)

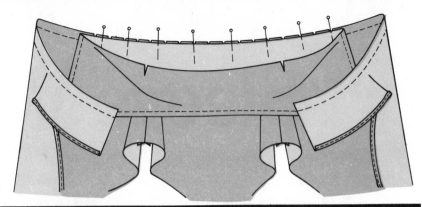

fig. 62

Position the facing over the collar, clipping the seam allowance if necessary. Fold down the upper collar seam allowance around the back of the collar. Stitch the collar to the neck edge following directional arrows. Do not catch the fold of the upper collar in the stitching. (fig. 63)

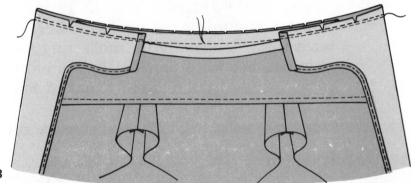

fig. 63

Trim, grade and clip the seam allowances. Turn the facing to the inside of the garment. Using the tip of the iron press the seam allowances up into the collar at the back of the neck. (fig. 64)

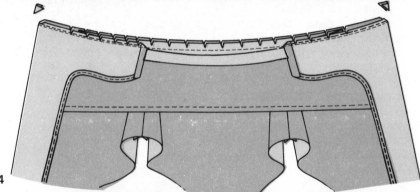

fig. 64

Arrange the neckline and collar as they will be when worn. Turn under the seam allowance at the back of the upper collar and pin in place so it just covers the neckline stitching. Catch the collar in place by hand. Turn under the ends of the facing and catch in place at the garment shoulder seams. (fig. 65)

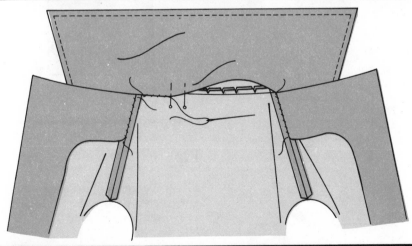

fig. 65

Sleeve Vents

Long sleeves with separate cuffs require some type of sleeve vent. Instructions are given below for three most commonly used vent finishes. Since they can be used interchangeably on most long sleeve patterns, the one you use for a particular garment is determined by the desired finished look.

The Patch Vent

The patch vent is easy to make and is ideal for knit fabrics because it has very little bulk and the raw edges of the patch require no special finish since knits do not fray.

Cut two patches of fashion fabric 1 inch (25mm) longer than the vent length and 3 inches (7.5cm) wide. Mark the vent location and length on the wrong side of each sleeve. (fig. 1)

Center the patch over the vent mark, right sides together and pin in place. (fig. 2)

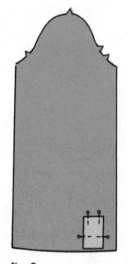

fig. 2

Tip

All sleeve vents should be constructed before the underarm sleeve seam is stitched.

Working on the wrong side of the sleeve, and using a short stitch length, stitch around the vent mark with a short stitch length. Start ⅛ inch (3mm) to the side of the vent line, stitch toward the end of the vent mark, take one stitch across the top of the mark and continue down the other side ending ⅛ inch (3mm) away from the vent line. (fig. 3)

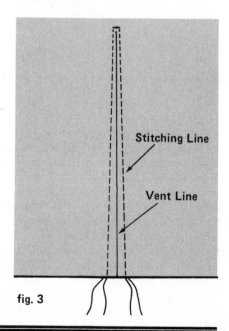

Stitching Line

Vent Line

fig. 3

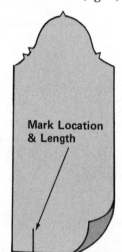

Mark Location & Length

fig. 1

Slash to the point of the V. (fig. 4)

Turn the patch to the wrong side of the sleeve and press. Roll the vent seam slightly to the underside. (fig. 5)

Hold the patch in position by topstitching around the vent opening. (fig. 6)

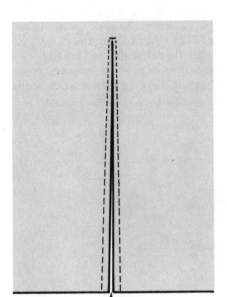

fig. 4   Slash

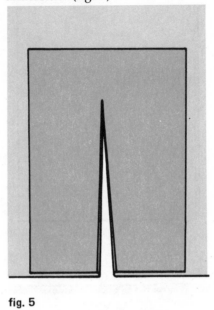

fig. 5

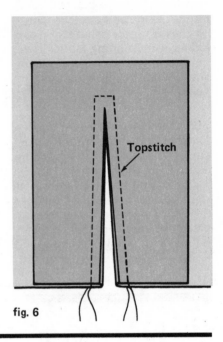

Topstitch

fig. 6

The patch can also be held in place by slipping strips of fusible web between the fabric layers and pressing. (fig. 7)

The patch vent finish can be used with woven fabrics but care must be taken with the cut edge of the patch to control fraying. Pink the edge with pinking shears. (fig. 8)

Or turn under a scant ¼ inch (6mm) and edgestitch around the three outside edges. (fig. 9)
(continued on next page)

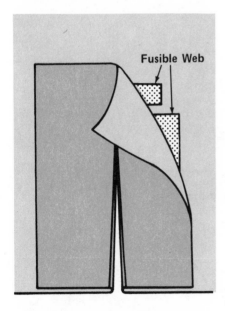

Fusible Web

fig. 7

fig. 8

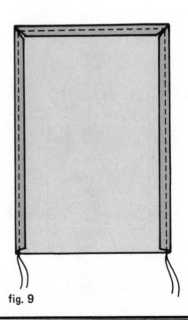

fig. 9

Woven fabrics which fray badly should have the patch completely faced before it is stitched to the vent area. Cut two patches from fashion fabric and another two patches from the same fabric or a lighter weight lining fabric. The patches should be ¼ inch (6mm) larger than the measurements given.

Pin the two patches right sides together and stitch around three edges with a scant ¼ inch (6mm) seam. Trim the corners as indicated and turn the faced patch right side out and press. Construct the vent by centering the faced patch over the vent mark on the right side of the sleeve. Stitch and finish as directed above. (fig. 10)

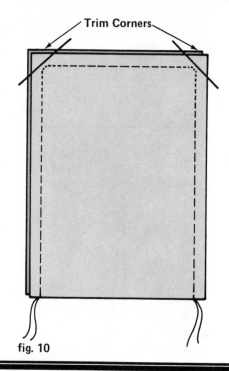

Trim Corners

fig. 10

Tip

Another way of controlling fraying edges of woven fabric patch vents is to apply a thin bead of Fray Check along the cut edge. This liquid seals the threads together to prevent fraying. From Scovill, Sewing Notions Division.

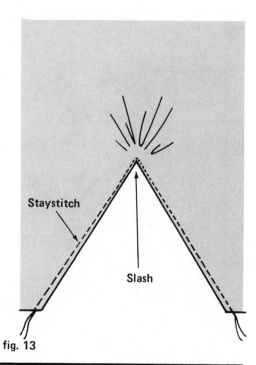

The Bound Vent

The bound vent is probably the most common vent finish found on shirts. The strip of fabric used to bind the vent opening is usually cut on the lengthwise grain of the fabric but can be cut on the bias for effect.

Mark the vent location and length on the wrong side of each sleeve piece. (fig. 11)

Cut two strips of fashion fabric that are 1 inch (25mm) longer than twice the vent length and 1½ inches (38mm) wide. Press over a ¼ inch (6mm) seam allowance along one long side of each strip. (fig. 12)

Staystitch around the vent mark starting and ending ⅛ inch (3mm) to the side of the vent mark. Slash the vent mark right to the stitching at the point of the V. (fig. 13)

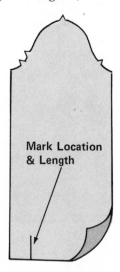

Mark Location & Length

fig. 11

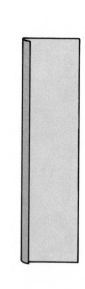

fig. 12

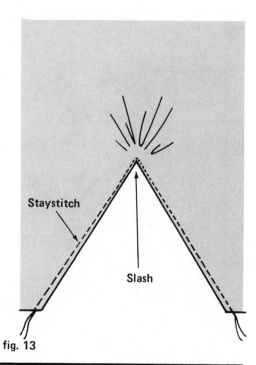

Staystitch

Slash

fig. 13

Position the right side of a vent strip against the wrong side of the slash, pulling the slash open to an almost straight line. The edge of the strip will be even with the edge of the slash only at the slash ends. The point of the V will be offset approximately ¼ inch (6mm). Pin in place. (fig. 14)

With the sleeve up, stitch the sleeve and binding together keeping just to the left of the staystitching and catching just a few fabric threads at the point of the V. (fig. 15)

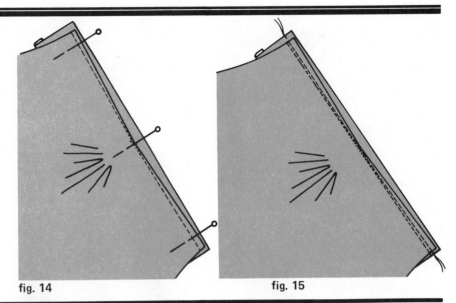

fig. 14   fig. 15

Fold the binding over enclosing the seam allowances. The pressed under seam allowance along the edge of the binding should just cover the stitching line. (fig. 16)

Hold the binding in place by edgestitching along the folded edge. (fig. 17)

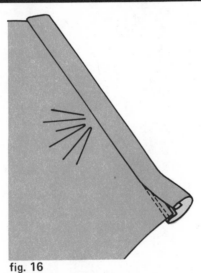

fig. 16

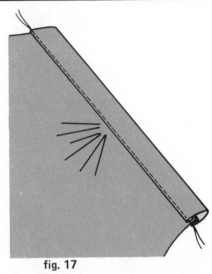

fig. 17

Pull the two sides of the bound vent out away from the wrong side of the sleeve. Stitch the top of the vent at an angle. This helps keep the vent in position when the garment is worn. (fig. 18)

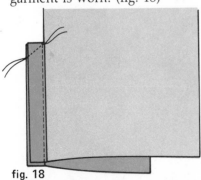

fig. 18

Tip

When applying a standard cuff to a sleeve with a bound vent finish, the upper part of the vent will be folded under against the sleeve and the under part of the vent will be pulled out away from the sleeve. Both sides of the vent should be folded under against the sleeve if a French cuff is being applied.

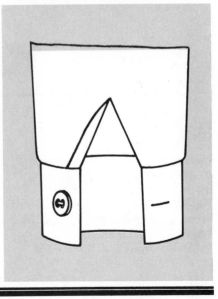

The Tailored Placket

The tailored placket is the type of sleeve vent found on tailored shirts and jackets. The tailored placket described here uses one pattern piece for the complete placket and is very easy to make. The pattern for the placket is given at the right. (fig. 19). Trace it off onto a separate piece of paper so you won't damage the book. The length of the placket can be adjusted for personal preference by adding or taking away from the bottom edge. The length given here is standard shirt placket length.

It is suggested that you make a sample placket on some scrap fabric before beginning work on the actual garment. This will take just a few minutes and will help you decide if the placket length is correct.

(continued on next page)

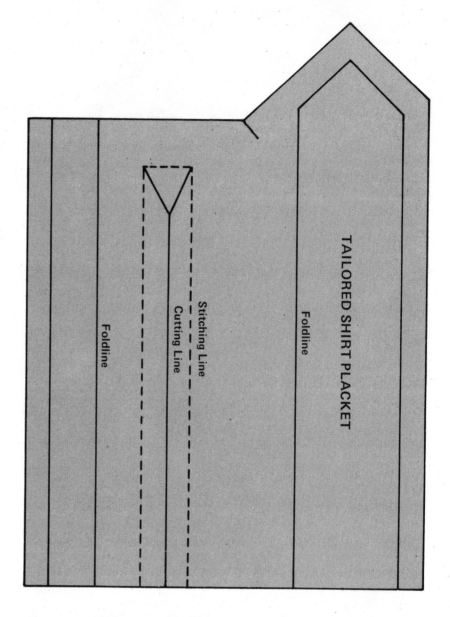

fig. 19

Foldline

Stitching Line

Cutting Line

Foldline

TAILORED SHIRT PLACKET

Tip

Tracing paper and a tracing wheel are the best way to mark the stitching box on the placket pieces. The E-Z Buckle Double Faced Tracing Paper and chubby Tracing Wheel make the job easy. Available from E-Z Buckle Co.

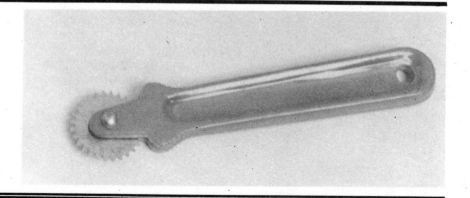

Cut out two placket pieces from your fashion fabric and mark each foldline with a small clip. Transfer the stitching box to the wrong side of each placket piece. (fig. 20)

Press over and baste a ¼ inch (6mm) seam allowance along both long edges and the point of each placket piece, clipping where indicated. (fig. 21)

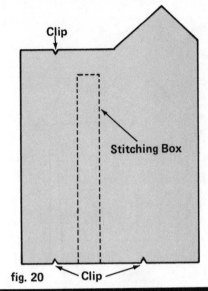

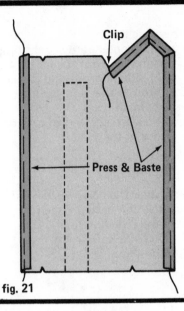

fig. 20

fig. 21

Press both sides of the placket pieces over along the foldlines. The basted edges of the placket should just meet the sides of the stitching box. (fig. 22)

Pin the right side of the placket piece against the wrong side of the sleeve so the stitching box is centered over the vent line. The pointed side of the placket should be toward the front of the sleeve. (fig. 23)

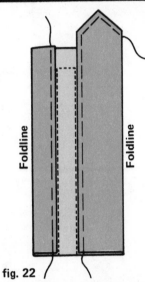

fig. 22

fig. 23

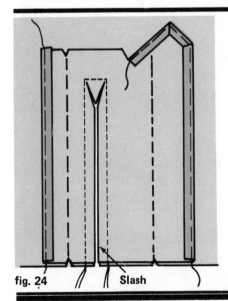

fig. 24   Slash

Stitch around the box with a short stitch length. Slash down the center of the box to within ½ inch (13mm) of the end and then cut into each corner. (fig. 24)
(continued on next page)

Tip

Using a sharp pair of scissors, always cut right to the stitching line when cutting open a box. Failure to cut right to the stitching will prevent the placket piece from turning smoothly to the right side.

Press each side of the placket toward the center of the vent along each seamline. Turn the sleeve to the right side and pull the placket piece through the vent opening. Press again so the seam allowances are pressed in toward the center of the placket.

Fold over the narrow side of the placket so the basted edge just covers the stitching line. Edgestitch the fold to the top of the vent opening. (fig. 25)

Fold over the pointed section of the placket so the basted edge just covers the stitching line. Pull the underneath section of the placket out of the way and edgestitch the fold of the pointed section just to the top of the vent opening. Pull thread through to the wrong side and tie. (fig. 26)

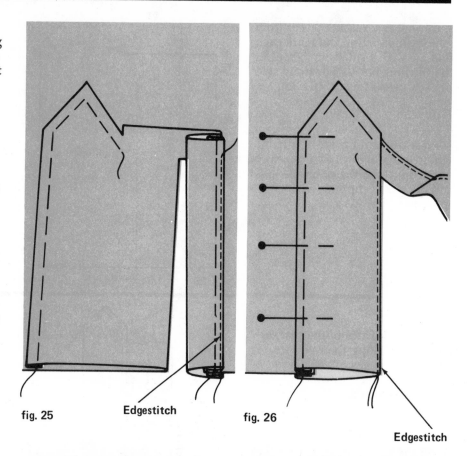

fig. 25   **Edgestitch**   fig. 26

Edgestitch

With the sleeve spread out flat arrange the placket in the finished position. Pin in place so the basted edge just covers the stitching line. (fig. 27)

Edgestitch the placket following the directional arrows. Pull the threads through to the wrong side and tie in a knot. (fig. 28)

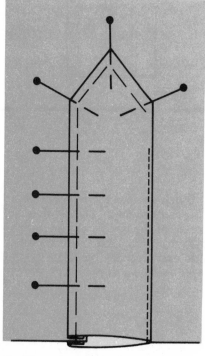

fig. 27

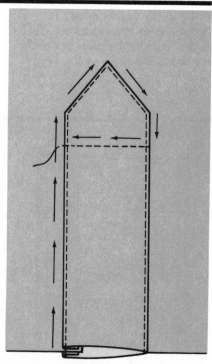

fig. 28

Sleeve Cuffs

The following instructions will help you make and apply perfect cuffs to all your long sleeved garments. Your cuffs can have accurate points and curves, facings that don't show through to the right side and smooth joining seams at the sleeve edge.

Cuff Interfacing

All cuffs need interfacing to give them body and keep them crisp. Use either a fusible or nonfusible interfacing of the weight that will give the desired finished look.

The interfacing should always be applied to the wrong side of the upper cuff piece so it lies between the visible part of the cuff and the seam allowances. This prevents "shadowing through" of the seam allowances.

One-piece cuffs should have interfacing applied only to the upper half of the cuff piece. The interfacing should extend ½ inch (13mm) beyond the foldline. Fusible interfacing should have all seam allowances trimmed away before application. (fig. 1)

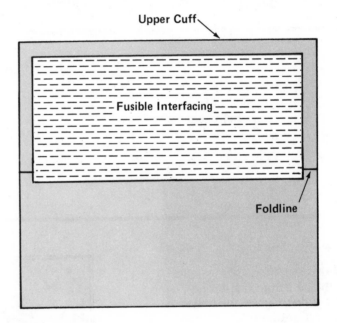

fig. 1

Nonfusible interfacing should be stitched in place just outside the given seamline and then trimmed close to the stitching. (fig. 2)

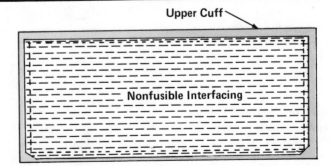

fig. 2

One-Piece Cuff Construction

Fold the cuff right sides together along the foldline pulling the cuff facing portion out beyond the upper cuff about ⅛ inch (3mm). Pin and stitch with the given seam width. (fig. 3)

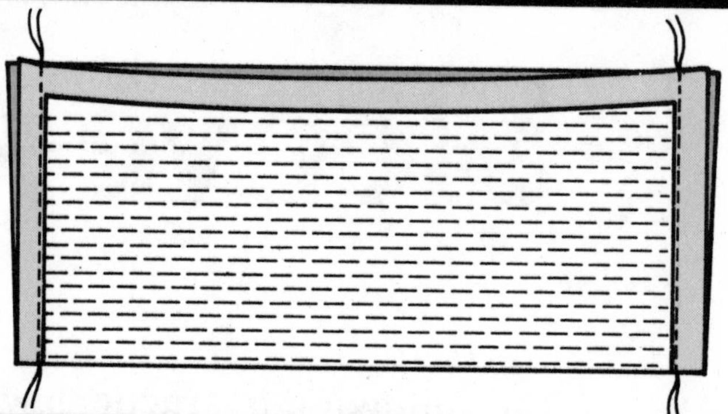

fig. 3

Grade the seam allowances and trim the corners. Press the seam allowances open with the tip of the iron. (fig. 4)

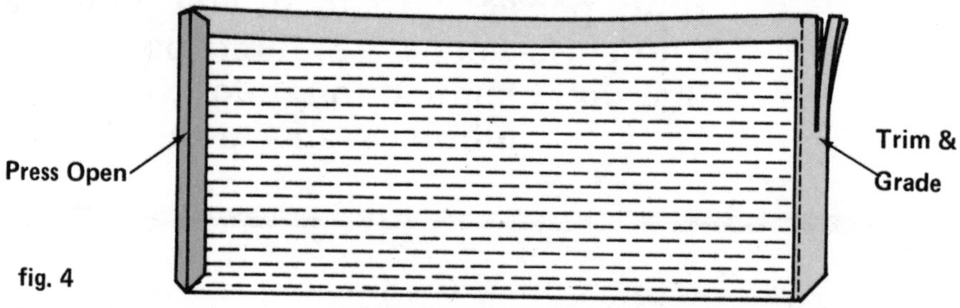

Press Open

Trim & Grade

fig. 4

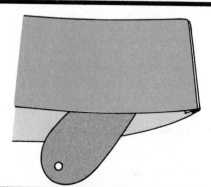

Turn the cuff right side out, using a point turner to help get sharp corners. (fig. 5)

fig. 5

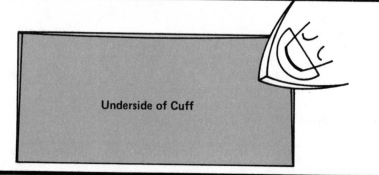

Press the cuff from the wrong side, rolling the seam to the under side of the cuff. (fig. 6)

Underside of Cuff

fig. 6

Tip

The seam allowances can also be pressed open on the Point Presser. This wooden pressing aid helps one achieve perfect edges on collars and lapels too. Available from Risdon Mfg. Co.

Two-Piece Cuff Construction

Pin the two cuff pieces right sides together pulling the cuff facing out beyond the upper cuff about ⅛ inch (3mm) on the three outside edges. (fig. 7)

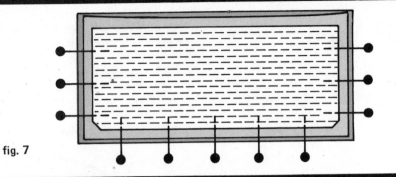

fig. 7

Stitch with the given seam width using a short stitch length around each corner for reinforcement.

Trim and grade the seam allowances notching any curves. Press the cuff in the flat position and then press open the seam allowances with the tip of the iron. Press all seam allowances over to the cuff facing side. (fig. 8)

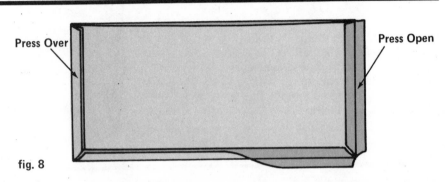

Press Over

Press Open

fig. 8

Turn the cuff right side out using a point turner to help get neat corners.

Press the cuff from the wrong side rolling the seams to the underside. (fig. 9)

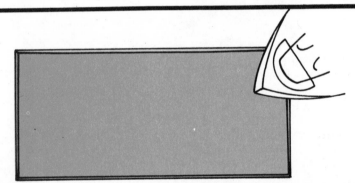

fig. 9

Tip

Always take one or more diagonal stitches across the points of square corners. The heavier the fabric the more diagonal stitches needed. This allows room for the seam allowances when they are turned inside the cuff.

Tip

Use the Dritz Point Turner to help you get a perfect cuff point without damaging the fabric. This tool also serves as a 4 inch ruler and a helper for making thread shanks when sewing on buttons. From Scovill, Sewing Notions Division.

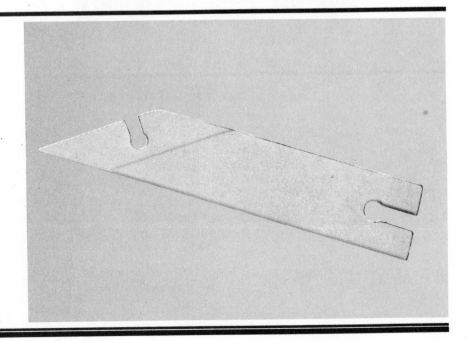

Cuff Application

The two methods of applying a standard cuff are the wrap method and the double stitched method.

Try each method to see which one you prefer. The double stitched method should be used when applying very narrow cuffs since it is impossible to wrap these and still have stitching room.

Prepare the sleeve for either application method by gathering or pleating in the sleeve fullness as the pattern indicates.

Trim and grade the seam allowance.

The Wrap Cuff

With the sleeve inside out pin the right side of the cuff to the right side of the prepared sleeve edge. Stitch just the upper cuff layer to the sleeve edge with the given seam width. (fig. 10)

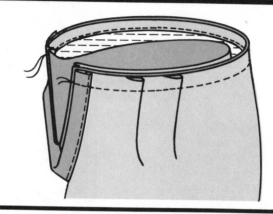

fig. 10

Wrap the cuff facing back around each end of the cuff so the right side of the cuff facing is against the wrong side of the sleeve. Open up the cuff seam allowances and fold them back around the cuff. Stitch for about 2 inches (5cm) along the original seam on both ends of the cuff. (fig. 11)

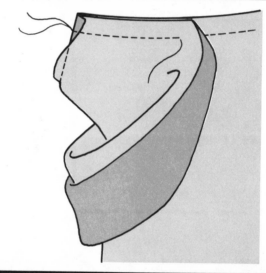

fig. 11

Close the unstitched portion of the cuff facing by hand (fig. 12), or by machine if you are going to topstitch the top edge of the cuff. (fig. 13)

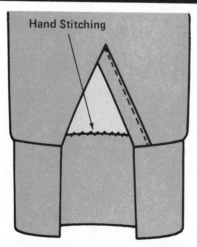

Hand Stitching

fig. 12

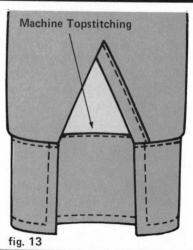

Machine Topstitching

fig. 13

The Double Stitched Cuff

Prepare the cuff as directed except press down the seam allowance along the top edge of the interfaced cuff piece and trim it to ⅜ inch (10mm) before you stitch the two cuff pieces together. (fig. 14)

Stitch, grade and trim the seam allowance; turn and press the cuff, rolling the seam to the facing side. (fig. 15)

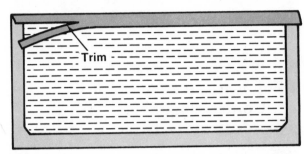

fig. 14

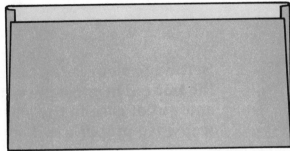

fig. 15

With the prepared sleeve right side out, pin the cuff facing to the sleeve edge, right side of facing to the wrong side of the sleeve. Extend each edge of the sleeve about ⅛ inch (3mm) beyond the edge of the cuff. (fig. 16)

Stitch the cuff to the sleeve with the given seam allowance starting and ending the seam ⅛ inch (3mm) narrower than the given width. Pull the folded edge of the upper cuff out of the way while stitching. Trim the seam allowance to ¼ inch (6mm). (fig. 17)

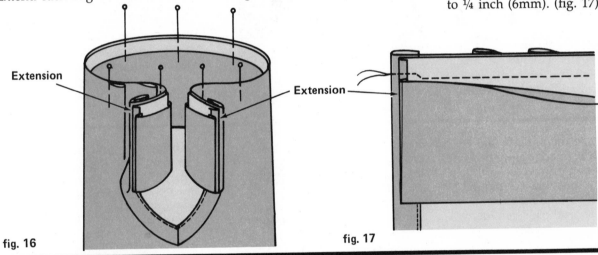

fig. 16

fig. 17

Turn the sleeve right side out and arrange the cuff in the finished position so the folded edge just covers the stitching. The seam allowances at the ends of the cuff should be pushed down into the cuff and pinned so the stitching is completely covered and no bump forms at the joining seam. (fig. 18)

Edgestitch the upper cuff to the sleeve, holding the cuff taut in front of and behind the presser foot to prevent puckers. (A free arm sewing machine is great for this procedure.) (fig. 19)

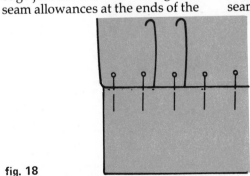

fig. 18

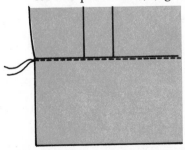

fig. 19

Set-In Sleeves

Setting in sleeves can be a snap if you know the tricks of the trade. The most important thing is to have the proper amount of ease in the sleeve cap. Controlling the sleeve cap ease properly will then give you a perfect sleeve.

Measuring And Adjusting Sleeve Cap Ease

Sleeve cap problems result when the pattern allows too much ease or the fabric isn't supple enough to handle the allowed ease. Soft natural fiber fabrics ease in better than synthetic fabrics with a firm finish. The sleeve cap ease of the pattern should be measured and adjusted if necessary to accommodate the differences in fabrics.

The recommended amount of sleeve cap ease for various fabrics is 1½ inches (38mm) ease for supple fabrics and 1 inch (25mm) ease for knits, firm wovens, permanent press fabrics and real or fake leathers.

Check the ease on your paper pattern before cutting the fabric. Making ease alterations on the pattern is much easier and more accurate than trying to make them on an already cut-out sleeve.

Determine the pattern ease allowance by overlapping the front and back pattern pieces until the shoulder seams line up; pin in place. Walk a tape measure around the armhole seamline, starting and ending at the underarm seam. This is easy to do if you place the tape measure on edge. (fig. 1)

With the tape on edge, measure completely around the sleeve seamline beginning at the underarm seam. The difference between the two measurements is the allowed sleeve cap ease. (fig. 2)

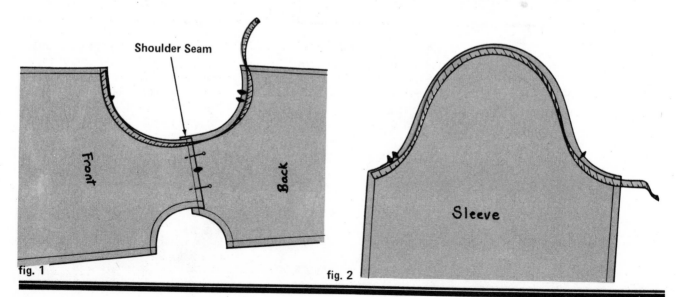

Shoulder Seam

Front

Back

fig. 1

Sleeve

fig. 2

Reducing Sleeve Cap Ease

The sleeve cap ease should be reduced if the difference between the two measurements is more than the ease amounts suggested.

Cut the sleeve pattern apart at underarm points. (fig. 3)

Reduce the sleeve cap ease by making one slash in the sleeve cap area for each ¼ inch (6mm) of excess ease. Keep slashes within the top curved portion of the sleeve. Cut to but not through the lower edge of the sleeve. (fig. 4)

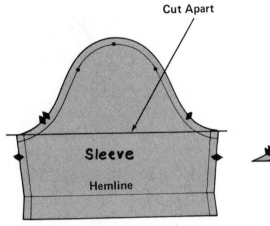
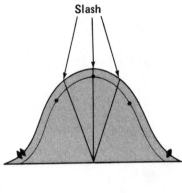

fig. 3

fig. 4

Overlap each slash up to ¼ inch (6mm) and tape in place. Check the sleeve measurement and adjust overlaps if necessary until you have the right amount of ease in the sleeve. (fig. 5)

Tape the two sleeve pieces back together and use this altered pattern to cut the fashion fabric. (fig. 6)

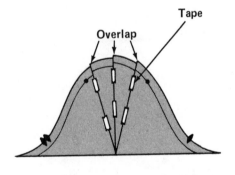
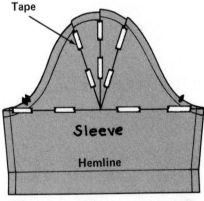

fig. 5

fig. 6

Tip

Use the 18 inch C-Thru Plastic Ruler when making these sleeve adjustments. It will help you draw accurate lines and is great for other alterations too. From the C-Thru Ruler Co.

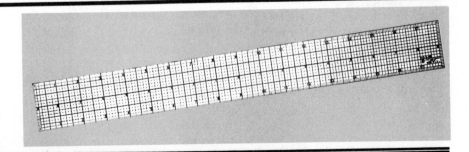

Controlling Sleeve Cap Ease

The ease of the sleeve cap must be controlled while the sleeve is being pinned and stitched into the armhole. The best method of control is to easestitch the cap of the sleeve from notch to notch. Do the easestitching in the seam allowance, close to the seamline so it won't show after the sleeve has been stitched into the armhole. (fig. 7) Easestitching is explained in the *Seams* chapter.

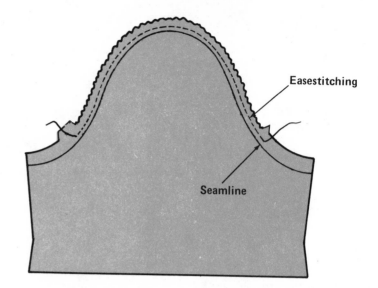

Easestitching

Seamline

fig. 7

Tip

Some fabrics will ease up more than others during the easestitching process. If your sleeve cap hasn't eased up enough pull up the bobbin thread with a pin every six or eight stitches until you get enough ease. If the fabric has eased too much, release some ease by breaking the thread every so often until you have the proper amount of ease.

Sleeve Application

There are two methods that can be used to apply set-in sleeves. The set-in method has the sleeve stitched into the armhole after the underarm seams of both the sleeve and garment have been sewn.

The shirt sleeve method is used almost exclusively on men's shirts. The sleeve is stitched to the armhole before any underarm seams are sewn. This method should not be used for anything other than a shirt sleeve unless a slight modification is made to the procedure. Otherwise the sleeve will not fit right in the underarm and will tear out easily.

The Set-In Sleeve

With the garment and sleeve right side out pin the sleeve into the armhole matching construction marks and seams. Place the pins at approximately ½ inch (13mm) intervals inserting them in the fabric at the given seamline for best ease control. (fig. 8)

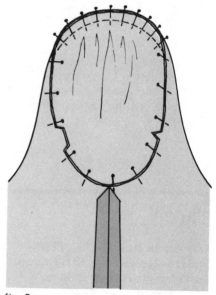

fig. 8

Start stitching at one notch; go all around the sleeve, past the starting point, and end at the second notch (fig. 9) This gives a double line of stitching in the underarm area for strength. Trim the seam allowances to ¼ inch (6mm) between the notches, and to ⅜ inch (10mm) around the top of the sleeve. (fig. 10). Overcast the trimmed seam allowance between the underarm notches with a wide zigzag stitch.

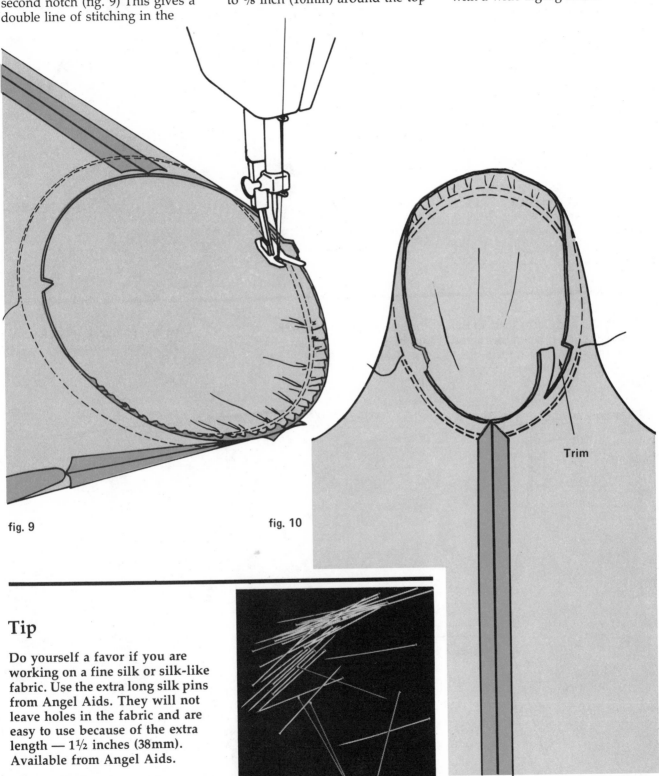

fig. 9

fig. 10

Trim

Tip

Do yourself a favor if you are working on a fine silk or silk-like fabric. Use the extra long silk pins from Angel Aids. They will not leave holes in the fabric and are easy to use because of the extra length — 1½ inches (38mm). Available from Angel Aids.

The Shirt Sleeve

This method of setting in a sleeve is used with shirt sleeves that have very little curve in the sleeve cap. The difference between the sleeve and armhole is usually very little so easestitching around the cap of the sleeve is not necessary.

Pin the sleeve to the armhole before any underarm seams are sewn, handling what little ease there is with the pins. (fig. 11)

Stitch the seam first with a straight stitch and then a zigzag. Trim the seam allowance close to the edge of the zigzag stitching. (fig. 12)

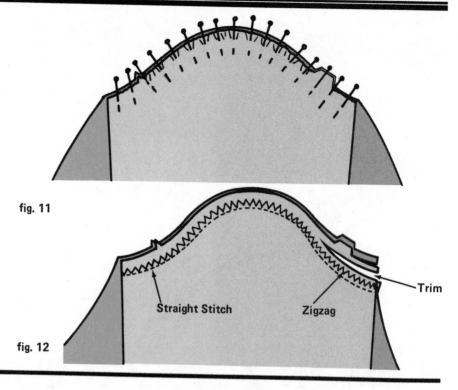

fig. 11

fig. 12

Straight Stitch   Zigzag   Trim

Stitch the underarm seam of the garment matching seamlines at the underarm point. Stitch from the hem of the garment out through the sleeve making sure the armhole seam is turned out into the sleeve. (fig. 13)

Do a row of zigzag stitching and trim the seam allowance. (fig. 14)

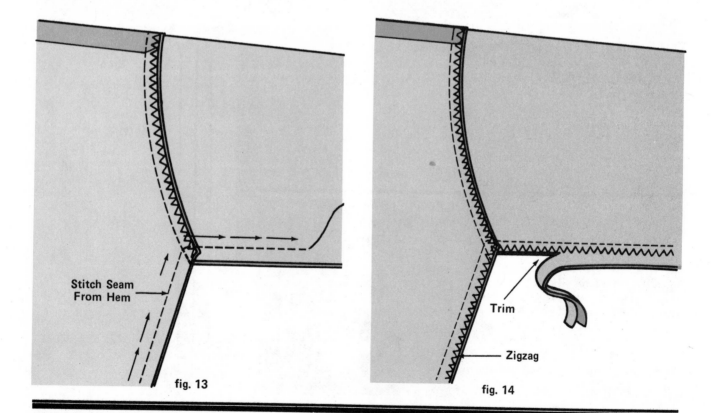

Stitch Seam From Hem

fig. 13

Trim

Zigzag

fig. 14

The Modified Shirt Sleeve

A combination of the set-in and shirt sleeve method can be used to set in many tailored sleeves. Easestitch the cap of the sleeve as previously directed and pin the sleeve into the armhole before any underarm seams are sewn — making sure you match all construction marks. Start stitching at one underarm notch and stitch around to the other. (fig. 15)

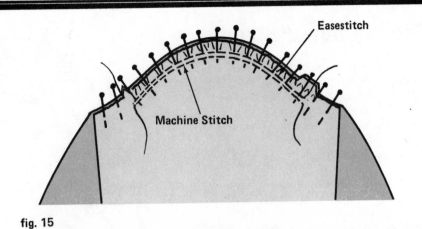

fig. 15

Stitch and press open the underarm seams of the garment and sleeve.

Complete the armhole seam in the underarm area. Trim the seam allowances to ¼ inch (6mm) below the notches and to ⅜ inch (10mm) around the top of the sleeve. (fig. 16)

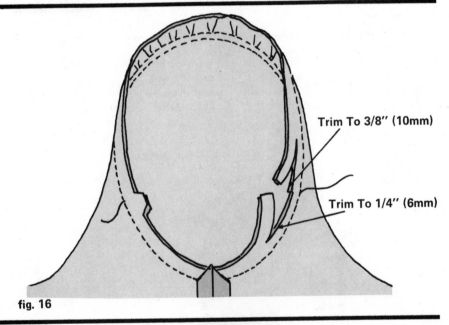

fig. 16

Overcast the trimmed seam allowance between the underarm notches with a wide zigzag stitch. (fig. 17)

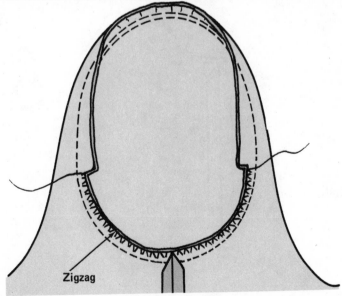

fig. 17

The Gathered Sleeve

Make two rows of machine basting between the gathering marks on the sleeve cap. One row should be along the given seamline and the other row ¼ inch (6mm) away in the seam allowance. (fig. 18)

Stitch and press open the underarm seam. Pull up both bobbin threads on each side of the sleeve cap to make the gathers.

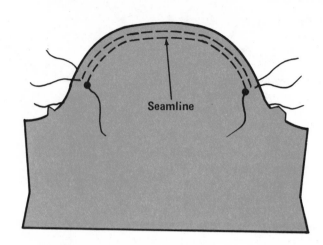

Seamline

fig. 18

Pin the sleeve into the armhole, right sides together, matching construction marks. Distribute the gathers evenly and pin in place. (fig. 19)

Stitch along the given seamline, making sure the gathers stay neat and even as you stitch over them. Do another row of stitching in the seam allowance ¼ inch (6mm) away from the first. Trim the seam allowance close to the second row of stitching. (fig. 20)

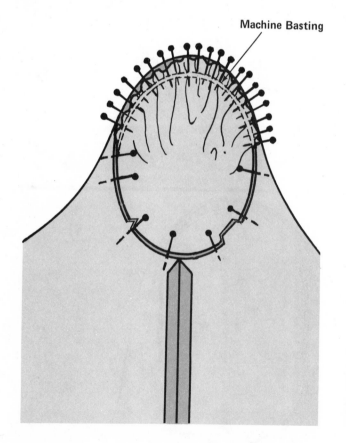

Machine Basting

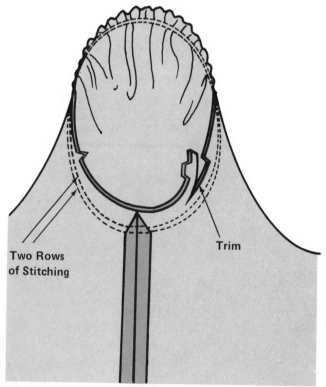

Two Rows of Stitching

Trim

fig. 19

fig. 20

Zippers

Regular zippers can be used for center slot or lapped zipper application at necklines, sleeves, waistlines, and center back or center front seams. Invisible zippers should be used mainly for back or side openings since they will bulge unattractively in center front applications in fitted or semi-fitted garments. However, they can be used in the front of loose, flowing garments without problems.

Anatomy Of A Zipper

Two basic types of zippers are the chain and the coil. The chain type zipper has either metal or plastic teeth and the coil type zipper has a nylon or polyester coil. It is lighter-weight and more flexible than the chain zipper. Both zipper types are made in many weights and either type is equally strong. Your choice will depend on the fashion fabric and color selection.

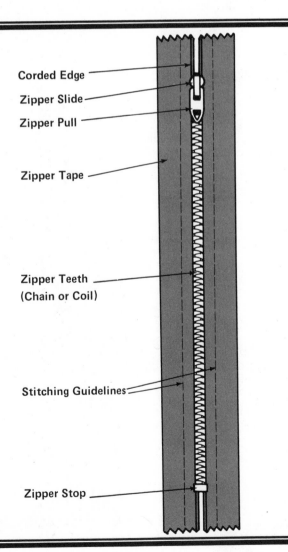

Corded Edge

Zipper Slide

Zipper Pull

Zipper Tape

Zipper Teeth (Chain or Coil)

Stitching Guidelines

Zipper Stop

Zipper Know-How

All zippers should be pre-shrunk before being sewn into a garment. This removes any shrinkage from the zipper tape and prevents puckers in the zipper seam after the garment is laundered. Soak the zipper in a basin of hot water for a few minutes, roll in a towel and allow to dry, or run the zipper through the washer and dryer when pre-shrinking the fashion fabric.

Neckline and waistline zippers which have a facing finish should have a hook and eye sewn to the top of the zipper opening for a neat finish. This means the zipper should be positioned an extra ⅜ inch (10mm) down from the neck or waistline seam to allow room for the hook and eye.

Insert zippers into the garment before any other seams have been sewn whenever possible. It is much easier to insert a zipper while the garment pieces can be laid out flat.

Trim cross-seam allowances severely when they occur in a zipper area to reduce bulk. (fig. 1)

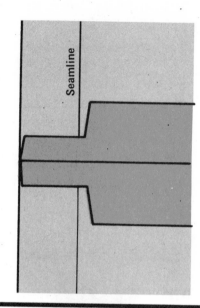

fig. 1

Enlarge seam allowances in the zipper area when necessary with strips of seam binding edgestitched to the existing seam allowances. (fig. 2)

Zippers can be shortened by securely hand stitching across the zipper teeth at the desired length. Trim away the excess zipper ¾ inch (20mm) below the stitching. (fig. 3) *(continued on next page)*

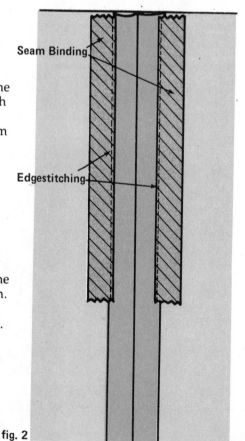

Seam Binding

Edgestitching

fig. 2

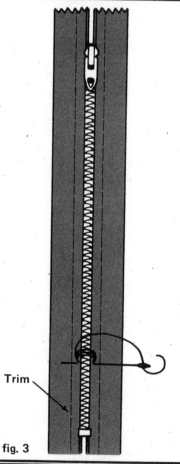

Trim

fig. 3

Zippers should be secured to the seam allowances of the garment by some form of basting before any permanent stitching. This can be done using one of the following methods.

Use hand basting. (fig. 4)

Use a strip of drafting or magic transparent tape. (fig. 5)

Tip

Self-basting zippers are now available which have thin strips of fusible material on each side of the zipper tape. Position the zipper on the seam allowances and press with a warm iron, following the manufacturer's instructions.

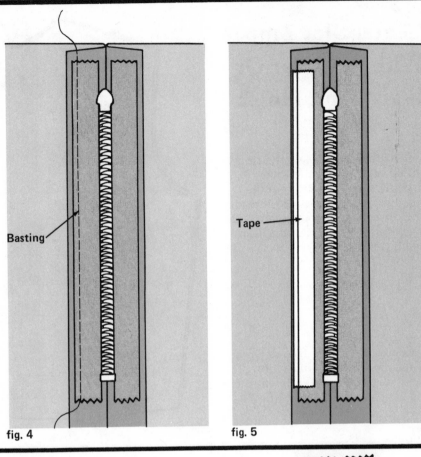

fig. 4   fig. 5

Secure the zipper to the seam allowances with a glue stick. Apply the glue to both edges of the right side of the zipper tape and press in position on the seam allowances, right side down. (fig. 6)

Strips of double-faced tape can also be used to hold zippers in position. Place the tape strip on the right side of the zipper tape close to the teeth. (fig. 7)

Position the zipper face down on the seam allowances and press in place. Make sure you don't stitch into the tape and remove it immediately after opening the zipper.

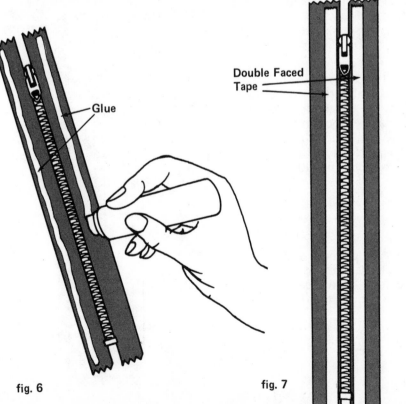

fig. 6   fig. 7

Center Slot Zipper With A Collar Or Waistband Finish

Stitch the seam below the zipper with a regular stitch length. Backstitch at the bottom of the zipper opening. Break the threads and close the remaining seam with machine basting. Press the seam open. (fig. 8)

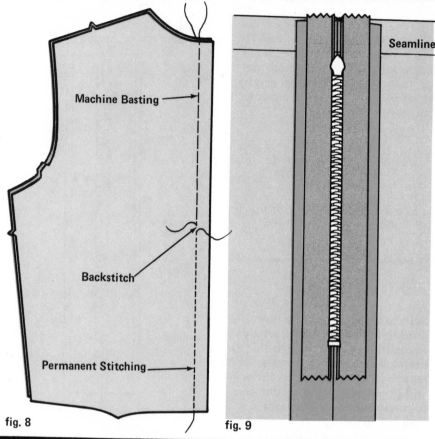

Machine Basting

Backstitch

Permanent Stitching

Seamline

fig. 8

fig. 9

Center the zipper face down on seam allowances with the top of the slide a seam width down from the edge of the garment. (fig. 9)

Baste the zipper to the left seam allowance only using one of the methods previously described. Using a zipper foot on the machine, edgestitch the right zipper tape to the right seam allowance only. (fig. 10)

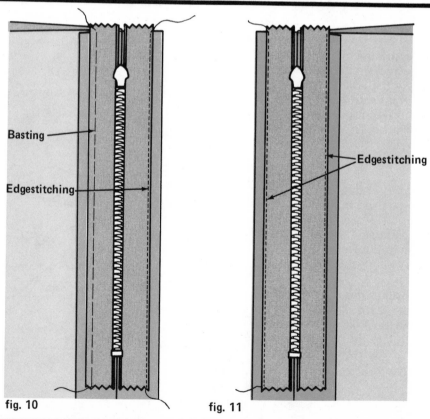

Basting

Edgestitching

Edgestitching

fig. 10

fig. 11

Refold the garment and edgestitch the left zipper tape to the left seam allowance only. (fig. 11) Remove any tape or basting thread.

On the right side of the garment, mark the bottom of the zipper teeth with a pin. Hand baste across the bottom of the zipper and up both sides ¼ inch (6mm) from the seam. (fig. 12)

Working on the right side, machine stitch each side of the zipper from bottom to top, starting at the garment seam just below the hand basting. Keep the stitching just to the side of the basting so it can be easily removed. (fig. 13)

Pull all threads to the wrong side and tie in a knot. Remove the machine basting from the center seam and the hand basting around the zipper. Press the zipper from the wrong side only.

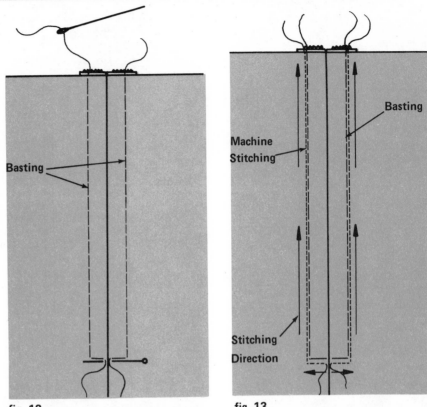

fig. 12

fig. 13

Center Slot Zipper With A Facing Finish

Stitch the seam below the zipper with a regular stitch length. Backstitch at the bottom of the zipper opening. Break the threads and close the remaining seam with machine basting. Press the seam open. (fig. 14)

Center the zipper face down on the seam allowances with the top of the slide a seam width plus ⅜ inch (10mm) down from the garment edge. (fig. 15)
(continued on next page)

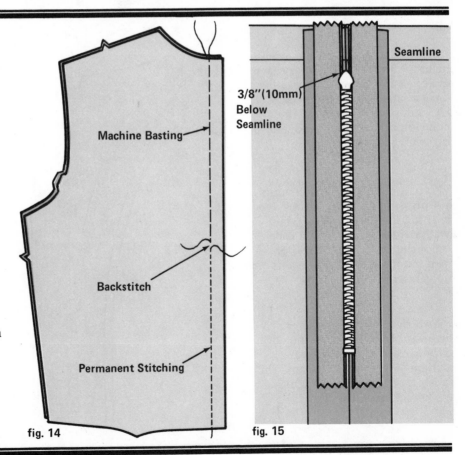

fig. 14

fig. 15

Baste the zipper to the left seam allowance only using one of the methods previously described. Using a zipper foot on the machine, edgestitch the right zipper tape to the right seam allowance only. (fig. 16)

Refold the garment and edgestitch the left zipper tape to the left seam allowance only. (fig. 17)

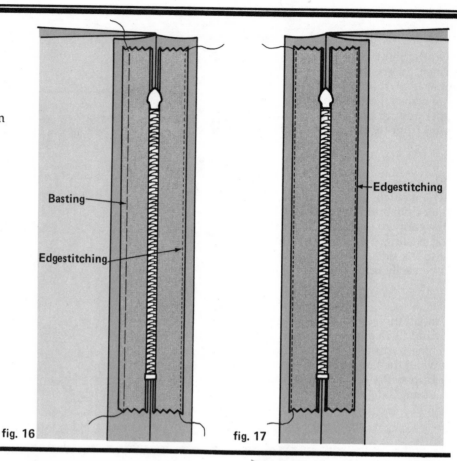

Basting

Edgestitching

fig. 16

Edgestitching

fig. 17

Remove thread from the top 3 inches (7.5cm) of the zipper seam and open the zipper to that point. Make a small clip at the top edge of both sides of the garment ⅝ inch (15mm) in from the edge of the seam allowance. (fig. 18)

Prepare the facing by stitching and pressing open the seams and finishing the lower edge. Trim away ½ inch (13mm) from each end of the facing. Stitch and press open the shoulder or side seams of the garment.

With right sides together stitch the ends of the facing to the edge of the garment seam allowance, taking a ¼ inch (6mm) seam. The zipper tape should be caught in this line of stitching. (fig. 19)

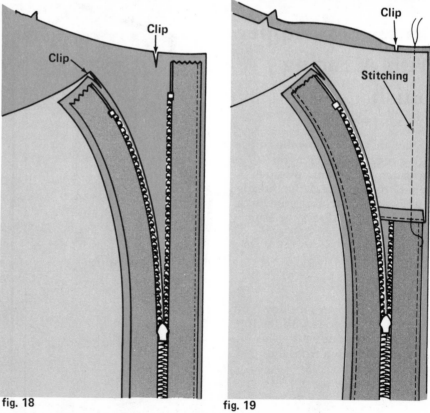

Clip

Clip

fig. 18

Clip

Stitching

fig. 19

Pin the facing in place matching construction marks and seamlines. Fold each side of the garment at the clip mark, enclosing the zipper in the fold. Stitch the facing to the garment with the given seam width keeping both sides of the opening folded at the clip marks. (fig. 20)

Trim and clip the facing seam and turn the facing to the finished position. Understitch the faced edge and press from the wrong side. (fig. 21)

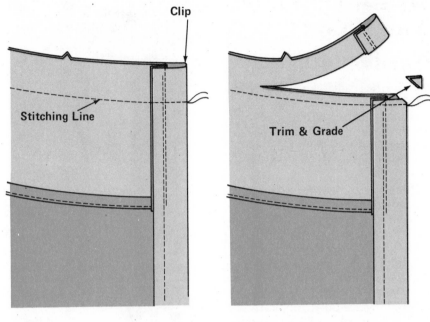

fig. 20   **fig. 21**

Close the top of the zipper opening with a few hand stitches so the folded edges just meet. Mark the bottom of the zipper teeth with a pin. Hand baste across the end and up both sides of the zipper ¼ inch (6mm) from the seam. (fig. 22)

Machine stitch both sides of the zipper from bottom to top, starting at the garment seam. (fig. 23)

Pull all threads to the wrong side and tie in a knot. Remove machine basting from the center seam and the hand basting around the zipper. Press the zipper from the wrong side only. Sew a hook and eye in place at the top of the zipper opening.

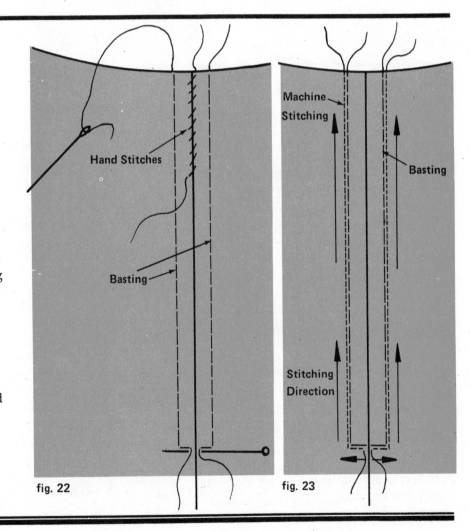

fig. 22   **fig. 23**

Lapped Zipper With A Collar Or Waistband Finish

Stitch the seam below the zipper with a regular stitch length. Backstitch at the bottom of the zipper opening. Break the threads and close the remaining seam with machine basting. Press seam open.

Open the zipper and place it face down on the left seam allowance with the top of the slide a seam width down from the garment edge and the edge of the teeth along the seam. Using a zipper foot stitch next to the zipper teeth, securing the zipper to the seam allowance only. (fig. 24)

Close the zipper, turn it right side up and edgestitch the fold of the seam allowance next to the zipper teeth. (fig. 25)

With the garment right side up and the zipper lying flat underneath the seam allowances, mark the bottom of the zipper with a pin. Hand baste across the bottom of the zipper and up the left side ⅜ inch (10mm) to ½ inch (13mm) from the seam. (fig. 26)

Machine stitch through all fabric layers and the zipper across the bottom and up the side. Keep the machine stitching just to the side of the hand basting. (fig. 27)

Pull both threads through the fabric to the wrong side and tie in a knot. Remove the machine and hand basting and press the zipper from the wrong side only.

Tip

The permanent stitching line for a lapped zipper can be marked with a strip of tape instead of basting. Position the tape so its left edge is ⅜ inch (10mm) to ½ inch (13mm) from the seamline.

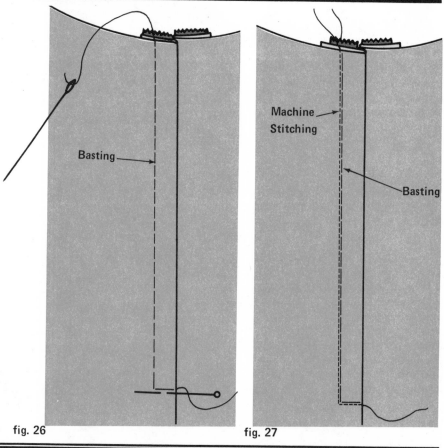

fig. 24   fig. 25

fig. 26   fig. 27

Lapped Zipper With A Facing Finish

When a facing finish is used at the top edge of a lapped zipper, the zipper is stitched to each of the garment pieces before they are stitched together.

Place the closed zipper face down on the right side of the right garment piece so that ⅛ inch (3mm) of fashion fabric extends beyond the edge of the zipper tape. The top of the zipper slide should be a seam width plus ⅜ inch (10mm) down from the edge of the garment. Using a zipper foot stitch from the zipper stop to the top of the zipper tape, pivot around the needle and stitch down the outside edge of the tape to the zipper stop. (fig. 28)

Stitch and press open the facing seams and finish the lower edge of the facing as the fabric indicates. The corresponding garment seams are not stitched at this point.

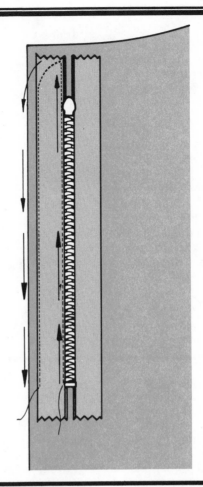

fig. 28

Unzip the zipper. Insert a pin from the wrong side of the garment so it comes through the zipper tape at the seamline and is on the tape side of the corded edge of the zipper. This will be the pivot pin. (fig. 29)

Position the facing along this garment piece right sides together. Push the pivot pin through the facing so it comes out at the facing seamline. Pull the lower edge of the facing ½ inch (13mm) beyond the edge of the garment. Sew from the bottom of the facing, starting in the center of the zipper tape and stitch up to the pivot pin. Remove the pin and take one diagonal stitch across the corner and then stitch along the top edge of the facing to within 1½ inches (38mm) of the unstitched garment seam. (fig. 30) *(continued on next page)*

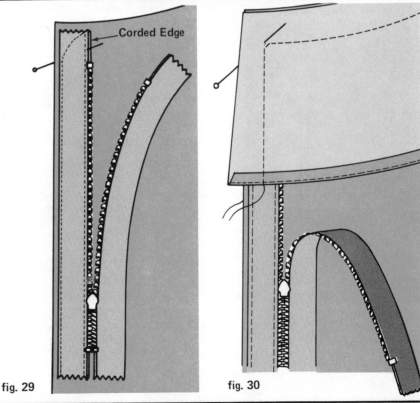

Corded Edge

fig. 29

fig. 30

Trim and clip the facing seam allowance and turn the facing to the inside of the garment. Press the faced edge, rolling the seam to the inside. (fig. 31)

Position the free side of the zipper on the seam allowance of the other garment piece, right sides together, with the edge of the zipper tape even with the seam edge. The top of the slide should be a seam width plus ⅜ inch (10mm) down from the top edge of the garment. Edgestitch the zipper tape to the seam allowance. (fig. 32)

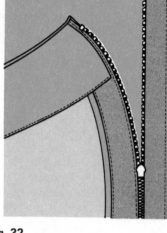

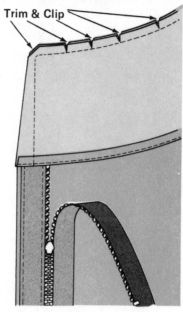

fig. 31

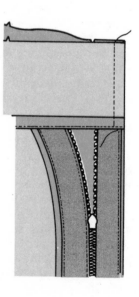

fig. 32

Close the zipper and sew the garment pieces together with a ⅝ inch (15mm) seam below the zipper. Start stitching just above and to the left of the visible stitching. Press the seam open. (fig. 33)

Position the facing against the garment right sides together, folding back the edge as shown. Make a small clip in the top edge of the garment ¾ inch (20mm) in from the edge of the seam allowance. (fig. 34)

Trim the end of the facing ⅞ inch (22mm). Stitch the trimmed edge to the garment seam allowance with a ¼ inch (6mm) seam. The zipper tape should be caught in this stitching. (fig. 35)
(continued on next page)

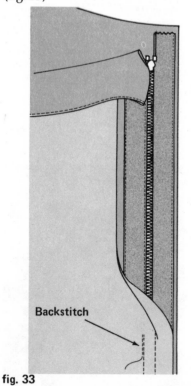

fig. 33

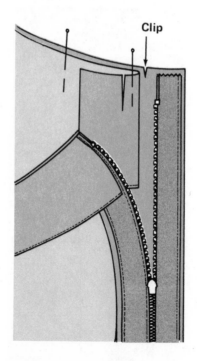

fig. 34

fig. 35

Fold the garment on the clip so the facing and zipper are sandwiched between the garment and facing layers. Stitch the facing edge with the given seam width ending 1½ inches (38mm) short of the unstitched garment seam. (fig. 36)

Turn the facing to the right side and close the zipper to see if the finished edges meet exactly at the top of the garment. Adjust the seam width if necessary.

Stitch and press open the shoulder or side garment seams and facing seams and complete the facing application. Trim, clip and understitch the facing seam. Turn the facing to the inside of the garment, rolling the seam to the inside and press lightly from the wrong side.

Close the zipper and pin the lap in place making sure the right side of the zipper is well-covered. Mark the bottom of the zipper teeth with a pin. Hand baste across the bottom and up the left side of the zipper ⅜ (10mm) to ½ inch (13mm) from the seam. (fig. 37)

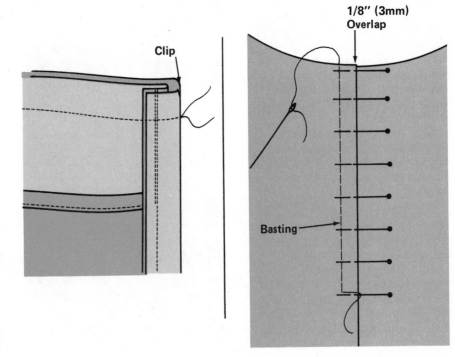

fig. 36

fig. 37

Remove the pins and machine stitch through all layers of fabric, across the bottom and up the side of the zipper. (fig. 38)

Pull both threads through to the wrong side and tie in a knot. Remove the basting and press the zipper area from the wrong side. Sew a hook and eye in place at the top of the zipper opening. (fig. 39)

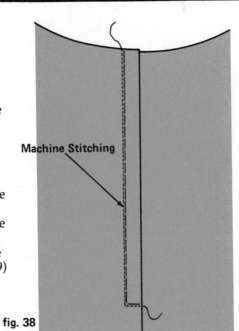

fig. 38

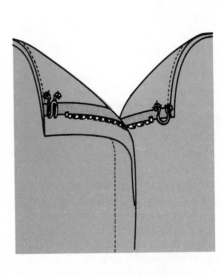

fig. 39

Hand Finished Zippers

A hand finished zipper adds a touch of elegance to fine garments. The process is called "hand pricking" and is quite easy to do. Hand pricking a zipper is sometimes the easiest way to finish the zipper application in plaid or striped fabrics. It is usually easier to control the matching of patterns across the zipper seam with hand pricking than with a machine stitched finish.

Install the center slot or lapped zipper following the previous instructions except do the final stitching by hand instead of by machine. Using a single thread of matching color bring the needle to the right side of the fabric. Insert the needle back one or two fabric threads and bring the needle out ¼ inch (6mm) ahead. Work around the entire zipper using this version of the hand backstitch. (fig. 40)

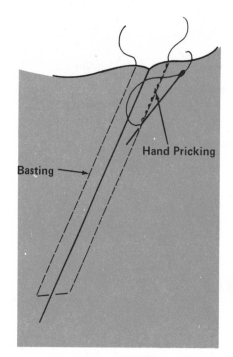

Basting

Hand Pricking

fig. 40

Tip

If you have long fingernails and find using a regular thimble difficult try a Tailor's Thimble with an open top. You get the protection where you need it but it doesn't interfere with your nails. Manufactured by Risdon Mfg. Co.

Invisible Zippers

Invisible zippers are applied with a special type of zipper foot that should be purchased at the same notions counter as the zipper. Each zipper brand has its own special foot — make sure you purchase one that is the same brand as your zipper. Follow the instructions given with the foot when attaching it to your machine.

An invisible zipper is applied to each side of the garment before the two pieces are stitched together. Stabilize the zipper seam area of stretchy fabrics by placing a strip of ½ inch (13mm) wide drafting or magic transparent tape down the garment piece about ¾ inch (20mm) in from the edge of the fabric. (fig. 41)

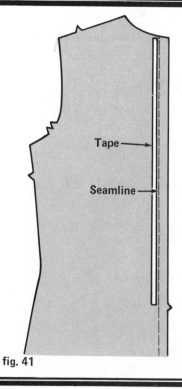

Tape

Seamline

fig. 41

Open the zipper and prepare it for insertion by gently unrolling the coil away from the zipper tape with your fingers. Press the tape next to the unrolled coil lightly with an iron so it will stand away from the coil.

Position the zipper face down on the right side of the left garment seam allowance so the top of the teeth is 1 inch (25mm) below the edge of the garment if you are using a facing finish, and a seam width below the top edge of the garment if you are applying a collar or waistband. The teeth of the unrolled zipper should be on the seamline. Garments with zippers extending up into collars or waistbands should have those items attached before the zipper is stitched in place. Follow the pattern instructions for exact zipper placement. *(continued)*

Hold the zipper in position with pins if necessary and fit the left hand groove of the special zipper foot over the zipper teeth. Backstitch at the top of the zipper tape and stitch the length of the zipper as far down as possible. Backstitch at the bottom. (fig. 42)

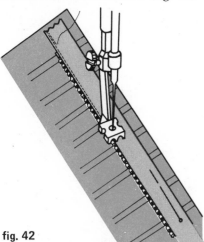

fig. 42

Close the zipper and mark with a pencil any cross seams or matching points of the fabric on the zipper tape. (fig. 43)

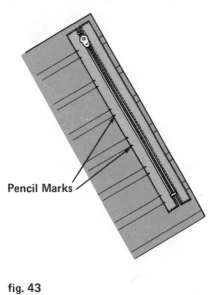

Pencil Marks

fig. 43

Open the zipper and position it face down on the right side of the other garment piece, matching any cross seams or fabric pattern points. Pin in place. (fig. 44)

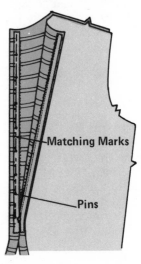

Matching Marks

Pins

fig. 44

Fit the right hand groove of the special zipper foot over the teeth. Backstitch at the top of the zipper tape, stitch as far down the zipper as possible and backstitch. (fig. 45)

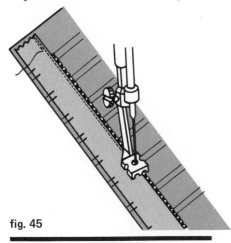

fig. 45

Tip

If the zipper tape shows on the right side of the garment after stitching each side of the invisible zipper, adjust the foot so the needle is closer to the coil and restitch each side.

Close the zipper and complete the garment seam by pushing the special foot all the way to the left. Pull the end of the zipper out away from the seam area and start sewing about ⅜ inch (10mm) above the end of the stitches and a scant ⅛ inch (3mm) to the left. Backstitch and close the remainder of the garment seam, making sure the edges are even at the bottom. (fig. 46)

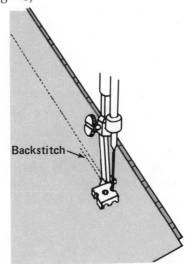

Backstitch

fig. 46

Hold the tape ends down by stitching each side only to the garment seam allowances. (fig. 47)

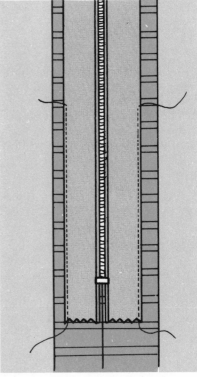

fig. 47

Invisible Zipper
With Facing Finish

Apply the zipper according to the above instructions. Clip the top edge of both garment pieces ⅝ inch (15mm) from the edge of the seam allowance. (fig. 48)

Prepare the facing by stitching and pressing open the seams and finishing the lower edge. Trim away ½ inch (13mm) from each end of the facing. Stitch these trimmed edges to the edge of both seam allowances with a ¼ inch (6mm) seam. (fig. 49)

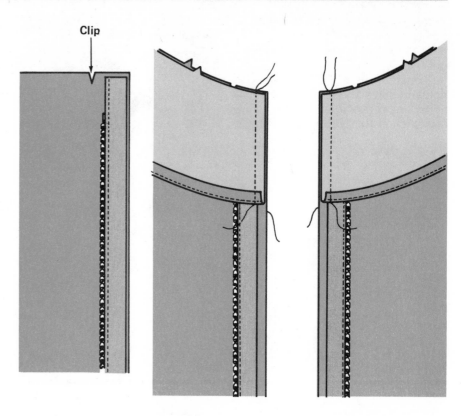

fig. 48   fig. 49

Pin the facing in place matching seams and construction marks. Fold each side of the garment at the clip marks enclosing the zipper in the fold. Stitch the facing in place with the given seam width. (fig. 50)

Trim and clip the facing seam and turn the facing to the inside of the garment. Understitch the facing seam and press the garment edge, rolling the seam to the under side. Sew a hook and eye in place at the top of the zipper. (fig. 51)

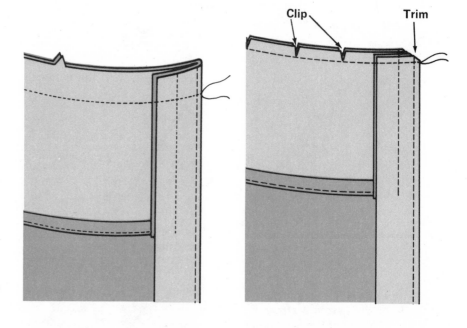

fig. 50   fig. 51

The Fly Zipper Application

The fly zipper is used on both men's and women's pants. The fly laps left over right on men's pants and is made with the same lap on many women's pants too. The lap can be made right over left if desired — just substitute left for right in the following instructions.

The following technique applies to pants patterns which have the fly facing cut as part of the pants front pattern. If your pattern has a separate fly facing pin it to the pants front pattern, overlapping the center front seamlines. Cut the fabric using this altered pattern. (fig. 52)

Reinforce the wrong side of the left fly facing, right up to the center front seamline, with a piece of fusible interfacing. (fig. 53)

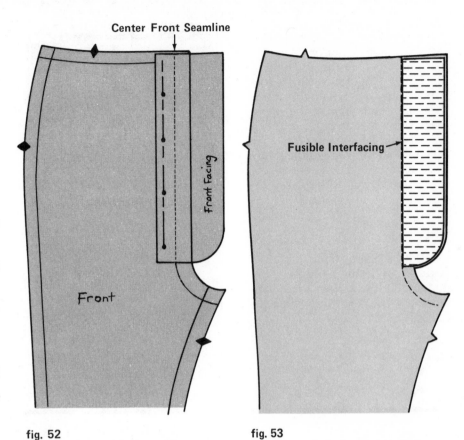

fig. 52   fig. 53

With right sides together, machine baste the center front of the pants down to the dot at the bottom of the zipper area. Break the thread, backstitch and permanently stitch the crotch seam below the dot to within 1 inch (25mm) of the end of the seam. Clip to the seamline at the bottom on the fly facing. (fig. 54)

With the pants fronts right sides together press over the left fly facing along the seamline. (fig. 55)
(continued on next page)

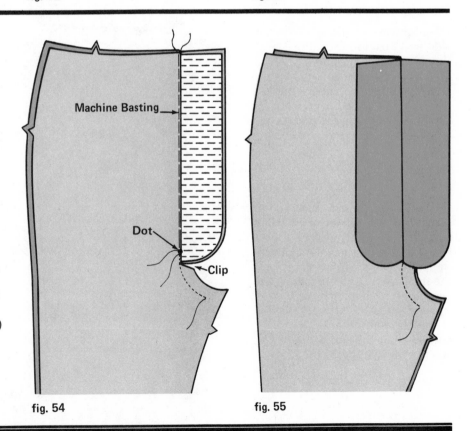

fig. 54   fig. 55

Place a zipper foot on the machine. Position the zipper face down on the right fly facing so the zipper stop is ¼ inch (6mm) above the dot at the bottom of the zipper area. The left edge of the zipper tape should be along the seam. Stitch the zipper tape to the facing as close to the teeth as possible. (fig. 56)

Turn the zipper right side up. With the fly facing folded underneath the zipper, press the fabric fold next to the zipper teeth. (fig. 57)

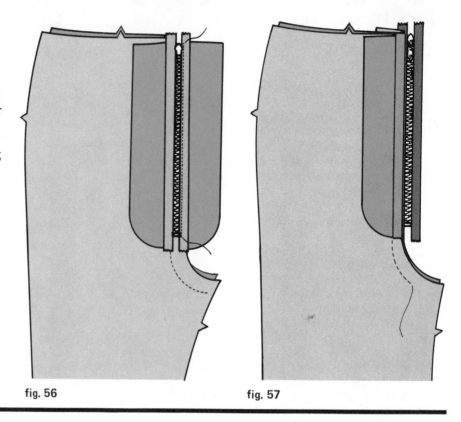

fig. 56　　　　　　　　**fig. 57**

Pull the left fly facing out to the side and position the zipper face down on it making sure it is pulled over as far as it can go. Pin in place and stitch the left zipper tape to the facing as close to the teeth as possible, removing the pins as you stitch. (fig. 58)

Unfold the pants fronts and place them wrong side up on a flat surface. Fold the fly assembly over to the left until it lies flat against the pants front. Pin in place. Do the final zipper stitching along the very edge of the zipper tape, curving smoothly to meet the dot at the bottom of the zipper. Backstitch at the end of the stitching for strength. (fig. 59)

Final Stitching

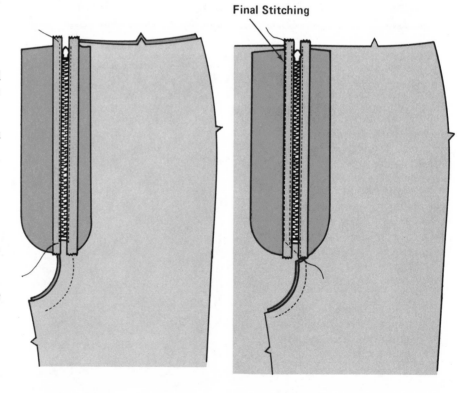

fig. 58　　　　　　　　**fig. 59**

Trim away the fly facing that extends beyond each side of the zipper tape. Remove the machine basting from the center front seam. Press the zipper area from the wrong side only. (fig. 60)

Prepare a fly shield from a strip of fashion fabric cut 3 inches (7.5cm) wide and 2 inches (5cm) longer than the finished zipper along the lengthwise grain of the fabric. Fold the strip in half lengthwise with wrong sides together and press.

Open the zipper and position the fly shield behind the underpart of the zipper with a ½ inch (13mm) lap. The top of the shield should be even with the top edge of the garment. Using the zipper foot, secure the fly shield by machine stitching along the fabric fold next to the zipper teeth. Stitch as far down into the zipper as possible and backstitch. (fig. 61)

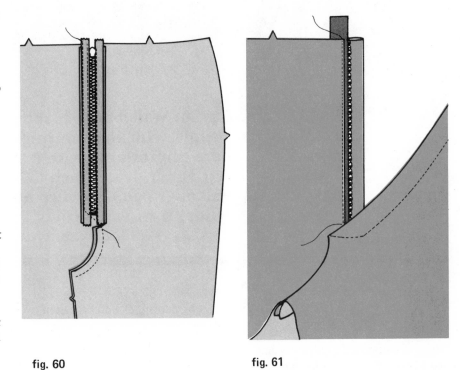

fig. 60

fig. 61

Close the zipper and bartack the end of the zipper stitching on the right side of the pants. Trim away any excess fly shield. (fig. 62)

Fold over the pants front until the edges of the fly facing and fly shield are exposed. Bartack through these layers about ¼ inch (6mm) above the zipper stop. This bartack prevents the bottom of the zipper from tearing out. (fig. 63)

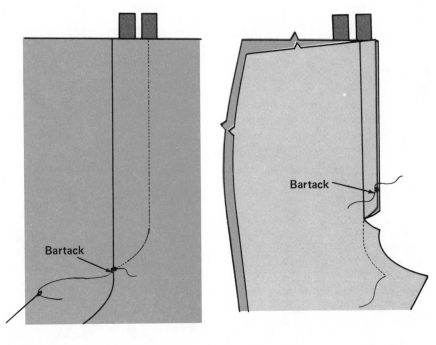

Bartack

Bartack

fig. 62

fig. 63

Waistbands

Whatever the type of waistband, it should always be comfortable. People with short or thick waists will always be more comfortable with a stretch type waistband that is not over 1 inch (25mm) wide. Long-waisted, slender people can comfortably wear wide, firm waistbands.

Types Of Waistbands

The tailored and pull-on elastic waistbands are the two most popular waistband finishes used on skirts and pants. The tailored waistband is set onto the garment and requires a zipper opening. It is used on knit and woven fabric garments and can be stretchy or firm depending on the type of waistband stiffening selected. The pull-on elastic waistband is used on stretchy knit garments and doesn't require a zipper opening. It can be a simple turned-over waistband finish or a separate waistband casing, both containing a piece of elastic.

Marking The Waistline

Before a waistband is applied to a skirt or pants, the actual waistline should be marked on the garment. This is best done by trying the garment on after the vertical seams have been sewn but before the zipper has been inserted, if the pattern calls for one.

Wearing the garment, pin the zipper opening closed and tie a string snugly around the waist. Adjust the garment until it hangs straight and the seams are properly positioned. (fig. 1)

Mark the natural waistline underneath the string with pins or chalk. You might find the natural waistline is not always even with the garment seamline.

Remove the garment and trim the top edge so just a seam width extends above the string marks. (fig. 2)

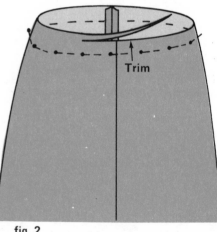

Trim

fig. 2

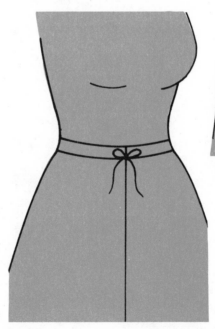

fig. 1

Tip

If you plan to use the same pattern again, trim the pattern matching the garment adjustment so it will fit perfectly the next time.

Waistband Length

Measure the waist circumference before removing the string and garment. This will determine the waistband length. Adjust garment seams if necessary for a comfortable fit at the waistline. (fig. 3)

If it is unnecessary to make any seam adjustments then use the waistband pattern as is. If adjustments are necessary make the same length adjustments to the waistband also.

fig. 3

Waistband Stiffening

There are various materials that can be used for waistband stiffening. Fusible interfacing can be used for both faced and fold-over tailored waistbands.

Waistbanding, which gives a firm, non-roll finish can be used for straight cut waistbands only. Waistbanding comes in various widths and is purchased by the yard.

Waistband elastic is used for stiffening and support in garments using the pull-on waistband finish. Buy only elastic recommended for waistband application, and marked dry-cleanable. Some elastic is too soft and will not hold the garment properly, and some elastic will not survive the dry cleaning process. The usual elastic width is 1 inch (25mm) but can be narrower or wider if desired.

Pull-on elastic waistbands can be used on knit garments if the difference between the person's waist and hip measurement is 10 inches (25.5cm) or less. If the difference is more, the waistband that is large enough to fit around the hips will be too large to fit neatly around the waist. A waistband with an opening should be used in this case.

Tip

One of the best waistbanding products available has the Ban-Rol name and can be purchased in two styles — firm and stretch. Available from Staple Sewing Aids Corp.

Faced Tailored Waistband With Interfacing

Cut the inner and outer waistband pieces and apply fusible interfacing to one or both pieces, depending upon the desired stiffness. (fig. 4) Stitch the waistband halves together. Then trim and press the seam open.

With right sides together, stitch the two waistband pieces together along the top edge. (fig. 5)
(continued on next page)

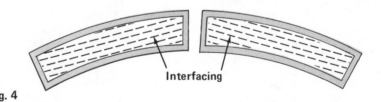

fig. 4

Interfacing

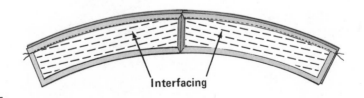

fig. 5

Interfacing

Grade and understitch the seam to within 2 inches (5cm) of each end. (fig. 6)

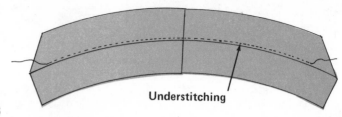

Understitching

fig. 6

Press over the seam allowance of the inner waistband and trim to ¼ inch (6mm). Baste in place if the fabric will not hold a crease. (fig. 7)

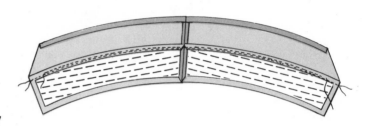

fig. 7

Pin the right side of the outer waistband to the right side of the garment, matching construction marks. Stitch with the given seam width and grade the seam allowances. (fig. 8 & 9)

Using the tip of the iron press the waistband and seam allowances up away from the garment.

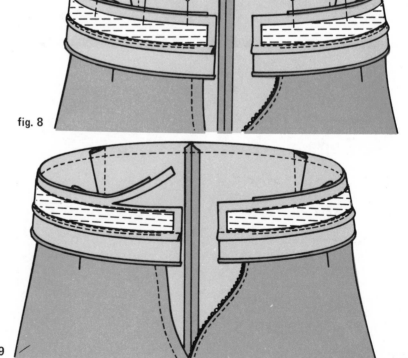

fig. 8

fig. 9

Fold the waistband pieces right sides together and stitch across each end with the given seam width. (fig. 10) Trim the seam allowances. Turn to the right side.

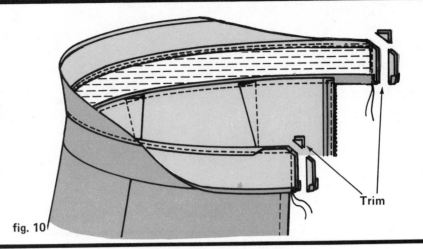

fig. 10

Trim

Turn the waistband to the inside of the garment and pin the folded edge so it just meets the seamline. Slipstitch the fold to the threads of the seamline only so no stitches show on the right side of the garment. (fig. 11) Finish the waistband with a skirt and pants hook and eye.

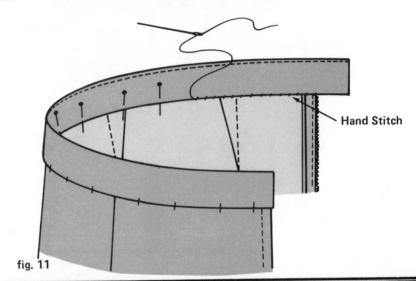

Hand Stitch

fig. 11

Fold-Over Tailored Waistband With Waistbanding

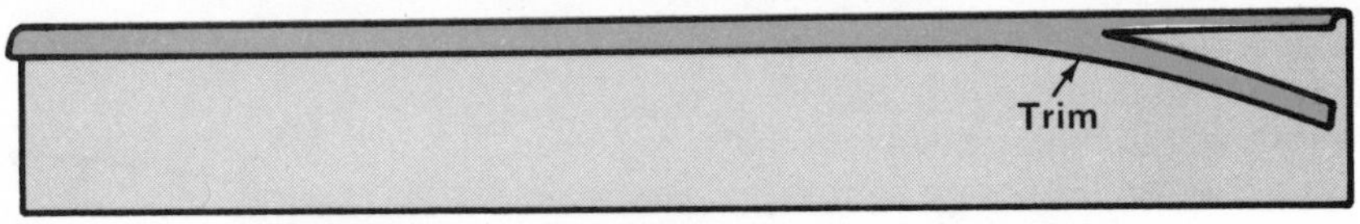

Press over the seam allowance along one edge of the waistband and trim to ¼ inch (6mm). Baste in place if the fabric will not hold a crease. (fig. 12)

Pin the right side of the waistband to the right side of the garment matching construction marks. Stitch with the given seam width. (fig. 13) *(continued)*

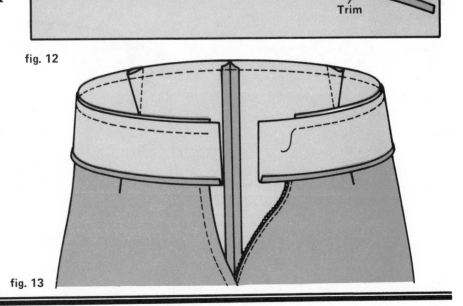

fig. 12

Trim

fig. 13

Cut the waistbanding material the length of the finished waistband and position it over the seam allowance so the lower edge is along the seamline. Stitch the lower edge of the waistbanding to the seam allowance only with a straight or zigzag stitch. (fig. 14) Grade the seam allowance.

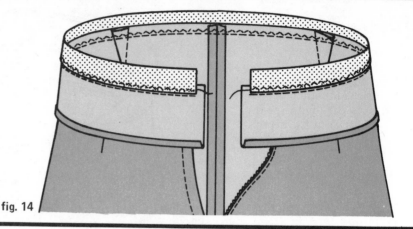

fig. 14

Fold the waistband in half, right sides together and stitch across each end with the given seam width. Do not catch the waistbanding in this stitching line. Trim the seam allowances. (fig. 15)

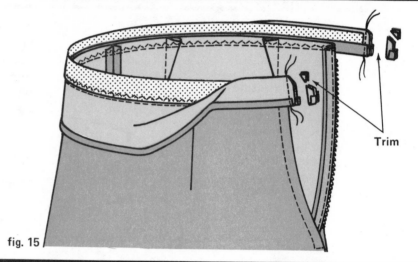

Trim

fig. 15

Turn the waistband to the right side, adjusting the corners with a point turner until squared. Pin the folded edge to the inside of the garment so it just meets the seamline. Slipstitch the fold to the threads of the seamline so no stitches show on the right side of the garment. (fig. 16) Finish the waistband with a skirt and pants hook and eye.

Tip

Waist Shaper, an iron-on waistband stiffening, can be used in the waistband instead of a waistband stiffening. Full instructions are on the package and it is a quick way to make a non-roll waistband. From Stacy Fabrics Corp.

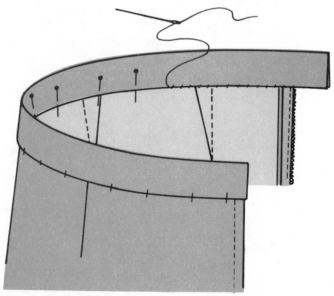

fig. 16

Turned-Over Elastic Waistband For Knits

Allow one elastic width plus ⅜ inch (10mm) above the natural waistline mark for this type of waistband finish instead of just a seam width. This gives the waistline the necessary width for the turned-over finish.

Leave a section of the center back seam unsewn. The top ¼ inch (6mm) should be securely stitched, and the opening should be the width of the elastic. (fig. 17)

Turn down the casing the width of the elastic plus ⅜ inch (10mm) and edgestitch the fold. (fig. 18) Stitch again ¼ inch (6mm) above the lower edge of the casing. Use a straight stitch, stretching the fabric layers slightly as you stitch or use a narrow zigzag stitch.

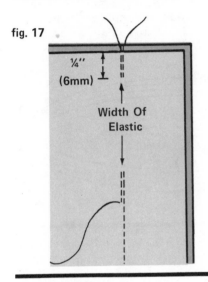

fig. 17

¼"
(6mm)

Width Of Elastic

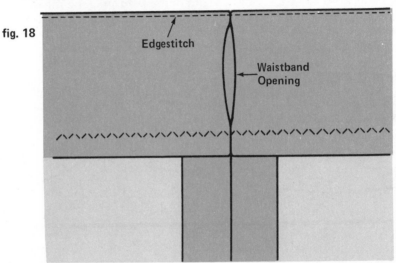

fig. 18

Edgestitch

Waistband Opening

Measure the elastic around the waist for a snug, but comfortable fit. Allow an extra ½ inch (13mm) for an overlap.

Insert the elastic into the casing.

Join the ends of the elastic with a ½ inch (13mm) overlap, stitching securely. (fig. 19)

Close the seam opening with a few hand stitches. Distribute the waist ease evenly around the elastic and secure the elastic at each seamline by stitching-in-the-ditch. This keeps the elastic in place and prevents twisting. (fig. 20)

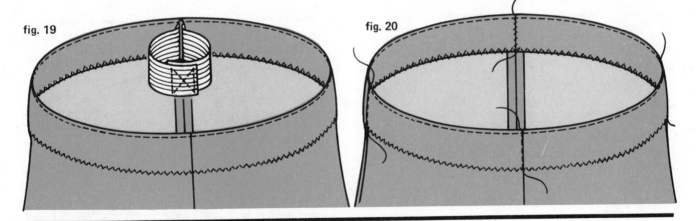

fig. 19

fig. 20

Tip

Fasten the ends of the elastic with a safety pin for the first few wearings and washings to make sure the elastic length is comfortable. Elastic sometimes shrinks or relaxes after the first washing. Do the stitching-in-the-ditch after the final length of elastic has been determined.

Separate Elastic Waistband For Knits

A separate elastic waistband gives a more finished look and is a must if you are going to wear the pants or skirt with a tucked in shirt or blouse.

Adjust the waist circumference of the garment so it is big enough to pull up over the hips but small enough to fit well around the waist. You don't want a lot of excess fabric at the waistline — it will gather and look baggy.

When marking the natural waistline allow ½ inch (13mm) above the string for a seam allowance.

Cut the waistband across the width of the fabric making it twice the width of the eleastic plus 1 inch (25mm). The length of the waistband should be actual waist measurement plus 1 inch (25mm).

Join the ends of the waistband with a ½ inch (13mm) seam, right sides together. (fig. 21) Press the seam open.

Measure the elastic for a snug fit around the waist allowing an extra ½ inch (13mm) for an overlap. Join the ends, overlapping ½ inch (13mm) and stitching securely. (fig. 22)

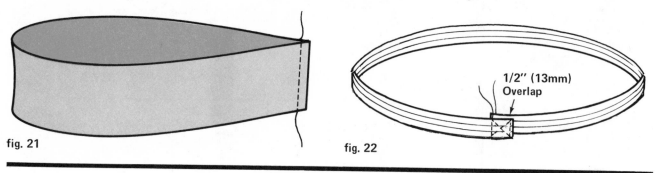

fig. 21

fig. 22

1/2″ (13mm) Overlap

Divide the waistband edge into four equal sections and mark with pins. (fig. 23)

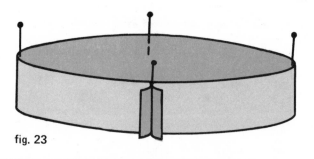

fig. 23

Divide the garment edge into four equal sections using the center front or center back seam as a starting point. Mark with pins. (fig. 24)

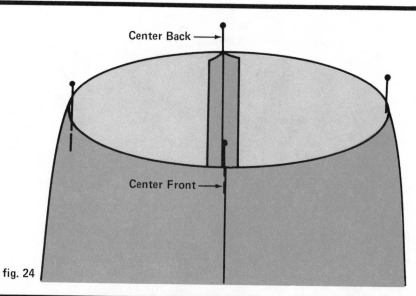

Center Back

Center Front

fig. 24

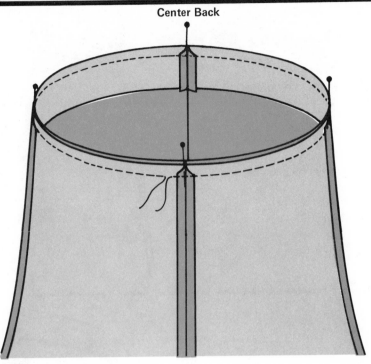

With the garment inside out, pin the right side of the waistband to the right side of the garment placing the waistband seam at the center back and matching up the pins. Stitch together with a ½ inch (13mm) seam. (fig. 25)

fig. 25

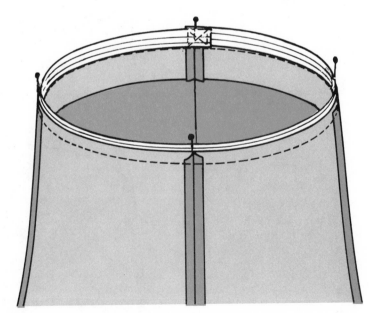

Divide the prepared elastic into four equal sections, marking with pins or a pencil. Pin the elastic to the seam allowance only so the lower edge is along the seamline. The pins should match the previous waistline divisions. (fig. 26)

fig. 26

Stitch the lower edge of the elastic to the seam allowance only with a big zigzag stitch. A straight stitch can also be used but the fabric and elastic must be stretched while sewing. (fig. 27)

Trim the seam allowance behind the elastic to ¼ inch (6mm). Be careful not to cut the elastic during the trimming.

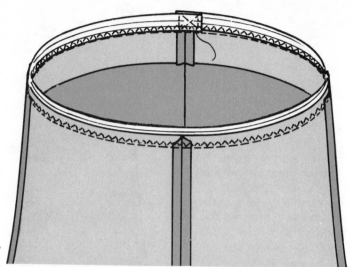

fig. 27

Fold the waistband over the elastic pulling it snugly to the wrong side of the garment. Pin in place at 3 to 4 inch (7.5cm to 10cm) intervals. Finish the waistband by stitching-in-the-ditch from the right side of the garment. (fig. 28)

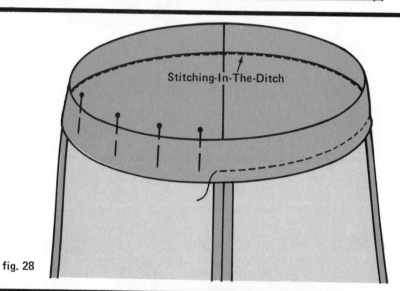

Stitching-In-The-Ditch

fig. 28

Trim away the excess seam allowance from the back of the waistband. Since knits don't fray you can trim to about ⅛ inch (3mm). (fig. 29)

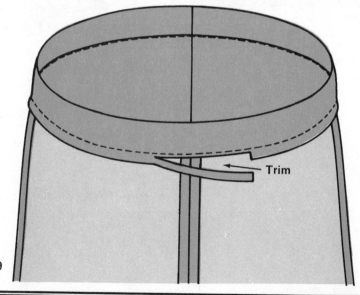

Trim

fig. 29

Buttonholes

Buttonholes, required on many garments, can be design features as well as functional. They can be worked by machine or bound. While the bound buttonhole is considered most elegant it isn't suitable for every type of garment. Machine buttonholes can be used on all types of garments.

It is a good idea to make a complete machine or bound buttonhole from scraps of your fabric before beginning them on the garment. Use the same types and number of layers that are found in the buttonhole area of the garment so you get a true picture of the finished buttonhole. Making a trial buttonhole allows you to check its size in relation to the button size, and confirm your choice of buttonhole type before it is too late to make a change.

Buttonhole Size And Location

Garments calling for a button closure will give buttonhole size and location information on the pattern. If you use the recommended size button, and length adjustments in the buttonhole area are not required, you can use the pattern information as is. Otherwise, the given buttonhole information must also be changed.

Buttonhole Length

The given buttonhole length on the pattern is determined by the size of the recommended button. If you choose a larger or smaller button you must change the buttonhole length the same amount as the size difference between the recommended and chosen button.

Adjust the length at the end of the buttonhole which is farthest away from the edge of the garment. (fig. 1)

Buttonhole lengths on patterns are given for the average flat button. If you choose a thicker button or a ball or half ball button you will have to increase the buttonhole size to accommodate the extra thickness.

Buttonhole length for thick buttons should equal the width plus the thickness for a bound buttonhole. The width plus the thickness plus ⅛ inch (3mm) must be added for a machine buttonhole. (fig. 2)
(continued on next page)

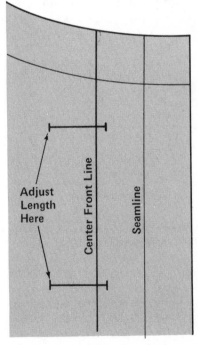

fig. 1

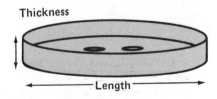

fig. 2

Buttonhole length for ball buttons should equal the button circumference. Measure this by wrapping a strip of paper around the button and then measuring the paper to find the correct buttonhole size. (fig. 3)

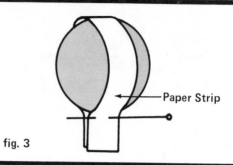

Paper Strip

fig. 3

In the case of a vertical buttonhole, the length will be adjusted at the lower end. (fig. 4)

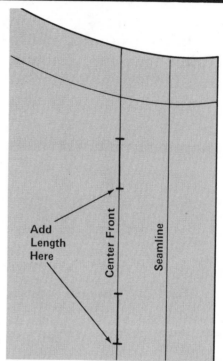

Add Length Here

Center Front

Seamline

fig. 4

In changing the length of a horizontal buttonhole, the space between the center front or center back line and the finished edge of the garment must also be increased or decreased the same amount. This maintains the proper relationship between the button and the edge of the garment and the proper amount of underlap.

Cut the pattern apart along the finished edge, whether it is a seamline or foldline, spread or overlap the two pieces the same amount as the difference in button size, and pin or tape the pattern pieces back together. (fig. 5) **Note:** the width of the facing should be increased or decreased the same amount.

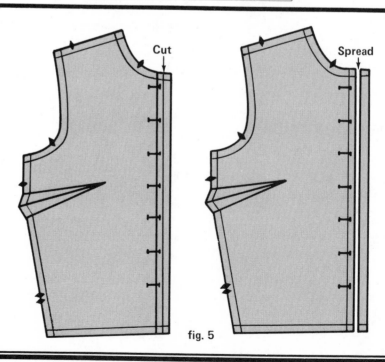

Cut

Spread

fig. 5

Buttonhole Location

The buttonhole location given on the pattern should be used as is unless a length alteration has been made to the pattern which affects the buttonhole area, i.e. lengthening or shortening the bodice. The buttonholes will have to be respaced so the distance between them again becomes equal.

Women's garments, with front button openings, should have a button placed at the fullest part of the bust in order to prevent gapping. This is especially important for women with large busts.

If the pattern doesn't give a buttonhole at that point you can adjust the buttonhole distance to allow for one. Or if impossible because of design problems, sew a snap fastener between the garment layers at that point.

Using larger or smaller buttons than the recommended size can also influence the space between buttonholes. For instance, small buttons should be placed closer together than large buttons.

When changing buttonhole locations, keep the distance between each button equal. Double check the spacing with a ruler before beginning the buttonholes.

Tip

Use the Simflex Buttonhole Gauge whenever you have to reposition buttonhole locations. Stretch it out so one space equals the desired buttonhole spacing and it will automatically measure all other spaces accurately. Available from Brewer Sewing Supplies Co.

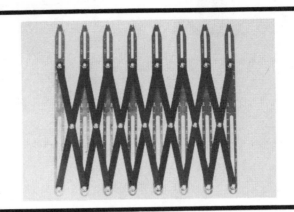

Machine Buttonholes

Machine buttonholes are the most common type of buttonhole and can be used on any kind of garment. They are made after the garment is finished. Accurate marking of the length and location is very critical to good machine buttonholes. An easy and accurate way of marking is to use pins and strips of drafting tape.

Position the pattern over the completed garment matching the finished edge and any seams. Push pins through each end of the buttonhole marks. Carefully pull the pattern away from the garment leaving pins in place. Check the pin placement with a ruler to make sure they are evenly spaced. Adjust any pins if necessary. (fig. 6)

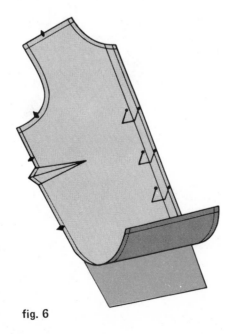

fig. 6

Tip

A cardboard cutting board or cork surface should be placed under the garment when using this technique to hold pins securely.

Tip

Always test how the tape comes off your fashion fabric before constructing the garment. If impossible to safely use the tape on fashion fabric, mark the buttonhole information on the garment pieces with hand basting before sewing any seams. Double check the accuracy of the basting with a ruler before proceeding.

Place strips of drafting tape down the outside of each row of pins, letting the tape touch each pin. Place small strips of tape across the first two strips at each pair of pins. Position the strips above the pins if your machine moves forward at the beginning of the buttonhole and below the pins if your machine moves backwards at the beginning of the buttonhole. (fig. 7)

Remove the pins and use this tape grid as a guide for the buttonholes. The vertical strips of tape will determine the buttonhole length and the horizontal strips will give buttonhole locations.

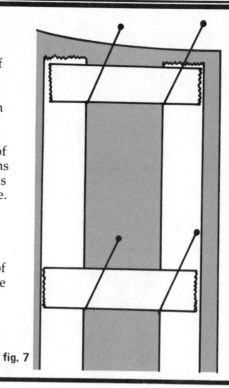

fig. 7

Start each buttonhole at the intersection of two tape strips. Use the edge of the tape as a guide but don't let the needle stitch into the tape. This may put a sticky coating on the needle and cause skipped stitches. (fig. 8)

Remove the tape grid immediately after the buttonholes are completed. Tape left on the fabric for a period of time can result in a sticky residue remaining after the tape is removed.

Tip

Machine buttonholes are usually worked with regular thread of a matching or contrasting color. If a heavier look is desired try threading two regular threads through the eye of the needle instead of just one. This is an easy way to get the look and strength of a corded buttonhole without the fuss.

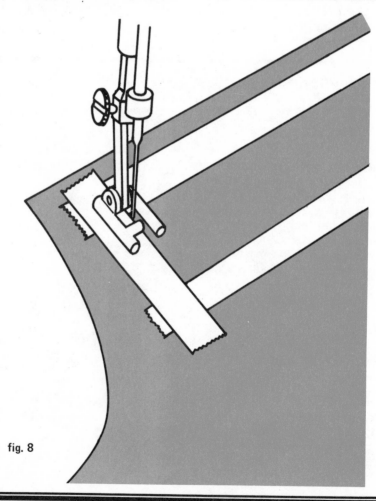

fig. 8

Carefully open each buttonhole from bartack to bartack with a pair of sharp, finely pointed scissors. Place a pin at each end of the buttonhole, in front of the bartacks, to prevent cutting through the ends. (fig. 9)

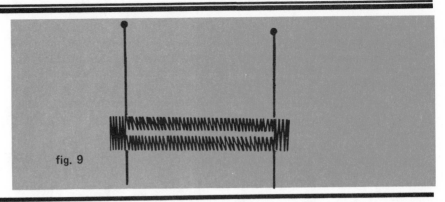

fig. 9

Tip

The Automatic Buttonholer makes perfect machine buttonholes every time. This attachment will fit most machines and automatically makes buttonholes of the same width and length even if your machine does not have a zigzag stitch. It also has a template to make beautiful keyhole type buttonholes. Manufactured by Griest Division MITE Corp.

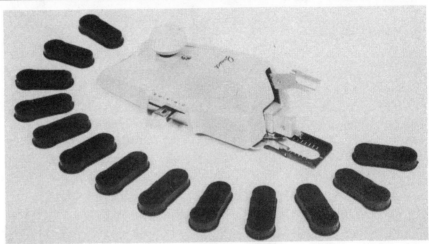

Tip

A pair of buttonhole scissors makes opening machine buttonholes a snap. Adjust the screw so the blade cuts the exact length. The notch at the back of the blade allows you to begin cutting there rather than at the tip of the scissors for a neater cut. Manufactured by Gingher, Inc.

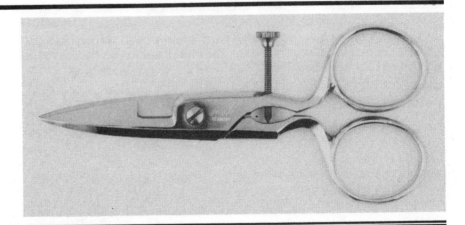

Bound Buttonholes

Bound buttonholes add an elegant touch to the finished garment. They are used mainly on women's clothing although you will sometime see bound buttonholes on some men's outer wear. Bound buttonholes are made before any other sewing is done on the garment. The backs of the buttonholes are finished after the facings are in place.

Accurate marking of the buttonhole length and location is very important to perfect bound buttonholes. Some sort of interfacing should back bound buttonholes unless the fabric is very heavy. Use a fusible interfacing only if the whole garment piece is going to be interfaced, otherwise a line will show on the right side where the interfacing ends. If the entire front of the garment isn't going to be interfaced then cut a strip of nonfusible interfacing 3 inches (7.5cm) wider than the buttonholes and 2 inches (5cm) longer than the buttonhole area. *(continued on next page)*

Pin or baste this interfacing strip to the wrong side of the garment piece on which the buttonholes will be made. (fig. 10)

Mark the buttonhole length and location on the wrong side of the garment piece by placing the pattern over the fabric, matching all cut edges. Push pins through

the ends of each buttonhole. Carefully pull the pattern away from the fabric leaving the pins in place. Double check the pin locations with a ruler to see if they are accurate. (fig. 11)

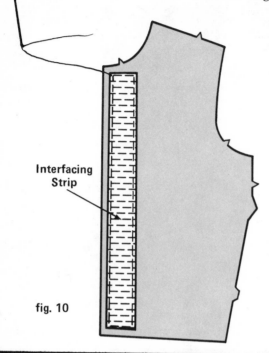

Interfacing Strip

fig. 10

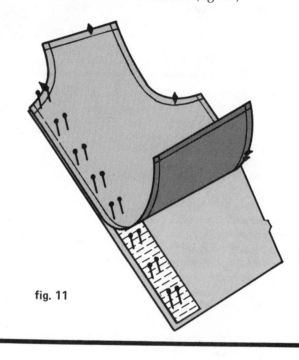

fig. 11

Tip

A cardboard cutting board or **some sort of cork surface should be placed under the garment piece when using this marking** **technique. This assures you that the pins will remain in place for accurate double checking.**

Using a ruler and marking pen or chalk pencil, draw a grid on the wrong side of the garment piece using the pins as guides. (fig. 12)

Machine baste along the grid lines so they show on the right side of the garment. Stitch both vertical lines and each horizontal line from the same direction so the grid remains square. (fig. 13)

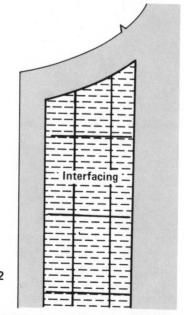

Interfacing

fig. 12

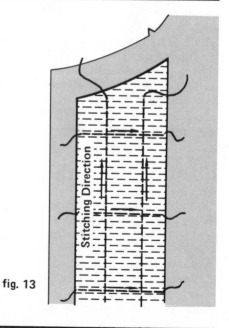

Stitching Direction

fig. 13

Buttonhole Construction

Complete each step of all bound buttonholes in a series rather than finishing each buttonhole independently. This gives a more uniform look to the finished buttonholes and helps you catch any construction errors before it is too late.

Use a short stitch length during the actual buttonhole construction — 20 stitches per inch or a 1.5mm stitch length. This helps you stitch accurately, gives square corners, and makes for stronger buttonholes.

Never backstitch during the buttonhole construction. It is very difficult to do accurately. Always pull the threads through to the wrong side and tie them in a square knot.

Cut a strip of fashion fabric for the lips of the buttonhole that is 1 inch (25mm) wide and long enough to give you two pieces for each buttonhole that are 1 inch (25mm) longer than the finished buttonhole length. Cut this strip on the lengthwise grain for knits and on the bias for woven fabrics unless a bias cut of a patterned fabric is not attractive.

Fold the strip lengthwise down the middle with wrong sides together and press. Stitch the length of the strip ⅛ inch (3mm) from the fold. If the fabric tends to fray, do several more rows of stitching. (fig. 14) **Note:** Garments made of heavy fabrics, such as coatings, should have ¼ inch (6mm) rather than ⅛ inch (3mm) allowed for the width of the lip. Cut the strip 1½ inches (38mm) wide and do the first row of stitching ¼ inch (6mm) from the fold.

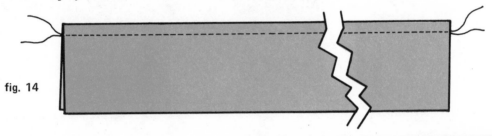

fig. 14

Working on the wrong side of the garment, staystitch a box around the horizontal mark that is ⅛ inch (3mm) from the center line on each side and directly on the vertical basted lines. Do not start the stitching in a corner. Count the stitches across the ends of the box so each side will be equal. (fig. 15)

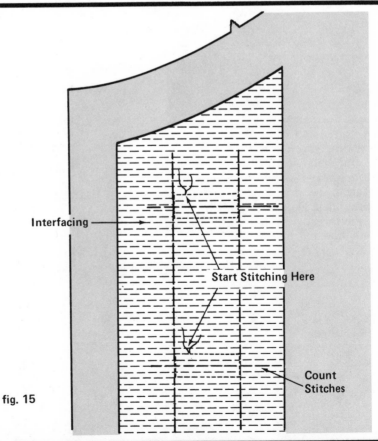

Interfacing

Start Stitching Here

Count Stitches

fig. 15

Cut the prepared buttonhole strip into equal pieces that are at least 1 inch (25mm) longer than the finished buttonhole length.

Position one strip on the right side of the garment so the strip stitching line lies directly on top of the bottom stitching line of the buttonhole box. Hand baste the strip in position. (fig. 16)

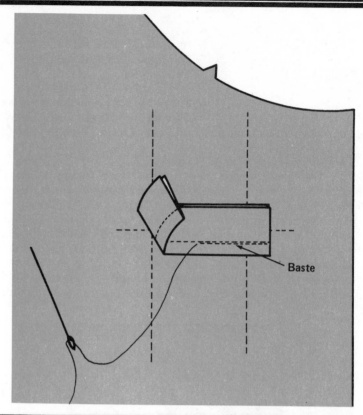

fig. 16

Turn the garment to the wrong side and machine stitch along the bottom line of the buttonhole box, starting and ending exactly on the vertical lines. Do not backstitch. Pull the threads through to the wrong side and tie in a knot. (fig. 17)

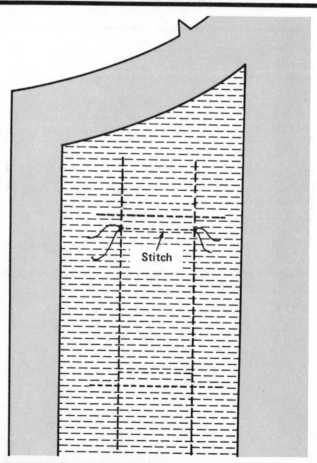

fig. 17

Pull the strip out of the way and position the other strip on the right side of the garment so the stitching line lies directly on top of the top stitching line of the box. Hand baste in position. (fig. 18)

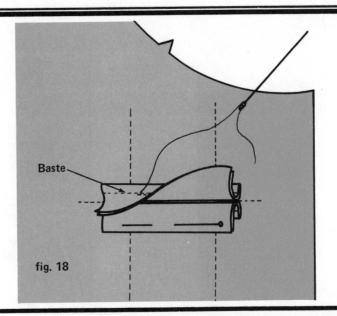

fig. 18

Turn the garment to the wrong side and machine stitch along the top line of the buttonhole box, starting and ending exactly on the vertical lines. Do not backstitch. Pull the thread ends through to the wrong side and tie in a knot. (fig. 19)

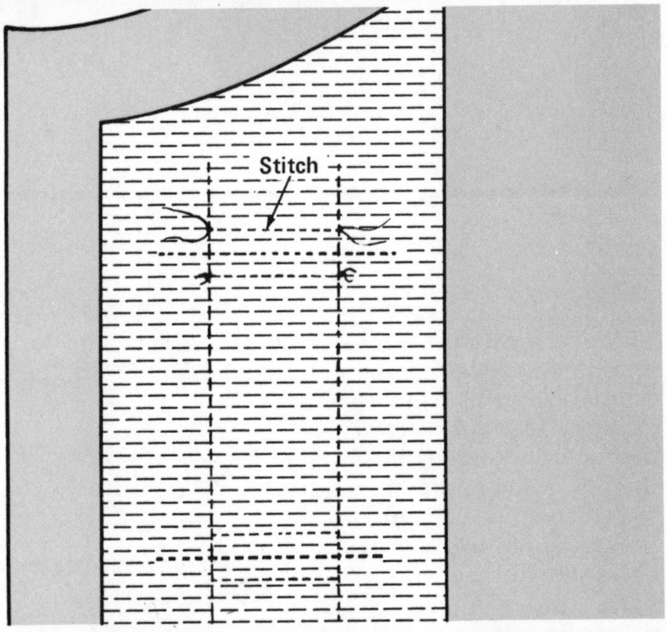

fig. 19

Open the buttonhole between the stitching lines being careful to cut just the interfacing layer and the garment fabric. Cut right to the corners of the box leaving a good sized wedge in each corner. (fig. 20) *(continued on next page)*

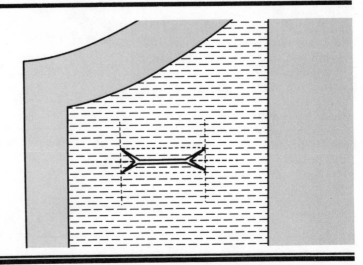

fig. 20

Turn both strips through the cut to the wrong side of the garment. Tuck the wedges to the inside, straighten the lips so they meet evenly and baste them closed. Steam press from the wrong side only. (fig. 21)

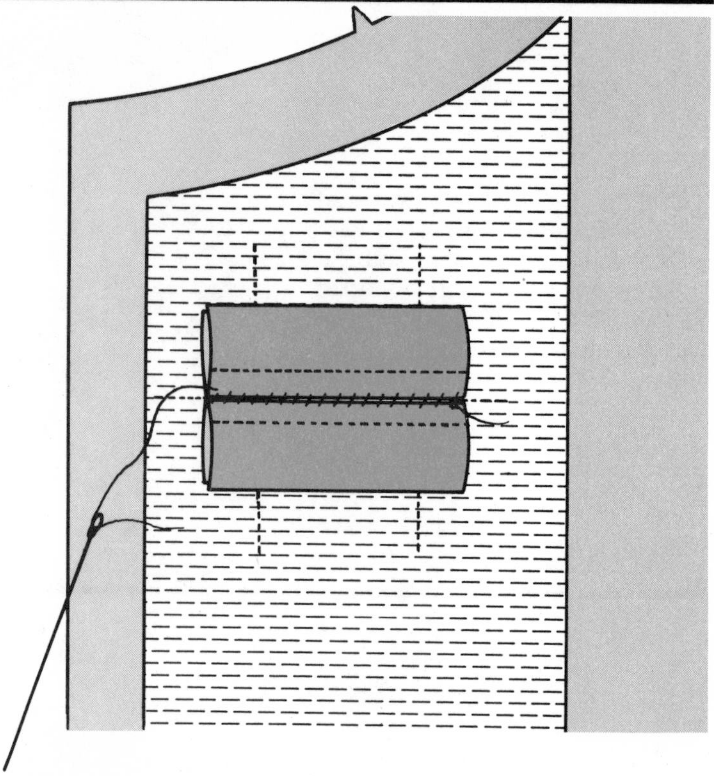

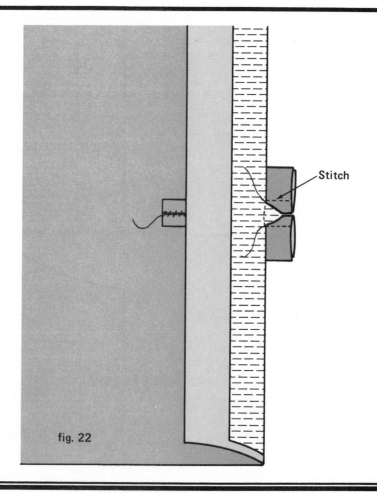

fig. 21

With the garment right side up fold back the edge until the buttonhole strips and wedge are exposed. Machine stitch across the base of each wedge catching it to the lips of the buttonhole. Curve the stitching line slightly toward the center of the buttonhole and backstitch for strength. (fig. 22)

Fold back the other side of the garment along the other edge of the buttonholes and stitch across the other wedges. Trim the buttonhole strips to about ¼ inch (6mm) all around. Hold the scissor at an acute angle so the cut is beveled rather than blunt. Steam press the buttonhole area from the wrong side only. The front side of the bound buttonhole is now finished.

Stitch

fig. 22

Facing Finishes

Construct the rest of the garment and finish the back of the buttonholes after the facing has been sewn in place. Use one of the following methods.

Method #1

Baste the facing in place around each buttonhole and stick pins through to the wrong side at each end of the buttonhole. Slash the facing open between the pins. (fig. 23)

Turn under the cut edges of the facing, forming a curve, and hem in place to the wrong side of the buttonhole. (fig. 24)

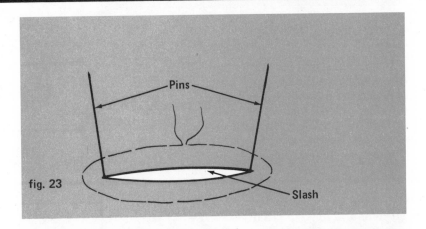

fig. 23

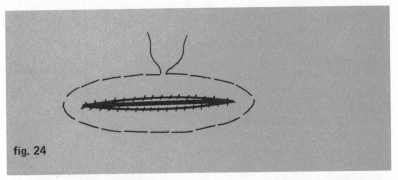

fig. 24

Method #2

Baste the facing in place around the buttonholes and stick pins through all four corners of the buttonhole. Slash the facing open as shown, cutting right to each pin. (fig. 25)

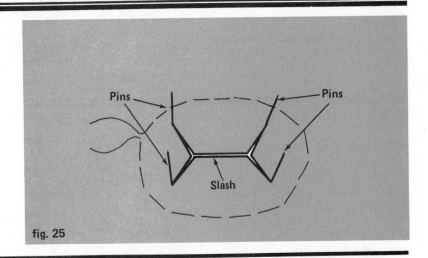

fig. 25

Turn under the cut edges of the facing forming a box, and hem in place to the wrong side of the buttonhole. (fig. 26)

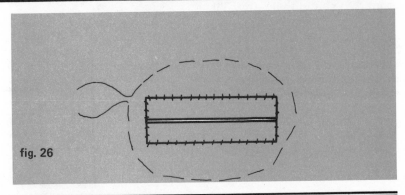

fig. 26

Method #3

Use this method for fabrics that fray easily. Pin the facing in place between the buttonholes and stick pins through the buttonhole ends. Put a mark on the wrong side of the facing where each pin goes through the fabric. (fig. 27)

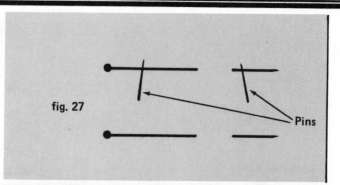
fig. 27

Pins

Pull the facing away from the garment and make a faced buttonhole opening using a patch of lightweight, tightly-woven or knit fabric, such as sheer tricot. Position the right side of the patch to the right side of the facing, but stitch from the wrong side of the facing so you can follow the marks at the ends of the buttonhole. Cut the facing open the length of the stitching and turn the patch to the wrong side of the facing and press. (fig. 28)

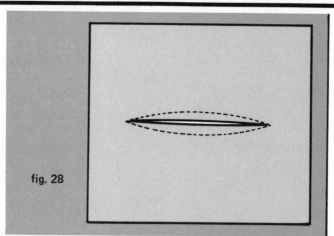
fig. 28

Finish the back of the buttonhole by hemming the edges of the faced opening to the back of the bound buttonhole. (fig. 29)

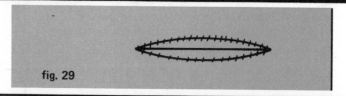
fig. 29

Method #4

This method can be used only on knit fabrics since the cut edges do not fray. Baste the facing in place around each buttonhole. Working on the right side of the garment, stitch-in-the-ditch all around the buttonhole. (fig. 30)

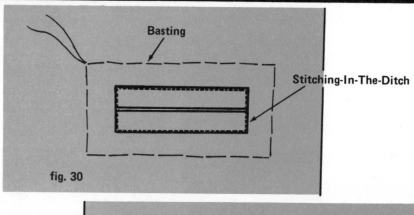
Basting

Stitching-In-The-Ditch

fig. 30

Working on the facing side, cut the buttonhole open as close to the stitching line as possible. (fig. 31)

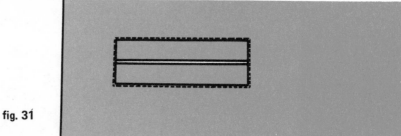
fig. 31

Buttons and Fasteners

Buttons and other types of fasteners help hold our clothes together while adding style or design. Often the "right" button can turn an ordinary garment into a strong fashion statement while the "wrong" button can make a garment look plain. Fasteners such as hooks and eyes, snaps and self-fastening tape are used when an invisible closing is required at the tops of zippers on waistbands and at collars.

Button Selection

Recommended button size is given with each pattern and is determined by the total look the designer wants to achieve. Any change from the recommended button size will necessitate corresponding changes in the buttonhole size and possibly the location too. For example, small buttons should be spaced closer together than large buttons. Refer to the *Buttonholes* section for this information.

Two basic types of buttons are the shank button and the shankless button. (fig. 1) Since patterns generally don't recommend one button type over the other the choice is up to you. However, there are a few facts to keep in mind when choosing buttons.

For example, shankless buttons should be sewn to the garment with a thread shank unless the garment edge is very thin, in order to allow room for the overlapping garment edge.

Also, buttons with shanks are not good choices for decorative buttons such as the type used on one side of a double breasted coat or at sleeve vents of tailored jackets. The shank holds the button away from the fabric causing it to droop.

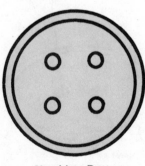

Shankless Button

Shank Button

fig. 1

Applying Buttons

Button location marks are given on most patterns. However, they should be double checked just prior to sewing the button in place to make sure they still correspond exactly with the finished buttonholes.

Regular thread can be used to sew on buttons although the heavier topstitching thread does a nicer job. Use just a single thread and run it through some beeswax to prevent tangles. Make sure the needle you choose is small enough to fit through the holes in the button.

Overlap the garment edges until center lines meet. Insert a pin through each buttonhole ⅛ inch (3mm) from the end closest to the finished edge of the garment. (fig. 2)

For vertical buttonholes, insert the pins ⅛ inch (3mm) down from the top end of the buttonhole. (fig. 3)

Carefully separate garment layers without disturbing the pins and secure each pin to the garment fabric. Sew each button to the garment where the pin enters the fabric. (fig. 4)

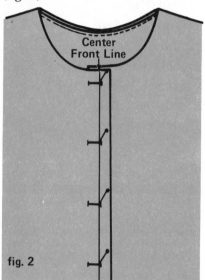

fig. 2

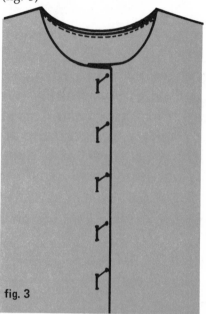

fig. 3

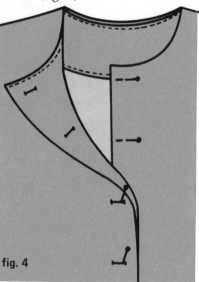

fig. 4

Shankless Buttons

Shankless buttons should have a thread shank constructed while the button is being sewn in position for all but the thinnest garments. This keeps the garment from pulling around the buttonhole. The length of the thread shank should equal garment thickness plus ⅛ inch (3mm) ease.

Take a couple of small stitches where the pin marks the button location and then bring the thread up through one hole of the button and down through another and into the fabric. (fig. 5)

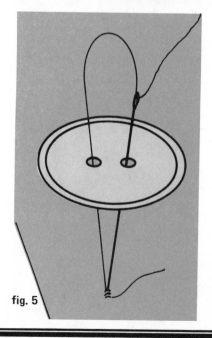

fig. 5

Slip a matchstick or round toothpick underneath the thread loop and work all the stitches over the stick in order to form the thread shank. (fig. 6)

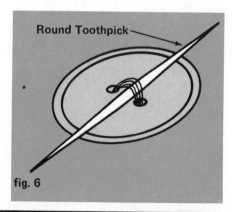

Round Toothpick

fig. 6

Remove the stick, pull the button to the end of the stitched loop and wrap the thread tightly around the stitches, forming the shank. Secure the thread at the base of the shank with a small knot. (fig. 7)

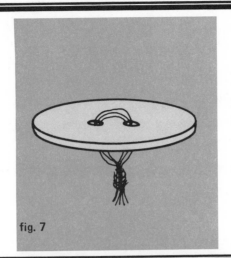

fig. 7

Tip

A quick way of securing shankless buttons is with a Lasso Loop in a matching color. Insert the plastic loop through the fabric and button as instructed for a strong attachment. These are best used on 2-hole buttons and are more suitable for sports and outer wear and children's clothes than on your finer garments. Makes a quick and easy emergency button repair too. Manufactured by Stacy Fabrics Corp.

Shank Buttons

Take a few small stitches where the pin marks the button location and position the button on the garment so the shank is parallel with the buttonhole. This keeps the shank from spreading the buttonhole open when the garment is closed. (fig. 8)

Take enough stitches through the shank to secure the button to the garment. Secure thread ends with a small knot between the garment and facing layers.

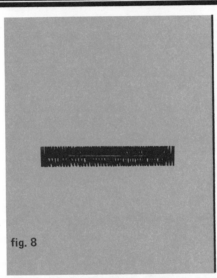

fig. 8

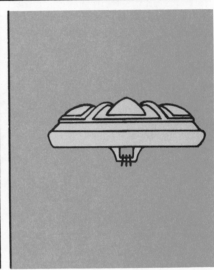

Some shank buttons will need a thread shank also if the garment fabric is very thick. The length of the combined button and thread shank should equal the garment thickness plus ⅛ inch (3mm).

Begin the button the same way as above but hold the edge of the button away from the garment with your fingers so thread loops are formed. Wrap the thread tightly around the stitches forming the shank. Secure the thread at the base of the shank or between the garment and facing. (fig. 9)

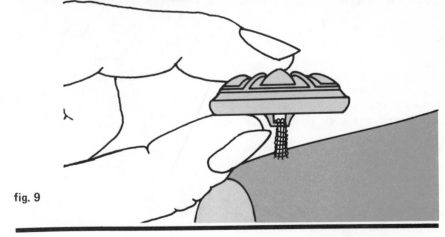

fig. 9

Tip

Button pins can be used to hold shank buttons in place. Insert from the wrong side of the garment so the hump in the pin fits in the button shank. This is a good way of securing buttons that have to be removed for cleaning. Manufactured by Risdon Mfg. Co.

Covered Buttons

Sometimes a fabric covered button is the best choice for a garment, particularly when it is difficult to find a good color match in a regular button.

Covered button kits are available at most notions counters. Follow the instructions carefully for perfect covered buttons.

Tip

Try the Maxant or E-Z Buckle covered button kits. They both come in various sizes and are easy to make. Maxant also offers covered buttons with gold or silver colored outer rims for a decorative touch.

Hooks And Eyes

Hooks and eyes are used at waistlines and necklines where there might be strain placed on the zipper or button closure. Standard hooks and eyes come in various sizes and colors. They usually have both the straight and round eyes included in the package. Straight eyes are used for lapped applications and round eyes are used when the edges of the garment just meet.

Special waistband hooks and eyes are stronger than regular hooks and eyes and come in one size with a black or nickel finish.

Tip

The Talon Skirt and Trouser Hooks and Eyes come in a sew-on or no-sew type. Instructions for application appear on the package. From Donahue Sales, Talon Division of Textron Inc.

Tip

If you want hooks and eyes to match your fabric, E-Z Buckle has them. They come in black, white, brass and nickel plus pastel and dark colors.

Lapped Application

Position and stitch the hook in place first, keeping the hook end close to the edge of the garment. Sew with overhand stitches around the holes and then across the end of the hook. Do not let the stitches show on the right side of the garment. (fig. 10)

Close the garment and mark where the hook touches the underlapped garment edge.

Position the straight eye over the mark with the curve going toward the garment edge. Secure with overhand stitches around the holes. (fig. 11)

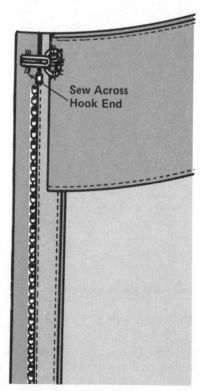

Sew Across Hook End

fig. 10

fig. 11

Centered Application

Position and stitch the hook in place first, keeping the hook end close to the edge of the garment. Sew with a few overhand stitches around each hole and then across the end of the hook. Do not let the stitches show on the right side of the garment. (fig. 12)

Position the round eye so it extends beyond the garment edge far enough to catch the hook. The garment edges should just meet.

Secure holes of the eye with overhand stitches and then take a few more stitches across the sides of the eye as close to the garment edge as possible to hold the eye securely. (fig. 13)

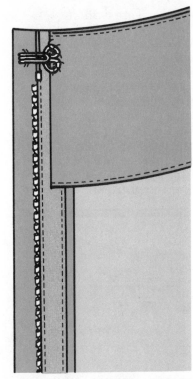

fig. 12

fig. 13

Tip

Try Bonnie Clasps instead of hooks and eyes when making a garment for a person with long hair. These small, plastic clasps will not snag long hair when placed at the neckline so children will love them. They are also useful whenever a regular hook and eye will not stay fastened because of lack of tension. Made by E-Z Buckle Co.

Waistband Hooks And Eyes

Use the special heavy waistband hooks and eyes whenever possible at the ends of skirt and pants waistbands. Large, regular hooks and eyes can also be used if two are placed along the edge of the waistband instead of just one. Position the hooks and eyes so the top of the zipper doesn't pull when the garment is worn.

Position and stitch the waistband hook and eye as described for the lapped application. Stitch through all the holes of the hook portion so it will be secure. (fig. 14)

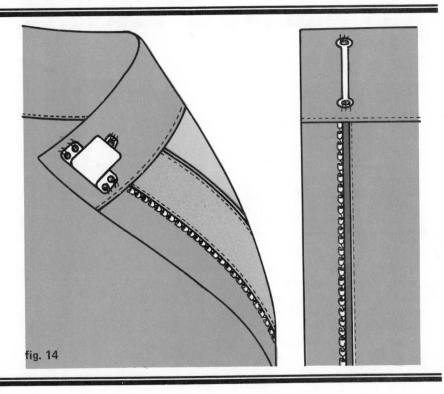

fig. 14

Snaps

Snaps are available in various sizes, colors and materials (metal and plastic). Some snaps are covered with fabric for an elegant touch. When using snaps, select a color compatible with your fabric and the smallest size that will do the job.

Snaps are used on garment areas where there is little strain. They are not strong enough for waistband application.

Use covered snaps on the areas of a coat or suit which will be visible when the garment is open. Buy pre-covered snaps or make your own following the instructions given in this section.

Snaps are usually used at an overlapping closure. However, a hanging snap can be used on a closure where the garment edges just meet such as a center slot zipper application.

Tip

E-Z Buckle makes covered snaps in four colors to be used on fine coats and suits. Look for them at your notions counter.

Lapped Application

Sew the ball half of the snap to the overlapping garment edge securing each hole with overhand stitches that don't show on the right side of the garment. (fig. 15)

Close the garment and mark the point where the ball touches the underlap fabric. Secure the socket part of the snap over that mark, with overhand stitches (fig. 16)

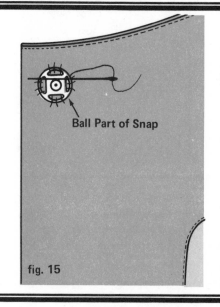

Ball Part of Snap

fig. 15

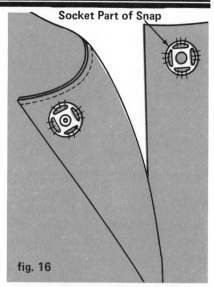

Socket Part of Snap

fig. 16

Hanging Snap

Use this snap application where the edges of the garment just meet. Sew the ball half of the snap as close to the garment edge as possible. (fig. 17)

Secure one hole of the socket part of the snap to the edge of the garment. (fig. 18)

Tip

Try using clear Nylon Snaps when using the hanging snap technique. They are almost invisible and are machine washable and dry cleanable. From Belding Lily.

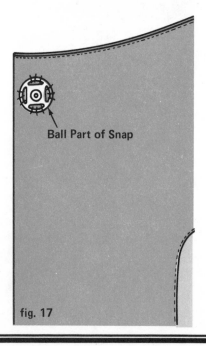

Ball Part of Snap

fig. 17

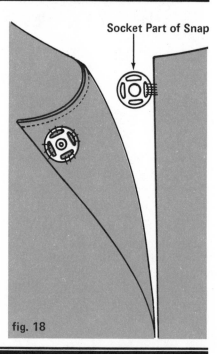

Socket Part of Snap

fig. 18

Covered Snaps

Use a size 3 or 4 snap for this application. Cut two circles of lining fabric twice the diameter of the snap. Stitch around the edge of each circle with a small running stitch. Make a small hole in the center of each circle. (fig. 19)

Force the hole over the ball of the snap and pull up the running stitches drawing the fabric tightly around the snap. Fasten the thread securely on the underside of the snap. (fig. 20)

Place the other fabric circle over the other snap so the hole is directly over the socket. Pull up the stitches drawing the fabric tightly around the snap. Secure on the underside. (fig. 21)

Stitch the covered snap parts to the garment as previously directed.

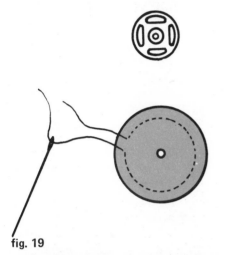

fig. 19

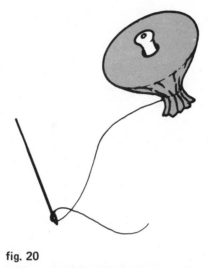

fig. 20

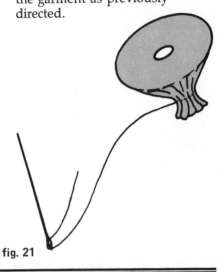

fig. 21

Self-Fastening Tape

Self-fastening tape can be used in place of buttons, zippers and hooks and eyes. It comes in various widths and colors and is sold by the yard and in packages. Self-fastening tape is also made in small circles and squares for spot application. Self-fastening tape is strong, easy to open and has some adjustability.

Position the loop portion of the tape on the overlapping portion of the garment, and stitch in place by machine or hand if you don't want stitches showing on the right side of the garment. (fig. 22)

Secure the hook portion of the tape to the underlapped portion of the garment by machine or hand. (fig. 23)

fig. 22

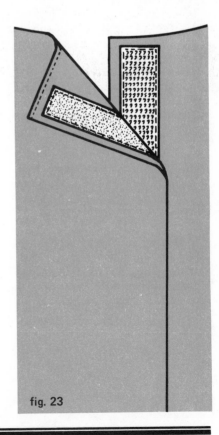

fig. 23

Four-Part Snaps

Four-part snaps can be used in place of buttons and zipper closings on many garments. They can be applied individually, as with the decorative snaps, or in a series on a pre-made snap tape. Four-part snaps come in different sizes and should be selected according to the thickness of your garment fabric. Make sure you select the proper size when buying the snaps.

Four-part snaps are quite strong and one or two layers of interfacing fabric should be placed between the garment and facing fabric to support the snaps. Test a snap on some fabric scraps before constructing the garment to see how much support the snap requires. Too little support will allow the snaps to pull through the fabric.

Individual Application

Carefully mark the snap position on both garment layers. Do this by sticking a pin through the overlapped garment and then marking where the pin enters each garment layer with a pen or pencil. (fig. 24)

Apply each portion of the snap using the instruction included in the package or use one of the new snap setting tools now available at most notions counters.

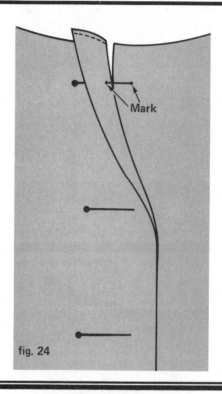

Mark

fig. 24

Tip

The Klik•A•Plier is a multi-use fastener tool that makes setting plain and decorative four-part snaps a breeze. It also applies eyelets and heavy duty snaps and the price makes it well within the reach of most home-sewers. Manufactured by Risdon Mfg. Co.

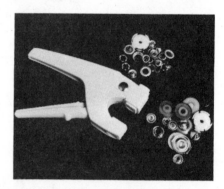

Tape Application

Machine stitch each side of the snap tape to the garment edges making sure the opposing snaps match up exactly. Turn under the cut edge of the tape and secure with machine stitching. (fig. 25)

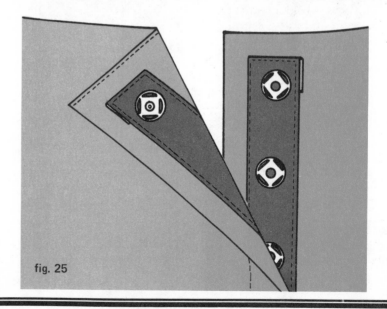

fig. 25

Hems

Hems add the final touch to your garment. They should never show on the right side unless a decorative type hem is being used. Woven fabrics need to have the edge of the hem finished in some way before it is turned up and finished. Knit fabrics generally don't need hem finishes unless the fabric frays. There are many types of hem stitches and the one selected will depend on the fabric and type of hem.

Hem Widths

The hem width should be considered after you have marked the proper hem length on the garment. Suggested widths are given in the accompanying chart. Trim your garment accordingly.

Tip

The Dritz Pin-Type Skirt Marker is one of the most accurate and easy to use tools on the market today. A special channel at the top of the clamp automatically inserts the pin at the proper position to mark an even hem. Available from Scovill, Sewing Notions Divisions.

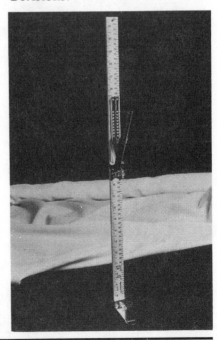

		Hem Width Chart
Dress or skirt	Straight A-line Full	2½"-3" (6.3cm-7.5cm) 1½"-2" (38mm-5cm) ½"-1" (13mm-25mm)
Pants		1½"-2" (38mm-5cm)
Shirts and Tops	Tuck-in Pull over	¼"-½" (6mm-13mm) 1"-1½" (25mm-38mm)
Sleeves		1"-1½" (25mm-38mm)
Jackets and Coats	Lightweight Heavyweight	1½"-2" (38mm-5cm) 2"-3" (5cm-7.5cm)

Hem Preparation

After determining the desired garment length, trim the hem to the proper width. Snip the seam allowance to the seamline at the hem fold and trim the seam allowances below the hem fold to ¼ inch (6mm). This will reduce bulk in the hem area. (fig. 1)

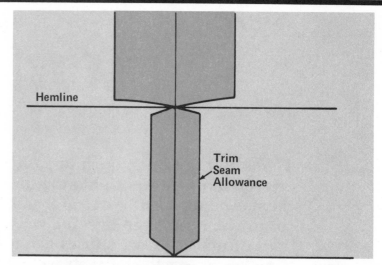

fig. 1

Hem Finishes

Finish the edge of the hem using one of the following finishes before hemming the garment.

Pinked and Stitched

Use this finish on fabrics that don't ravel very much. Straight stitch ¼ inch (6mm) below the top of the hem and then pink the edge. (fig. 2)

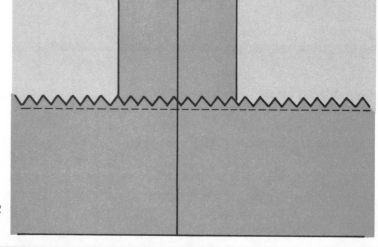

fig. 2

Turned and Stitched

Use this finish only on lightweight woven fabrics. Turn under ¼ inch (6mm) of the hem edge and edgestitch. (fig. 3)

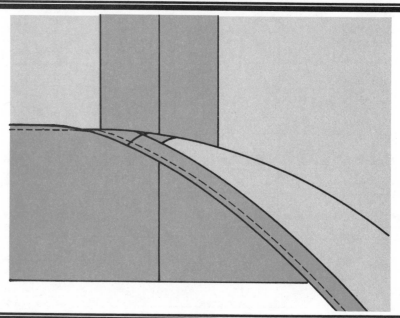

fig. 3

Overcast

Use this finish for fabrics that ravel easily. Straight stitch ¼ inch (6mm) away from the edge and then overcast the edge by hand or with the zigzag stitch on the machine. (fig. 4)

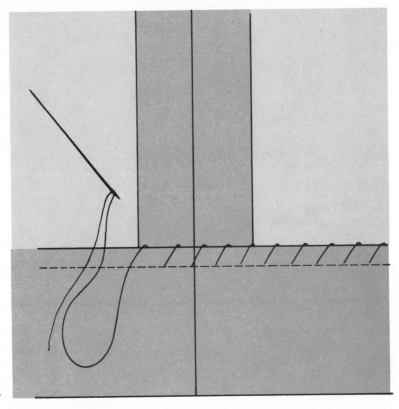

fig. 4

Bound Hem

Seam binding is used for loosely woven fabrics and washable garments that would be too bulky if the hem edge were turned and stitched. Use ribbon seam binding or stretch lace for straight hems and bias seam binding for flared or curved hems.

Overlap the hem edge one half the width of the seam binding and edgestitch the binding to the hem. (fig. 5)

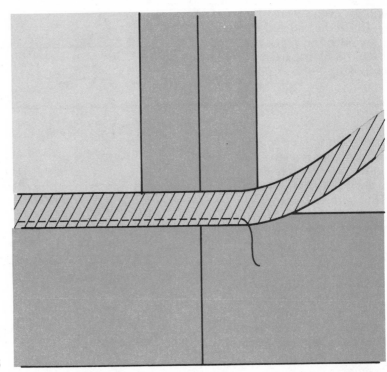

fig. 5

Hong Kong Finish

Bulky fabrics that tend to fray can be finished with the elegant Hong Kong finish. This is also a good finish to use on seam edges of unlined garments for a more finished look. The binding can be either purchased, single fold bias tape or ¾ inch (20mm) wide strips of bias cut lining fabric.

Stitch the binding strip to the hem edge with a ⅛ inch (3mm) seam, right sides together. Turn the strip over the hem edge to the wrong side. Secure the bias strip by hand or stitching-in-the-ditch. (fig. 6)

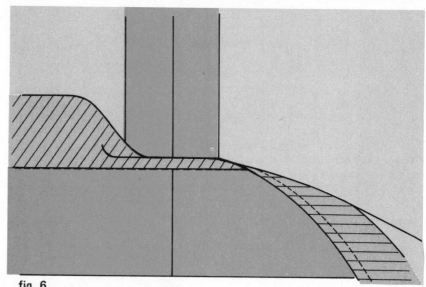

fig. 6

After finishing the hem edge fold the hem up in position basting along the fold to hold it in place. (fig. 7)

Tip

Use The Dritz Tailorette hem gauge when turning up the hem so you get it even. A small piece of chalk fits in the end and allows you to measure and mark at the same time. Available from Scovill, Sewing Notions Division.

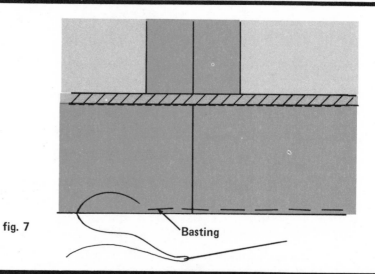

fig. 7

Basting

Press from the fold up, placing a strip of paper or large envelope between the fabric layers to prevent an impression on the right side of the garment. (fig. 8)

Tip

Small amounts of fullness at the top edge of the hem can usually be steamed out. The fullness found on A-line or flared hems should be controlled with a line of easestitching ¼ inch (6mm) from the hem edge.

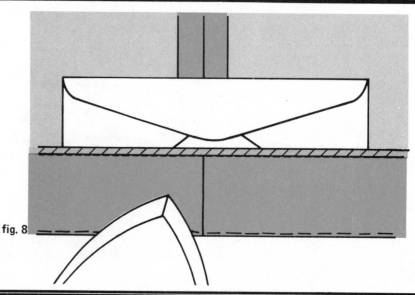

fig. 8

Hem Techniques

Two basic hemming techniques are the flat finish and inside hem. The flat finish has the hem edge sewn flat to the garment. The hem is stitched in place with a blindstitch, catchstitch, or slipstitch, depending on the hem finish used.

For an inside hem the hem stitches are done between the garment and hem layers, using either a catchstitch or blindstitch. This is the preferred method for your nicer knits and wovens. Because the garment and hem are lightly layered together the hem will never show a ridge on the right side of the garment, and will be invisible also on the wrong side.

Whichever technique is used never pull the hem threads tightly, or else the hem will show on the right side of the garment.

The Flat Finished Hem

The flat finished hem can be done with any of the following hem stitches.

Hemming Stitch

Working from right to left, take a stitch in the hem edge and then just catch a thread of the garment. (fig. 9)

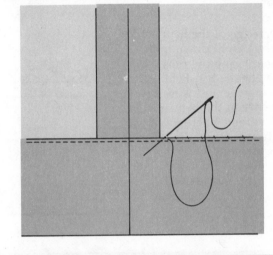

fig. 9

Catchstitch

This strong hem is good for children's clothes. It is also quite flexible and can be used on knits. Work from left to right, catching just a thread or two of the garment and hem edge. (fig. 10)

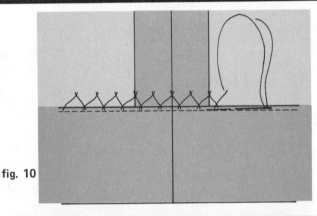

fig. 10

Slipstitch

This technique is used only on a flat finished hem that has been turned and stitched. Work from right to left. The needle runs along the hem fold, coming out periodically to catch a thread of garment fabric. (fig. 11)

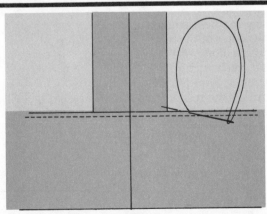

fig. 11

The Inside Hem Finish

The inside hem finish should be used on all your fine knits and woven fabric garments. When done properly it makes an invisible hem finish on both sides of the garment.

Pin the top edge of the hem about ½ inch (13mm) down from the hem edge placing the pins parallel to the hem edge. Fold down the hem edge and work a catchstitch between the hem and garment layers remembering not to pull the threads tight. (fig. 12) Insert the needle into the fabric opposite the direction you are hemming and the threads will cross over each other, locking each stitch.

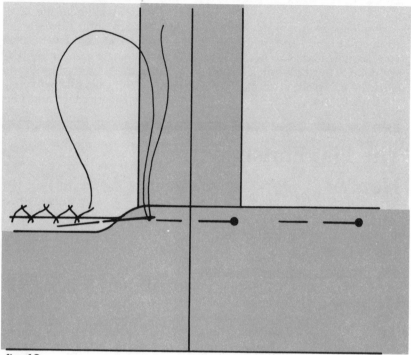

fig. 12

The Double Hem

The double hem is another version of the inside hem. It is used on wide hems of garments that are made of knit or heavy fabric, wherever a regular hem would sag and pull on the garment.

Fold and baste the hem edge. Baste down the center of the hem. Turn back the hem along this basting line and catchstitch the hem to the garment. Remove the basting and turn up the rest of the hem, securing it with another row of catchstitching. (fig. 13)

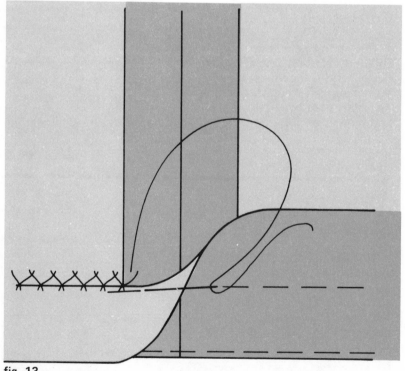

fig. 13

Machine Hems

While most hems on fine garments are done by hand, the machine hem, whether a machine blindhem or several rows of topstitching, can also be used. The machine blindhem is good for children's clothes and sportswear. The topstitched hem is used for decorative purposes and is also the only type of hem that looks nice on some of the lighter weight knits. Regular hand hem techniques will always show on these delicate fabrics.

Machine Blindhem

Each machine has different control settings for the machine blindhem. Check your instruction book for the specific instructions concerning your machine. Some come with a special presser foot.

Topstitched Hems

The topstitched hem is quick to do, and adds design interest as well as finishing the edge of the garment. Many casual sports clothes call for topstitched hems. They are also a good choice for knits, since you don't have to worry about finishing the hem edge first.

Finish the hem edge as indicated by the fabric. Mark and turn up a 1 inch (25mm) to 1½ inch (38mm) hem and pin in place. Do one or more rows of topstitching using a matching or contrasting thread. Use regular thread, topstitching thread, or two regular threads threaded through the eye of the machine needle. (fig. 14)

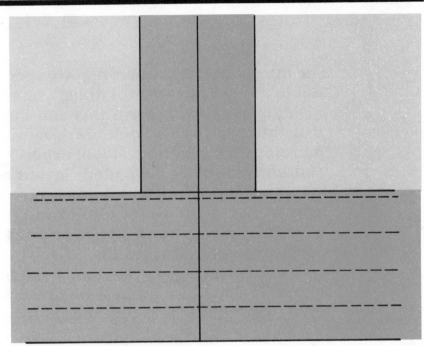

fig. 14

Fused Hems

Narrow strips of fusible web can be used to hold hems in place. Cut a strip of web ¼ inch (6mm) narrower than the hem, or use pre-cut strips of web. Insert the web between the hem and garment fabric, making sure it is about ¼ inch (6mm) short of the hem edge. Fuse in place following the manufacturer's instructions. (fig. 15)

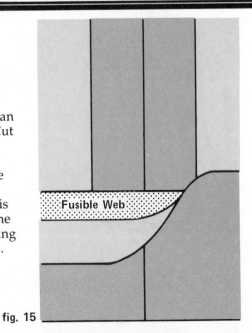

Fusible Web

fig. 15

Tip

Always test fuse a hem on a scrap of fabric to see if the fused web hem will be invisible on the right side of the garment. Some fabrics tend to let the web show through giving the hem a glued look or leaving a visible line of demarcation.

Working With Special Fabrics

The fabrics in this chapter require special attention but after learning a few helpful hints, you will be able to use plaids, sheers, border prints and the other fabrics mentioned in this book. Each fabric has its own characteristics requiring a bit of expert help. With plaids and border prints, the pattern layout requires special attention. Once the layout is done correctly, the garment is put together by simply following the guide sheet.

With sheers, pattern choice and seam technique determine successful results. Pile fabrics have special layout and pressing instructions. Read the section in this chapter of particular interest to you at the moment and then don't hesitate to buy the fabric of your choice.

Plaids

If you are working with a plaid fabric choose a pattern with simple, classic lines and few seams. The plaid will make the garment interesting without trim or tricks. Few seams show the plaid to better advantage. The art work in the counter catalog will show a plaid fabric if the design is good for plaids. If the description says, "no allowance for matching plaids or stripes" you can still use a plaid if you buy extra fabric and lay out the pattern carefully matching the plaid at the seams. If it says "not suitable for plaids or stripes" don't try it because the seams will not match. (fig. 1)

fig. 1

Plaids may be printed or woven. Avoid printed plaids. They are seldom printed straight and cannot be matched at the seamlines. Buy plaids that look the same on both sides. They are woven and can be matched.

Make any fitting adjustments on the paper pattern before you lay it out on the fabric. You must know the exact size and length of each pattern piece in order to match the plaids perfectly.

Plaid designs may be even or uneven along the length and/or width of the fabric. You must first determine what type of plaid you have as this will affect the pattern layout. "Even" plaids repeat color bars and lines symmetrically around the center of the plaid block while "uneven" plaids do not. A plaid can be even in one direction while being uneven in the other. Or it can be even or uneven in both directions. (fig. 2)

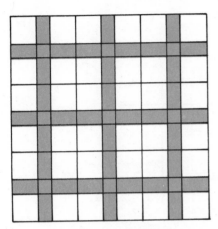

**Even Lengthwise
Even Crosswise**

fig. 2

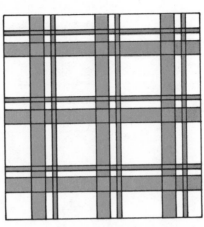

**Uneven Lengthwise
Uneven Crosswise**

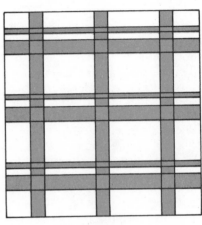

**Uneven Lengthwise
Even Crosswise**

If the evenness or unevenness of a plaid is not readily apparent, it can be determined by folding the fabric down the center of a plaid block, first on the lengthwise and then the crosswise grain. The color bars and lines should match exactly along the edges. (fig. 3 & 4)
(continued on next page)

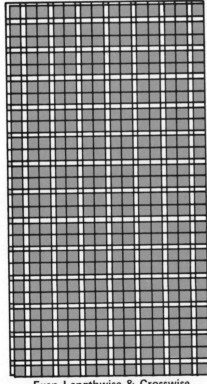

fig. 3 **Even Lengthwise & Crosswise**

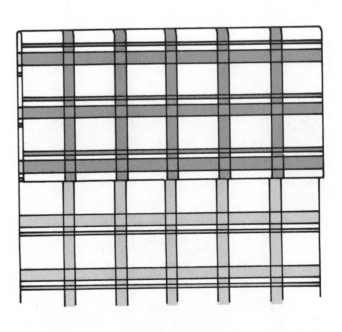

fig. 4 **Uneven Lengthwise**

Always use a "with nap" layout for plaid fabrics that are uneven in either direction. In other words the tops of all pattern pieces should be facing in one direction. A "without nap" layout can be used for plaids even in both directions.

You will usually need extra yardage for the pattern layout when working with plaid fabrics. More is needed for large plaids; less for small plaids. A good rule of thumb is to buy the yardage indicated for the "with nap" layout plus three times the length of the plaid repeat. The repeat is the combination of color bars and lines that occur regularly along the length of the fabric. (fig. 5) Large plaids may require up to 1 yard (0.95 meters) of extra fabric.

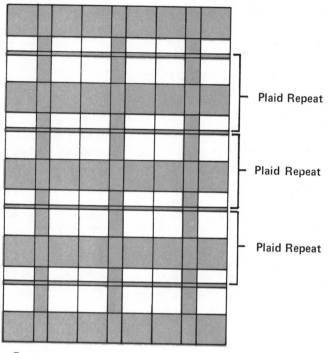

Plaid Repeat

Plaid Repeat

Plaid Repeat

fig. 5

Plaid Layouts

Spread out the full width of the fabric on a table or other large flat surface. Stand back so you can see the dominant color bars or drape the fabric on yourself and look in a mirror. The dominant color bar should be in the center front. (fig. 6) If there are two color bars of equal intensity, balance them on either side of the center front. (fig. 7) This placement is important. If the dominant color is positioned wrong, the optical illusion of the plaid will be distorted and the garment will look uneven. The same dominant color bar can be used at the center of the sleeve and at the center back, if possible.

fig. 6

fig. 7

It is best to cut plaid fabric a single layer at a time. Then you are sure both garment pieces are cut identically. When two garment pieces must be cut from the same pattern piece, such as the back bodice or sleeves, cut one with the pattern printing right side up and the other with the printing turned underneath. This makes sure you get a left and right garment piece.

Pattern pieces to be cut on a fold should be flipped over at the foldline after cutting out one half. (fig. 8)

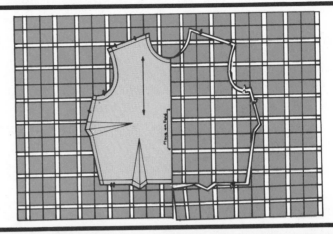

fig. 8

Place the main, front pattern piece on the fabric, first making sure it lies on the dominant color bar or bars as desired. Position the adjoining pattern pieces next, making sure they match the first pattern piece at notches and corners. (fig. 9). Remember you are matching seamlines, not cutting lines, when you are laying out the pattern so keep this in mind as you position the pattern pieces.

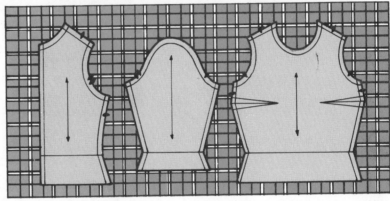

fig. 9

Tip

Patterns with underarm bust darts must be matched from the hem edge up. The area above the dart will not match. If you match from the underarm point down, the area above the dart will match up. The long seam below the dart will be mismatched.

Position the sleeve pattern on the fabric so the front of the sleeve matches the front of the armhole. (fig. 10)

The sleeve will not match the garment at the back but the look is acceptable. *(continued on next page)*

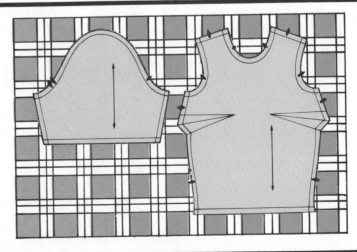

fig. 10

Cut small detail pieces, such as patch pockets, pocket flap, cuffs or applied belts, after the main garment pieces have been cut. A good way to match these pieces is to lay the pattern on the cut-out garment piece matching construction marks. Extend the plaid lines of the garment piece onto the paper pattern with a ruler and pen or pencil. Mark the lines according to color. (fig. 11)

Place the paper pattern on the plaid fabric matching the drawn plaid lines with the lines of the plaid fabric. Pin and cut. (fig. 12)

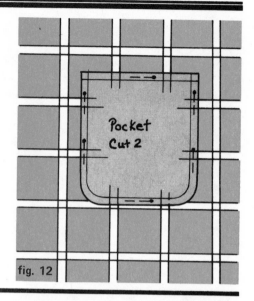

Pocket Pattern

fig. 11

Pocket Cut 2

fig. 12

On a jacket and skirt or dress with a waistline seam the pattern pieces should be placed so the vertical color bars are continuous (fig. 13)

Horizontal color bars should be evenly spaced the garment length. Place the waistline mark of both the top and bottom pattern pieces on the same horizontal plaid line. This is important if both pieces are cut on the straight grain. If the skirt is cut on the bias, the spacing will not be as critical. (fig. 14)

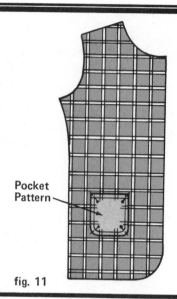

fig. 13

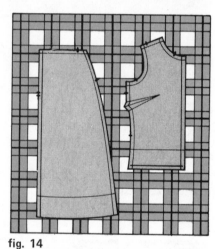

fig. 14

The plaid design can go around the body in the same sequence as the fabric. However, if you have a plaid that is even lengthwise but uneven crosswise, a balanced effect can be achieved at the center front and back by placing the pattern pieces as shown, (fig. 15) creating a center back or front seam if necessary. (fig. 16)

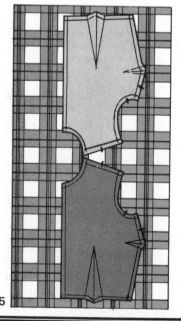

fig. 15

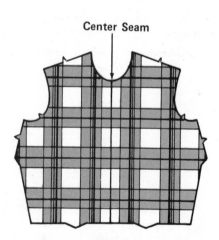

Center Seam

Resulting Balanced Effect

fig. 16

An uneven plaid fabric with no right or wrong side can be balanced by cutting two pieces and not turning the pattern over when cutting the second piece. (fig. 17) You will then sew a right to a wrong side and achieve a balanced effect. (fig. 18) If the pattern calls for a center front fold, convert it to a seam by adding a ⅝ inch (15mm) seam allowance and stitching on what was the foldline.

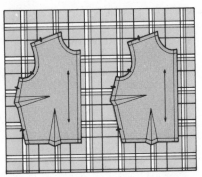

fig. 17

fig. 18 Resulting Balanced Effect

Stitching Plaids

Plaids must be perfectly matched along seamlines. One of the following methods will help you accomplish this, but try each one first on a fabric scrap to see which one works best with your particular fabric.

Pin Method

With right sides against each other pin the fabric layers together making sure the pins enter the fabric exactly at the seamline. The pins must also enter the fabric at the same place on matching plaid lines on both layers. (fig. 19) Stitch, removing the pins along the way.

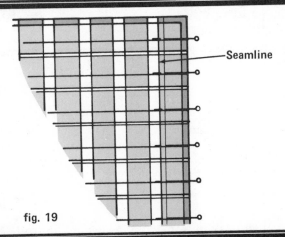

Seamline

fig. 19

Tape Method

Use the narrow, double faced tape, available at most notions counters, to baste the seams together before stitching. Position the tape just to the right of the seamline on the right side of one seam allowance. (fig. 20) Position the other garment piece right sides together with the plaid lines matching and secure in place with the tape. Stitch the seam, being careful not to catch the tape in the stitching. Remove the tape and press the seam open. (fig. 21)

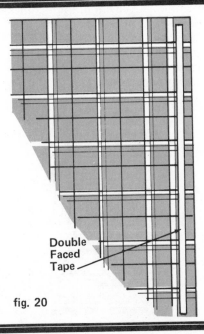

Double Faced Tape

fig. 20

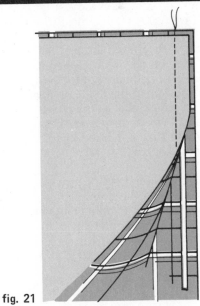

fig. 21

Slip Baste Method

Slip baste the seam before machine stitching. Fold under the seam allowance of one fabric layer.

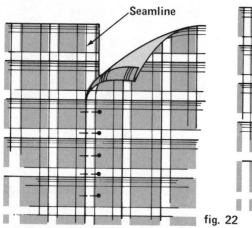

Seamline

Overlap the fold to meet the seamline of the other fabric layer, matching the plaid lines; pin in place. Hand stitch the two layers together by running the thread just along the fold of the upper

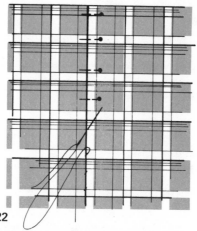

fig. 22

layer and then catching just a thread of the bottom layer periodically. (fig. 22) Unfold the fabric and machine stitch along the seamline. Remove the basting stitches. (fig. 23)

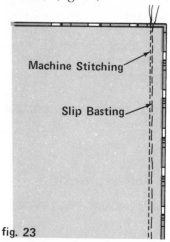

Machine Stitching

Slip Basting

fig. 23

Stripes

Most of the instructions pertaining to plaids are equally true about stripes. Obviously stripes only run in one direction so

there is less to be concerned about than there is with plaids during the layout.

Choose a pattern with simple, classic lines that will show the stripe to an advantage. Check the catalog copy to be sure the pattern is suitable for stripes. If it is not,

the copy will say, "not suitable for plaids or stripes."

Make any fitting adjustments on the paper pattern before you lay it out on the fabric. You must know the exact size and length of each pattern piece in order to match the stripes perfectly.

Horizontal stripes run from selvage to selvage; vertical stripes run the length of the fabric. Stripes may be printed or woven. Be very careful with printed stripes since they may be off-grain. Horizontal stripes especially are apt to "bow" in the middle of the fabric or slant and not be parallel to the cross threads. Woven stripes are best. Anything that is marked "yarn dyed" is woven.

Part of understanding stripes is in recognizing the dominant color bar and using it to an advantage. Drape the fabric around you and

look in a mirror. The dominant horizontal stripe should not come at the apex of the bust or the biggest part of the hips. Move the draped fabric up or down until the horizontal stripes are in the most flattering position. (fig. 24)

The dominant color bar on a vertical stripe should be used at the center front. Good use of stripes makes the difference between a professional or nonprofessional garment. (fig. 25)

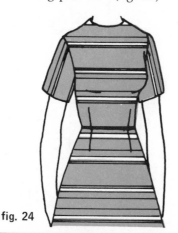

fig. 24

fig. 25

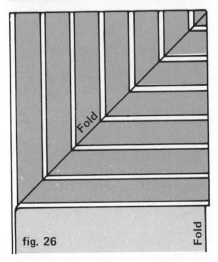

fig. 26

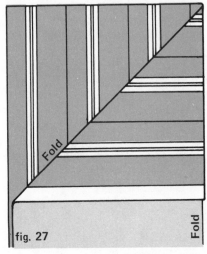

fig. 27

Determine which kind of stripe you have by folding the fabric along a stripe and then folding back a corner. Balanced stripes will match along the turned back edge. (fig. 26)

Unbalanced stripes will not match along the turned back edge. (fig. 27)

Extra fabric is usually necessary when using striped fabric so you can get a perfect match at the seamlines. Narrow stripes with a narrow repeat will need less extra fabric than wide stripes with a wide repeat. Balanced stripes generally need less extra fabric than unbalanced stripes. Many times the only way to determine the exact amount of yardage is to lay out pattern pieces on the fabric before it is cut from the bolt. Many stores permit this.

Stripes are balanced or unbalanced. Balanced stripes are easy to cut while unbalanced stripes require more thought.

Stripe Layouts

A horizontally balanced stripe is easiest to match. Place the grain arrow on the lengthwise grain and move the pattern pieces up or down until the stripes match at the notches and corners. (fig. 28). You can use a "without nap" layout for balanced horizontal stripes.

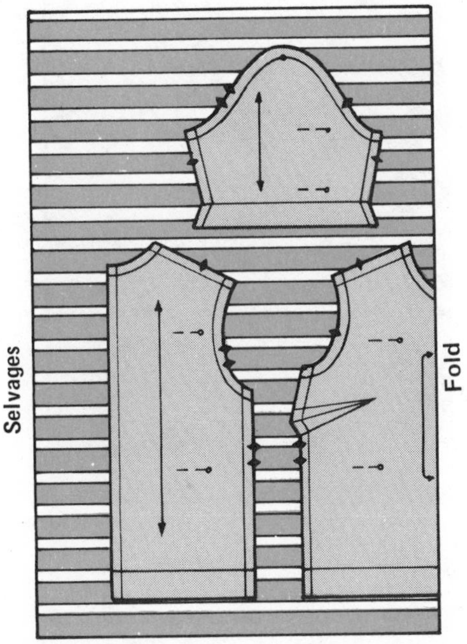

Position pattern pieces so the hemline falls along the dominant stripe unless this placement will make the dominant stripe also fall at the full part of the bust or hips. If the hem has much of a curve, the center front and back of the hem should be on the dominant stripe for the proper optical illusion. Match the bodice front and back from the hem up so the stripes will match below the bust dart.

Balanced vertical stripes are also quite easy to lay out. Make sure the pattern grainline is on or parallel to a stripe, and position the dominant stripe so it goes down the center front and back. The seamline at the front of the sleeve should match the seamline at the front of the armhole. (fig. 29) If you are making a two-piece garment make sure the stripes are unbroken at the joining point. A chevron of stripes will form at the side seams of A-line skirts and dresses. *(continued on next page)*

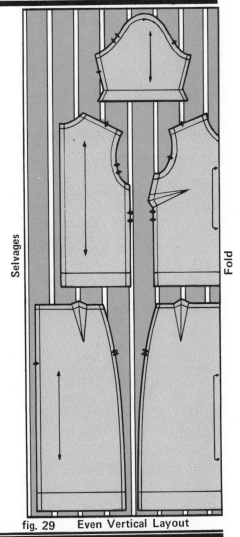

fig. 28   Even Horizontal Layout

fig. 29   Even Vertical Layout

When working with unbalanced horizontal stripes follow the same rules for balanced horizontal

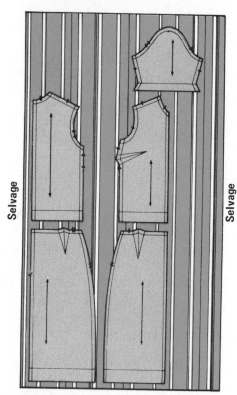

fig. 30

stripes except use a "with nap" layout. Also, make sure the stripes run continuously down the figure when cutting a two-piece outfit from an unbalanced horizontal striped fabric. You want the stripe at the hem of the jacket to match the stripe it meets on the skirt.

Unbalanced vertical stripes are cut as shown. First position the center front on the desired stripe and match the center back placement to the same stripe. Match the seamline of the bodice front. The stripes will generally not match at the side seams nor chevron along an A-line. (fig. 30)

A mirror image of the stripes can be created when working with unbalanced vertical stripes if each half of the front and back is cut as shown. If the center front or center back does not have a seam you must create one by adding a ⅝ inch (15mm) seam allowance and then use the original foldline as the seamline. This technique can not be used if the fabric requires a "with nap" layout. (fig. 31)

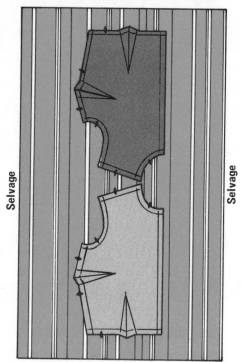

fig. 31

Match and stitch striped fabrics using the same methods given for matching and stitching plaids.

Diagonals

There are more diagonals around than you might realize, but most of them are so subtle they can be treated as a solid color fabric. Denim and gabardine are twill weaves and therefore diagonals, usually not requiring special care. The diagonals that do require special care are diagonal designs printed on, or woven, or knit into the fabric.

Diagonals are best made up in patterns with straight lines. That means straight skirts and set-in sleeves; no dolman or raglan sleeves and no A-line skirts. The copy in the counter catalog will indicate by omission which patterns can be used. Also, patterns or instructions that say "obvious diagonal fabrics are not suitable" should not be used.

Pattern Layout

Diagonal fabrics require a "with nap" layout and will usually require extra fabric for matching. The amount of extra fabric will be determined by the width of the diagonal repeat and the size of the pattern pieces. Do a trial layout in the store if possible so you know just how much fabric is required.

Position the pattern pieces so the diagonal runs from the lower left to the upper right or vice versa. The important thing is to be consistent throughout the garment. Diagonal stripes or prints may not be on the exact bias of the fabric but usually close enough to allow you to cut collars and ties parallel to the design lines. This way the design runs around the neck, matching at the center front or back. (fig. 32)

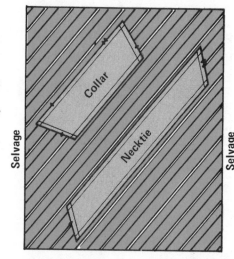

fig. 32

Use the same methods for matching and stitching diagonal fabrics as given for plaids.

Border Prints

Border prints are great fun, providing a chance to show your creativity. A border print is a narrow or wide print that runs the length of the selvage rather than an all-over print that runs across the width of the fabric.

Border prints are often seen at the hem of a dirndl or straight skirt but they can also be used in other ways. If the print can be turned upside down, use it at the hemline of a dress and then cut the top of the dress and the sleeve from the border. The dress from the bust to the hip will have less print than the hem and shoulder area.(fig. 33)

A border print that isn't too wide can be effectively concentrated at the center front of a button front dress. It might also be possible to use part of the print there and the rest at the hem.

Choose the pattern according to your fabric. A print covering half the fabric width that goes in only

fig. 33

one direction should probably go on a skirt or dress with a straight hem. The print may not work on a skirt with a curved hem. When the border print has no directional design and is not very wide you can try one of the suggestions given above.

Most border prints are at least 45 inches (115 cm) wide. That is enough length for almost any pattern piece except a floor length dress cut in one piece. Check the finished length of the garment on the back of the pattern envelope to be sure your fabric is wide enough.

Use a pattern with simple lines. It will show the print to better advantage than one with many seams. The print is the fashion story so don't compete with it by using a pattern with lots of detail.

Make all fitting and length adjustments on the pattern before doing the layout. The placement of the hemline is one of the most important layout decisions.

Pattern Layout

To decide on the amount of fabric needed, measure the widest part of the pieces to be placed on the border. Double the measurement of pieces that are to be cut twice or on a fold. Add

these measurements for the needed yardage. Pieces not cut on the border will usually fit above the border pieces. (fig. 34)

Because the border is printed along just one selvage, you will not be able to follow the pattern

layout unless it is designed for border prints. Don't panic! Each pattern piece will tell you whether it goes on a fold or straight grain or bias. Pieces that go on the straight grain must go at right angles to the selvage instead of parallel to it. Folds also go across the fabric at right angles to the selvage.

Position the hemline carefully, leaving enough fabric to turn under a hem. There is usually a narrow band of solid color fabric for this purpose.

Make sure the front and back match at the side seams if a border print is used at the bottom of the garment.

Stitching border prints is no problem once the proper layout and cutting is done. Just follow the pattern guide sheet.

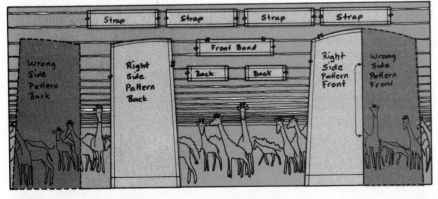

fig. 34

Sheer Fabrics

Sheers are usually thought of for warm weather, but they can also be used for lovely dressy clothes for festive winter occasions, and of course, wedding dresses. Sheers are soft or crisp. The best example of a soft sheer is chiffon or georgette. The crisp sheers are dotted swiss or organdy. These aren't all the sheers by any means but they help you visualize what we mean by sheer fabric. Many sheers that were formerly made of silk or cotton are now made of synthetic fibers or a blend of fibers. This means easy care and fewer wrinkles.

The object when making a sheer garment is to maintain the sheer look. When possible, bind a raw edge instead of facing it since facings cast a shadow and will detract from the sheer look. Trim seam allowances to make them as narrow as possible. Finish all seams and darts carefully so there are no dangling threads or knots that show.

Sheers generally look best when there is fullness designed into the pattern. Billowy sleeves and full skirts give a soft feminine look. Crisp or soft, a tightly fitted blouse or dress will put too much strain on a sheer fabric. If some part of your chosen pattern is fitted then underline that part with another fabric of the same color and treat the two fabrics as one when sewing.

Patterns designed for sheers list sheers among the recommended fabrics. The art work will show a sheer dress; the slip may or may not be part of the pattern. You do not have to limit your choice to patterns showing only sheers, but do pick a simple design. A dress with too much detail and many seams will not enhance a sheer fabric.

A blouse or dress calling for a button closure looks nice if you use button loops and ball buttons on a slash. (fig. 35). If a conventional lapped button closure is desired, use an interfaced shirt band type of closure rather than a simple fold back facing as this type of finish will show through the front of the garment. (fig. 36)

fig. 35

fig. 36

Pattern Layout

If your sheer fabric is slippery or distorts easily, such as chiffon, spread a sheet on the cutting surface before doing the layout. The fabric will cling to the sheet making the layout and cutting process much easier.

If the selvage puckers, snip it every few inches (cm) until it relaxes and is as long as the body of the fabric.

Follow the pattern layout, but eliminate neckline and armhole facings wherever possible. Bias strips will then be cut from fabric scraps to bind the neckline or armhole edges.

Allow for an extra deep hem on dirndl skirts. The prettiest width is from 4 to 8 inches (10 to 20.5cm).

Interfacing will be required for the collar and cuffs. It will look best if the interfacing color matches the fabric so use a lightweight lining fabric of the same color instead of regular interfacing fabrics. Small opaque areas, such as interfaced collars and cuffs contrast nicely with large sheer areas.

Sometimes it is desirable to cut the front bodice double. It will then serve as its own lining and interfacing. Just place the front fold or seamline on a fabric fold and cut. Handle the double bodice as one piece of fabric during construction. (fig. 37)

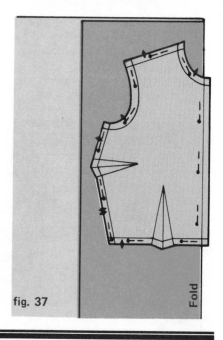

fig. 37

Fold

Cutting and Marking

Keep one hand flat on the pattern and fabric as you cut with the other hand. Soft sheers need this technique for a smooth, straight edge.

Transfer construction marks to the fabric with chalk or tailor tacks using silk thread. Test chalk on a fabric scrap first to see if it can be brushed off easily.

Stitching

Use fine synthetic, cotton or silk thread for stitching sheers. Lingerie thread works great. Use a size 9 or 11 (60 or 75) needle with a sharp point.

Backstitch at the beginning and end of each seam if it does not show on the right side. Otherwise leave long thread ends; thread a needle and take a few small hand stitches to secure the threads.

If the seam tends to pucker hold the fabric taut as it goes under the presser foot. Another solution is to sandwich the fabric layers between tissue paper while stitching. (fig. 38) This prevents the fabric from puckering and getting caught down in the needle hole.

Use the straight stitch throat plate on your sewing machine when straight stitching sheer fabrics. The small hole works better than the wide zigzag hole and helps make a better seam.

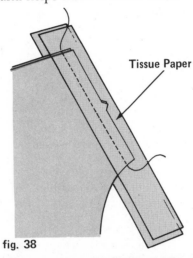

Tissue Paper

fig. 38

Tip

Belding Lily offers a roll of Tissue Tape that is just right for stitching sheers. It is marked with various seam widths and can be used on other difficult-to-stitch fabrics.

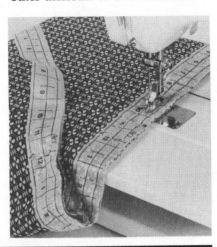

Seam Techniques

Test the following seam techniques on fabric scraps to see which one works best for your particular fabric. Sometimes a combination of seam types can be used on the same garment. Use whatever works best for a particular situation.

Basic Seam

Stitch a plain seam. Stitch again ⅛ inch (3mm) away and trim the seam allowance close to the stitching. (fig.39). Use this type of seam only on fabrics that don't ravel easily.

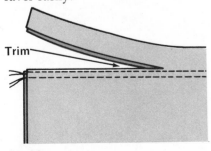

Trim

fig. 39

Enclosed Seam

A French seam or the flat-felled seam can also be used for seaming sheers. Follow the instruction in the *Seams* chapter for these seam techniques.

Zigzag Seam

Use a narrow zigzag seam when stitching the edges of collars, cuffs, pocket details and facings. Support the seam by stitching over a lightweight filler cord. Trim away the seam allowance close to the edge of the stitching. (fig. 40)

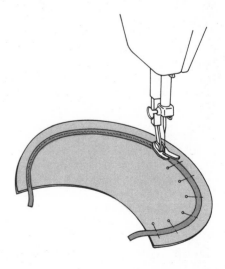

fig. 40

Darts

Use the continuous thread dart described in the *Shaping The Garment* chapter when stitching darts in sheer fabrics. Darts should be as inconspicuous as possible.

Construction Techniques

Whenever a zipper is required, use a feather weight zipper and do the final stitching by hand for a softer look.

Snaps look nice if they are covered with a layer of sheer fabric before being stitched in place. See the *Buttons And Fasteners* chapter for covering instructions.

Tip

The invisible Nylon Snap from Belding Lily is great to use on sheer fabrics. It blends in with the fabric color so you can hardly see it.

When facings are eliminated at neckline and armhole edges, a bias binding is required. Cut the bias strips six times the desired finished width and the length of the neckline or armhole. Cut the strips from fabric scraps, piecing together if necessary.

Staystitch the garment edge ¾ inch (20mm) from the cut edge and trim away the ⅝ inch (15mm) seam allowance. (fig. 41)

Fold the bias strip in half lengthwise, wrong sides together. Place the strip on the right side of the garment matching the raw edges and stitch. The distance between the stitching and cut edge will be the same as the finished width of the binding. Fold the bias over the raw edge and slipstitch to the line of machine stitching. (fig. 42)

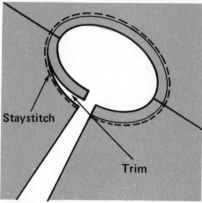

fig. 41

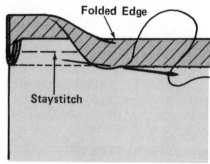

fig. 42

Hems

A deep hem on a straight skirt looks nicest if made double. Allow twice the finished hem width when cutting. Fold up half the hem allowance and then fold again. Catch in place with a blind hem.

Garments with curved hems should hang 48 hours before hemming. Allow for just a narrow hem allowance. Turn up ⅛ inch (3mm) and slip the needle through the fold taking a small stitch in the garment. Do several stitches and pull the thread causing the hem to roll. (fig. 43)

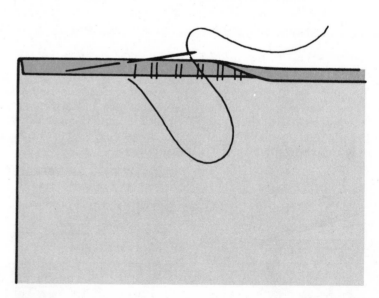

fig. 43

Lace

Lace is the loveliest and most feminine of fabrics or trims. An entire garment or part of a garment may be made of lace. It may also be used for trim. Today there is great freedom in fashion to be creative in using your own ideas. The pattern catalogs show lace on wedding gowns and perhaps jackets or shawls, but with your imagination, lace can have many uses.

Lace is easy to use and the results are impressive. The object with lace, as with sheers, is to keep the sheer look. Plan to wear a slip in the same color as the lace if the fabric is too revealing. Change the straps to a sheer fabric also so they show as little as possible. No interfacing is used with lace although very fragile lace may be backed with a sheer fabric for strength.

Choose a pattern with simple lines since the fabric will add the interest. Make an all-over lace garment or use the lace for detail areas such as yokes, collars, cuffs and sleeves. Many fabrics combine well with lace. For example, a good combination includes a soft fabric such as crepe.

A suggested use for the finished edge found on many lace fabrics is to use it along the edge of neckline or sleeve ruffles as well as the hem edge of the garment. (fig. 44)

Follow the yardage requirements given on the pattern envelope if you are making an all-over lace garment. If you are using lace for just some of the pattern pieces determine the needed yardage by laying the pattern pieces out on the fabric while in the store.

fig. 44

Understanding Lace

Lace comes as wide as fabric and as narrow as ½ inch (13mm). It may have one or two scalloped or finished edges that can be used as the finished edge of the garment. (fig. 45)

fig. 45

Pattern Layout

Sometimes you will have to modify the pattern layout to take advantage of the finished edges of lace fabric. A trial layout on a fabric of a similar width will help you plan your final layout and estimate the amount of fabric needed.

There is no grain when laying out pattern pieces on wide lace but there is a design to be considered. Decide which part of the design is to be centered and displayed most prominently. Center the front, back and sleeve pattern pieces, taking advantage of the design and the repeat. Check for "one-way" designs lengthwise and crosswise and lay out the pattern pieces accordingly.

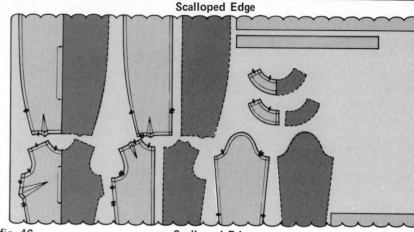

Scalloped Edge

fig. 46   **Scalloped Edge**

When one or both edges of the lace are finished, lay the pattern out as for a border print. For a blouse, the bottom of the sleeve and any ruffled edge should go along the finished edge of the lace. If the blouse is not to be tucked in, the hemline of the front and back should go on the finished edge. Straight skirts should also take advantage of the finished edge. Position the hemline of the skirt along the finished edge of the lace, as for the blouse. (fig. 46)

Note: Both edges may be finished, but with different designs. All skirt hems should be on one side and all blouse and sleeve hems on the other.

If the lace design is close and connected you can cut away the connecting threads and make your own scalloped edge. (fig. 47) Cut garment pieces to be backed from lace and backing fabric. Backing fabric should be sheer and not detract from the lace. Baste the cut pieces together and treat them as one during the garment construction.

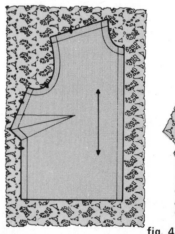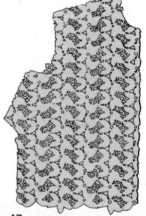

fig. 47

Marking

Marking lace is best done with tailor tacks. Tracing carbon shows and pins may fall out. Chalk may work but test it first on fabric scraps to see if it will brush off.

Stitching

Seams and darts are stitched as for sheers. French seams work for fine lace; the double stitched seam is best for heavy lace. The thread and needle size will depend on the weight of the fabric.

Use strips of tissue paper under lace fabric when stitching if it tends to catch in the feed dog. Use strips on top also or a roller foot if the lace catches on the toes of an ordinary presser foot.

Tip

Try the Tissue Tape made by Belding Lily if you have difficulties stitching lace fabric. Sandwich the fabric between two strips of tape and it won't catch on the feed dogs or toes of the presser foot.

Hems

Hems, where the scalloped edge is not used, should be finished with a double strip of net. Allow for just a ¼ inch (6mm) hem allowance and cut the net twice the width of the finished hem. Fold in half and match the raw edges to the skirt edge. Do two rows of machine stitching and turn the net to the inside slipstitching in place. (fig. 48)

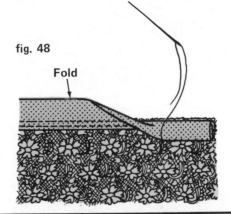

fig. 48

Fold

Pressing

Set the iron for the fiber content of the lace; test on fabric scraps. For a heavy lace, spread a terry towel on the ironing board. Press the lace on the wrong side only to avoid flattening the design.

Narrow Lace Application

Narrow lace can be sewn flat to the garment with a running hand stitch or machine zigzag. If the lace ends do not go into a seam, turn under ¼ inch (6mm) before stitching.

When narrow lace is used for an edging, finish the raw edge of the garment with a narrow hem or turn under the raw edge to the right side of the garment and stitch the lace over it. Use a running hand stitch or machine zigzag. (fig. 49)

Narrow lace can be inserted into other fabrics for a decorative, sheer look. Baste the lace in position. Cut away the garment fabric underneath leaving enough for a narrow rolled hem. Stitch by hand or machine. If a machine zigzag is used, a hem is not needed. (fig. 50)

(continued on next page)

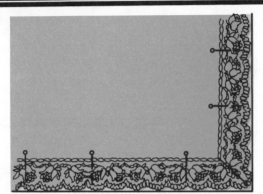

fig. 49

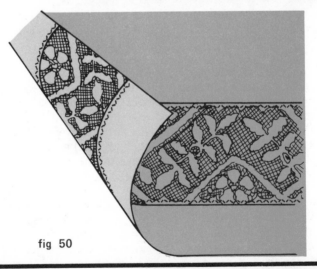

fig 50

Tip

Small, straight handled Trimming Scissors work best when cutting fabric away from lace. They will do a much better job than your regular shears. From Joy Scissors, Division of Cole Consumer Products.

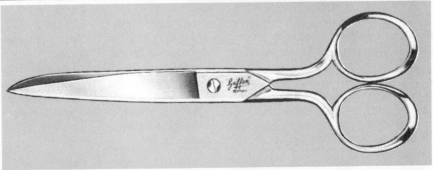

Narrow lace is often ruffled and used around collar and cuff edges. Cut the lace two or three times the measurement of the outer edge of the collar or cuff, depending on the desired fullness. Some lace will have a thread along one edge that can be pulled up for gathering. If not, use the longest machine stitch and pull up for gathers as described in *Shaping The Garment*.

Pin the lace to the edge of the collar or cuff with the gathered line on top of the seamline and the finished edge of the lace toward the inside of the garment piece. Taper the lace to nothing at the edges and baste in place. (fig. 51) Pin the facing in place, right sides together and stitch following the guide sheet for finishing

techniques. Use this method whenever lace is stitched between two layers of fabric so it extends out beyond the finished edge.

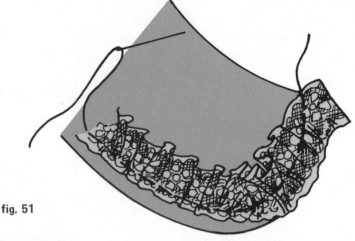

fig. 51

Napped Fabrics

Velvet, velveteen and corduroy are the fabrics we usually think of in this category. They are frequently grouped together because the construction of the fabrics is similar. Suede cloths are also napped fabrics. These fabrics should be cut using a "with nap" layout. Pieces that are cut incorrectly will look as though they were made of fabric from a different dye lot.

Velvet is soft, silky and has a rich sheen. The pile makes it beautiful and delicate. Velvet is usually reserved for special occasion clothes partly because it cannot take strain and hard wear and because it can be expensive.

Velveteen and corduroy on the other hand are desirable for all kinds of clothes. Corduroy has wide ribs, narrow ones or none at all. Ribless corduroy looks like velveteen. Both fabrics wear well, are easy to use, are reasonably priced and suitable for all ages.

Suede cloths can be of a matted, knit or woven construction. They come in light to medium weights and a variety of colors difficult to find in real suede. Easier to care for, suede cloths are usually less expensive than real suede making them more practical.

There are really no restrictions on choosing patterns for napped fabrics. They are suitable for dresses, pants, skirts, jackets and coats. Although weight and drapability of the fabric should be suitable to the chosen pattern style. (fig. 52)

Since you must use a "with nap" layout when working with napped fabrics it is best to have a "with nap" yardage notation in the yardage requirements. You will then know there is a "with nap" layout on the pattern guide sheet. When the pattern does not give a "with nap" yardage notation you will have to examine the given layout diagram and estimate how much extra yardage will be needed when you lay out the pattern pieces all in one direction.

fig. 52

Pattern Layout

Pattern pieces may be placed on the fabric so the nap runs up or down the finished garment. (fig. 53) If the nap runs up, the garment will have a deeper, richer color, but it may wear better if the nap runs down because we tend to smooth our clothes down when we adjust them or sit down.

Run your hands over the fabric to find the nap direction. When the fabric feels soft and silky you are going with the nap; rough and bristly, against the nap. Draw arrows on the wrong side of the fabric with chalk to indicate the direction of the nap. (fig. 54)

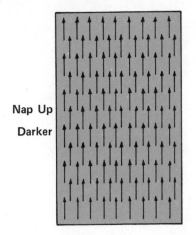
Nap Up
Darker

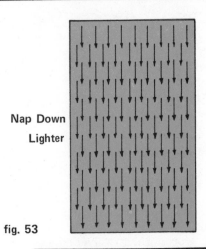
Nap Down
Lighter

fig. 53

Tip

Use the Dritz Tailor's Chalk to mark nap direction on the wrong side of the fabric. It comes in its own plastic holder with a built-in sharpener. Your fingers will stay clean and the chalk sharp. From Scovill, Sewing Notions Division

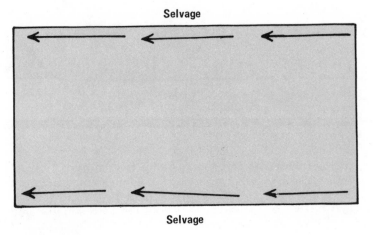

Selvage

Selvage

fig. 54

Fold the fabric with the right sides together for the pattern layout and make sure all the pattern pieces are placed so the tops face one direction. (fig. 55) *(continued on next page)*

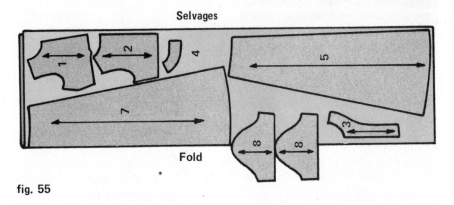
Selvages

Fold

fig. 55

Napped fabrics should never be folded on the crossgrain for the pattern layout. However, the layout guide may tell you to cut across the width of the fabric and reverse one layer so the nap on both pieces goes in the same direction. Your nap direction arrows will help you position these pieces. (fig. 56)

Use fine, sharp silk pins when pinning the pattern to napped fabrics. Sometimes long, thin needles, instead of pins, work best when working with velvet so you don't damage the pile.

Underlining velvet is sometimes necessary to support this delicate fabric and protect it against strain and wrinkles.

Tip

Angel Pins — fine, extra long silk pins are ideal for napped fabrics with a pile. Their extra length keeps them from falling out of the fabric and their fineness prevents fabric damage. From Angel Aids.

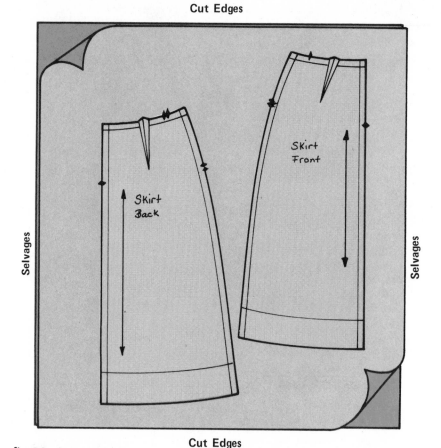

fig. 56

Facings and Interfacings

Cut facings from lining fabric if your fashion fabric is very heavy. This is recommended for the necklines, armholes and sleeve edges of velvets and velveteens.

Interface the garment where necessary but don't use fusible interfacing on velvet since the pressure and heat necessary for a good bond will damage the pile.

Fusible interfacings can be used on velveteens, corduroys and suede cloths but the interfacing must be applied to the whole garment piece rather than just an edge, as in a blazer type jacket with a rolled lapel. Fusing interfacing to just part of the garment piece will leave a line on the right side of the fabric.

If the garment is to be washed, facing fabric, interfacing and any linings must also be washable.

Marking

Test any marking procedure on scrap fabric before trying it on the garment to make sure it shows and doesn't damage the fabric. Tracing carbon and a tracing wheel can usually be used on velveteen, corduroy, and suede cloth. It is best to use tailor tacks on velvet. Use silk thread if possible or fine lingerie thread so you will not make marks in the fabric.

Stitching

Use a thread and needle size compatible with the weight of your fabric. Test seam a scrap of fabric to see if any pressure adjustments have to be made. Sometimes you will have to lighten the pressure on the presser foot if it leaves marks along the seam, especially if you are topstitching.

Do not topstitch velvet; the machine will always leave marks. Do any topstitching around zippers or garment edges by hand.

Many napped fabrics need to be basted together before stitching to prevent the top layer of fabric from "creeping" ahead of the bottom layer. Hand baste using a fine needle and a silk thread.

Stitch with the direction of the nap as much as possible.

Finish the edges of napped fabrics that tend to ravel with a hand overcast or machine zigzag stitch. This is especially important if the garment is to be washed.

Pressing

Pressing requires extra care when working with napped fabrics. Steam rather than press so you don't flatten the pile or napped surface.

Steam seams open with the tip of the iron. Allow the fabric to cool and the moisture to evaporate before you move it about on the ironing board.

Prevent seam allowances and dart ridges from showing through to the right side by using a seam roll or strips of paper placed between the seam allowance or dart and the wrong side of the fabric. (fig. 57 & 58)

Protect the right side of deeply napped fabrics when pressing by placing a needle board, terry towel, or piece of the same fabric on the ironing board. The right side of the napped fabric will not be damaged during the pressing. (fig. 59)

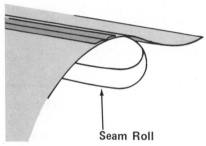

Seam Roll

fig. 57

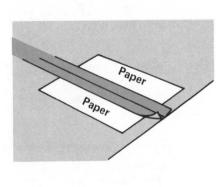

fig. 58

Needle Board

fig. 59

Knits

Knits are widely available today and are easily handled by all home-sewers — novice or experienced. Knit clothes are comfortable to wear, easy to care for and sew. You do not need a special machine or sewing equipment to work with knits.

Knits are divided into two groups: stable and stretchable. Stable knits have little stretch and are recommended for many pattern designs.

Stretchable knits require special patterns clearly marked in the pattern catalogs. Use only stretchable knits with these patterns. This is not a matter of design but a question of fit. Patterns designed for stretchable knits depend on the stretch in the knit for body ease (wiggle room).

Stretchable knits have various amounts of stretch. Patterns for these knits will have a gauge printed on the envelope back so you can test the stretch of the knit before buying, to be sure the needed stretch is there. (fig. 60)

Other facts to consider when choosing a pattern for knit fabrics are that soft pleats or gathers work well for most knits but knife edge pleats do not unless they can be professionally set.

Also soft clingy knits look best with some fullness. This avoids the "stuffed sausage" look. (fig. 61)

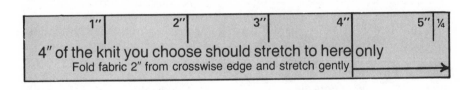

| 1″ | 2″ | 3″ | 4″ | 5″ | ¼ |

4″ of the knit you choose should stretch to here only
Fold fabric 2″ from crosswise edge and stretch gently

fig. 60

fig. 61

Understanding Knits

There are many types of available knits such as single knits, double knits, warp knits and interlocks. The technical differences are usually not important. What is important, in addition to the amount of stretch, are the following points:

Fabric care information is given on the hang tag or bolt end. You will also be given a small label which will outline the proper cleaning procedure. (fig. 62) Keep this information handy for future reference.

The recovery of the knit after it has been stretched is very important. Check all knits by stretching them along a crosswise fold and then letting them go. (fig. 63)

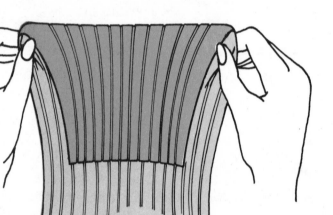

fig. 63

If the fabric quickly snaps back to the original size the recovery is good; if it does not the recovery is poor and that fabric should not be used where it will receive any stress — such as in straight skirts, pants or fitted dresses.

Some knits will stretch during construction and will sag when worn. Buy them knowing you will have to tape seams, staystitch and line pants and skirts. These steps will take a little longer but are not hard to do.

Medium to heavy weight knits of a firm or closely knit hand can be used for tailored garments. Lightweight, loose knits are fine for the soft look.

Pre-Care

Knits should be pre-shrunk before cutting. This is important for three reasons.

Many knits, especially the natural fiber ones, shrink when washed or cleaned. It is better to remove this shrinkage before you cut the fabric than end up with a too small garment after the first washing.

All knits have to relax after they have been cut from the bolt. They are wound on the bolt under tension at the mill and are stretched slightly in the process. Pre-shrinking the fabric before cutting gets rid of this stretching, otherwise you will think the fabric has shrunk after the first washing.

Many knits contain an excess of finishing materials which can build up on your machine needle as you sew, causing skipped stitches. Pre-shrinking the fabric gets rid of these chemicals.

If your knit is machine washable then pre-shrink the fabric using the same water temperature and machine cycle you will use for the finished garment. Use a fabric softener in the final rinse or add a fabric softener sheet to the dryer to remove wrinkles and cut down on static electricity.

If your knit has to be dry cleaned, pre-shrink it in your home dryer. Put the dry knit fabric into the dryer with wet clothes (knit T-shirts are best). Run the dryer ten minutes on a delicate cycle if possible. Remove the knit yardage from the dryer and spread on a flat surface until the moisture evaporates.

Pattern Layout

Some knits have a permanent crease along the center fold. If the crease remains after pre-shrinking, re-fold the fabric for the layout so the crease does not fall on any garment piece. If you must use the area with the permanent crease, try pressing the crease using a press cloth moistened with a solution of two parts water to one part white vinegar. Test first on a fabric scrap to make sure the knit is colorfast.

Keep all fabric on the table as you lay out and cut, keeping the excess neatly rolled at one end. Some knits will stretch if allowed to hang off the end of the table and the garment size will not be true after cutting.

Most knits stretch lengthwise

and crosswise; some just crosswise. Position the pattern pieces so the greatest stretch goes around the body. (fig. 64)

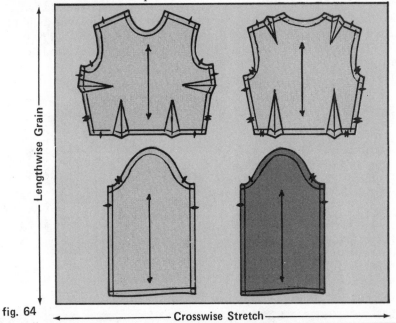

fig. 64 ← Lengthwise Grain → ← Crosswise Stretch →

Use a "with nap" layout for your knits. Most knit fabrics will show a subtle color change of seams if some pattern pieces are cut one way and some the other way. This is especially true of solid color knits.

The lengthwise grainline is sometimes difficult to find on knits. It is indicated by a lengthwise rib on the fabric. Mark it with a line of thread basting so you can see it better when pinning the pattern pieces in place. (fig. 65)

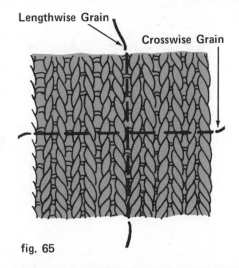

Lengthwise Grain
Crosswise Grain

fig. 65

The lengthwise grain will have to be ignored when working with striped knits since the stripes are not exactly perpendicular to the lengthwise rib. Match the stripes across the pattern piece and don't worry about the lengthwise grain; it is better to match the stripes.

Cut striped knits or other knits that have to be matched from a single layer of fabric. Remember to cut one piece with the pattern printing right side up, and one with the printing down. Solid color knits or fabrics that don't need to be matched can be cut double.

Cutting

Use sharp regular shears or shears with a serrated blade. Barber shears can be used if available. Do not cut out with pinking shears.

Marking

Test the usual marking methods on fabric scraps to see which works best with your knit. If you are going to use tracing carbon try the tracing wheel with the smooth edge for a better mark. Tailor tacks will sometimes be the best solution for loosely knit or heavily textured knits.

Interfacing

Use interfacing wherever the pattern calls for it. Some interfacing fabrics have crosswise stretch making them ideal for knits. Use either fusible or non-fusible interfacing. However, the fusibles are especially good for knits because they can be eliminated from the seam allowance, reducing thickness at the garment edge.

Stitching

Use either a ballpoint or sharp needle for sewing knits. The size will depend on the fabric weight. If you use a sharp needle, make sure it is sharp. A damaged or dull needle will cause holes or runs in your garment.

Use a polyester or polyester/cotton thread when sewing knit fabric. These threads are strong and have some built-in stretch which will make for a strong seam.

Staystitch knits only at waistline seams of fitted garments and necklines where a separate collar is to be applied. All other seams will be stitched with a seam with give so you retain the comfort of the knit fabric. Knits that threaten to stretch out of shape should have the seams reinforced with twill or seam tape, as shown. (fig. 66) This applies mostly to shoulder seams.

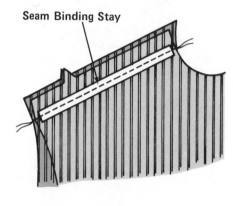

Seam Binding Stay

fig. 66

Stitch with a balanced tension using any of the seam techniques given in the *Seams* chapter. Hold threads at the beginning of each seam so they don't get caught in the bobbin area. (fig. 67)

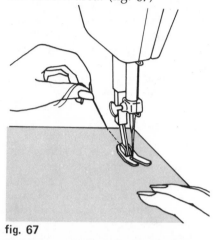

fig. 67

Pressing

Test the iron temperature on fabric scraps. Synthetics will melt if the iron is too hot and some wool will shrink.

Acrylic knits will darken when steam pressed. Allow the fabric to dry completely and come back to its normal color before moving it on the ironing board, or it will stretch out of shape.

Press with an up and down motion to avoid distorting the fabric. Use brown paper strips under darts and seam allowance to avoid impressions on the right side. (fig. 68)

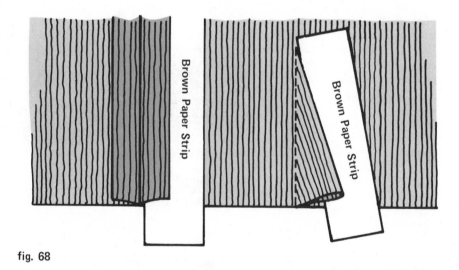

Brown Paper Strip

Brown Paper Strip

fig. 68

Construction Hints

Most knits do not ravel, and seam allowances can be left unfinished or trimmed close to the stitching for a neat finish.

Hems in knits can be done with a machine blind hem or multiple rows of topstitching for a decorative effect. For a truly invisible hem, use the inside hem finish.

Allow garments made from very stretchy knits to hang for 24 hours before marking the hem.

If you are making buttonholes with an automatic buttonhole attachment, put a piece of thin plastic over the buttonhole area before slipping it under the attachment. Remove the plastic before stitching and replace it before taking the work out from under the attachment. This will avoid snagging the fabric.

Buyer's Guide-- Fabrics

Fabrics are a joy to the person who understands how to buy and work with them. Knowledge about fabrics is readily available, but it is not always related to the needs of the home-sewer. We want to give you the essential information you need to buy, use and care for today's textiles.

Today's fabrics bear little relationship to yesterday's fabrics. Present terminology is a bit sloppy and confusing. For instance, polyester is a common word, but do you and your neighbor mean the same thing when you say polyester? Polyester is not the name of any one fabric; polyester is a fiber that is made into yarn and then knit or woven into many different types of fabric. Qiana is another word that is used to mean a specific fabric but it is really DuPont's trade name for a type of nylon fiber. It is useful for the home-sewer to know the difference between generic names such as nylon or polyester and trade names such as Qiana and Dacron.

Fabrics are made from yarn and yarn from fiber. Fibers can be natural or man-made. Listed below are the fibers most often available to the home-sewer and the consumer who buys clothes ready-made.

Natural Fibers

Cotton   Silk
Linen   Wool

Man-Made Fibers

Rayon   Nylon
Acetate   Polyester
Tri-acetate   Acrylic
Spandex

The natural fibers are familiar to everyone. Rayon, acetate and tri-acetate are man-made fibers and are derived from chemically treated cotton linters or wood pulp. The other man-made fabrics are produced by a chemical process from petroleum, coal, oil, water and other raw materials.

It may seem that there are many more man-made fibers than those listed, but in reality, there are many brand names for these fibers. DuPont calls their polyester Dacron. Eastman Chemical calls their polyester Kodel. Monsanto Chemical produces an acrylic which they call Acrilan. Because some brand names have become part of our language, it is important to clarify the difference between the generic name and the brand name. The Federal Trade Commission recognizes nylon, polyester, acrylic and spandex as generic names for four different fibers. They say the generic name must appear on hang tags, labels and in advertisements along with the brand name.

Of course, the manufacturer would like you to recognize his brand name, but from the home-sewer's point of view, it is only necessary to recognize the generic name. If you know how to take care of one brand of nylon, you know how to care for all brands.

Fibers are spun into yarn and yarn is woven or knit into fabric. Weave as well as the fiber help us identify fabrics and determine their suitability for our projects. Also, the weave of the fabric is the source of many familiar names.

Three basic weaves for making fabric are plain, twill and satin. The plain weave is strongest of the three. It is the over and under potholder you made as a child. The lengthwise threads of the fabric, known as the warp, are the strongest. The crosswise threads are known as the weft or filling threads. The plain weave has many variations such as the basket weave, rib weave and pile. Examples of plain weave fabrics are: batiste, broadcloth, chambray, flannel, dress linen, challis, shantung and taffeta.

Plain Weave

The twill weave is almost as durable as the plain weave. It has a diagonal look when examined closely because the filling threads cross the warp threads in a stair-step fashion. Examples of twill weave fabrics are: denim, gabardine, chino, ticking, birdseye and surah.

The satin weave is least durable because a filling thread "floats" over several warp threads. It may also be woven with the warp thread floating over the filling threads. The beauty of the fabric rather than durability is usually the aim. For that reason the satin weave is done primarily in silk, rayon or lustrous man-made fibers. Examples of satin weave fabrics are: Brocade, slipper satin and damask.

Fabric types can be made in several different fibers. Flannel, gabardine and broadcloth are all woven with cotton, wool or man-made fibers. The weave gives the fabric its characteristic look, but the fiber determines the type of garment, the care and to a great extent, the price. We all recognize the difference between cotton flannel and wool flannel or cotton broadcloth and wool broadcloth.

Some fabrics, known as blends, have more than one fiber. Cotton and polyester is a widely used blend. By blending fibers in a fabric we get the best characteristics of both fibers. In a cotton/polyester blend we get the absorbency of the cotton and the strength and crease resistance of the polyester. Blends also help stabilize fabric prices. When the price of cotton climbs you will be apt to find a blend of 65 percent polyester and 35 percent cotton. When prices stabilize on both fibers, the blends are apt to be 50 percent and 50 percent.

Another way of creating fabric from yarn is knitting. Knits were not available to the home-sewer until 15 years ago. The advent of patterns designed for knits, zigzag sewing machines, ball point needles and synthetic thread have encouraged the home-sewer to try lingerie and bathing suits as well as dresses and sportswear in knits.

There are two basic types of knits: warp knits and weft knits. Warp knits tend to be flatter and tighter than weft knits. There is horizontal stretch but little vertical stretch in warp knits. Tricot is an example of a warp knit. Weft knitting is similar to hand knitting. It has stretch in both directions but more across the width of the fabric than the length.

It is unwise to generalize about knit fabrics because the whole industry is growing and changing so fast. Tricot is a good example of this change. It used to be for lingerie only. Today tricot knits in a heavy weight are being used for men's wear and outer garments. Actually, the fiber used for knit fabric, the weight of the knit and the amount of stretch are the important things to the home-sewer. These factors determine the construction techniques and are discussed in the chapter *Working with Special Fabrics*.

There is a category of fabrics known as non-wovens because the fibers are chemically matted together instead of being woven or knit. Felt was the original non-woven, but today you will find non-woven interfacings and luxury non-wovens such as Ultra Suede fabric.

When fabric has been knit or woven, it is known as greige goods and goes to the converter for the final stages of manufacturing. Dyeing and printing are functions of the converter, but unique to today's fabrics are the finishes applied by the converter. They make life easier for all of us and include crease resistance, flame resistance, water repellancy, stain repellancy, permanent press and other features. The consumer has learned to expect fabrics that perform in totally new and much more satisfactory ways.

Many of the finishing processes involve a resin bath. In other words, chemicals are applied to the fabric and then it is heat cured to make the finish durable. A negative factor in these finishes is that the high-speed finishing machinery may pull the fabric off grain. The crosswise threads are no longer at right angles to the lengthwise threads. There is no way to correct the grain when a durable resin finish has been applied. However, the hang of the garment will not be affected if the fabric is off 1 inch (25mm) or less because the finish will hold the crosswise threads in position. Off grain plaids and stripes with a durable resin finish cannot be matched at the seamlines. Since the fabric cannot be straightened it should not be purchased.

Care Prior To Cutting

This brings us to the question of grain perfect fabrics and whether or not an effort should be made to straighten the fabric. Is it really that important to have grain perfect fabric? Yes, we think it is because the garment will never hang perfectly if the fabric is off grain.

Your first step is to check the grain and decide whether it is true.

Twill Weave

Satin Weave

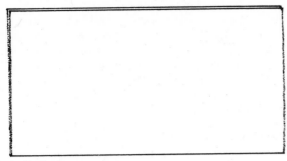

Grain Perfect

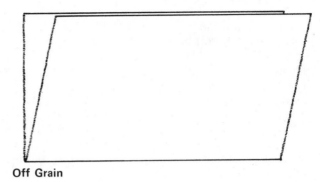

Off Grain

To do this, snip the selvage close to the cut edge and tear a strip across the width of the fabric on both ends. Many fabrics cannot be torn; if it doesn't tear, pull a thread on both ends and cut, following the thread. Now fold your fabric with right sides inside and match the selvage edge. If you have a perfect rectangle, your fabric is grain perfect and you are ready to go ahead with your project.

If the cut edges of the fabric do not match it is not grain perfect and must be straightened, if possible, before cutting. Remember, off grain fabrics that have a durable press finish cannot be straightened; do not buy them.

Baste the torn or cut edges together and then pre-shrink the fabric in the washing machine using a gentle cycle. After washing, put it in the dryer, or spread it out on a flat surface, smoothing out wrinkles and patting the fabric into shape.

If the fabric cannot be washed, take it to a dry cleaner and explain the problem. What you want him to do is straighten the fabric by steaming it back into shape. He cannot do this unless you have basted together the cut edges. We recommend having the cleaner straighten the fabric because he has live steam and usually has a work surface big enough to accommodate the whole piece of fabric.

Tips On Buying Fabric

Choosing the right fabric for the pattern is the most important decision you will make regarding your sewing project. Using ready-to-wear fabrics as a guide is the most reliable way to arrive at a good choice. Also check the suggested fabrics on the pattern envelope.

When you have found the fabric you think you want remember other considerations. Does it carry a brand name? This is an indication of quality. However, check the fabric to make sure there are no flaws in the surface or, if it is a print, in the printing. As we have said before, printed plaids, stripes and geometric designs are frequently crooked and do not follow the crosswise threads of the fabric. This is a serious flaw that no amount of cutting and sewing can correct and it is best not to buy the fabric.

Next, read the care label. Federal law requires that a care label be attached to all fabrics and ready-to-wear garments. Fabrics usually have a bolt end label, but you may be handed a separate label to sew into your garment which is even better. Just be sure you are willing to give the fabric the kind of care recommended on the label.

Buying Interfacings and Linings

Buy interfacings and linings when you buy fabrics. The back of the pattern envelope will give the interfacing yardage but the type and weight of is up to you.

Interfacing is used to support the fabric and keep it from stretching in areas such as collars, cuffs and under buttonholes. It should not change the appearance of the fashion fabric. In other words, don't use a very stiff interfacing in a soft fabric unless you want extra crisp collars and cuffs. A very soft interfacing in a heavy fabric is not good because it will not support the fabric where needed. Drape interfacing and fabric over your hand and see what the effect is. Try this with several different interfacings and decide which one is best for your purpose. What seems confusing at the beginning becomes clear as you acquire more sewing experience. The right interfacing can make the difference between a professional-looking garment and one that looks home-made.

Interfacing may be fusible or nonfusible. (See the *Interfacings* chapter). The fusibles are bonded to the fabric with an iron. They are quite soft before bonding so the drape test won't be completely accurate; the bolt end label will tell you whether the interfacing is dress or suit weight. Instructions come with the interfacing and must be carefully followed in order to get a perfect bond. Most of the fusibles are easy to handle and well worth the minutes spent bonding them to the fabric.

There are also special stretchable interfacings for knits. They will support and give with the knit without changing the appearance of the fashion fabric.

Interfacings come in white, black and a natural color. Choose the one that will not show through your fashion fabric. No one should be aware of the interfacing when the garment is worn.

Be sure the interfacing has the

same care instructions as your fashion fabric — that it can be washed and dried or dry cleaned the same way. If you have pre-shrunk your fashion fabric or are about to, pre-shrink the interfacing too. Woven fusibles should be soaked in a basin of warm water and allowed to drip dry. Non-woven fusibles do not have to be pre-shrunk.

Special fabrics are made for lining garments but you can also choose from an endless array of lightweight blouse or dress fabrics. Two things should be kept in mind when selecting a lining: make sure it is relatively thin and lightweight so it won't affect the fit of the outer shell, and choose one that has a fairly slick surface so you can get into and out of the garment easily.

Solid colored and printed fabrics are available for linings. The choice is up to you. Making a blouse out of the same fabric you use to line a suit is a good way to get a coordinated outfit. This is especially attractive if the fabric is a striking print.

Fabrics By Mail

When the stores in your home town don't have the fabric you want, try one of the mail order firms. Remember though, it takes time to get the swatches through the mail and then order the fabric you need. Following are thumbnail sketches of some firms and the fabrics they carry. A complete list would be impossible because new companies constantly join the mail order ranks. These companies either have a minimum charge for swatches, deductible from the first order, or they have a subscription service for which you pay a flat sum and receive four to six mailings a year.

Britex Fabrics, 146 Geary Street, San Francisco, CA 94022. All credit cards accepted. $2.00 charge for swatches. Britex sent us quality fabric swatches, some basics and some interesting novelty fabrics. Their "personalized swatch

service" will try to find the fabric you need if you fill out and return the questionnaire enclosed.

Fabrics in Vogue, Ltd., Suite 303 East, 200 Park Avenue, New York, NY 10017. Subscription of $10.00 a year includes six mailings. These are advertised as the fabrics found in *Vogue Patterns* magazine. In other words, these are the fabrics used in the photographs in the magazine. Do not expect to find all the fabrics in the magazine. Do expect frequent substitutions such as polyester crepe for silk crepe or "this plaid cotton replaces original fabric which is unavailable." Supposedly *Vogue* editors have approved all substitutions. The fabrics they do have are nice but you must decide whether a $10.00 subscription is worthwhile.

Gem Fabric Centers, 5806 Burnet Road, Austin, TX 78756. Refundable $2.00 charge for swatches. New exciting fabrics — the ones you've been reading about in the fashion magazines. Swatches are small but there is a generous number of them. Easy to order. Not inexpensive but about what you would expect to pay for new, better fabrics.

Herbert Gladson, Ltd., 45 West 45th Street, New York, NY 10036. $3.00 refundable charge for swatches. Attractive, well mounted swatch card; easy to order. Classic fabrics but good coordinates. Prices are average.

Left Bank Fabric Co., 8354 West 3rd, Los Angeles, CA 90048. $5.00 charge for swatches, refundable. Better fabrics with reasonable prices in most cases. They sent 30 good size swatches; however there were no care instructions for any of them. They will try to match or find whatever you need.

Leiter's is not precisely a mail order company. However if you write to Box 978, Kansas City, MO 64141 they will put you in touch with their nearest representative who will show you their fabrics in her own home.

Maxine Fabrics, 417 Fifth Avenue, New York, NY 10016. $1.00 charge in the U.S., $2.00 outside of the U.S. Charges are refundable. Maxine puts together a line of classics and interesting new fabrics. There is a generous selection of small swatches with complete information and reasonable prices.

Natural Fiber Fabric Club, 521 Fifth Avenue, New York, NY 10017. $10.00 yearly subscription. Good professional service. For starters they will send you 24 basic swatches such as velveteen, poplin, voile and shantung that can be ordered in a range of colors. Then you will receive four sets of seasonal swatches at the beginning of each season. Swatches are a generous 2x3 inches. You also receive a handy sewing aid catalog. Subscribers get 20 percent off all prices for fabric and sewing aids; including sale prices.

Sawyer Brook, Box 194, Orford, NH 03777, $2.00 charge. One of the best coordinated and most appealing fabric collections we have seen. Prices are very reasonable. Nice classics with some interesting novelty fabrics. They even have coordinated knitting yarn if you want to make a cardigan to go with your ensemble. Information is really complete. You can order with confidence.

Thai Silks, 393 Main, Los Altos, CA 94022. $2.35 refundable charge, but this will vary with the type of swatches you order. They have interesting imported fabrics and a lot of things other than silk. Prices seem reasonable but it is well to remember that silk varies in quality. It is difficult to wade through all the printed pages they send and find the information that goes with each swatch group. We could find no care instructions and fabric widths are sometimes missing. This would probably be a good source if only they were better organized.

Buyer's Guide--
Patterns

We have said a great deal about the big four pattern companies — Vogue, Butterick, McCall's and Simplicity — but there is a whole group of small, interesting, new and not so new pattern companies that may have exactly what you want for a particular project. These companies are not trying to be all things to all sewers; they are usually specialists in one area. They may not have huge catalogs, but they do have a number of different designs. If they are not available in your area, write to them for information.

Authentic Patterns, P.O. Box 4560, Fort Worth, TX 76106. They specialize in western wear and square dance clothing patterns for men, women and children. These are multi-size patterns with a good guide sheet. You can buy a man's western shirt pattern for $2.00 and if you want to use it again buy a different yoke for a different look for 75 cents.

Burda Patterns, 2750 South Cobb Industrial Blvd., Smyrna, GA 30080. This is a German company, well known in Europe, that features European styling. Their multi-size patterns are reasonably easy to follow. However, Burda has no seam allowance on the patterns. They feel strongly that patterns should be adjusted and then seam allowance added. There is some merit in what they say but

it takes some concentration to remember to add seam allowance to every edge of every pattern piece.

Donner Designs, P.O. Box 6747, Reno, NV 89513. Donner specializes in ski wear kits that include not only pattern and fabric but insulation and everything else you need to make jackets, pants, and overalls for the entire family. They also have separate patterns and fabric. The colors are beautiful and the finished product in their catalog looks very professional. Certainly you can save money. Invest 50 cents in their catalog. These are multi-size patterns with excellent guide booklets.

Folkwear, Box 98, Forrestville, CA 95436. Folkwear produces timeless authentic patterns from Europe, the East and the United States. The people who wore these lovely clothes originally didn't worry much about fit and you won't have to either. One size fits almost everyone, even men and women in one pattern for the Cheese Maker's Smock. Instructions are good and there is interesting background information on each design. Many of the designs call for embroidery and trim. Patterns are printed on heavy paper because they hope you will use them more than once. Folkwear is sold in museum shops as well as fabric and department stores.

Jean Hardy, 2151 La Cuesta Drive, Santa Ana, CA 92705. Jean Hardy patterns are all American. The knit patterns are multi-size and they recommend using the size that is right for the stretch in your knit. Instructions for measuring and sewing are clear and easy to read. Patterns for wovens are based on standard pattern measurements. They have patterns for all kinds of sportswear, including two English riding jackets with riding pants or jodhpurs. One of the jackets and pants comes in children's sizes.

Kwik Sew Patterns, 300 6th Avenue North, Minneapolis, MN 55401. This company has a complete line of patterns — everything from sleepwear to outerwear. Their multi-size patterns are printed in color which makes them easy to follow. The guide sheets are written in a clear, concise style from the home-sewer's point of view.

Spadea, 2 Bridge Street, Milford, NJ 08848. Spadea has been around a long, long time. They make perforated, not printed, patterns. In other words, construction marks, notches etc. are cut in the tissue. Beginners may find this a bit difficult but their styles have an interesting couture look. Spadea is in fabric and department stores and in some newspapers weekly.

Little Miss Muffet, Inc., 6709

Glenbrook Drive, Knoxville, TN 31919. This company specializes in lovely smocked children's clothes with a few for women. It offers both kits and patterns. You don't have to start with a dress; small items like pillows or a delightful Christmas ornament are also available.

Sew Easy Lingerie, 1625 Hennepin Ave., Minneapolis, MN 55403. Sew Easy has patterns for slips, panties, bras, girdles, sleepwear and bathing suits. Their patterns are sold wherever their fabric and trims are sold, but they also do a mail order business. They have everything you need to make lingerie items. This is worth looking into because most lingerie is easily and quickly made for much less than it costs in stores.

SureFit Patterns, 65 Oak Street, Norwood, NJ 07648. SureFit computer patterns are an easy way to get a good fit. You measure as instructed by the company and order the patterns you want. You'll receive a plastic pattern made to your measurements. They guarantee perfect fit without further adjustments on your part. You only measure once unless you gain or lose weight. They store the measurements in the computer so you can reorder when new styles come out. The plastic patterns are durable and easy to use with a tracing wheel and carbon. Write for their four-color catalog and the measurement blank. They have expanded their line considerably and have several new dress designs.

The big four pattern companies have departments that answer consumer mail and deal with consumer problems. Since these companies are so well known we are only giving their addresses.

Butterick Fashion Marketing, 161 Sixth Avenue, New York, NY 10013. Write to them for both **Vogue** and **Butterick.**

McCall Pattern Company, 230 Park Avenue, New York, NY 10017

Simplicity Pattern Company, 200 Madison Avenue, New York, NY 10016

Jean Hardy Western Wear No. 190 & 520

Folkwear Afghani Dress No. 107

Buyer's Guide-- Notions

Anyone who has walked by a well-stocked notions counter has been impressed and perhaps dismayed by the sheer number of items on display. An experienced sewer will have no problem making selections but the beginner can become confused by the variety of notions. How does one decide which items are basic, necessary sewing tools and which items should be added gradually over a period of time?

We suggest, for the beginning sewer, a list of basic sewing tools necessary for the first project. Suggestions are also given for "nice to have" items that can also be purchased if the budget allows. Items not on the basic list can be added gradually.

Basic Sewing Tools

Bent-handled shears — 7 to 10 inch
Pins
Pin Cushion
Chalk Pencil or Tracing Paper and Tracing Wheel
Pack of assorted size Hand Needles (sharps)
Thimble
Tape Measure

"Nice To Have" Tools

Plastic Straight Ruler — 12 to 18 inch
Plastic Curved Ruler
Trimming Scissors — 4 to 6 inch
Seam Ripper
Beeswax
Sewing Gauge
Point Turner

Notions departments should be shopped on a regular basis to review new product developments. Trying out new items is part of sewing fun, but you should be aware that some of the latest notion items might not live up to their publicity. This Buyer's Guide will help you decide what to try or ignore. We discuss not only basic sewing tools but other notion items that will help you with your sewing projects.

Since new items are being developed constantly, this listing cannot be complete. When you find a new or unfamiliar sewing notion, carefully analyze the product; read the instructions and ask yourself these questions. Does the basic concept make sense? Will it simplify or improve a sewing task? Are the instructions easy to follow? Do the benefits to be obtained justify the expense? If the answer is yes to all these questions, try the new item. If you can't answer yes to all the questions, think twice before spending your money.

Remember, not everything performs as advertised, so be cautious in your purchases. Ask store personnel about their experience with a given product. Let them know if and why you aren't satisfied with a certain notion item. Exchange notion discoveries and information with your sewing friends so you are well informed and can make wise purchasing decisions.

The Buyer's Guide has been

divided into two sections. The first section — Sewing Aids — covers handy items to use during the construction process. Of course, no home-sewer needs or has space for all the notions mentioned. However, we give the information that makes it possible for you to choose the notions that will work best for you.

The second section — Notions Incorporated Into The Garment — includes items such as thread, zippers and buttons. Information given will help you select the right style or type of notion item for your project as well as suggested uses for each type of notion.

Sewing Aids

Cutting Tools

Scissors top the list of your basic sewing needs. You will need a good pair of bent-handled shears, 7 to 10 inches long, for cutting fabric. Make sure you buy left-handed shears if you are left-handed. Small trimming scissors, pinking shears and thread nippers are "nice to have" tools. Electric scissors may be suitable for many sewers.

When shopping for your sewing scissors be particularly aware of quality. Every pair of scissors is relatively expensive, so for a slightly higher price you can buy ones you'll enjoy using. They will also last a lifetime with proper care. Buy the best you can afford since they will be used extensively during your sewing career and make sure they are used just for sewing projects.

There are many good brand name scissors, some American and some imported, which are made of the best steel and come with a reasonable warranty. Don't buy a pair of scissors unless you can try out the actual pair you've selected on various fabric samples. Most reputable stores will allow this test. Don't be satisfied with trying the store's sample pair. Not every pair of scissors in a certain line is sharp. Occasionally a bad pair will pass through final inspection. Also, be aware of how the scissors feel in your hand. They must be the right size and feel comfortable.

Lightweight scissors are new in the market. Most top brand names in scissors make a lightweight version of bent-handled shears. They are comfortable in a woman's hand, especially if she is a beginner. However, they might feel quite unusual to the experienced sewer and require some adjustment.

Bent-Handled Shears

There are four sizes of popular bent-handled shears (7, 7½, 8 and 10 inches) so see which size is best for you. While 8 and 10 inch shears are the most popular standard size, 7 or 7½ inch shears are just as sharp and accurate and may be more comfortable for small hands. The new lightweight, bent-handled shears should not be overlooked. If you prefer them to the traditional shears be sure they are heavy enough to cut through the types of fabric you select.

Wiss bent-handled shears, in 6, 8 and 10 inch sizes, are made in the U.S.A. of fine steel and can be resharpened to as-good-as-new. Made by Wiss - The Cooper Group. The company will provide, on request, information on where they can be sharpened in your area. Other acceptable sources of bent-handled shears are: Gingher, Inc.; Joy Scissors, Division of Cole National Corp.; Marks International; United Cutlery, and Kingshead. Approximate Retail Price: (Wiss 8") $13.50

Left-Handed Shears

Wiss makes their 7½ inch cutting shears in left-handed styling. The handles fit the left hand comfortably and the blades are reversed in slant, making cutting much easier for the left handed person. Made by Wiss - The Cooper Group. Other acceptable sources of left-handed shears are: Donahue Sales, Talon Division of Textron, Inc.; Gingher, Inc.; Marks International; United Cutlery, and Kingshead. Approximate Retail Price: (Wiss) $14.00

Lightweight Shears

Lightweight shears have been developed to a degree of efficiency that matches heavy ones. It may be a little difficult to get used to the feel of them if you have worked for years with standard cutting shears. Try the Talon 8 inch Light One with neatly shaped and fitted tortoise shell handles for less of a shock in the change-over. They also come in the 7 inch size for smaller hands. From Donahue Sales, Talon Division of Textron, Inc. Other acceptable sources of lightweight shears are: Gingher, Inc.; Kingshead; Fiskars by

Normark; Rex Cutlery, Division of Cole National Corp.; Wiss - The Cooper Group, and Marks International, Inc. Approximate Retail Price: (Talon 8") $9.50.

The same Talon 8 inch Light One shears for right handers are also made in a left-handed model. Distributed by Donahue Sales, Talon Division of Textron, Inc. Other acceptable sources of lightweight shears for lefties are: Wiss - The Cooper Group; Rex Cutlery, Division of Cole National Corp.; Marks International, Inc., and Fiskars by Normark. Approximate Retail Price: (Talon 8") $9.50

Pinking Shears

Pinking shears come in various sizes, left- or right-handed, and regular or lightweight. Choose the size and weight most comfortable for you, and try them on various scraps of fabric to make sure they cut smoothly. They will be a bit stiffer than regular shears.

Wiss pinking shears come in three sizes, including the big professional size. Wiss has larger teeth than comparable shears from other manufacturers. There is an obvious advantage to a deeper cut — it will stop the ravelling of loosely woven fabrics better than shallow cutting shears. Wiss also makes a scalloping shear, more decorative than useful, but it achieves the same non-ravel edge as the large-tooth shears. Available from Wiss - The Cooper Group. Other acceptable sources of pinking shears are: Gingher, Inc.; Joy Scissors, Division of Cole National Corp.; Kingshead Corp., and Marks International. Approximate Retail Prices: (Wiss pinking) $16.50; (Wiss scalloping) $17.50

Wiss Bent-Handled Shears

Talon Light One

Wiss Pinking Shears

Scovill Electric Scissors

Gingher Buttonhole Scissors

Scissors II Quipper

Not all pinking shears come in a left-handed model, but Joy Scissors makes an 8½ inch pinking shear for lefties. They are made from good nickel and chrome plated surgical steel. Since right-handed pinking shears are especially difficult for left-handed people to use, these are worth waiting for even if you have to special order them. Joy Scissors are made by Rex Cutlery. Other acceptable sources of pinking shears for the left-handed are: Gingher, Inc.; Wiss - The Cooper Group, and Marks International, Inc. Approximate Retail Price: (Joy) $16.50

A sturdy 8 inch pinking shear doesn't have to be heavy. The Scissors II has the steel blades and molded handles of the other lightweight shears in the same line, and cuts sharply for at least 15 years according to their warranty. They're made in the U.S.A. by Rex Cutlery. Another acceptable source of lightweight pinking shears is Marks International, Inc. Approximate Retail Price: (Scissors II) $15.00

Trimming Scissors

Small trimming scissors or shears are handy to keep at the sewing machine or ironing board for trimming and clipping jobs. Choose from straight-handled trimming or embroidery scissors, small bent-handled shears or the new, lightweight scissors or shears in smaller sizes.

Good quality, straight-handled scissors are made from hot-dropped, forged surgical steel with nickel and chrome plating. They will have fine and accurate

points giving years of service. Joy Scissors, made by Rex Cutlery, offers fine quality embroidery scissors from 3½ to 6 inches and straight-handled scissors in 5 and 6 inch sizes. Other acceptable sources of straight-handled scissors are: Gingher, Inc.; Marks International, Inc.; Wiss - The Cooper Group; United Cutlery, and Kingshead. Approximate Retail Prices: (Joy 3½") $8.00; (Joy 5") $8.50.

Trimming and clipping jobs are easy to do with a pair of small, 6 inch bent-handled shears. They are made from the finest quality steel and have sharp, accurate points. Wiss - The Cooper Group makes a fine quality pair of small shears for your trimming and clipping needs. Approximate Retail Price: (Wiss) $12.00

There is little reason for making small scissors or shears in a light weight except that it's fun to have a matching set of cutting tools. However, they have one disadvantage over conventional weight scissors and shears — they do not have as fine a point. You can choose from equally good Scissors II by Rex Cutlery, or Talon, from Donahue Sales, Talon Division of Textron, Inc. Other acceptable sources of lightweight scissors and shears are: Fiskars by Normark; Kingshead, and Marks International, Inc. Approximate Retail Price: (Scissors II) $7.00

Electric Scissors

Electric scissors are excellent for sewers who have arthritis or a damaged wrist or hand. These compact scissors are available in

one or two speeds and can handle most fabric weights. Some have cords but others are battery powered which makes them even easier to use. Practice on scrap material will help acquire ease in handling electric scissors.

Dritz Single Speed Electric Scissors are readily available and will do a good cutting job on most fabrics. They are distributed by Scovill, Sewing Aids Division. Approximate Retail Price: $15.00

Buttonhole Scissors

Buttonhole scissors are small and sharp with a special design allowing them to cut open buttonholes without cutting the garment fabric at buttonhole ends. They have an adjustable screw allowing for different length buttonholes.

Fine quality buttonhole scissors are available from Gingher, Inc. They work on all weights of fabric and make a tedious job easy. Other acceptable sources of buttonhole scissors are: Marks International, Inc., and Wiss - The Cooper Group. Approximate Retail Price: $13.00

Thread Nippers

Thread nippers are handy little gadgets to keep near your sewing machine for cutting stray threads and small clipping jobs.

The inexpensive Quipper by Scissors II is an easy-grip (works in either hand) pair of thread nippers. It comes with a 15 year guarantee from Rex Cutlery, Division of Cole National Corp. Other acceptable sources of thread nippers are: Marks International,

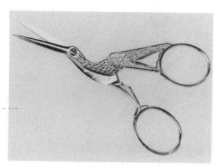

Joy Stork Scissors

Inc.; Wiss - The Cooper Group; United Cutlery; Fiskars by Normark, and Scovill, Sewing Notions Division. Approximate Retail Price: (Quipper) $6.00

Tiny Sewing Basket Scissors

If you carry a small sewing or embroidery bag or basket you will need tiny scissors for snipping thread. Joy Scissors makes the traditional gold-plated stork scissors which are sharp, attractive, and have a fine point. You might prefer Joy Folding Scissors, which take up even less space than the stork scissors and prevent accidental snagging. Both are from Joy Scissors, made by Rex Cutlery. Other acceptable sources of stork scissors and folding scissors are: United Cutlery; Marks International, Inc., and Scovill, Sewing Notions Division. Approximate Retail Price: (Joy "stork") $6.50

General Purpose Scissors

If the family is using your good sewing shears to trim carpets, cut leather and snip electrical wire, buy them a pair of Cut Anything Shears. They are designed to cut through almost anything except very heavy metal or wood. They're light and easy to handle for large or small hands and will save your sewing shears a lot of grief. Available from E-Z Buckle, Inc. Another acceptable source of general purpose shears is: Wiss - The Cooper Group. Approximate Retail Price: $6.00

Cutting Boards

A folding cutting board is a valuable cutting aid. If the family dining table has to serve as your cutting table, cover it with a cardboard cutting board to protect its surface. Or lay the cutting board out on the floor or a twin size bed for a convenient cutting surface.

The Superboard by Dritz opens to 40 by 72 inches and folds away to a convenient 12 by 40 inches. It is marked in 1 inch squares with metric equivalents. There are also lines for cutting bias, and patterns for drawing circles and scallops in several sizes. Made by Scovill, Sewing Notions Division. Approximate Retail Price: $5.50

One primary purpose of measuring is to make garments fit properly. The E-Z Pattern Cutting Board has simplified working with the flat, two-dimensional pattern, making it more understandable in terms of the three-dimensional figure. If you measure for a size 12 top and a size 14 skirt, you will find adjusting your pattern much simpler on this board. There are also inch and centimeter grids, bias and scallop patterns and an armhole curve for easy reference. A product of E-Z Buckle, Inc. Approximate Retail Price: $5.00

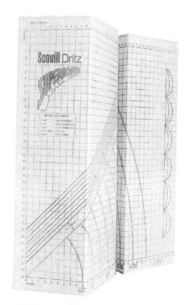

Scovill Dritz Superboard

Weights

A fabric or pattern weight can be any heavy ashtray or other household object, but a set of six weights from Bo Sew Accents will do an even better job. They are plastic covered, smooth on one side with thumb tacks on the other. The tack side is especially good for holding very heavy fabrics to a cutting board. If the fabric is more delicate, use the smooth side. You can keep the fabric grain straight and hold the pattern in place without pins by using several of these weights at strategic spots. Approximate Retail Price: $6.00

Pins

Pins are classified according to length, diameter and metal. Size numbers correspond to pin length in 1/16 inch measurements. For example, a No. 16 pin is 16/16 inches or 1 inch long. A No. 20 pin is 20/16 inches or 1¼ inches long. The smallest diameter or finest pin is a silk pin. The next size up used for home-sewing is a dressmaker pin with a diameter slightly larger than the silk pin. Most pins are made from brass or steel and have nickel plating to prevent oxidation. Stainless steel pins with maximum corrosion resistance are available in some pin types. Pins with large glass or plastic heads are good for pinning patterns onto fabric. Do not use them for basting since they break sewing machine needles. The head holds the entire pin up too high for the machine foot to go over easily. Always buy fine quality pins since bargain pins can damage fine fabrics.

Pins For General Use

Clinton Silk Pins come in brass or steel — the steel pins seem slightly sharper and can be picked up with a magnet. The advantage of brass is it will not rust. Clinton Ball Point Pins are also steel, in the same size, but with points especially good for knits. From Scovill, Sewing Notions Division.

Scovill Clinton Pins

E-Z Pin Cushion

Risdon Pin Dispenser

Other acceptable sources of pins for general use are: Coats & Clark; Donahue Sales, Talon Division of Textron; Penn Products Co., and Risdon Mfg. Co. Approximate Retail Prices: Under $1.00

Clinton Plastic Head Pins come in a variety of sizes, from the Small Head ones that are extra fine to the Jumbo (1½ inches long) and the Super (1¾ inches long). All of these are good for pinning patterns on fabrics of varying weights, from fine voiles to heavy woolen coatings. They are not to be used for cross-in basting to be run through the machine. Their only advantage is that the plastic head does not tear through a paper pattern. From Scovill, Sewing Notions Division. Other acceptable sources of large head pins are: Coats & Clark; Donahue Sales, Talon Division of Textron; Penn Products Co., and Risdon Mfg. Co. Approximate Retail Prices: Under $1.00

Pins Professionals Prefer

If you or any of your friends are going to Switzerland, buy Iris Silk Pins. They are, unfortunately, not sold in the U.S.A. They are extra fine, extra long steel pins that have the most delicate points imaginable. A pin now available in this country, imported from Switzerland, is the Angel Pin. It is almost identical to, if not the same as, the Iris Silk Pin. Be careful when using these pins since they

break rather than bend when placed under stress. Never sew over them with the machine. A piece of pin could break under the machine needle and fly into your eye. Angel Pins are available from Angel Aids. Approximate Retail Price: $2.00

Pin Cushions

Keeping your pins organized and in one or more convenient places is the job of pin cushions. Use as many different types as you need to keep your sewing area neat and efficient.

The little tomato pin cushion with an emery strawberry attached has been around for a long time and is still a useful piece of equipment. The emery cleans and sharpens needles better than anything else and the cushion keeps its firmness a long time. The E-Z Pin Cushion has a needle threader attached as an added attraction. Available from E-Z Buckle Co. Other acceptable sources of this type of pin cushion are: Penn Products Co.; Risdon Mfg. Co., and Scovill, Sewing Notions Division. Approximate Retail Price: (E-Z Buckle) Under $1.00

Wrist Pin Cushion

Some people would not be without their wrist pin cushions, others find they get in the way. A good one for the price is the Belding Wrist Pin Cushion, fabric covered and on a plastic band.

Other acceptable sources for the wrist pin cushion are: Scovill, Sewing Notions Division; Risdon Mfg. Co.; E-Z Buckle, and Penn Products Co. Approximate Retail Price: (Belding) Under $1.00

Pin Dispenser

The Magnetic Pin Dispenser from Risdon Mfg. is a good substitute for the traditional pin cushion. A large opening at the top of the plastic container is surrounded by a magnet which keeps pins in place, ready to be picked out. Of course, steel pins must be used for the magnet to work. The dispenser comes supplied with large head pins. This new type of pin holder is great for picking up spilled pins or individual pins scattered around on the cutting board. Made by Risdon Mfg. Another acceptable source of magnetic pin caddies is: Scovill, Sewing Notions Division. Approximate Retail Price: (Risdon) $2.20

Hand Needles

Hand needles are classified according to type and size. Needle sizes go from 1, the largest, to 12, the smallest. The sizes generally used for dressmaking are 5 through 10. Sharps are the needle type used for dressmaking. Betweens, which are shorter than Sharps, can also be used for fine sewing jobs. Milliners needles are

SEWING MACHINE Needle Sizes						
American	10	12	14	16	18	19
Metric	70	80	90	100	110	120
Fabric Weight	Delicate	Medium Light	Medium	Medium Heavy	Heavy	Extra Heavy

longer than Sharps and Betweens, and are useful for the long quick stitches used in hand basting. Darners and Crewel needles have longer eyes than Sharps, Betweens or Milliners and may be easier for some people to thread.

When you find a good brand of needles like Clinton, you should get several types in assorted sizes. Or if you don't sew often, buy their assortment pack containing different types and sizes. No one type of needle is designed to do every job. The quality of the brand matters when selecting hand needles. Clinton also makes ballpoint needles for use on stretch fabrics. From Scovill, Sewing Notions Division. Other acceptable sources of hand sewing needles are: Risdon Mfg. Co.; Coats & Clark, and Boye Needle Co. Approximate Retail Prices: Under $1.00

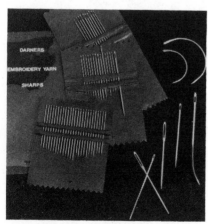

Scovill Hand & Repair Needles

Sight Saving Needles

It's easier on your eyes to slip thread into the needle's eye from the top of Belding's Self Threading Needles than it is to push the end of the thread into a conventional needle eye. These needles are not made in the slimmest sizes but are good utility needles; especially for quick mending jobs such as basting. Available from Belding Lily Co. Other acceptable sources of self-threading hand needles are: Coats & Clark; E-Z Buckle; Penn Products Co.; Risdon Mfg. Co., and Scovill, Sewing Notions Division. Approximate Retail Price: (Belding) Under $1.00

Repair Needles

The seven assorted Repair Needles from Dritz will help you mend everything in the house your ordinary needles can't handle. The package contains upholstery and carpet needles and two sizes of curved needles. Available from Scovill, Sewing Notions Division. Other acceptable sources for similar needle assortments are: Risdon Mfg. Co., and Penn Products Co. Approximate Retail Price: (Dritz) Under $1.00

Leather Needles

Glover or leather hand needles should be used whenever you sew leather or leather-like fabrics such as Ultra Suede fabric. These needles have a sharp wedge point that slides through the fabric easily and makes hand sewing a snap. Risdon Mfg. Company packages four leather needles in assorted sizes. Use the finest size when working with leather-like fabrics. Another source for leather hand needles is: Scovill, Sewing Notions Division. Approximate Retail Price: (Risdon) Under $1.00

Sewing Machine Needles

The proper size and type of machine needle is necessary to create perfect seams. Needle size should coordinate with thread size (fine needles for fine thread — large needles for heavy thread) and the point type should be chosen relative to the fabric.

The two most common types of needle points are the ballpoint,

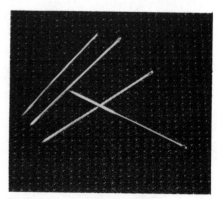

Risdon Leather Hand Needles

suitable for knits and elastic fabric, and the cutting or sharp point, suitable for some knits and all woven fabrics. Leather needles have small wedge shaped points that enable the needle to cut through the leather easily.

Needle sizes are standard among manufacturers and fall under the American and/or Metric numbering system. Refer to the chart for needle size equivalents.

Needles wear out so they should be replaced often, sometimes after every garment. Points become dull from ordinary wear or by hitting pins or metal zipper parts. Dull or bent needles can cause skipped stitches or damaged fabrics.

Special Sewing Machine Needles

Schmetz Needle of Germany has developed special needles for specific fabrics or sewing problems. They offer special swim and ski wear needles, a no-skip, stretch fabric needle, a topstitch/basting needle, a Jeans needle for sewing heavy denim fabric and a needle with a slit in the eye for people with impaired sight. Double and triple machine needles can be used for decorative stitching. Two or three threads are used on top of the machine while one thread is used in the bobbin. Schmetz Needle of Germany makes fine quality needles of this type. Look for Schmetz Needles at fine fabric stores and most sewing machine shops. Approximate Retail Prices: Under $2.00

Pressing Equipment

One important group of sewing aids is your pressing equipment. A well made garment should be pressed during construction. Proper use of the right pressing aid will help create a professional look. The basic pressing necessities are an ironing board and a good steam iron. Other pressing aids can be purchased as money and space allows.

Dressmaker's Hams

A Dressmaker's Ham is a useful item at the ironing board. It allows you to build in body shape as you press a garment during construction. It is especially valuable when tailoring a garment. The Risdon Dressmaker's Ham is sturdy, lightweight and will not absorb moisture or mildew. Available from Risdon Mfg. Co. Approximate Retail Price: $7.00

A new Tailor's Ham with interesting curves weighs less than one pound and fits into the June Tailor Hamholder. Both hands can consequently be free for handling the fabric and iron. The two pieces are sold separately but make a good combination for those who need something larger than a Pressing Mitt for tailoring. Both products are available from June Tailor, Inc. Approximate Retail Prices: (Ham) $8.50; (Hamholder) $7.00

Pressing Mitt

You may not want to invest money or space for a large Dressmaker's Ham, but you should at least have a Dritz Pressing Mitt for rounding the ends of darts and pressing curves into hiplines. The mitt can be slipped onto the left hand so that, with the iron in the right hand, you have double action in a pressing motion. You can also lay the mitt down on the ironing board and use it like a small ham. Available from Scovill, Sewing Notions Division. Other acceptable sources for Pressing Mitts are: The Risdon Mfg. Co., and June Tailor, Inc. Approximate Retail Price: (Dritz) $3.00

Tailor's Clapper

The Risdon Tailor's Clapper is made of smooth hardwood with a grooved side for a comfortable hand grip. It is used to flatten bulky facing, collar and lapel edges. It will also smooth buttonholes and set pleats. An essential tool for fine tailored garments the clapper is made by Risdon Mfg. Co. Other acceptable sources of Clappers are: June Tailor, Inc., and Scovill, Sewing Notions Division. Approximate Retail Price: (Risdon) $4.00

Point Presser

The combination Point Presser & Pounding Block made by Risdon is the perfect tool for helping you get exact points on collars, cuffs and lapels. It can also be used to flatten garment and facing edges. It is two tools in one — a point presser and clapper. Made of

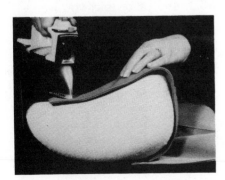

June Tailor Tailor's Ham

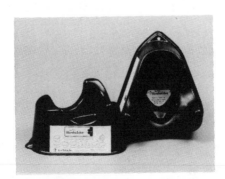

June Tailor Hamholder

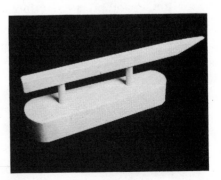

Risdon Point Presser/Pounding Block

June Tailor Seam Roll

Scovill Dritz Folding Sleeve Board

June Tailor Velvaboard

smooth hardwood, it won't snag even your finest knits. Made by Risdon Mfg. Co. Another acceptable source of Point Pressers is: June Tailor, Inc. Approximate Retail Price: (Risdon) $9.00

Seam Roll

The June Tailor Seam Roll measures 14 inches long and is a great help when pressing open seams of sleeves, pants legs and other hard-to-get-at places. It also prevents seam impressions from showing on the right side of the garment because of its curved surface. Covered with two types of fabric, it is sturdy yet lightweight and easy to handle. From June Tailor, Inc. Other acceptable sources of seam rolls are: Risdon Mfg. Co., and Scovill, Sewing Notions Division. Approximate Retail Price: (June Tailor) $7.00

Sleeve Boards

If you have limited space and can't set up a full size ironing board in your sewing area, you should own the Dritz Folding Sleeve Board. You can set it up on the end of a cutting table or on your dresser and press everything from a skirt seam to a narrow sleeve on it. It folds to store and replacement covers are available. From Scovill, Sewing Notions Division. Other acceptable sources for folding sleeve boards are: Risdon Mfg. Co., and June Tailor, Inc. Approximate Retail Price: (Dritz) $10.00

Needle Board

Napped fabrics need special care

when pressing to prevent crushing or damaging the pile. The Dritz Needle-Board provides just the right surface for pressing delicate velvets without leaving iron marks. The board measures 5"x13" and good instructions are included in the package. Available from Scovill, Sewing Notions Division. Approximate Retail Price: $20.00

Velvaboard For Napped Fabrics

A new twist to the traditional needle board is the Velvaboard from June Tailor. This flexible pad measures a big 12"x16" so you won't have to reposition the garment so often when pressing. It holds steam in the bristled pad and reflects it back up into the fabric for super steam pressing. Available from June Tailor, Inc. Approximate Retail Price: $10.00

Pressing Cloths

There are few home sewing jobs that require the old-fashioned heavy pressing cloth. The Dritz Vue-Thru Pressing Cloth has the advantage of allowing you to see what you are pressing — not getting in an extra wrinkle or folding back a seam. It is scorch proof and works especially well with a steam iron. Available from Scovill, Sewing Notions Division. Other acceptable sources of lightweight pressing cloths are: E-Z Buckle; Risdon Mfg. Co., and June Tailor, Inc. Approximate Retail Price: (Dritz) $2.00

The non-woven Jiffy Press Cloth can be used dry with a steam iron but is especially good for wet use. It is not as easy to see through as the woven type of lightweight cloth but it absorbs water much better and more evenly. It also has enough bulk to protect the soleplate of the iron from hook-and-eye fasteners or other items which might scratch it. Made by Staple Sewing Aids Corp. Approximate Retail Price: Under $1.00

June Tailor, Inc. has a special pressing cloth to be used when top pressing napped fabrics. Called the Bristled Pressing Cloth it should be used to protect velvets, corduroys and other napped or pile fabrics whenever pressing on the right side is required. It allows steam to pass through to the fabric and prevents flattening, marking or matting. Available from June Tailor, Inc. Approximate Retail Price: $6.00

Pressing Pad

If you use this super size (21x35 inches) Cushioned Pressing Pad from June Tailor, Inc. you won't need an ironing board. It can be used on any flat surface and also comes in a smaller size (12x16 inches) which is ideal for travel. The reversible pad is cushioned and absorbent on one side, and firm and non-absorbent on the other so it can be used for all kinds of pressing jobs. It prevents a shiny, flattened, over-pressed look. It is great for pressing needlework projects too. Approximate Retail Price: $5.00

Uni-Pressboard

The Uni-Pressboard is an all-in-one pressing tools that takes over the functions of many separate tools. It serves as a tailor's ham, sleeve board, point presser, seam roll and clapper. If your sewing space is limited this might be just the tool for you. Available from Elizabeth Mohr Jones Ph.D. Approximate Retail Price: $19.00

Tailor Board

June Tailor, Inc. offers a multi-curved pressing board which comes in a folding and non-folding model. The Tailor Board allows for the proper pressing of facing edges, lapel points and curved seams which can be difficult to do with just an ordinary iron and ironing board. Special fitted covers are available to fit the curved edge whenever a cushioned pressing surface is desired. Approximate Retail Price: $15.00

Iron Soleplates

The Iron Safe is a perforated, metal soleplate covered with a thick coating of Teflon that can be attached to the bottom of a conventional steam iron with a metal spring. It protects fabrics from scorching, allows you to press on the right side without the need of a pressing cloth and prevents fusible materials from sticking to the bottom of the iron. This is a super iron accessory for anyone who does a lot of dressmaking. Made by Jacobson Products. Approximate Retail Price: $6.00

Iron All by Stacy is a soleplate attachment for your iron that prevents scorching and fabric shine. You will never have to use a pressing cloth to protect your fabrics if you have this perforated soleplate cover attached to your iron. Made of a space-age material it has one disadvantage. It does not have a slick surface like the Iron Safe and will collect debris from fusible materials. Be careful when using it with fusible interfacings and fusible webbing. Made by Stacy Fabrics Corp. Approximate Retail Price: $4.00

Seam Presser

The Osrow Steamstress II is a lightweight plastic steamer, less expensive than other steam irons, and useful for the kind of sewing room press-as-you-go operations that make your garments look professional. It steams well, is guaranteed never to scorch, and should be kept exclusively as sewing room equipment. One advantage it has over most steam irons is that it can be used in a vertical position to train the folds in draperies, or touch up a hem of a garment hanging on a dress form. It is great for pressing napped fabrics such as velvet since the steam does the work and doesn't damage the nap. Made by Osrow Products Co., Inc. Approximate Retail Price: $17.00

Travel Iron

There is no need for a large awkward iron in the sewing room, especially with modern easy care fabrics. The General Electric Deluxe Spray, Steam & Dry Travel Iron puts out a generous amount of steam, yet is small enough to use with ease on women's and children's clothes. It has the additional advantage of an "open-throat" handle so that the point can slip into the tiniest corners. The water is not stored inside the iron but in a detachable plastic bulb which makes it possible to use tap water without the slightest danger of corrosion. Available from General Electric, Small Appliances Division. Approximate Retail Price: $27.00

Iron Cleaner

Use Dritz iron-off to clean your iron. This iron cleaning paste can be used on the soleplate of a hot iron to remove residue from iron-on fusibles, interfacings and patches. It will also clean fabric deposits, melted synthetics and starch build-up. Iron-off is non-toxic, non-abrasive and non-flammable. Available from Scovill, Sewing Notions Division. Approximate Retail Price: $1.50

Cover Fastener

Pressing jobs are easier if the ironing board cover is smooth and taut. A set of Cover Fasteners from Travco will give you the desired surface and they can be used again when you have to replace a worn cover. Available at most hardware stores and housewares counters. Approximate Retail Price: Under $1.00

Cord Holder

Keeping the iron cord out of your way while pressing at the ironing board can be difficult. The Iron Cord Holder from Travco will solve this problem nicely. It attaches to the edge of the ironing board with a screw clamp and has a long flexible arm with a clamp on top to hold the cord. The arm folds down against the board for easy storage so you can leave the cord holder in place indefinitely.

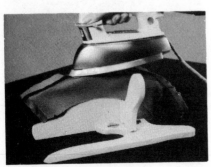

June Tailor Tailor Board

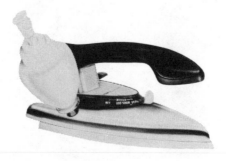

G.E. Travel Iron

Available at most hardware stores or housewares counters. Approximate Retail Price: $1.80

Measuring And Altering Tools

Measuring tools are necessary for accurate sewing. Before you cut out a garment you will need to alter your pattern or at least check the measurements. You also need to measure the grain line for straightness when pinning the pattern to the fabric. For measuring needs there are a number of aids including tape measures, rulers (straight and curved), T-squares and cutting boards with measurements. For all small measuring jobs such as hems and buttonholes there are also special tools. And now that the metric system is increasingly used, many aids for adjusting to that system are on the market.

Measuring for fit requires the use of more than a tape measure and a good dressmaker's curve; it also requires a proper understanding of the flat two-dimensional pattern. The "personalized" dress form is not the cure for fitting problems that many home-sewers think it should be. It may help you see problem areas that are hard to see in the mirror but it is rigid and does not breathe, so there is always the danger of overfitting. A dress form can be of more help to an advanced seamstress with a better understanding of what she can and cannot expect of it.

Tape Measures

An efficient tape measure should be 60 inches long and strong enough to withstand normal wear and tear. The Dritz Lifetime Tape Measure is made of sturdy fiberglass and has a replacement guarantee against stretching or tearing in normal use. It also has inches on one side and inches plus centimeters on the other. Made by Scovill, Sewing Notions Division. Other acceptable sources for durable tape measures are: E-Z Buckle, and Risdon Mfg. Approximate Retail Price: $1.00

This little 60 inch tape measure snaps back into its colorful plastic case. While of little use in the sewing room it is great to keep in your purse for checking fabric width or other measurements in the store. The Spring Tape Measure is available in several colors and is manufactured by Risdon Mfg. Co. Another acceptable source for a 60 inch spring type tape measure is: Scovill, Sewing Notions Division. Approximate Retail Price: $1.25

Rulers

A yardstick designed for pattern alteration and layout is much better for sewing than a plain wooden yardstick. The Fashion Square can turn into a T-square, or a triangle or an L-Square and then lock into position for an easy to use yardstick. It is also made of see-through plastic. From Fashionetics Inc. Approximate Retail Price: $4.00

The Fashion Ruler is a good professional tool for pattern alteration and other uses. The curve is suitable for drafting or redrawing the armhole, crotch or neckline curves. The straight edge has handy parallel slots. The smaller Mini Ruler version is useful for children's clothes. It is also favored by quilters and others who must draw or trace curved designs. Both from Fashionetics Inc. Approximate Retail Prices: (Ruler) $4.00; (Mini Ruler) $2.00

Pattern alterations, length adjustments and buttonhole spacing are easily done with the 18 inch long plastic ruler made by C-Thru Ruler Co. It is two inches wide and has the entire surface marked off in a ⅛ inch grid, which is great for all kinds of measuring problems. It's also a handy ruler for general household needs. Manufactured by C-Thru Ruler Company. Approximate Retail Price: $1.75

The 4 inch wide Dritz See-Thru Dressmaker's Ruler is equipped with parallel slots at several widths for marking out bias strips, straightening grainlines, and many other uses. It is marked in inches and centimeters, both along the 15 inch edge and across the ends. Made by Scovill, Sewing Notions Division. Approximate Retail Price: $2.00

Sewing Gauges

The simplest and most utilitarian of measuring devices is what many home-sewers need for

Scovill Dritz Lifetime Tape Measure

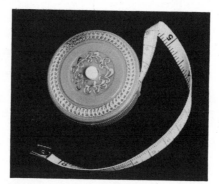
Risdon Spring Tape Measure

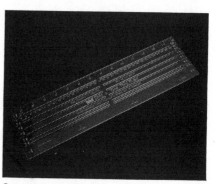
Scovill Dritz See-Thru Ruler

little jobs. The Singer Sewing and Knitting Gauge has all the necessities and no frills. The slider works with precision; there are markings in both inches and centimeters, and it can also be used by knitters. It is properly priced at the low end of the range of all the types of gauges on the market. It is made in the U.S.A. for the Singer Sewing Co. Other acceptable sources for this 6 inch Sewing Gauge are: E-Z Buckle; Risdon Mfg. Co., and Scovill, Sewing Notions Division. Approximate Retail Price: Under $1.00

This Talon gauge will probably do more jobs for the price than any other similar product available. Besides a smooth-running slider, metric and inch measurements, and an end which makes an excellent point turner, it has a layered metal slot at the other end for holding buttons at the correct shank depth while they are being sewn in place. There are three possible depths for varying thicknesses of fabric so that all the shanks will be uniformly controlled. It has a hole in the slider and one in the point for pin and pencil, also a feature of many other gauges, which acts as a simple compass for drawing scallops and other curves. Made by Donahue Sales, Talon Division of Textron. Another acceptable sewing gauge of this type is available from Risdon Mfg. Co. Approximate Retail Price: (Talon) Under $1.00

Talon Universal Gauge

Talon Buttonhole Spacer

Buttonhole Spacers

Especially on knits and fabrics which do not have an obvious grain, it is often difficult to line up and mark the length of buttonholes accurately. The Talon Buttonhole Spacer and Sizer makes it possible to adjust the angle and length of the buttonholes accurately. It also helps achieve an even distance between buttonholes. Made of metal, the Talon Buttonhole Spacer and Sizer is clearly marked in metric and inches. The only drawback is that the sliding piece could fit a little tighter to the main piece. Distributed by Donahue Sales, Talon Division of Textron. Approximate Retail Price: Under $1.00

The Simflex Gauge from Brewer Sewing Supplies Co. makes marking buttonhole spaces a snap. Stretch the gauge until the spaces are what you need, then lay it on the garment and mark each point for equal buttonhole spaces. Approximate Retail Price: $3.50

Fitting A Pattern

Fashionetics Fash-on is especially useful in achieving a personal basic pattern, and for those people who need to see three-dimensionally. It is a fine, supple material which irons on to the back of a pattern, making it possible to work with the pattern as though it were a muslin. It may be difficult to use on yourself but is great in a classroom situation, or if you have a good dress form. From Fashionetics Inc. Approximate Retail Price: $3.00

The Dritz My Double dress form is a wire mesh form which hooks together over your body and can be pushed and molded into your shape. Mounted on a stand and covered with an elasticized cover, it is as successful as any body-fitted dress form. However, the custom-made professional dress form is best. Made by Scovill, Sewing Notions Division. Approximate Retail Price: $50.00

Fashionetics Fash-On

Pattern Tissues

Mend-A-Pattern from Fantastic Fit Products consists of a 12 yard by 3 inch roll of pattern tissue and a glue stick which can be used to lengthen, alter or mend paper patterns. This makes the job much easier because the tissue strip is marked off in one-inch intervals. Available from Fantastic Fit Products. Approximate Retail Price: $2.00

Give new life to your favorite pattern and reinforce new ones with Pattern Saver — a press-on backing. It can be used for home decorating and craft projects. Pattern Saver is pre-packaged and comes in 8.2 feet by 22 inch (2.5m by 56cm) sizes. It is available from Pellon Corp. Approximate Retail Price: $2.30

You need tracing material when working with multi-size master patterns and Perma-Trace is a good choice. This strong, see-through material can be used to make new patterns and duplicate old, worn-out patterns. It can also be sewn up for trial fittings. It comes pre-packaged and is 13.1 feet by 25 inches (4m by 63.5cm). Available from Pellon Corp. Approximate Retail Price: $1.80

Marking Tools

Most notions manufacturers have worked hard in the last few years to perfect marking tools. On some fabrics, such as thick tweeds, you will still have to rely on thread tailor tacks, made patiently by hand. However, most other fabrics can usually be marked by tracing paper, dressmaker's pencil or one of the new washable marking pens. One type of marking device will not work on all fabrics, so be prepared to invest in several types of marking tools for your various sewing projects. Fortunately, marking tools are not expensive.

Tracing Papers

Tracing paper is one of the easiest and most convenient methods of transferring pattern construction marks to fabric. However, even though most packages are marked "Washable and Dry Cleanable," that applies only if the marks have not been pressed sometime during the construction process. They will wash or dry clean out of some fabrics after being pressed, but you only find that out by pre-testing a fabric scrap or completing the garment and then waiting to see what happens during the initial washing or cleaning. Tracing paper comes in two types; carbon-coated on one or both sides. The double-coated paper is handy to use when marking two layers of fabric at one time by slipping it inbetween the wrong sides of the fabric layers. Packages of tracing paper contain three to five different colors. Choose the selection that best fits your sewing needs. Acceptable sources for tracing paper are: E-Z Buckle Co.; Penn Products Co.; Risdon Mfg. Co.; Scovill, Sewing Notions Division, and Singer Co. Approximate Retail Price: Under $1.00

Tracing Wheels

The chubby plastic handle of the Gold Label Tracing Wheel makes it easy to hold and control. The wheel is serrated for a clear dotted line on the fabric. Be sure to use it on a cutting board or there will be a dotted line on your table top. Available from E-Z Buckle Co. Other acceptable sources for serrated tracing wheels are: Penn Products; Risdon Mfg. Co., and Scovill, Sewing Notions Division. Approximate Retail Price: (E-Z Buckle) Under $1.00

For some purposes such as certain embroidery designs and applique, you might prefer a smooth line to the dotted one given by a serrated wheel. The Belding Smooth Edge Tracing Wheel will give you a smooth line. It has a handle with a finger guide that makes it easy to control direction. An added aid is a magnet which will pick up stray pins. From Belding Lily Co. Other acceptable sources for smooth tracing wheels are: Penn Products Co.; Risdon Mfg. Co., and Scovill, Sewing Notions Division. Approximate Retail Price: (Belding) Under $1.00

Tailor's Chalk

The square plastic holder for Dritz Tailor's Chalk keeps your hands and the chalk clean. The chalk is, therefore, usable a lot longer. There is also a built-in sharpener in the holder which keeps the edge of the chalk sharp. Refills are available in a package of three colors. From Scovill, Sewing Notions Division. Other acceptable sources of tailor's chalk

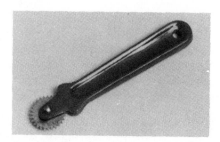

Gold Label Tracing Wheel

are: E-Z Buckle Co.; Penn Products Co., and Risdon Mfg. Co. Approximate Retail Price: (Dritz) Under $1.00

The Dritz Tailor's Chalk Pencil is similar to a mechanical pencil in that it can be refilled. However, the pencil line is not fine and this pencil is not as easy to use as the regular Dressmaker's Pencil which can be sharpened easily. From Scovill, Sewing Notions Division. Other acceptable sources for a chalk pencil are: E-Z Buckle Co.; Penn Products, and Risdon Mfg. Co. Approximate Retail Price: (Dritz) Under $1.00

Dritz Powder Chalk Refill is intended for use in the chalk skirt marker but it is also useful to quilters. The pink is dark enough to show up on white to mark out quilting designs, and the white will show on most colors. It is sprinkled through perforated patterns to mark a faint line which can be brushed out after stitching. From Scovill, Sewing Notions Division. Another acceptable source for powdered chalk is Risdon Mfg. Co. Approximate Retail Price: (Dritz) Under $1.00

Marking Pencils

The Fashionetics Dressmaker Pencil is yellow — one of the easiest colors to see on any other color or white. It's the right size for any pencil sharpener so the point can be kept perfect. It has a brush eraser on one end. From Fashionetics Inc. Approximate Retail Price: Under $1.00

It's handy to have a blue pencil for light colored fabrics, and white for dark ones in one pencil. The Talon Marking Pencil has one color at each end and a small, separate brush for dusting the marks off the fabric. It is made like a wooden pencil and can be sharpened in a standard pencil sharpener. You can have a point delicate enough for any use. From Donahue Sales, Talon Division of Textron. Approximate Retail Price: Under $1.00

Marking Pens

Finding a removable marking device dark enough to see on all fabrics had been a problem for years. The water soluble Marking Pen has bright blue ink that immediately disappears when touched by a damp cloth or a drop of clear water. Therefore, you can now mark the right sides of fabrics without worrying about mark removal later. Available from Risdon Mfg. Co. Approximate Retail Price: $2.00

Hand Sewing Tools

Since some garments cannot be entirely completed with machine stitching, hand sewing is required of every seamstress. Having the proper tools will make this work easier and faster. Of course, among the most important items needed for hand sewing are a good light and comfortable chair.

Thimbles

Not only the collector, but the serious seamstress can enjoy silver, gold or enameled thimbles from The Sewing Corner. Some thimbles can be personalized with monograms, and many come in a range of sizes. An inexpensive set of good aluminum ones from Austria in several styles and sizes is available. Approximate Retail Prices: From $10.00

If your excuse for not wearing a thimble is that your nails are too long, try a tailor's thimble. A practical silver one with no top is available from The Sewing Corner. It takes time to learn to use this type of thimble effectively, but European tailors have worked successfully with them for many years. Other sources for the open end thimble are: Risdon Mfg. Co.; and J.H.B. Imports, Inc. Approximate Retail Price: $2.00

If you find that a metal thimble is difficult to use, try a Leather Thimble. It is shaped like the top of your finger and stays snugly in place without the bulk of a regular metal thimble. Available in two sizes from The Sewing Corner. Approximate Retail Price: $1.00

If you have done a long stretch of hand sewing, you may notice that the forefinger of your hand is rough and sore at the end. You can protect that area with a finger shield, just as you protect the middle finger of your right hand with a thimble. The shield is lightweight celluloid and expands to fit any size. It can be ordered from The Sewing Corner. Approximate Retail Price: $1.00

Needle Threaders

Dritz Needle Threaders come three to a package so that you can have one anywhere you need it. They are metal with thin flexible wires that pull thread through any needle, hand or machine. Available from Scovill, Sewing Notions Division. Other acceptable sources for needle threaders are: Penn Products Co., and Risdon Mfg. Co. Approximate Retail Price: Under $1.00

Seam Rippers

The Talon Deluxe Seam Ripper is sharp, easy and safe to use. It is good for your hands and fabric. There is a small plastic ball on the end of the piece that slides along the fabric making it almost impossible to slip. The sharp point on the other piece is great for ripping out individual stitches one at a time. It comes with a cover for safe storage in your sewing basket. Distributed by Donahue Sales, Talon Division of Textron. Other acceptable sources of the seam ripper are: Risdon Mfg. Co.; E-Z Buckle, and Penn Products. Approximate Retail Price: Under $1.00

Dritz not only makes a standard large ripper with all the features you need, but also makes the Dritz Compact Seam Ripper. The ripper is 3½ inches long with its safety cover. It will work as effectively as the large ripper, including cutting open machine stitched buttonholes. From Scovill, Sewing Notions Division. Approximate Retail Price: Under $1.00

Magnifier

If you have trouble seeing very fine handwork or embroidery, keep an E-Z Magnifier around your neck. The feet on the magnifier rest on your chest to make the angle of the glass comfortable, leaving both hands free. From E-Z Buckle, Inc. Approximate Retail Price: $7.50

Assorted Thimbles From The Sewing Corner

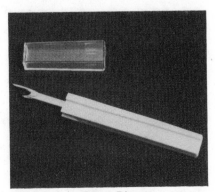

Talon Deluxe Seam Ripper

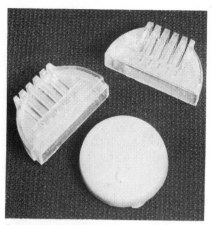

Scovill Dritz Beeswax & Holder

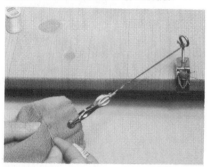

The Sewing Corner Sewing Bird

Mobilite 95 Hi-Intensity Lamp

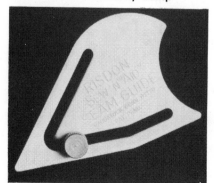

Risdon Seam Guide

Beeswax

Waxing is an old technique for making thread smoother and stronger. The Dritz Beeswax and Holder makes the wax easier to use and keeps it clean and unbroken. From Scovill, Sewing Notions Division. Other acceptable sources for beeswax are: E-Z Buckle; Risdon Mfg. Co., and Penn Products Co. Approximate Retail Price: Under $1.00

Sewing Bird

Sometimes you need a third hand when doing hand sewing jobs. A Sewing Bird fills this role whenever the need arises. You may be lucky enough to have an antique Sewing Bird which clamps onto a table and holds fabric in its metal beak. An updated version of the bird is available through The Sewing Corner Catalogue. Approximate Retail Price: $3.00

Bright Lighting

The Mobilite 95 Hi-Intensity lamp is useful wherever you sew, including at your sewing machine. It directs a good, strong light on your work and not in your eyes. The swing arm helps you to spot it exactly where it is needed. There is a high and low switch to adjust the intensity of the light. From Mobilite Inc. Approximate Retail Price: $19.50

Machine Sewing Aids

There are a few special tools designed to ease and speed your machine sewing which are not in the basic group of sewing aids. Some of them are used to solve stitching problems created by special fabrics and others help in basic seam construction. All of these items are nice to own.

Seam Guide

A fully adjustable seam guide that screws onto the bed of your sewing machine is available from the Risdon Mfg. Co. It can be used for any seam width during straight stitching, or for curved seams, scallops and topstitching. If you need help making even seams, this guide may be just the answer for you. Approximate Retail Price: $1.00

Dust Cover

If you leave your sewing machine out of the case or cabinet for any length of time it is a good idea to have a plastic dust cover handy so it stays clean. One size fits all machines and it is much handier than putting your machine away each time after using it. Available from The Sewing Corner. Approximate Retail Price: $1.30

Magnifier

If you have difficulty threading your machine needle the F-L-E-X-I-B-L-E Sewing Machine Magnifier is for you. It sticks on the front of the sewing machine and can be pulled down into position when needed but folds up out of the way when not in use. Manufactured by Universal Sewing Notions, Inc. Approximate Retail Price: $2.50

Construction Tools

This section covers all the notion items which are helpful during various stages of garment construction. Some are indispensable while others are a matter of personal preference.

Long Loop Turner

When working with a large amount of spaghetti trim, it is best to learn to turn the trim over its own cord. The Belding Loop Turner works for short lengths of fabric and for narrow ones. The chief problem is in keeping the latch securely fastened as you pull. Other acceptable sources for loop turners are: E-Z Buckle, Inc.; Risdon Mfg. Co., and Scovill, Sewing Notions Division. Approximate Retail Price: (Belding) $1.25

Machine Pin Cushion

A new pin cushion is available that has a plastic suction cup on the bottom. It will stick to any smooth, hard surface such as the head of your machine or a table. Grandma used to wrap a strip of flannel around the head of her machine to hold pins. This stick-on pin cushion will do the same job. Available from Jean Hardy Pattern Co. Approximate Retail Price: $1.70

Bodkins

Bodkins have been used for centuries to thread ribbons and elastic into casings. The Dritz Ezy-Pull Bodkin works on a pincer principle, with small, firm saw-teeth in the prongs of the pincer. On the bodkin is a ring which slides to tighten the pincers so that they will hold against almost any amount of pull. By Scovill, Sewing Notions Division. Other acceptable sources for this type of bodkin are: Risdon, Mfg. Co., and Penn Products Co. Approximate Retail Price: Under $1.00

Point Turners

The Dritz Point Turner is a handy plastic tool that helps you turn sharp points without damaging your fabric or poking holes through the points.

In addition to turning points, this tool will help you form thread shanks when sewing on buttons. It is also a 4 inch ruler. Made by Scovill, Sewing Notions Division. Approximate Retail Price: Under $1.00

The Multipurpose Point and Tube Turner from Fashion Services, Inc. is an unusual looking tool that helps you turn perfect points on collars, lapels, pocket flaps and belt ends. It looks like a miniature pair of ice tongs. It can also be used to turn belts, spaghetti straps, buttonhole loops and other narrow turning jobs. Approximate Retail Price: $6.00

Buttonholers

The slot in the center of this Belding Bound "Buttonholer" is to help form a straight line while stitching buttonholes. The disadvantage of this item is that it does not have enough range for different types of machine feet or wider buttonholes. From Belding Lilly Co. Approximate Retail Price: $2.00

If your sewing machine is not equipped to make buttonholes, you can buy a Greist Automatic Buttonholer as a good substitute. This device fits most machines, straight stitch or zigzag, and comes with five templates for four plain buttonholes and one keyhole buttonhole. Extra templates are available for other plain and keyhole buttonhole sizes as well as an eyelet. The Buttonholer automatically measures each buttonhole so they all come out exactly the same length and look professional. Made by Greist Division, MITE Corp. and available at most sewing machine shops. Approximate Retail Price: $16.25

Buttonhole Cutter

The Buttonhole Knife and Cutting Block from Bernina Sewing Machine Company provides an easy method of cutting open a series of buttonholes. Back the buttonhole with the cutting block and use the small sharp knife to accurately cut open any size buttonhole. Also available from E-Z Buckle, Inc. Approximate Retail Price: $3.00

Hole Punch

Use the Dritz Awl whenever you need to punch small holes in fabric, leather or plastic before inserting eyelets or heavy duty snaps. It has a large, comfortable wooden handle, and protective guard for safe storage. Available from Scovill, Sewing Notions Division. Approximate Retail Price: $1.25

Scovill Dritz Ezy-Pull Bodkin

Scovill Dritz Point Turner

Bernina Buttonhole Cutter

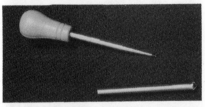

Scovill Dritz Awl

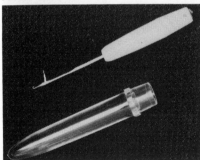

Risdon Knit Fixer

Help For Your Knits

Though knits are considered the miracle fabric of our time, they have the annoying problem of snagging. Snags should never be cut off since cutting will cause holes or runs. The Knit Fixer from Risdon Mfg. Co. will safely pull the snags to the wrong side of the garment where they won't show. Other acceptable sources for a snag fixer are: E-Z Buckle, Inc., and Scovill, Sewing Notions Division. Approximate Retail Price: $1.00

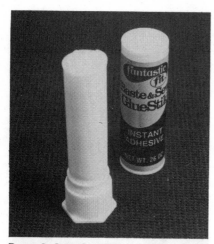

Baste & Sew GlueStik

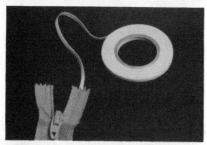

Talon Stick and Stitch Basting Tape

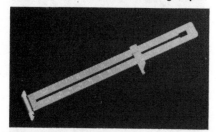

Scovill Dritz Tailor-Ette

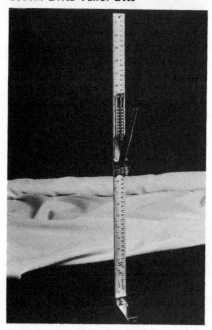

Dritz Pin-Type Skirt Marker

Basting With Glue

Some fabrics must be basted before sewing. You can save a lot of time if you use a glue stick rather than a needle and thread. The Baste & Sew GlueStik, from Fantastic Fit Products, is strong enough to hold seams, trims and patch pockets in place during stitching. It will also wash out completely leaving no trace. Other acceptable sources for a glue stick are: E-Z Buckle, Inc., and Dennisons (look for this brand at drug and stationery stores). Approximate Retail Price: (Baste & Sew) $1.40

Stop Fabric Fraying

Fray Check, a colorless liquid which seals cut edges of woven fabrics, has many applications in the sewing room. Squeeze a thin line of Fray Check along seam and hem edges to prevent fraying, or along collar and cuff edges of completed garments that are beginning to wear. The dried liquid is invisible and will withstand repeated washings and dry cleanings. From Scovill, Sewing Notions Division. Approximate Retail Price: $1.50

Sewing Tapes

Various types of sticky tapes are useful in the sewing room. Some are made especially for home sewing while others are general purpose tapes that adapt well to many sewing jobs.

If you have trouble keeping an accurate ⅝ inch (15mm) seam or a ⅛ inch (3mm) stitching edge, try Belding adhesive Tape Stitch or Belding non-adhesive Tissue Tape. Tape Stitch is ¾ inches wide and bright yellow. Tissue Tape is 1¼ inches wide, marked off in ⅛, ¼, and ⅝ inches. They prevent fabric slip and keep your stitching straight. Made by Belding Lily Co. Approximate Retail Prices: (Tape Stitch) $1.25; (Tissue Tape) $1.00

Talon Stick and Stitch Basting Tape is very narrow and can be used as double-sided or single-sided holding tape. Double-sided, it holds braids, zippers, and other trimmings in place for stitching. This sewing aid bastes plaids with more accuracy than is possible with needle and thread. If you don't peel the outer guard strip off, you can use it as a topstitching guide. From Donahue Sales — Talon Division of Textron. Another acceptable source for double-faced tape is: Risdon Mfg. Co. Approximate Retail Price: (Talon) Under $1.00

Drafting Tape made by the 3M Co. has many uses in the sewing room. Mark right or wrong sides of look-alike fabrics with tape strips. Tape-baste zippers or patch pockets in place, or use long strips of tape as a topstitching guide. The ½ inch width size is a popular choice, and the light sticky surface will not transfer to or mar most fabrics. However, we suggest you always test the tape on a fabric scrap first. Avoid stitching through the tape which might make your machine needle sticky. Approximate Retail Price: Under $1.00

Hemming Tools

An even, neat hem is very important for the custom look that is so desirable. Various gauges and hemming aids are available for hemming by hand or machine.

The Dritz Tailor-Ette is a 6 inch plastic gauge with an adjustable slider and piece of tailor's chalk built into the end. This gauge will help you measure and mark hem depths at the same time. It is not as durable as comparable metal gauges and sometimes has rough edges that are annoying. However, the built-in chalk is convenient. From Scovill, Sewing Notions Division. Approximate Retail Price: Under $1.00

The best way to make a hem level and even is to have a friend mark it with a Dritz Pin-Type Skirt Marker. It can be set for a wide range of inches from the floor. There is a channel through the clamp at the top through which a pin is slipped while the clamp holds the fabric firmly in place. From Scovill, Sewing Notions Division. Another acceptable source for the pin-type skirt marker is: Risdon Mfg. Co. Approximate Retail Price: (Dritz) $5.50

Without help from a friend to mark your hems, you can mark them yourself with powdered chalk and a squeeze-bulb made by Scovill. You can also use the Dritz 3-Way Skirt Marker with pins or chalk. From Scovill, Sewing Notions Division. Approximate Retail Price: $5.50

Sewing Boxes And Storage

Sewing Boxes can be a mixed blessing. There are the kind you pick out yourself because they suit your space and needs, and there are the unfortunate variety that come as gifts from well-meaning friends. If you have drawer space for your sewing needs, you may prefer the notions trays instead of a box. You may want a "parlor" sewing box to store the items you work on by hand in the evenings. For most of us the best storage box is a roomy, easy-to-clean box with a tray or two. Fortunately, these are usually the least expensive variety.

The Wil-hold line of sewing boxes are strong, sturdy, easy-to-clean, and made of colorful heavy duty plastic. The large 2-Tray Sewing Chest has carefully arranged room for all the scissors, small notions and thread in one tray, and movable dividers in the other. The lower section is large enough to carry some work-in-progress. The latch is secure, and the top handle folds down out of the way. There is a smaller version of this sewing box with one tray, called the Sew Case. It is nice for a beginner or someone who only does a little

light mending. The Wil-hold sewing boxes are available in variety stores at very reasonable prices. They are made by the Hugh H. Wilson Co., Div. of Wilson Mfg. Co. Approximate Retail Prices: (2-Tray) $5.00; (Sew Case) $3.00

A clear plastic tray with compartments for items such as thread, bobbins and scissors prevents a hopeless jumble. If you have a lot of equipment, you'll find two trays fit handily into most dresser or cabinet drawers. The minute you open the drawer, all items will be immediately visible. Made by Scovill, Sewing Notions Division. Approximate Retail Price: $2.50

The Dritz Vue-Thru Thread Box holds 26 spools of thread (any size spool), plus pins and other odds and ends. The box is small enough to sit on your machine or sewing table without being in the way, and you can see what's in the box at a glance. The companion piece to the thread box is the Dritz Bobbin Box which holds 32 bobbins, always visible through the clear plastic top. Both are made by Scovill, Sewing Notions Division. Approximate Retail Price: (Thread Box) $2.75

E-Z Buckle Inc. markets a clever plywood sewing box which comes disassembled. Putting it together with its own wooden pegs is child's play and no tools are needed. It does require more sanding and finishing than the instructions lead you to believe, but it can be stained, painted, decoupaged, or decorated as you wish. It makes a nice personalized gift sewing box, or a parlor sewing box for your own use, finished to match your decor. In price, it falls between utilitarian plastic boxes, fancy baskets and parlor boxes. Approximate Retail Price: $10.00

There are always a few patterns that you cannot bear to throw away. If you keep them in a Wil-hold Pattern File, they will be available and easy to find when

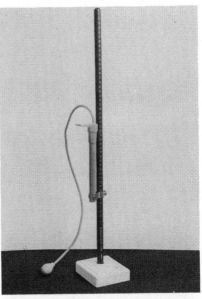

Dritz 3-Way Skirt Marker

Wil-hold 2-Tray Sewing Chest

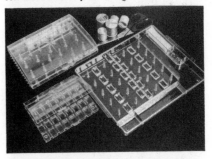

Scovill Dritz Vue-Thru Boxes

Wil-hold Pattern File

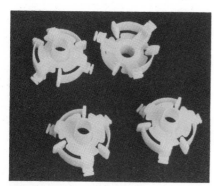

Scovill Handi-Bobs

you want to reuse them. This file holds up to 30 standard size patterns and has four movable dividers for identification of types. The inexpensive file is made of the same easy-to-clean plastic as the Wil-hold sewing boxes. It is sturdy and practical as well as functional. Made by the Hugh H. Wilson Co., Div. of Wilson Manufacturing Co. Approximate Retail Price: $2.70

Keeping bobbins matched with the thread spools can be a frustrating job. Thread color may look the same, but unless you always use the same brand thread, you may not match exactly. Mismatches can cause stitching problems. Push a Handi-Bob into the spool top, and then snap the matching bobbin in place for neat storage. The Handi-Bob will fit most bobbins. Available from Scovill, Sewing Notions Division. Approximate Retail Price: Under $1.00

Use vinyl hanger bags with shelves which are meant for storing purses and shoes. These storage bags work equally well for fabrics, yarn, or projects-in-progress. Henry A Enrich & Co. makes several sizes in the Model Home Windo-Kleer line, sold at department and variety stores. Approximate Retail Price: From $13.00

Underbed chests make use of unused space in a small apartment or house. Use them for fabrics and patterns which are too heavy for the hanger bags. "Dead storage" shouldn't be so dead that you can't

remember what's up there on the top shelf, so store your out-of-season fabrics in clear vinyl boxes on the top shelf. With or without compartments, they're available in the Model Home Windo-Kleer line by Henry A. Enrich & Co. in closet accessory departments. Approximate Retail Price: From $10.00

Notions Incorporated Into The Garment

Besides handy gadgets that make your sewing easier and more fun, there are other gadgets that make the finished garment better and more professional. The more the field of fabrics expands, the more the notion field must expand. Trimmings must be compatible with fabrics in weight, in washability, in performance, and in color. Many of the matching problems are obvious. For example, you are not going to put a heavy brass zipper into a delicate voile dress, or bind a shiny satin robe with a cotton bias binding. Other problems are more subtle, including the choice of threads, seam bindings, and buttons.

There must be a starting point for making decisions about notions to be incorporated into the garment. The back of the pattern will provide necessary suggestions including the number and size of buttons, the length and type of zipper, types of needed seam tapes, trimmings and elastic. Within certain bounds you may vary these. For example, choose one or two more buttons, slightly different in size or select a longer zipper length if you know you're going to step into your clothes rather than pull them over your head.

Thread

No garment can be made without thread. Probably no other

sewing notion has gone through as many changes as thread in the past decade. We have heard "pure polyester," "cotton wrap," "machine embroidery," and a host of other designations for what was once a one-kind-only product that allowed very few choices.

Finding the right thread for you and your sewing machine is a matter of personal testing and manufacturer's recommendations. Testing threads by yourself can answer more questions than anyone else can answer for you. Before you test threads, be sure your machine is in top condition or you will not be giving the thread a chance. Be especially careful to have the correct needle size for the test thread. The special threads for heavy duty use and topstitching will not run through the eye of small machine needles. You will have to try one of the larger size needles — 14/90 to 16/100. Also, be sure that you have the correct needle type for the fabric — sharp, ball point, leather point.

Some thread fibers are much tougher than fabric fibers and will not only outwear them but can actually cause fabric damage by cutting through the delicate fabric fibers. Polyester fabrics should be stitched with polyester thread so that the wearing qualities are equal. As a general rule, it is best to stitch natural fibers with natural fiber thread, and synthetic fibers with synthetic fiber thread. The cotton wrap/polyester core thread crosses the boundaries between natural and synthetic fibers and is a general purpose thread that can be used safely on most modern fabrics.

New threads for special purposes, and some older types which have only recently returned to the scene, make decorative sewing much more fun. There are topstitching threads, buttonhole twist, and machine embroidery thread in good variety. Many of the companies who have rediscovered the usefulness of a wide variety of thread types are now printing good instructional material on these threads and how to use them to the best advantage.

If you cannot find such material at your local store, write to the thread company. Addresses are provided in the *Directory of Sources and Manufacturers* at the back of this book.

Belding Lily makes the largest selection of thread in every type and fiber. They manufacture a very good polyester thread, mercerized cotton threads, and a line of excellent silk thread and silk buttonhole twist. A partial list of Belding threads includes those mentioned above plus cotton quilting thread, cotton button and carpet thread, black and white cotton thread in sizes 8 through 60, heavy duty polyester thread for home sewing, polyester buttonhole twist for buttonholes and topstitching, and a clear monofilament nylon thread for invisible stitching and bead-work. Many types of Belding Lily thread come on spools in two or three sizes for extra economy. Approximate Retail Price: Under $1.00

American Thread Company's imported Suisse long-fiber polyester thread is smooth in finish and easy to use for hand or machine sewing. It comes in topstitching weight, color-matched to the lighter weight. The only drawback to either weight seems to be a tendency to unravel as you thread the needle, sometimes making that process difficult. From American Thread Co. Approximate Retail Price: Under $1.00

Gütermann Thread

Gütermann pure polyester thread is imported and marketed in this country by Talon. A very good cotton-wrap polyester-core thread, and a good mercerized cotton thread is also by Talon. The Gütermann thread comes in standard weight, smooth and strong, and in a handsome buttonhole or topstitching weight. Both are wound on nifty spools with a patented arrangement for holding the end of the thread neatly in place and preventing its unwinding in the sewing box. From Donahue Sales, Talon Division of Textron, Inc. Another source for fine imported polyester thread in two weights is: Molnlycke, Inc. Approximate Retail Price: Under $1.00

J & P Coats Dual Duty Plus thread has been improved since it first appeared on the market. The polyester-core, cotton-wrap thread is smoother and runs more evenly in the machine than the original product. It now comes in a

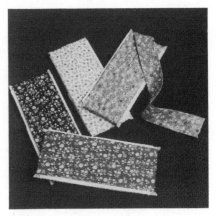

Talon Fancy Tapes

nice showy topstitching weight and a fine machine embroidery weight as well as the standard all-purpose sewing thread. Made by Coats & Clark Sales Corp. Approximate Retail Price: Under $1.00

Tapes And Trims

Tapes and trims serve many purposes, from holding items together to decorating the fabric surface. This group of notions also represents ever-changing color and fashion trends and reflects the types of fabric in use at any given time. In this group we include decorative as well as utilitarian tapes. You can also interchange decorative braids, tapes, and edgings for dressmaking with the ones for home decorating.

The most basic utilitarian tape is cotton or polyester twill tape — but even that has undergone a few happy changes recently. You will soon be seeing the ½ inch width in a selection of fashion colors, for

Belding Lily Polyester and Silk Threads

the imaginative seamstress to use in decorating sportswear and home furnishings. If you don't like the first product you see, shop around until you find something more to your taste and needs.

The washable peasant braids with pretty embroidery designs are so numerous it is impossible to cover each one. A few of the smaller ones come packaged by the same companies who package bias tape, rick rack, and other decorative braids and edgings. There are many places which sell the same familiar brands as well as imports by the yard. If you are using these on a washable garment it would be wise to pre-shrink them by dipping in warm water.

We mention the brands that are most widely distributed, reliable, and have the best range of colors. That doesn't mean that there are not other good brands of bias tape, twill tape, rick rack, etc. In this line we mention mostly Wrights because they are excellent and widely available. Talon also has a strong line of these items in equally good quality, though they are the followers in new trends rather than the leaders. A few items you will find mentioned are exclusively Talon's — at least for the moment. There are other lines, some quite reliable and some that should be examined with care. If you are doubtful of the quality of a bias tape, check the weave to see if it is as fine as the weave in the quality brands mentioned. The turned edge should not be skimpy. Don't hestitate to do comparison shopping for these small items since they can make or break the professional look you want.

There is a huge array of seam bindings, lace seam bindings and bias seam bindings. Some come in several widths, folded or flat, and in a variety of colors. Color and performance must be compatible with your fabric.

Iron-on bindings are not as popular as they were when they first came out because they did not really live up to their promises. We recommend them only for

emergencies and on fabrics that are hard to control. Sew them later before they go through many washings or dry cleanings.

Bias Tapes

Cotton or cotton/polyester bias tapes are endlessly colorful, useful, and decorative. The selection from Wrights includes the standard widths, ½ inch and ⅞ inch in a full range of colors. The same tapes come in calico prints, checks, and other fashion designs, changing with the years. You can depend on the good quality of the fabric and the stability of the dye in these products. From Wm. E. Wright Co. Approximate Retail Price: Under $1.00

Wrights Bias Tape, always the largest line of cotton or cotton/polyester bias available, has added a new and very helpful extra wide double fold. It has always been a little tricky to handle the narrow double fold except on very thin firm fabrics. Now binding the edge of quilted mats or robes will be easier, and the extra width gives more pizazz to children's clothes and aprons and many other decorative items. Made by Wm. E. Wright Co. Approximate Retail Price: Under $1.25

Rick Rack

Wrights polyester Baby Rick Rack, Medium Rick Rack, and Jumbo Rick Rack are dyed to match so that you can use more than one width on the same garment for added accent. Most colors are also coordinated with the bias tape so that they can be used together. From Wm. E. Wright Co. Approximate Retail Price: Under $1.00

Seam Or Hem Tape

A good soft, flexible polyester tape for finishing hems and seams is Wrights Soft and Easy. It isn't too slippery, handles well, and has woven lines to help you stitch

straight. It also is nice looking and comes in plenty of colors. There is an iron-on version of it, slightly more expensive and not really worth it. There is also a bargain pack of the regular tape, containing nine yards at a reduced price per yard. From Wm. E. Wright Co. Approximate Retail Price: Under $1.00

Dainty Edgings

The alternative to seam tape — ⅝ inch flexible lace seam or hem edging — is nice for all the sheers and soft fabrics now in fashion. There are several good brands, including Talon, Belding Lily, and Wrights. The last two mentioned have also added two other useful lace edgings, hem facing — 1¾ inches wide — and a nifty folded lace edging. If you've ever tried to fold lace over the edges of the seams on a pretty peignoir, you will know just how welcome is this addition to seam finishing. From both Wm. E. Wright Co. and Belding Lily Co. Approximate Retail Price: Under $1.25

Wrights Lace Edging

Twill Tape

Most of the trimming companies make white and black twill tape, (usually 100 percent polyester) in a variety of widths. It is strong, sturdy material that will hold and prevent ripping or wear and tear in most situations. The narrow size tape is an excellent seam-stay for the crotch of pants and the armholes of jackets. The wider widths are especially useful in home decorating. Talon now has Fancy Tape, a ½ inch twill tape in six bright fashion colors. It can be used as outside trimming in any place that you might use the embroidered peasant braids, or as pull strings and ties in a gathered waistline or the top of a pretty laundry bag. From Donahue Sales, Talon Div. of Textron Inc. Approximate Retail Price: Under $1.00

Zippers

Zippers — the great fastening discovery of the 20th century — have now blossomed into a fashion item. Every since they were invented, great effort was made to make them more lightweight and flexible, and as invisible as possible. This has been accomplished with the introduction of synthetic zipper coils and polyester tapes, and the development of the invisible zipper. Zipper closings are now suitable for the finest, most

Talon Zippers

lightweight knit and woven fabrics. But, in a fashion reversal, zippers are also being sported big and brassy and bright. Whatever your style, zippers are one of the most important notion items incorporated into your garments.

Talon means zippers to many people who sew. Though the company has diversified into other notions, their zipper line is large and very good. They make a premium quality polyester/nylon zipper and a lighter weight for knits. They make two weights of metal jacket zippers, and elaborate ones that open from either end or work on reversible jackets. They make slipcover zippers, extra long and extra strong, and big brassy jeans zippers. The only problem is finding a store which carries the full selection you'd like to see. From Donahue Sales, Talon Division of Textron, Inc. Approximate Retail Price: Under $1.25

Novelty Zippers

Big colorful plastic zippers are fun for sportswear, beach bags, and items that require a showy zipper. YKK makes a full line of colors in this type of zipper with a big ring on the slide. The plastic teeth are so attractive that they should be exposed, making the zipper a lot easier to install. From YKK U.S.A., Inc., Home Sewing Division. Approximate Retail Price: Under $2.00

Invisible Zippers

The Unique Invisible Zipper, now marketed by YKK, has long been the best in truly invisible zippers. It has never been possible to make them lightweight enough for use in the backs of soft dresses but they are great for pants, skirts, and some home decorating. From YKK U.S.A., Inc., Home Sewing Division. Approximate Retail Price: Under $1.00

Flexible Coil Zippers

The nylon coils of the Belding Lily zippers are set in a

polyester/rayon tape, very flexible, very washable, and delightfully trouble-free. The same company makes a lightweight nylon coil zipper in separating style, especially good for sweaters. They also make a line of metal zippers, comparable in performance to their competitors. From Belding Lily Co. Approximate Retail Price: Under $1.50

Self-Basting Zipper

Wrights Soft & Easy Self-Basting zipper is 100 percent polyester and the lightest weight tape possible. It's a fine zipper for knits and sheers, and for those who like iron-on basting or basting tape, it has this feature built in. There is a narrow strip of a heat-fuse substance along each edge of the tape which will help to stabilize it in slippery fabrics. From Wm. E. Wright Co. Approximate Retail Price: Under $1.50

Waistband Stiffening And Belting

Several types of products are available to add support and stiffness to skirt and pants waistbands. Some are completely stable while others have some built-in stretch for extra comfort. Choice is determined by personal preference and fabric type.

The newest stiffening and belting is pre-cut fusible interfacing strips with fold and stitching guidelines. They are great for women's and children's waistbands of all types.

Belting is available in various widths and makes custom belts an easy task. It is available by the yard or in kits which include a buckle of some type.

For many years it seemed impossible to find good reliable waistband stiffeners. Most notions counters stocked belting that was not suitable for waistbands on skirts or slacks. Now the Ban-Rol waistbands are available by the yard in several styles and widths. There is the original firm, but thin, stiffener with smooth selvage edges in four widths. If you prefer the smooth look of a man's band with what is called a "curtain" finish inside, there is a 1½ inch stiffener for women, and two varieties for men. They come in solid and stretch form in several colors. There is also Ban-Rol men's ribbed elastic and a sheer Super Stretch in several widths for women. All of these perform well, depending entirely on what you want of a waistband in both effect and feel. All Ban-Rol waistband products are distributed by Staple Sewing Aids. Approximate Retail Price: Under $2.00

Waistband Interfacing

Waist Shaper, a pre-cut, non-roll, fusible interfacing for waistbands is one of the best new products. It comes in two widths, 1¼ inches and 2 inches. The seam allowances have been eliminated, and the foldline is perforated for a perfectly even waistband. The package, which contains enough interfacing for three average waistbands comes with excellent instructions. From Stacy Fabrics Corporation. Approximate Retail Price: $1.50

Pellon's Fuse'n Fold is a stabilized, non-woven, fusible interfacing strip which makes professionally finished waistbands. It has slots along each edge to indicate the seamline and foldline for accuracy. Fuse'n Fold is also available in other widths and weights for shirt plackets, cuffs and straight facing applications. Each package contains three yards. From the Pellon Corporation. Approximate Retail Price: $1.00

Make Your Own Belts

Firm, belting material is available by the yard in various widths and two colors from E-Z Buckle, Inc.; Penn Products; Risdon Mfg. Co., and Scovill,

Sewing Notions Division. Use this material to make custom covered belts. Most of these companies also offer the belting packaged in a kit with a plain or covered buckle and eyelets. Approximate Retail Price: (E-Z Buckle) Under $1.00

Elastic

Stretch fashion brings the need for all sorts of elastic. Many waistlines are comfortably elasticized. Elastic in necklines and wrists eliminates the need for buttons or zippers. Entire bodice or waist insets can be stitched with elastic thread for a smocked look. Specialty types of elastic such as lingerie and swimwear are also readily available for people who like to sew these items.

Always read elastic package instructions to make sure you are getting the right type of elastic needed for your particular garment. Not all elastic will survive dry cleaning or a dip in the pool. Make sure the package states the elastic is suitable for your particular use.

Good Basic Elastics

We are mentioning only one brand, Scovill, in basic elastics because it is a readily available one, carded and by the yard. However, you will find much the same types in Talon, Risdon, and other brands. The three types of fiber used in the Dritz or Scovill StayLastic line are nylon and polyester — both recommended for swimwear — and rayon for other uses. There is also a soft rayon Baby elastic which is especially good for girls' puffed sleeves and panty legs. By Scovill, Sewing Notions Division. Approximate Retail Price: (Packaged) Under $1.00

The person who sews for a family will appreciate elastics designed for a soft waistline or a good replacement job on pajamas and boxer shorts. The pajama elastic comes in two types which are wide and comfortable. The

lingerie elastic is lacy and comes flat or folded to go over the upper edge of a petticoat. All from Scovill, Sewing Notions Division. Another acceptable source for these types of elastic is Risdon Mfg. Co. Approximate Retail Price: Under $1.00

Scovill elastics cover the range of possibilities from the Victorian Vienna Oval Elastic to a sharp looking new Fashion Elastic in white and 13 colors. There is application for the colored elastic in children's clothes and sportswear. The oval has less use for most of us but is invaluable in doll clothes and some lingerie applications. From Scovill, Sewing Notions Division. Approximate Retail Price: Under $1.00

Elastic Thread

Sewing successfully with elastic thread is a matter of experience. With the popularity of the shirred look, more sewers will be trying elastic thread on sewing projects. Experiment with the thread with various fabric scraps to see just how it will handle in your machine and how much shirring effect you will get. The thread diameter, stitch length, weight of the fabric and bobbin tension all affect the finished look. Elastic thread is available from: E-Z Buckle, Inc.; Penn Products Co.; Scovill, Sewing Notions Division; Swiss-Bernina; Risdon Mfg. Co.,

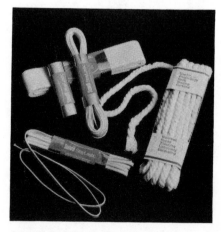

Scovill Staylastics & Cording

and White Sewing Machine Co. Approximate Retail Price: Under $1.00

Cording

Cords and covered cording are used more with home decorative sewing than with fashion sewing. However, they can make a fine accent for necks, waists, and hemlines. Plain cable cord comes in many sizes, all of which can be covered with fabric to be used as piping around a neckline, on a pocket edge, or to finish a yoke. The finest cord can be used in a bound buttonhole to make it firmer, giving it a decorative effect. Covered corded pipings, packaged or by the yard, can be found in notions and home decorating departments. Use the pre-covered corded piping for contrast accent —a much speedier operation than cutting and making your own from contrasting fabric. There are decorative cords that can be used for belts and tie fastenings; and the plain cable cord can be completely covered to make spaghetti cording to be used in the same way.

Cable Cord

Cable cord is one product that has remained the same over the past years. It is still 100 percent cotton, comes in a number of sizes, and is available from many manufacturers. It is harder to find it sold by the yard than in blister packs. However, the home decorating department in some stores sells it in large quantities at slightly less cost. When you want to make your own matching or contrasting corded piping, be sure you are getting a good brand of cotton cable cord, such as Scovill, which comes under their StayLastic line, although it has no elastic in it. From Scovill, Sewing Notions Division. Approximate Retail Price: $1.00

Corded Piping

The same good bias that is used in Wrights bias tapes is also made up into corded piping, regular and maxi. Use it to finish any faced edge with a touch of color. It comes in the same colors as the tape so that all sorts of mix-and-match decorations are possible. Made by Wm. E. Wright Co. Approximate Retail Price: Under $1.00

Buttons

Buttons can be decorative or purely functional. They are available as sew-through or shank type, on cards or in bulk. Buying carded buttons is convenient but sometimes not the best buy if you need only five buttons and the card has eight. Bulk buttons allow you to choose the exact number needed, and are usually cheaper for the same quality button. When buying buttons, look for the correct size, washability, or dry cleanability, and whether it is a sew-through or shank type button.

Button Molds

Two companies make rustproof aluminum button molds with a good trick for handling slippery fabrics. The mold has no teeth and the back slips in smoothly. The trick is in a small rubber cup which holds the fabric firmly as you push the top of the mold into it. There is a little tool with which you push the button back in and then the whole thing pops easily out of the rubber mold. Made by E-Z Buckle,

Inc. and Maxant Corporation. Approximate Retail Price: (Maxant) $1.00

Brass button molds from Dritz have a soft plastic back that slips in the mold easily, once you have attached the fabric to the teeth around the edge of the top piece. This is relatively easy except when working with stiff fabrics or sheers that must have a layer of lining included. It is an improvement in ease of handling over the all-metal molds with teeth. They are, of course, rustproof, washable, and dry cleanable, but that is true of button molds from any reputable notions manufacturer. From Scovill, Sewing Notions Division. Approximate Retail Price: $1.00

Pinettes

So many beautiful shanked buttons should not be washed or dry cleaned, which makes them lose their luster or the jewels. But who wants to snip them off and sew them on each time the garment is dirty? Clinton Pinettes will hold shanked buttons securely on all but the heaviest fabrics. The little hump in the pin allows both button and pin to lie flat, without a wrinkle in the fabric. From Scovill, Sewing Notions Division. Approximate Retail Price: Under $1.00

Bachelor Buttons

E-Z Pivot Bachelor Buttons are

Scovill Dritz Buttons To Cover

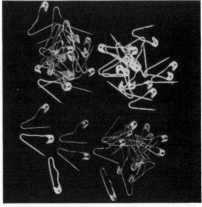
Scovill Clinton Pinettes

handsome heavy metal buttons that we associate with western denim suits. They can be hammered onto the garment with no extra tool at all. It is wise to place a piece of cardboard on each side to prevent damage to the button or the surface on which you're working. Made by E-Z Buckle, Inc. Approximate Retail Price: $1.00

Bachelor Button from Maxant Corporation provides an instant solution to the lost shirt button. The white plastic buttons have an attached shank which slips through the fabric to hold it in place until repairs can be made. A good item for a man to keep in his office, car and suitcase. Approximate Retail Price: $1.00

Lasso Loop is a quick, easy way to attach buttons to garments when a needle and thread aren't handy. Made from 100 percent nylon, these loops will not wear through like thread and can be used with either shank or sew-through type buttons. While we don't recommend this product for buttons on your finer garments, it is a good solution for children's coats and emergency repairs on most any garment. Packed 40 loops to a plastic box, in three different colors, this is another good product to keep in your purse, car or suitcase. Made by Stacy Fabrics Corporation. Approximate Retail Price: $2.00

Fasteners/Buckles

Decorative four-part snaps have been expanded from an item used only on work clothes and children's clothes to the realm of fashion sportswear. They are colorful, imaginative and come in more than one size. The methods of attaching them are better and easier, and often more secure than the earlier types. You can use a simple tool that you hit with a hammer, a plier-type tool that does more than just apply snaps, or a standing piece of machinery that is extremely fast and accurate.

The purely practical fastenings,

such as hooks-and-eyes, simple snaps and self-fastening tapes, are produced by a number of quality manufacturers. They all come in various types and sizes so you should be able to find just what you need.

One thing should be kept in mind about the various types of fasteners. Most types use a numerical size system that is standard throughout the industry with the exception of simple snap fasteners. They come in eight different sizes, but each marked size is not the same from one manufacturer to another. If you run out of snaps in the middle of a project make sure you buy the same brand in the same size.

Four-Part Snaps

High style four-part snaps in bright colors, fun and funny imitations of buttons, old-west metal, and checked gingham give you an easy way out of the buttonhole problem. The largest selection with the best distribution is the Clinton Ginger Snaps line. If you use such items infrequently, you will not need to buy any fancy attaching tool. You can use a spool and small household hammer and the directions on the package. If you use many such items, you may want to buy the Dritz Clinton Gripper Plier Kit. All from Scovill, Sewing Notions Division. Other acceptable sources for decorative four-part snaps are: Risdon Mfg. Co., and E-Z Buckle, Inc. Approximate Retail Price: (Clinton Ginger Snaps) Under $1.00; (Gripper Plier Kit) $4.50

Heavy Duty Snaps

Heavy Duty or Jumbo size snaps are a fashion item for jeans and outerwear. They are easily applied with a hammer and simple setting tool, or one of the plier-type fastener tools. E-Z Buckle, Inc. and Scovill, Sewing Notions Division, offer the greatest variety of styles and colors with E-Z Buckle carrying a two-sided snap for reversible garments. Risdon Mfg. Co. offers snaps in basic

gold, nickle, black and white. Approximate Retail Price: (Risdon) $2.25

Eyelets

Eyelets in two sizes and assorted colors are available from E-Z Buckle, Inc.; Penn Products Co.; Risdon Mfg. Co., and Scovill, Sewing Notions Division. Each offers a small applicator to be used with a hammer or you can use one of the large plier-type tools. Approximate Retail Price: Under $1.00

Fastener Tools

If you plan on using many four-part snaps, eyelets and large, heavy duty snaps, you will find that Risdon's Klik-A-Plier tool kit does a professional job of attaching them. The tool is considerably less expensive than many comparable ones. The only drawback — and this applies to many similar tools — is that it takes about an hour of reading directions and putting the proper pieces together before you begin. Therefore, unless you plan to install snaps and eyelets on a wholesale basis, you are better off tapping them in place with a simpler method. Made by Risdon Mfg. Co. Approximate Retail Price: $6.00

Scovill is offering a new multi-fastener tool which can be used for all sizes of four-part

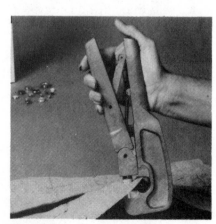

Scovill Dritz The Fastener

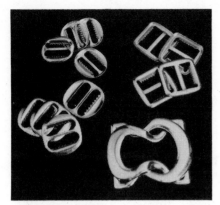
E-Z Metal Buckles

Talon Waistband Hooks & Eyes

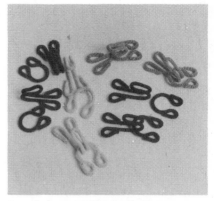
Scovill Covered Hooks & Eyes

snaps, eyelets and heavy duty snaps. It has many small interchangeable parts which require careful reading of the instructions to learn how to use them, but it does the application job nicely. Some objections to this tool might be the size, which is rather large for a woman's hand, and the price. It is more than twice the price of Risdon's Klik-A-Plier which does pretty much the same job. The Fastener is available from Scovill, Sewing Notions Division. Approximate Retail Price: $14.00

Buckles

E-Z Buckle, Inc. makes a marvelous range of buckles, from the most mundane to top fashion finishes. Three indispensable types for straps, belts, bags, children's clothes, and many other uses are the D-rings that make a simple slip-through fastening — the Ivy League buckles with teeth which are used on the side straps of men's vests, and the popular overall buckles which come in a variety of looks. The low price on these functional buckles will make you think of many other ways to use them. All from E-Z Buckle, Inc. Other acceptable sources for overall buckles are: Risdon Mfg. Co., and Scovill, Sewing Notions Division. Approximate Retail Price: Under $1.00

High fashion buckle assortments with coordinating belting of vinyl, fabric, macrame or decorative elastic are available

from many companies. Some of the nicest buckle kits we have seen come from B. Blumenthal and Co. under the Blumenthal, La Mode, or Le Chick name. Approximate Retail Price: From $2.00

Inexpensive belting and buckle kits, complete with eyelets for particular styles, enable you to make matching belts which stand up well and can be washed or dry cleaned. If your sewing machine balks at going through the heavy belting, you may find that turing the edge under and finishing by hand on the back is best. Even if you want a topstitch finish, you may find that doing this first prevents trouble with the point and with any pull on the fabric. E-Z Buckle, Inc. makes several styles. Other sources for covered belt kits are: Scovill, Sewing Notions Division, and Maxant Corporation. Approximate Retail Price: (E-Z Buckle) From Under $1.00

Hooks & Eyes

Regular hooks and eyes come in black, white, nickle or brass. Now E-Z Buckle, Inc. offers them in pastel and other dark colors so you can match them with your garment fabric. Nylon covered, they come carded in either the pastel or dark color assortment. Approximate Retail Price: Under $1.00

The type of no-sew heavy waistband hooks on men's

trousers can now be applied by home-sewers with nothing more than a pair of household pliers. Talon markets them in rustproof steel, four to the package. They are useful replacement items on trousers that have had the original ones pulled off or damaged. They are perfect for rough-and-tough clothes for all the family. From Donahue Sales, Talon Division of Textron Inc. Other sources for no-sew hooks and eyes are: E-Z Buckle, Inc.; Scovill, Sewing Notions Division, and Penn Products Co. Approximate Retail Price: (Talon) Under $1.00

All reputable notions companies seem to market Skirt and Trouser Hooks & Eyes on a card — some silver and some black. They are sew-on items for which we suggest heavy duty thread to prevent the metal from cutting the stitching. They lie flat and are less readily damaged in dry cleaning than conventional hook-and-eye fasteners. Other sources for this type of hook and eye are: E-Z Buckle, Inc.; Penn Products Co.; Risdon Mfg. Co., and Scovill, Sewing Notions Division. Approximate Retail Price: (Talon) Under $1.00

Large size, covered hooks and eyes are available from Risdon Mfg. Co. and Scovill, Sewing Notions Division. Use them on fur or cloth coats, collars and fur pieces. Available in black and white. Approximate Retail Price: Under $1.00

Clasps

Bonnie Clasps, lightweight plastic fasteners in two colors and three sizes, can be used in place of regular hooks and eyes, and pants and skirt hooks. They lock securely without needing tension to keep them closed, so they are ideal for tall turtlenecks with center back openings. Since they close by one side sliding into the other, they won't catch long hair — a problem faced many times when a conventional hook and eye is used at the back of a neckline. Available from E-Z Buckle, Inc. Approximate Retail Price: Under $1.00

Covered Snaps

Silk covered snaps in a large size are available in black, beige, brown or white from E-Z Buckle, Inc. Use them as hidden closures on your fine suits and coats for a custom touch. Approximate Retail Price: Under $1.00

Invisible Snaps

Belding Lily Nylon Snaps are perfect for sheers, jerseys and places where snaps should not be seen. They are washable, dry cleanable, and as simple to sew as any conventional snap. They must not be touched with a hot iron. Manufactured in England for Belding Lily. Approximate Retail Price: Under $1.00

Fur Tacks

E-Z Fur Tacks are simple to install and hold a detachable fur collar firmly in place over any coat collar, with no damage to the coat. The spiked section should be sewn onto the underside of the fur collar with heavy duty thread. The spike then pushes through the coat collar, and the small firm metal clasp slips onto the end of the spike. Made by E-Z Buckle, Inc. Approximate Retail Price: $1.00

Snap Tape And Hook And Eye Tape

Every notions company markets these products, usually in white, black and cream. They all seem equally good, and the prices on them differ very little when they are sold in blister packaging. Most manufacturers will supply these items to stores in reels for sale by the yard. For many uses, such as home decoration you may find the tape easier to work with in long lengths than by piecing together the packaged lengths. Buying by the yard is also slightly cheaper than the packaged variety. Approximate Retail Price: Under $1.00

Self-Fastening Tape

Velcro® is a trade name that was heard for so long before it had competitors that most of us never realized it wasn't the generic name for the product. It remains one of the best new products of the century with many inventive uses. There is now a packaged spot form of Velcro fasteners that comes in more colors than are available in the by-the-yard type. The only objection we find to these spots is that they have a sticky self-basting back which is not easy to sew through. Once on your garment however, they're fine. Distributed by Donahue Sales, Talon Div. of Textron, Inc. and Scovill, Sewing Notions Division. Approximate Retail Price: Under $1.00

Dritz Flexloc is a narrow self-fastening tape with an iron-on backing. It seems to hold well when ironed on, and could be used this way for items which do not need to be washed or dry cleaned frequently. It can also be sewn after having been ironed in place. There is no sticky quality to the bonding agent. The closing surface works well. Made by Scovill, Sewing Notions Division. Approximate Retail Price: $1.75

Thinner Fasteners

Conso Cric-Crac is thinner, a little wider, and just as strong as the original self-fastening tape. It is sold by the yard, and is less expensive than competitive brands. It was developed for home decorating, but is equally good for clothing. Developed by Conso Products Co. Approximate Retail Price: $2.40 per yard

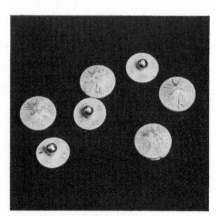

E-Z Silk Covered Snaps

Velcro Brand Fasteners

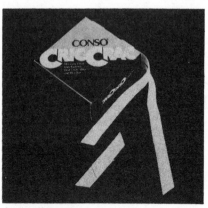

Conso Cric-Crac

Baubles & Bangles

The line is too big to cover completely but we can say that if it's glitter and glamour you want, look at the E-Z Buckle line. There are E-Z Jewels, so simple that they can be set with tweezers or small pliers. There are two inexpensive setting tools for rhinestones — one also sets gold or silver studs. Refills come in great variety. Both machines are simple to operate. All from E-Z Buckle, Inc. Approximate Retail Price: From $1.00

Lacing Tips

Lacing for eyelet closures can be purchased ready-made, or you can make it yourself from fabric scraps. Give the ends of either kind of lacing a professional look with Metal Tips. Easy to apply, they are available in gold or nickel and can also be used on the ends of cording belts. From E-Z Buckle, Inc. Approximate Retail Price: Under $1.00

Fusibles

Fusible notion items are used during garment construction and for decoration. Care must be taken when applying them to the garment so the bond is perfect. Follow the manufacturer's instructions exactly for best results. Some fusible products don't work well with some fabrics, and if the garment is to be washed or dry cleaned often, another method of attachment may be more satisfactory.

Fusible webs are another interesting development in the sewing world. After testing a number of brands, it would be hard to find any appreciable difference, except in width, price and packaging. So, it's a buyer's market. The wide Fusible Web from Pellon, and Stitch Witchery from Stacy Fabrics, are especially convenient for large appliques. Other names that are prominent in the pre-packaged

Pellon Fusible Web

web are Jiffy Fuse by Staple Sewing Aids Corp, and Poly Web from Coats & Clark. Approximate Retail Price: (Stacy) $1.00

Garment Repair

The notions manufacturers have designed a wide variety of mending items. You can buy replacement pockets, knit cuffs, toggle fastenings, and many other useful repair items. There are iron-on patches for the knees and seats of jeans, leather elbow patches, and wide bias hem facing for the growing schoolgirl's skirt. One nice thing about many of these patches and repair items is that they are designed to be fun and attractive. They often enhance rather than detract from the original garment.

Patches

Mending patches can be plain, colorful, and decorated. They come in denim and corduroy fabrics. They seem to be of equal quality from several of the major companies. Wrights Bondex line is large, and has a lot of happy prints and embroidered denims. E-Z Buckle makes plain mending tape in colors and cutouts of hearts, stars, butterflies, and other shapes. Talon also has mending patches in plain, print, and corduroy designs and fabric. Most iron-ons are good emergency items but for permanence it's best to stitch them. Other sources of

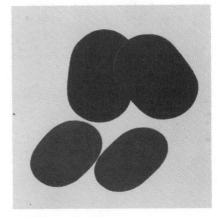

E-Z Elbow Patches

iron-on patches are: Scovill, Sewing Notions Division and Penn Products Co. Approximate Retail Price: Under $1.00

E-Z Elbow Patches come in genuine leather in two sizes. They last forever and make a man's sport jacket or sweather look rough-and-tough. They are perforated around the edges for easy sewing so they can be stitched on by hand with handsome heavy thread. From E-Z Buckle, Inc. Approximate Retail Price: Under $2.00

Pockets

It's usually too much trouble to replace an entire pants pocket.

Wrights Bondex Iron-On Pockets

E-Z Insta Letters

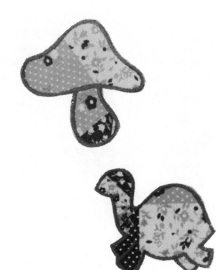

E-Z Appliques

Initials

Insta Letters by E-Z Buckle, Inc. are solid no-nonsense, heat-transfer letters, available in white, red, black, and navy. If used as directed, they work and wear well. Because the Insta Letters are inexpensive, you can buy enough double alphabets to make up any phrase.

The same company makes heat transfer glitter initials which do not work well. The same is true of their rubberized heat transfer Calico Patchwork & "Fun" Initials. There is a tendency for both of these items to peel off many fabrics, in spite of careful handling. All three are from E-Z Buckle, Inc. Approximate Retail Price: From Under $1.00

Pockets wear out at the bottom where keys and change are kept. With the Bondex Iron-On half pocket, you simply trim off the worn lower part of the pocket, and iron the new piece in place according to directions. We suggest stitching for extra security. From Wm. E. Wright Co. Approximate Retail Price: Under $1.00

Knit Replacements

E-Z Knitted Cuffs, Collars, and Waistbands are not only good for replacing worn parts on winter jackets, but have other uses. They can be used to extend the length of a child's jacket or his sleeves if he outgrows his clothes before he wears them out. The collar can be

added to a jacket that doesn't have cuddly warmth around the neck. The cuffs can also be sewn up inside of sleeves that are too wide at the bottom where wind blows up the sleeve. All from E-Z Buckle, Inc. Approximate Retail Price: Under $2.00

Toggle Buttons

At least one toggle always seems to wear out on that handsome sport jacket. Even if you can't find a toggle replacement to match the others on the garment, you can get an entire new set. E-Z Buckle Toggles come in several styles and lengths and will renew your favorite jacket. From E-Z Buckle, Inc. Approximate Retail Price: Under $2.00

Appliques

There are so many available appliques, iron-on and sew-on, that we cannot cover them adequately. Both E-Z Buckle and Wrights have large lines of embroidered and fabric appliques, from tiny flowers to bandana-print patch pockets. Streamline Button has entered the field with Cute Capers words in calico. Approximate Retail Price: From Under $1.00

A Loving Touch

Labels with sweet messages add a loving touch to the items you make for others. They are called Love Labels and are as well-made as the labels in the best designer clothes. It might even be fun to use them on the outside of a tote bag or belt. Made by B. Blumenthal & Co., Inc. Approximate Retail Price: (7) $1.00

E-Z Knit Replacements

E-Z Toggle Button

Blumenthal Love Label

258

Buyer's Guide-- Sewing Machines

A sewing machine may be one of the most valuable pieces of equipment in the household. It is essential for anyone who wants to create interesting, original clothes and home decorations. The experienced home-sewer regards a good machine as a necessary tool, recognizing that its performance helps keep the clothing budget within reasonable limits and tailor bills at a minimum.

Choosing The Right Sewing Machine

With so many sewing machines on the market, selecting the one that is best suited for your needs and your budget will require study. The purchase is usually considered a long-term investment, and to make your selection easier, CONSUMER GUIDE® has tested and evaluated 28 machines from 15 manufacturers. We hope to give you a better idea of what is in the marketplace and how each model performs. Your final decision, however, should be made only after you have actually tried out different makes and models in the same way you would road-test a car before making a selection.

Determining the right sewing machine for your needs is a matter of matching the capability and cost of the various machines to the sewing you consider essential and pleasurable. Price will undoubtedly be a major factor. It is possible to spend over $1000 for a complex model programmed electronically with many controls, many built-in stitch patterns and an automatic buttonholder. At the other end of the scale, you can spend just over $100 and get a basic zigzag model with stretch capacity. As a rule, the more expensive models have more stitch patterns as well as more sophisticated controls. Sometimes you are paying a premium for added patterns along with the same controls found in cheaper models in the same line. You must then make the decision whether those extra patterns are worth the extra money.

For a beginner, one of the simpler zigzag models with basic stitches and few controls to master would be a wise choice. It is sensible to spend about a year developing your sewing skills and seeing how much pleasure you get from creating clothes for yourself and your family before investing in a complicated, expensive machine.

If you are an experienced sewer, you are probably looking for a new model with more capability than exists on your old machine. You want one which has the stitch patterns to make professional looking seams on stretchables, knits and synthetics. You'll want to test the many utility and stretch stitches, taking into account which patterns you'll be using frequently and which occasionally. Be on the lookout for a certain amount of similarity in some stitch patterns on machines that offer a large selection. You may find the machine is a very expensive item if it has many decorative and utility stitches you will never use.

Do you want a free arm machine or a flatbed model? All manufacturers offer a free arm model, usually costing slightly more than their basic flatbed model, but the cost may be worth it because of the ease it gives to many sewing jobs. Try both kinds before you make a decision.

If you are the type of person who is always on the go, take a look at the new medium and lightweight portables that come complete with carrying cases and are easily transportable. Elna seems to have an edge on the lightweights with the Elnita weighing only 11 pounds and the Lotus slightly more at 14 pounds. These are sturdy machines, but the heads are slightly smaller. Another machine, not quite as light but still portable, is the Bernina Nova 900. It is a whole sewing center; when the case opens from the side, sewing aids and accessories are fitted on its doors. Several other machines have carrying cases with room for spools of thread and accessories in a compartment under the handle.

Almost any machine, whether it converts to a free arm, or has a flatbed head, can be installed in a carrying case for portability, but it may also be so heavy that you'll only use the case as a cover for storage. Cases are made of soft vinyl, transparent plexiglass, wood and plastic. A few cases enclose the machine entirely, latching securely at the base.

Many sewers with plenty of room prefer to have the machine installed in a console which can double as another piece of furniture when the machine is not in use. A console has the advantage of making the mounted machine very stable so there is less chance of vibration when sewing at top speed. A console also places the machine bed at the right sewing height, gives convenient storage space for accessories and notions in the drawers, and provides an extra work surface. Some consoles are designed to accommodate free arm models as well as flatbeds. The head is pulled up to a higher level when the free arm is needed for tubular sewing.

Consoles have some disadvantages, however. Many are designed without adequate knee room, and some models are not stable. Another inconvenience we have noted is the difficulty of inserting and removing the bobbin case in a flatbed, especially when it is mounted vertically in the shuttle. When the bobbin sits in the shuttle horizontally (as it does on the Singer and Elna models) or on an angle (Necchi) this task is considerably easier to accomplish.

Buying Procedure

Whether you are seriously considering a top of the line model or an inexpensive machine — new or used — there are basic questions to consider before committing yourself to a purchase.

First, make sure the dealer is established and has a reputation for good service. Besides the nationally known machines there are unbranded machines sold by individual dealers and by large chain stores who put their own names on them. Usually these machines are lower in price and often are made by well-known companies; some are not, however. If you are thinking of buying an off-brand model be sure it has a guarantee and that servicing can be done at locations in other parts of the country should you happen to move.

Questions to ask the dealer are:

1. Does the machine have wide distribution throughout the country and can it be serviced easily? Are parts available? If out of stock are they readily resupplied?

2. How long is the guarantee and what does it cover? Is it in writing? Who backs it — the manufacturer, distributor or dealer? In case the dealership changes hands or you move to another section of the country will the guarantee be honored?

3. What kind of maintenance does the machine require? Is it only periodical cleaning and oiling at home or must the motor be factory serviced at intervals? Can a console be serviced at home? Are cleaning tools and oil included with the machine?

4. Is the operator's manual clear and illustrated? Does the dealer offer free instructions or sewing lessons to help the purchaser become acquainted with the machine's potential?

Straight Stitch

Zigzag Stitch

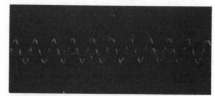
Tricot Stitch

Buttonhole Sewing

Knit Stitch

Feather Stitch

If you are satisfied with the dealer's answers, the next step is to examine the model carefully.

1. Are the controls placed for convenience, easy to read and easy to handle? Are you comfortable using them?
2. Is the lighting good or does it cast unwanted shadows in the sewing area? Is the bulb easy to replace? Does the face plate get very hot if the bulb is located behind it?
3. Is the foot control (or knee pedal) comfortable to use and does it press easily? Does it have a non-skid material on the back to keep it in place on an uncarpeted floor?
4. If you are buying a free arm unit does the extension table come off easily? Is it stable and sturdy when in place? Must the table be removed to gain access to the bobbin area? Is the free arm slender enough to accommodate small tubular sewing?
5. Is there good visibility around the needle area or does the face plate have so much overhang that it is difficult to thread the needle?
6. If there is a carrying case, is it sturdy? Is the machine light enough to actually be portable?

To see how the machine performs, sit down in front of the needle in a comfortable chair and sew. If you have never used a machine before, ask a friend who is familiar with sewing to shop with you. Don't rely on the fabric the dealer provides for test-stitching. It's almost always a piece of stiff muslin or heavy cotton which makes the stitch quality of any machine look good. Bring your own packet of test fabrics — a sheer (chiffon or voile), a tricot (perferably nylon), an acrylic knit, a polyester double knit, a woven cotton, a lightweight wool and a heavyweight wool. If you don't have scraps of all these fabrics take along nylon, double knit and two weights of wool to see how the machine responds to fabrics of different weights and fiber content.

Begin as the instruction manual usually lists the operations; wind the bobbin and thread the machine from the needle and bobbin. Ask these questions as you check out the performance:

1. How easily is the machine threaded?
2. Does the bobbin wind easily? Does it cut off automatically when full? Does it thread into the case handily and is it easy to mount and remove from the shuttle?
3. Is the shuttle area accessible?
4. Does the bobbin hold an adequate supply of thread?
5. Is there any bobbin "chatter" — as though it were loose when the machine is being run?
6. Is the tension control good or must it be readjusted for each new weight of fabric? Must you regulate the bobbin tension for a balanced stitch?
7. Does the machine run without vibrating? Is the motor quiet and does it respond instantly when the foot control is pressed? Is there any coasting after releasing the control?
8. If there are built-in stitches, how easy are they to dial? If there are insertable cams, are they easy to mount and remove from the cam holder?
9. Does the stitch capacity fit your needs? Is there a stretch stitch?
10. If there is an automatic buttonholer, does it make stitches of uniform density on both sides, and strong bartacks?
11. Does the machine backstitch easily with good quality of stitch?
12. Are the presser feet easily removed and mounted again?
13. Does the machine sew well on various fabrics with various thread contents?
14. Does the bobbin jam?
15. Is the machine easy to sew on, and are you comfortable with it?
16. Is the machine easy to clean and oil? Are there many oiling points and are they accessible? Is the needle plate easy to remove so the feed dogs can be cleaned?
17. Does the selection of accessories and aids include a zipper foot, a seam ripper, a screw driver, and a good assortment of needles?

Obviously, if your answers to more than a few of these questions are negative, you should look at another model or brand. No matter what the price range, you should not have to compromise on such vital features as tension control, stitch quality or capacity and the general response of the machine. Careful shopping for the features you want should help you find a machine that will give good performance for many years.

Sewing Machine Features

All new home sewing machines work basically the same, each having the ability to straight stitch, zigzag and make some sort of buttonhole. The differences between makes and models of sewing machines are in the number and types of features. Some features will be important to you, others may not, but they will help determine your machine choice.

Basic Features

Free Arm-Flatbed

Some machines have a free arm and others have a flatbed. The free arm enables you to stitch around sleeves, cuffs and other curved areas and also makes many patching jobs easier. All free arms are not the same size. Some are small in circumference and others are large. Some have a flat, instead of the more conventional round, shape. The smaller free arms offer more maneuverability than the larger free arms.

SEWING MACHINE FEATURES

Model	Free Arm	Flatbed	Extension Table	Built-In Stitches	Cams	Reverse Control	Adjustable Pressure	Drop Feed Dog	Motor Speeds	Bobbin Cut-Off	Bobbin Case	Snap-On Presser Feet	Buttonholer	One-Motion Threading	Carrying Case	Approximate Retail Price
Bernina 810	Y	N	N	6	N	L	N	Y	2	Y	V	Y	Y	Y	Y	$620.00
Bernina Nova 900	Y	N	Y	6	N	B	N	Y	1	Y	V	Y	Y	Y	Y	$770.00
Bernina 830	Y	N	Y	20	N	L	N	Y	1	Y	V	Y	Y	Y	Y	$990.00
Brother Odyssey 8060	Y	N	Y	7	N	L	N	Y	2	Y	V	N	Y	Y	Y	$350.00
Elna Elnita SP	Y	N	N	3	N	D	N	N	1	N	H	N	Y	Y	Y	$390.00
Elna Lotus T SP	Y	N	Y	8	N	D	N	N	1	N	H	N	Y	Y	Y	$620.00
Elna SU Air Electronic	Y	N	N	6	18	D L	N	N	1	Y	H	N	Y	Y	Y	$1200.00
National 776	Y	N	Y	28	N	B	Y	Y	2	Y	V	N	Y	N	Y	$550.00
National 350	Y	N	Y	10	N	L	Y	NA	1	N	V	Y	Y	N	NA	$600.00
National EL 300	Y	N	Y	15	N	L	Y	Y	NA	N	V	Y	Y	N	NA	$700.00
Necchi Silvia 584	Y	N	Y	4	N	L	Y	Y	2	N	A	Y	Y	Y	Y	$690.00
Necchi Silvia 586	Y	N	Y	10	N	L	Y	Y	2	N	A	Y	Y	Y	Y	$800.00
Nelco La Belle II 645F	Y	N	Y	8	N	B	Y	Y	2	Y	V	Y	Y	N	Y	$400.00
New Home 910	Y	N	Y	28	N	B	Y	Y	2	Y	V	Y	Y	Y	Y	$700.00
Penney 6520	N	Y	N	6	N	B	Y	Y	1	Y	V	N	N	N	N	$200.00
Penney 6905	Y	N	Y	7	N	B	Y	Y	1	Y	V	N	Y	N	Y	$300.00
Pfaff 209	Y	N	Y	3	N	L	N	Y	1	Y	V	N	Y	Y	Y	$400.00
Pfaff 1222E	Y	N	Y	10	N	L	N	Y	1	Y	V	N	Y	Y	Y	$998.00
Riccar 806	Y	N	Y	6	N	B	Y	Y	1	N	V	Y	Y	Y	Y	$550.00
Riccar 808 E	Y	N	Y	26	N	B	Y	Y	1	N	V	Y	Y	Y	Y	$770.00
Sears Kenmore 1525	Y	N	Y	12	N	L	Y	Y	1	Y	V	N	Y	Y	N	$240.00
Sears Kenmore 1780	Y	N	Y	12	30	L	Y	N	1	Y	H	Y	Y	Y	N	$430.00
Singer Fashion Mate 248	N	Y	N	N	15	B	Y	N	1	Y	H	Y	Y	N	N	$150.00
Singer Athena 2000	Y	N	Y	22	N	B	Y	N	2	N	H	Y	Y	Y	N	$950.00
Universal Standard 7000	Y	N	Y	5	N	B	Y	Y	1	Y	V	Y	Y	Y	Y	$470.00
Viking 5710	Y	N	Y	5	N	B	Y	Y	1	N	V	Y	Y	Y	Y	$500.00
Viking 6460	Y	N	Y	N	8	B	Y	Y	2	N	V	Y	Y	Y	Y	$870.00
White 710	Y	N	Y	26	N	L	Y	Y	2	Y	V	Y	Y	Y	Y	$800.00

Key: Y = yes; N = no; NA = information not available; B = button; L = lever; D = dial; V = vertical; A = angle; H = horizontal

Extension Table

While a flatbed machine provides more working surface around the needle, all the free arm models tested, (with one exception) came with an extension table that would increase the working surface of the basic free arm. The Bernina 810 has a free arm extension table but at an extra cost.

Built-In Stitches

Major manufacturers stopped making straight stitch machines a few years ago in favor of the more versatile models which zigzag and do many other decorative and utility stitches. All the reviewed machines will straight stitch, zigzag and have from three to 28 other built-in stitches. Some machines will have the capability of doing more stiches by combining two of the built-in stitches, or purchasing extra pattern cams. Most machines utilize the built-in stitch mechanism. Machines using cams for their various stitches are not difficult to use, but you do have to hunt through a stack of cams each time you want to change to another stitch. One advantage of the cam system is that you can usually purchase additional cams which will increase the stitching pattern capacity of your machine.

Reverse Stitching

All the machines tested had reverse stiching capabilities using a button, lever, dial or a combination of controls. All the machines would reverse stitch as long as the button, lever, or bar was operated. Machines with a dial control could be set for continuous backstitching at a given stitch length.

Pressure Regulator

The majority of the machines tested (almost all of those made in Japan) have controls which regulate the amount of pressure exerted on the presser foot. In some machines this seems to be critical, especially when sewing on lightweight fabrics which have a tendency to swerve under the needle; in other models we couldn't detect much difference when the pressure regulator was changed except for darning. Machines without a separate pressure regulator have a universal pressure system that handles all types of fabric at the built-in setting. We feel these systems functioned well.

Feed Dogs

The feed dogs, those tooth units underneath the needle, can influence how evenly the machine feeds the fabric under the pressure foot. Basically, there are three types of feed dogs — the cross-grooved metal teeth, the diamond-shaped metal teeth and those made of a composition material or hard rubber. Almost every machine has a lever that drops the feed dogs below the needle plate for darning or free-form embroidery. In lieu of this control, a smooth needle plate cover is usually provided which takes the feed dogs out of action. One advantage of dropped feed dogs is that you can smoothly slip bulky or easily snagged fabric under the presser foot if the feed dogs have first been lowered out of the way. Remember to raise them up again when you start to sew.

Speed Regulator

Usually a foot control accompanies a machine head as the speed regulator for the motor. If the model you select doesn't have one included you will have to buy a console or special carrying case that provides a control, either foot or knee, and possibly the connections for the motor and control as well. Of course, the cost of the control and console or case must be added to the initial price of the machine.

Foot Control

Any foot control should be wide enough to support the upper part of the foot. It should not skid around on the floor. Some controls have a switch which lets you change motor speed. Other controls govern the speed of the motor by the amount of pressure exerted on it. Whichever type of control you have, it should respond immediately to pressure and not coast along when the pressure is released.

Bobbin Case

The bobbin case should be easily accessible. Some bobbins are positioned vertically, some horizontally and one brand (Necchi) on an angle. Horizontally placed bobbins are easier to insert than vertically placed bobbins. Most of the vertically placed bobbins require a separate bobbin case. Plastic, see-through bobbins are a help because you can see how much thread is left on the bobbin without having to take it out of the case.

On the majority of machines we tested, bobbins are wound on the top of the arm and automatically cut off winding when the bobbin is full. If your bobbin doesn't cut off automatically, you will have to watch it carefully so it doesn't overfill. On a few models, the bobbin wound on the right side of the machine with the bobbin tension guide in back of the machine. These were awkward and hard to thread. Probably the best system is Singer's in which the bobbin is wound in place from the upper thread while the machine is still threaded. However, it doesn't have an automatic cut off.

Presser Feet

Snap-on feet, which mount on a common shank, eliminate the necessity of changing a set screw each time a new presser foot is needed. Some machines have much more space between the raised presser foot and feed dogs than others, a point which we think is important; bulky fabrics can be fitted under the foot without crushing them. Some presser foot lifters have the added plus of lifting even higher than the "up" locked position to take care of heavy materials. A white area on the shank, directly behind the needle eye, is found on the presser feet on some machines. This increases visibility when threading the needle.

Tension Adjustment

A slight adjustment of upper thread tension is acceptable to obtain good stich balance on different fabrics, but a wide variation should not be necessary. Most bobbin tensions can be adjusted if necessary for specialized stitching, but in the majority of cases they are set at the factory and should not be changed for ordinary sewing.

Buttonholes

All machines tested have the capacity of making a bartack buttonhole. Most machines make an automatic, no-turn buttonhole while some make a manual buttonhole which requires the fabric to be pivoted around the needle. Sometimes the satin stitch is pre-set so it is not possible to adjust it. We prefer the machine that allows a change in the stitch length in case the satin stitch is too dense or too spread out. In some of the more expensive machines the mechanism takes over entirely and with no dialing necessary other than the first setting.

Threading

One-motion threading is a convenience on most of the tested machines. This allows you to thread the machine without having to insert the thread through any closed eyelets; the eyelets have grooves or slots which allow you to slip the thread in place.

Lighting

Good lighting is essential for good sewing. Some light bulbs, mounted behind the machine face plate, are located so high up that much of the light is lost behind the plate. One of the best systems is on the National, which has two lights; one under the center of the arm and another behind the face plate. Some machines have a light only under the center of the arm which sheds light on the base of the machine but very little around the needle area.

Special Features

Power Switch

Some machines have a safety power switch which is an important feature. On some machines it is coordinated with the light switch — the machine can't be started whenever the light is turned off. The Elna SU Air Electronic has the best system. When the motor switch is turned on, a separate warning light also is lit which is not connected to the sewing light. This feature can prevent some unpleasant accidents.

Color Coding

Some controls on some machines are color coded. All you do is match up a certain color on the various dials when you want a special stitch. This is much easier to do than trying to remember which mark goes where when they all look similar.

Pattern Indicator Wheel

The Pfaff and Bernina have a pattern indicator wheel that shows the beginning of a pattern design with one full revolution making a complete design. This helps you start and stop your decorative stitching at the proper places.

Even Feeding

Every machine should feed the fabric evenly, but it is sometimes difficult to match plaids and stripes when sewing two layers of fabric without careful basting or pinning. Three companies — Singer, Pfaff and Riccar — have special presser feet which keep the layers of fabric perfectly aligned to the end so matching is possible without excessive preparation beforehand.

Pattern Elongator

Some machines are equipped with a pattern elongator dial which enables you to stretch out or compress decorative stitch patterns so they look different. This is handy only if you do a lot of decorative stitching.

Backstitching

Instant backstitching is available on the National models 350 and EL 300. A lever, when pushed up, makes several tiny stitches backwards to fasten a seam. When the lever is pushed down the machine reverse stitches in the same length of stitch as the forward setting.

Needle Stop Control

Another unique feature of the National EL 300 is an electronically controlled lever which programs the needle to stop out of the fabric with the take-up lever at its highest point or makes the needle remain in the fabric for easy pivoting. The Riccar 808E also has a similar device.

Bobbin Mounting

Necchi has mounted its bobbin in the shuttle race on a slant without the need of a separate bobbin case. It is easy to insert and the transparent bobbin made checking the bobbin thread a snap.

Pneumatic Foot Control

Instead of a regular foot control the Elna SU Air Electronic has a pneumatic control; a rubber button on a larger base that contains no electrical parts. When depressed, it activates the electronics in the machine. A lever can be moved to reduce speed at any given point while sewing with the motor at full power. This is an advantage when stitching heavy fabrics.

Four-Way Presser Foot Lifter

One of the unique features of the Pfaff 1222E is the Stopmatic action of the presser foot lifter. It is a special bar that can assume one of four positions. One position allows the take-up lever and needle to go to their highest position so the fabric can be removed from the machine. It also disengages the machine for bobbin winding at this point. Another position raises the presser foot but allows the needle to remain in the fabric so it can be pivoted around the needle. A third position lowers the presser foot and the lowest position is used to raise the bobbin thread to the surface when you have just threaded the machine.

Chain Stitch

Several machines tested have the capacity to make a chain stitch, a good temporary stitch if one is careful to fasten the end so it will not pull out easily. Setting up the chain stitch requires rethreading the top thread through special guides next to the take-up lever and replacing the bobbin with a special attachment.

Questionable Features

CONSUMER GUIDE® found certain features that did little to enhance the performance of the machine.

Needle Threaders

The needle threaders on Pfaff and Necchi machines were more of a nuisance than a help. It seemed much simpler to thread the needle manually than to operate the threading machanism.

Stitch Balance Controls

Machines from at least three different manufacturers had stitch balance controls for adjusting the density of satin or buttonhole stitches, primarily so both sides would be uniform. The concept is noteworthy since many of the buttonholes we made had a tendency to be dense when the mechanism stitched in reverse for one of the sides. But these controls were ineffective for the most part, no matter how they were adjusted.

Chain Stitching

Several makers included chain stitching for temporarily joining a seam or for decorative stitching. We thought it was a nuisance to have to rethread the machine and remove the bobbin for a chain looper attachment just to make a seam that could be pulled out very quickly. Indeed, if we weren't careful, it would unravel as soon as it was detached from the machine. Making a line of chain stitching for belt loops was equally unsatisfactory.

Long Basting

Actual speed basting with stitch lengths up to one inch (25mm) could be accomplished on both Necchi and Bernina models. Several other manufacturers, however, recommended basting in a less satisfactory manner. We had to make a stitch, raise the needle and pull the fabric manually as far as desired, lower the needle, make another stitch and pull again. Somehow, it seemed much easier to merely use the longest stitch length for basting, and settle for a shorter temporary stitch rather than go through the process of pulling to make each stitch.

Inadequate Controls

The spring loaded lever with a stopper on either side, which had to be adjusted to regulate stitch width, was difficult to set. Other controls which were awkwardly or inconveniently placed also rated low marks. We saw no reason to hide the pressure controls behind the face plates (in one case, directly behind the light bulb) or on the back of the arm. The control to drop the feed dogs was sometimes set next to the bobbin case behind the shuttle cover. On one model, that control was placed in back of the free arm making it especially difficult to reach when the extension table was in place.

Presser Feet & Accessories

Each machine will come with a number of presser feet and machine accessory items. An instruction book should also be included with the machine.

Many presser feet have been

designed to add to the machine's versatility. Almost all of the presser feet are hinged so they can "walk" over pins placed at right angles to the seam. Most of the feet snap on and off a common shank, and are easier to set in place than the designs that must be mounted around a set screw.

Every modern machine has a zigzag or all-purpose foot and a straight stitch foot. Many models come with a straight needle plate also which has a single hole for the needle to penetrate instead of the wide slot of the all-purpose needle plate, which accommodates the swing of the needle for zigzag stitching. The straight needle plate is very useful for straight stitching on lightweight fabrics which have a tendency to become caught in the wide zigzag slot and can be difficult to remove without damaging the fabric.

Depending upon the manufacturer, the buttonhole foot often resembles the zigzag all-purpose foot with the toes slightly wider apart. The sled type buttonholer usually has two advantages — it has markings on the side so buttonholes can be gauged and made the same length, and it has a mechanism for making corded buttonholes. Brother has an ingenious foot design; the sled detaches from the inner plastic foot by removing a stopper on the back, and the inner part then attaches buttons.

Several makers have a blindstitch presser foot that makes the operation considerably easier. The fold of the hem is held against a metal center ridge for guidance which helps control the fabric. A few manufacturers have a separate metal piece that mounts over the all-purpose foot and performs the same function.

Some models have feet which appear to be identical when viewed from the top, but turned over, the soles are different. The one used for woven fabrics will have a slight, broad groove on the bottom while the foot intended for stretchable fabrics and lightweight woven materials will have a completely flat sole.

Another useful foot is the overlock foot which is fashioned with a wire on the side to prevent knits from curling when an overcast stitch is being used. A two-way zipper, or cording foot, is always better than one which can only be used from one side. We also noted specific feet for stitching close to the invisible zippers which we thought was very practical.

Other accessories usually included with the machine are; machine oil, lint brush, bobbins, machine needles and one or two small screw drivers. Some machines will also have a double needle, needle threader, seam ripper, spare light bulb and darning plate.

Maintenance

A top quality sewing machine will last for years with little or no professional servicing if it is given the proper care at home. As with any machinery, it must be maintained to perform efficiently. It's a simple task to remove the needle plate, open the shuttle door, and with a soft brush remove any lint, dirt or loose threads to prevent unnecessary tangling or irregular stitching. The shuttle area and the feed dogs should be cleaned fairly often, after about 15 hours of sewing.

Periodic lubrication will keep the machine running smoothly and quietly. In every instruction manual a section is devoted to instructions on where and how often to apply a small amount of oil. Some machines even have the oil points marked in red so the sewer doesn't have to consult the manual to remind her where a drop or two of oil is needed. Most of the machines include a small container of light oil suitable for the lubrication. If the model does

not have oil among the sewing accessories, ask the dealer what kind of oil is recommended. Do not attempt to use an all-purpose oil because it might contain ingredients that would be harmful to the machine and clog the moving parts.

One machine, Viking, has a rather unique sealed system requiring no lubrication. No matter what the brand, when not in use, the machine should be covered so dust and dirt cannot accumulate.

Problem Solving

Whenever there is a breakdown of the machine, chances are that it has been caused by incorrect handling. The following list will identify problems and give probable causes. Using this information, try to remedy the problem yourself before calling a repair man.

Skipped Stitches

Needle is not inserted properly.
Needle point is blunt or broken.
Needle is the wrong type.
Thread is of poor quality or wrong content for fabric.
Machine is incorrectly threaded.
Incorrect presser foot is used.
Pressure is incorrect on presser foot.

Top Thread Breaks

Machine is threaded incorrectly.
Tension is too tight.
The needle is blunt or crooked.
Poor quality of thread has knotted.
The thread is caught on or under the spool pin.
The thread is too heavy for the needle size.

Lower Thread Breaks

Bobbin case is not inserted
    correctly.
Bobbin is not threaded properly
    into the case.
Bobbin tension is too tight.

Needle Breaks

Needle is not inserted correctly.
Needle clamp screw is not
    sufficiently tightened.
Needle is damaged.
Fabric is too heavy for needle size.
Fabric is being pulled by the
    operator.

Seam Puckering

Presser foot pressure is incorrect.
Upper and lower threads are of
    different sizes.
Threading is incorrect.
Bobbin is wound too full.
Needle is too large for fabric.
Wrong stitch length is used.

Irregular Stitching and Feeding

Presser foot pressure is too light.
The thread is of poor quality.
Bobbin is threaded incorrectly.
Thread remnants are between
    tension discs or under the
    bobbin case tension spring.

Machine Runs Noisy or Rough

Lint and oil have built up in hook
    or under needle plate.
Machine needs oiling.
Needle is damaged.
Wrong kind of oil has been used.
Stitch length and width dials are
    set incorrectly for stitch pattern
    used.

Poor Quality Stitch

A poor quality stitch is usually
caused by unbalanced thread
tension. All sewing machines have
two threads; the upper one which
is threaded through the needle
and one which is wound around
the bobbin. When the needle
pierces the fabric, the top thread is
locked in a loop with the bottom
thread. When the top and bottom
threads are locked evenly, with no
pull or stretch and no loops
showing on either side of the
fabric, the tension is correct and
balanced.

Every sewing machine has a dial
that will loosen or tighten the
upper thread tension. The
resistance through which the
thread moves as it feeds from the
spool to the needle is reduced or
increased, and the thread becomes
looser or tighter as it locks in the
fabric. Usually adjusting the upper
thread tension is sufficient to bring
a stitch back into balance. The
tension control is so precise on
many machines we tested that it
was unnecessary to make any
changes when stitching various
types of fabrics. On many
machines it is possible to regulate
the bobbin tension by turning a
screw on the bobbin case, but this
adjustment is seldom necessary.
Most bobbin tensions are
regulated at the factory and should
be turned only for specialized
stitching when elasticized thread
or heavy cord is wound around
the bobbin.

When the lower thread shows
on the top or the seam puckers,
correct the balance by loosening
the upper tension or dialing to a
lower number. When the upper
thread shows on the bottom, in
loops, the upper tension should be
set at a higher number to tighten.

Sewing Tips

A sewing machine is an
exceptionally fine tool that should
be treated with care and respect.
Here are some useful suggestions
to help you enjoy your machine to
the fullest.

1. Read the instruction book
    carefully.
2. Ask your dealer for a complete
    demonstration of the machine
    before purchasing it. If he
    offers lessons take advantage
    of them even if you are an
    experienced sewer. It will help
    you understand the potential
    of your machine.
3. Be sure you are acquainted
    with all of the controls before
    starting to sew.
4. Have a good supply of sharp
    and ball point needles on
    hand, in several sizes.
5. Position your chair so you are
    sitting directly in front of the
    needle, not in front of the
    center of the machine.
6. Always turn the hand wheel
    toward you when adjusting
    needle height, never away
    from you. Make sure the
    thread take-up lever is at the
    highest point before removing
    the fabric from the machine.
7. When changing from one
    machine operation to another,
    be sure to check all of the
    controls to make sure you have
    changed them to their new
    setting.
8. Do not change needle
    positions when the machine is
    running or when the needle is
    in the fabric. This might break
    or bend the needle.
9. If the shank of the presser foot
    doesn't have a white area for
    better visibility while
    threading the machine, hold a
    piece of white cardboard
    behind the needle to see the
    eye more clearly.
10. If the foot control has a
    tendency to slide around on an
    uncarpeted floor, place a pad
    or a small throw rug under it to
    keep it from skidding.
11. Always keep the accessories
    and sewing aids in a container
    nearby for quick changes of
    presser feet.
12. When using the twin-needle,
    be careful not to set the zigzag
    width so wide that the needle
    breaks.
13. After oiling, run the machine
    slowly for a few minutes,
    stitching on a cotton cloth that
    can be discarded. Wipe off any
    excess oil and start to sew on
    your current project.

Sewing Machine Test Reports

Bernina Matic 810

The Swiss-made Bernina Matic 810 is a lightweight free arm machine with a handle on top of the arm to make it portable. The carrying case is a soft plaid vinyl which covers the machine snugly and has an open slot to circumvent the handle. When the machine is not in use, the accessories, sewing aids and foot control are stored in an attachment box which fits around the free arm. An extension table can be purchased separately.

Although the 810 does not cost as much as the other Berninas tested by CONSUMER GUIDE®, it has some of the same quality features as the other models. The features include a self-adjusting tension, one motion threading, front loading bobbin, jam-free central bobbin hook and built-in stitch patterns. Besides the straight stitch, there are the zigzag, blindhem stitch, serpentine or running stitch, universal stitch, stretch stitch and vari-overlock stitch. A pattern selection panel is located on top of the arm and operated by a lever.

Easily visible on the front is a small window marked with a plus and minus on either side of a center line to indicate tension adjustment. The tension wheel for manual adjustment is on the arm, but the manufacturer recommends that the tension be readjusted with the wheel only for special purposes.

The stitch width regulator has two spring settings used to make semi-automatic buttonholes. When the settings are dialed they click so the sewer knows she has the correct size for either side of the buttonhole or the bartack. The fabric must be turned 180 degrees around after the first side is made to stitch the first bartack, and then proceed with the second side and bartack.

Among the utility stitches are several fine stretchables, and we are particularly pleased that the universal pattern has been included on the 810. This very elastic stitch was created expressly for sewing on fabrics suitable for girdles and bra insets. We tested several seams on lycra and were delighted with the stitches; they stretch not only vertically but also horizontally. The stretch stitch pattern was equally successful when we tried it on a loopy mohair knit and a cotton knit. The stitched seams gave as much as the fabric. This is not a straight stitch, it is like a small zigzag that makes a larger zag at intervals. It did not tear or shred the fabric the way some stretch stitches do. Because we kept the stitch width and length at a minimum, we were able to make fine enough seams so they could be pressed flat.

For the sewer who wants to make lingerie, the vari-overlock pattern will join and finish a seam at the same time. By using the special presser foot designed with a thin bar on the right side to prevent curling, we made an enviable seam both on tricot and batiste. Another quick seam on jersey or tricot that will also join and overcast in one operation is the blindstitch pattern, but with the regular zigzag presser foot. It is important to remember that the cut edge must be on the left, and the needle should actually go slightly off the fabric when it swings completely to the left.

The running or serpentine stitch (a series of small stitches in a wavy line) is best suited for darning broken areas in a fabric. We were able to almost invisibly mend a slight tear in a sheet by setting the stitch to the widest and the length almost to zero. For darning socks or other tears, it is also possible with the darning ring to weave a hole shut. By dropping the feed dogs, the sewer is in complete control of the direction of stitching and can guide the fabric back and forth without having to turn it. With a little practice, we turned

out a decently darned sock. The trick is to lay down the first row as close to the edge as possible, and to maintain the right speed.

Besides making utility patterns, the 810 can also baste with stitches up to one inch (25mm) in length. For one inch (25mm) stitches, it is necessary to use the magic needle which has two eyes, the upper one threaded for this purpose. It causes the machine to skip a couple of stitches, thereby making a long basting stitch.

We sewed on sheer nylon, polyesters, double knits, heavy denim, four layers of coating and leather and never had to adjust the tension. It was fascinating to watch the tension indicator, which never wavered from the center marking of 'normal,' in the window. Of course, we did have to adjust the stitch length for the various thicknesses. The stitch quality was excellent, and there was no coasting when we released the foot control.

The buttonholers are 'semi-automatic,' according to Bernina, which means that the garment has to be turned around at a 180 degree angle after the first side or 'bead' is made. Our buttonholes were strong and the satin stitch density was even on both sides. We did, however, pre-test the stitch as suggested in the instruction book to find the right setting on the stitch length regulator. The spring settings marking the ideal position on the stitch width control were easy to locate because there is a definite click at 1.75 for the side stitching and another at 3.5 for making bartacks. The range on the control is from zero to four. Our corded buttonholes were professional looking and strong. We had to follow the directions very carefully, which meant putting the needle into the fabric, laying the gimp left of the needle and lowering the presser foot. Before making the first bartack and after turning the fabric, we carefully laid the gimp parallel to the first side and steadied it with a finger as we made the first bartack and the second side.

It would be easier if the settings on the stitch length control were not so close together. Even the slightest turn of the rotary knob on the end of the lever can mean a noticeable effect on the stitch, especially in the range between zero and one. The size range is very good, though, away from the fine regulation on the shorter end. We counted 16 stitches to the inch when we set the lever at 1.5; when we set it at 4, the longest, we sewed seven stitches to the inch.

With only hooks and grooves, upper threading is a one-motion operation from the spool stand on the upper arm back to the eye of the needle. When the bobbin is full, it stops automatically as it is wound on top of the arm. Threaded in its case, the bobbin is ready to be placed vertically under the needle plate.

The motor has two speeds which can be set by a switch at the base of the machine. If you feel that more control is necessary for the work you are doing, you can set the control to "minimum" and the motor slows to half speed. The foot control is large enough to accommodate the whole foot comfortably.

As on the other Berninas, the lighting is adequate but not great. The bulb lights the needle area but mostly on the left side leaving the right slightly shadowed. It's a simple matter to change the bulb because the face plate is hinged to swing out so there is no bother unscrewing screws and lifting it up and around a switch.

The presser feet included with the machine all snap on by means of flipping a small lever on a shaft in back of the needle. They include: a zigzag foot, two-way zipper foot, blindstitch foot and darning foot. All but the darning foot have a white inset on the front that gives more visibility for the sewer when threading the needle. Other accessories to the machine are: six bobbins, a small screw driver, a special screw driver for removing the needle clamp, a straight edge gauge for marking buttonholes and hems, a seam ripper, darning ring, cleaning

brush, one package of assorted needles and a tube of oil.

The Bernina Guide instruction book which accompanies the machine is a sewing course in its own right. Even so, you will want to take advantage of the lessons offered by the dealer to become well acquainted with the many operations the machine can perform. Besides illustrating the various stitches, it also shows other available presser feet — such as a tailor tacking foot and an embroidery foot.

A limited 20-year warranty is included with the machine which covers all mechanical parts plus a two-year warranty for electrical parts.

Special capabilities of the 810 are darning and free-form embroidery and monogramming. With other optional presser feet that can be purchased, it can also tailor tack, sew on buttons, hem, gather, hemstitch and darn with wool. A twin-needle can also be used for decorative stitching.

The 810 is called the economy model by the manufacturer, but we would consider it expensive in comparison to many other machines which are near the low end of their lines. It is a quality product, and one that will give any sewer many years of pleasant stitching.

Approximate Retail Price: $620.00

Bernina Nova 900

The latest model in the Bernina line, the Nova 900 with the Swing Box, is well-engineered with a carrying case that has to be a *tour de force* in design. Because all of the accessories are fitted onto the case, there is no need to fumble through a box trying to find the right presser foot for the job or locate a new needle. Everything is within your grasp, mounted in its own niche or bracket, including three reels of spun-polyester Metrosene thread. The thread is excellent, but when the supply runs out, you

will have to find an outlet that sells thread on reels rather than on spools to fit on the three long, upright prongs that are built-in.

The case appears to be quite sturdy, and the inside front is handsomely lined in a red plush fabric. The ingenious frog fastener is equally strong. The case easily swings open and clears the table by about an inch. We attached the two case parts together, back to back, with the fastener for less swing and more stability as the instruction book suggested. Removing the case was easy; a lever was pushed to release a catch and the case could stand by itself near our sewing area.

With the Swing Box attached, however, it was awkward to manually turn the balance wheel when we had to raise the needle. The case is molded around the balance wheel and, when open, the molded edge is very close to the wheel.

The machine ran smoothly and quietly with no vibration throughout our testing. We made seams on chiffon, voile, polyester knits, denim, suede and heavy blanketing, and the stitch quality was excellent. The tension automatically adjusted to the thickness of the fabrics.

As on other Berninas we have tested, the utility stitches were excellent, especially among the stretchables. We tried the vari-overlock on a mohair knit. It not only produced a relatively flat

seam with edges neatly overcast, but also an elastic one. Another, identified as the stretch seam, is similar to a fine zigzag that makes a larger zag at intervals. It pressed flat like the straight stretches we have seen but unlike many of them, this stitch pattern goes forward only, not forward and then back a stitch or two. It can also be ripped out without damaging the fabric if a mistake is made.

Besides functioning as a blind stitch for hemming, the same pattern can also be used effectively to make a quick elastic seam, joining and overcasting at the same time. On a tricot seam, the blind stitch was a fast way to perform both tasks.

We liked the readability and accessibility of the controls on the Nova better than on other Berninas. There is no need to get up and peer at the top of the arm to make sure the correct stitch pattern has been dialed. The stitch selector with the utility patterns and the five stages for the automatic buttonholes is large and well located on the front of the arm so we were able to make a fast selection effortlessly. All patterns are shown by diagram and are also keyed either by letter or number. The stitch width regulator is conveniently placed directly below the control that changes needle positions. Being able to set the needle not only left and right but also half-left and half-right meant that it was handy to insert an invisible zipper, sewing very close to the teeth.

The control that regulates the stitch length is also an adequate size for handling with a wide scope. From zero to 1.5, which takes up about one-third of the dial, it is possible to make very fine adjustments. The best setting for making a good satin stitch on cotton shirting seemed to be 0.3 on our machine. To give an idea of the range, at a setting of 1.5 we counted 18 stitches per inch (25mm), and for the longest stitch, a setting of four yielded six and a half stitches per inch (25mm).

From the spool stand to the

needle, upper threading is a one-motion task going through open eyelets and slots with the tension disc positioned on the left of the take-up lever. The bobbin winder is on top of the arm to the right and a tension disc to the far left. The wound bobbin shuts off automatically when full.

Seven presser feet come with the Nova and they all snap on and off a common shaft. They are hinged to accommodate varying thicknesses of fabric and all but one have a white inset to give better visibility when threading the needle. Besides the zigzag foot, there are: a buttonhole foot, embroidery foot, darning foot, two-way zipper foot, overlock foot, and a blind hem foot. Every foot has a number on it for guaranteed identification. Besides all of the various utility and stretch stitches, it is possible to make a long basting stich by threading the upper eye on the "magic" needle just like the 830. It will make a stitch up to one inch (25mm) long with the blind stitch pattern selection. One stitch is skipped because of the unique needle.

The slide-on extension table, with a fuzzy sort of material around the inner edge is held firmly around the free arm by use of four pins which slide into corresponding holes on the machine proper. The table has no support on the left so it too is a free arm.

The electronic foot control gives full needle power at any speed through any thickness of fabric. On the Nova, Bernina has departed from its usual design for speed regulation. This control has a large button mounted on a square base with a rim of rubber on the bottom with grippers which keep it from sliding about on the floor. This control is about half the size of the ones on other Bernina models and accommodates only the ball of the foot.

There was no variation in the density of the satin stitch on either side. The precision buttonholer works the same as the one in the Electronic 830. There are five positions ending with the finisher, which locks the threads with several quick stitches. The trick of tightening the bobbin tension by running the thread through an eyelet on the case makes a smooth, more compact buttonhole. The design of the presser foot has simplified the process of making a good foolproof corded buttonhole. With an extra toe in the center we looped the gimp around it, drew both ends to the back under the foot and the machine took over. All that was needed to finish it was to clip the ends of the gimp when the last bartack was made and threads locked.

The illumination on the Nova could be better. The bulb is positioned under the face plate and throws light to the left of the needle, leaving the right and center of the free arm more or less in shadow. Changing the bulb is difficult. The face plate must be removed by releasing a screw and then lifting it off, around the light switch.

Two instruction books come with the 900. The first is a good manual of operating instructions which identifies the parts of the machine and shows how to use the controls and stitch patterns. It is also very helpful in telling how to maintain the machine by cleaning and oiling. Excellent photographs show how to remove the hook and clean the hook race. The second manual is the Bernina Guide booklet which also gives a diagram of the machine followed by a short sewing course on all possible operations within the Nova's stitch capacity. For each procedure there is a diagram of the foot needed and the correct control settings. Our Guide must have been produced for machines sold in Switzerland (the patterns are slightly different according to the operating manual), because our model did not have the universal stitch among its patterns although that stitch was illustrated on page ten. We also noted a mistake on page 20 which directed us to use the scallop seam (D) although the drawing did not look like a scallop. We wonder if Bernina didn't mean the bow or serpentine seam

instead which is in the 'D' position on our machine, the scallop being on 'E'.

The machine comes with a limited 20-year warranty on mechanical parts plus a two-year warranty on electrical parts.

Bernina says the Nova is "compact in size," but since it has a regular-sized head, we decided they must be using the word "compact" to describe how it goes snugly into the fitted Swing Box rather than referring to a smaller model.

The Nova is not an inexpensive machine and does not have the wide range of decorative stitch patterns we have found on other less expensive machines. It is beautifully designed however, with outstanding assets and superbly engineered. The controls are easily understood whether the sewer has had years of experience or not. Bernina believes the customer should take lessons offered from the dealer to realize the full potential of the machine. For the person who wants a portable, the lightweight Nova 900 would be at the top of our list.
Approximate Retail Price: $770.00

Bernina 830

Called the Bernina Electronic, this free arm machine comes complete with a legless slide-on table for added work space and a portable carrying case. The sturdy red accessory box contains sewing aids which include six bobbins, 11 presser feet, an extension foot, darning hoop, quilting guide, seam ripper, special screw driver for changing needles plus another utility screw driver, extra needles, a twin-needle, a plastic gauge for marking buttonholes or hems, a lint brush and oiler.

A new electronic foot control on the 830 now makes it possible to have full needle power at any speed whether sewing at 1150 stitches per minute or going slowly stitch by stitch. The motor

switch on the previous 830s which had two settings, slow and fast, has been replaced on this latest model.

This top-of-the-line model has just about every stitch pattern, all built-in, that the most demanding sewer could ask for and among them are five very good utility stretch stitches.

For example if you want to make a girdle, the universal stitch allows stretching in all directions. For ski pants or other garments which require elastic seams, the stretch stitch (four on the pattern selector) makes neat, flexible and nearly flat seams without tearing or damaging such fabric as helenca. We also liked the overlock that can overcast and stitch a seam in one operation on knits or wovens with no excessive stretching or curling. Another utility stitch that had considerable merit for reinforcing the edges and mending a T-shirt was the serpentine or running stitch.

The 15 decorative stitch patterns are an equally impressive lot giving the sewer a broad field in which to be creative. It seems unnecessary to spend money buying expensive ornamental trimmings when one has a machine with this capacity. Rows combining several different patterns will produce some interesting effects. If you really want an imaginative border, stitch two of the same patterns (such as a triangle or semi-circle) opposite one another in mirror image by turning the fabric completely

around after the first row is completed and stitching the second row right next to it. Matching two half patterns exactly to create a perfect whole could be difficult if it weren't for the ornamental pattern indicator with a rotating disc which shows in its window exactly how nearly complete is the motif.

All controls are quite accessible and clearly marked so each operation can be carried out with the minimum of fuss and bother. The only control we couldn't change quickly and easily was the stitch pattern indicator. Located on the arm's top, the 21 patterns are printed close together and next to a slot. In order to select one you must move a lever along the slot until it is lined up with the right pattern. It was not always easy to determine if we had found the right niche for our selection. We had to get up from the seat to ascertain if the selector was in the right position. Several times we were wrong. Presumably, one gets used to the closeness of patterns on the indicator and makes the right selections without getting up.

The electronic foot control gives full power at all speeds. Even when we were cautiously stitching over the bulk of a flat falled seam while hemming a pair of blue jeans, the motor didn't seem to be laboring. We were also able to stop without coasting. The foot control is designed to hold the entire foot at all times. It is large and stable and stayed in placed on a tile floor.

The quality of stitch was excellent. We were able to stitch through a single layer of muslin, two layers of denim and finally, four thicknesses of heavy wool coating and the tension automatically adjusted to each thickness.

Bernina has designed some very fine presser feet all of which are hinged to adjust to different thicknesses of fabric, and at least five have the white inset in the shank to help the sewer see the needle's eye better when threading it. All of the feet have numbers imprinted on them

giving positive identification when the sewer refers to the instruction book for an individual operation. The presser foot is pictured and its number given so there is not much chance of getting the wrong one. One of the most impressive feet is the overlock which looks somewhat like a one-sided zipper foot but has a thin wire on the right side which the needle clears and keeps the edge of tricot or jersey from curling. The convenient zipper foot can be used from either side. Another well-thought-out design is the buttonhole foot with a middle prong that is used to carry cord when corded buttonholes are in order. The cord is looped around the center prong, both ends are pulled under the foot to the back and the machine automatically satin stitches over the cord without being held. We did some fast tailor-tacking with the special foot for that purpose which has a thin vertical ridge through the middle, causing the thread to pass over it to make loops instead of locking firmly against the fabric. When our two layers of fabric were tacked together along dart lines, it was child's play to pull the two pieces slightly apart so the loops could be clipped leaving the pieces of thread to mark the lines in each layer.

In the past we have had less than satisfactory results with blind stitching hems by machine and have felt that perhaps it was a technique one perfected after practicing for years. It was, therefore, a delight to produce a good hem using this stitch pattern with the Bernina. The needle jumped over to the fold of a lightweight flannel catching just a thread so there was practically no evidence of the stitch on the right side of the skirt. At least part of this success story has to be attributed to the unique presser foot with a steel ridge running down the center. With the hem edge placed under the foot so the fold of the fabric rests against this ridge, it's relatively simple to do.

Upper threading starts from the back of the arm where the spool

stand sits and is done in one motion through slots and guides until one reaches the eye of the needle. The bobbin winder is on top of the arm with an arrow imprinted on the tension disc to show which way the thread should circle it. An automatic cut-off stops the winding when the bobbin is full.

An unusual feature of this machine is the presser foot lifter which lets the sewer raise and lower the presser foot with her knee pressed against the tubular control. When turning sharp corners, finishing a seam or when our hands were busy holding the fabric, this control was invaluable. It does, however, take some coordination because you are using the same leg for the foot control as you are for the lifter. Until we got used to it we found ourselves occasionally pressing on the knee control while stitching. The result was a less than perfect stitch because the pressure on the lifter had released the tension slightly. It should be noted that the foot lifter is there to make sewing easier and can be easily removed without affecting the operation of the machine.

Buttonholes are made automatically as you turn the dial to five positions. We made professional-looking bartack buttonholes, both with and without cord, in less time than it took to mark their positions with tailors' chalk. Because the fifth position finishes the buttonhole with several small securing stitches, it was unnecessary to knot any threads. The satin stitch setting on the stitch length control at the short end may vary slightly with each machine and its density should be checked according to the fabric used. The control is so finely regulated that adjustment is minimal. On our machine the rotary knob had to be reset from the suggested "six o'clock" position to "half-past five" for the best satin stitch when we made buttonholes on polyester and cotton.

A great asset on the 830 is its even feeding ability without benefit of any extra foot or gadget. We were able to stitch a seam on a horizontally striped polyester knit and have the stripes match exactly with no undue amount of perpendicular pinning. Testing further, the ends of seams on hard-to-manage Qiana also came out evenly. The manufacturers tell us this is due to the triangular teeth of the feed dogs.

The machine's capacity to baste is a real time saver. We basted a long side seam on a terry beach robe without a pucker, all in a matter of seconds. This operation can be a great boon in tailoring when marking necessary plumb lines for fitting at center front, back, sleeves, chest and waistline.

The free arm is narrow and well-shaped to take any kind of tubular stitching from sleeves to sock darning. The slide-on extension for added work surface fits snugly in place with a small lever. Because this extension is legless on the left side, the sewer can use it to stitch up narrow pants' leg seams or any other tubular sewing of a wider nature.

The Bernina Guide instruction book which accompanies the machine is very good with diagrams and photos showing the correct and incorrect way to proceed with each operation. It would be difficult to go wrong; the right presser foot with numbers is shown and every necessary setting of the machine is meticulously printed in red for each operation, including the appropriate needle and thread number. In addition, on almost every page where a new technique is introduced, there is a life-sized drawing of a swatch with the stitch pattern discussed. When the new owner takes the sewing course recommended by the Bernina dealer, samples of stitches are made and mounted on these replicas for the customer's future reference. The Guide goes further than just illustrating how to operate the machine; it also shows some excellent short cuts such as how to gather with elastic thread or the best way to make a smooth patch.

The machine comes with a

limited 20-year warranty on mechanical parts plus a two-year warranty on electrical parts.

The design of this fairly quiet machine is simplicity itself with its off-white and black sleek lines. The controls are attractive and everything, including the foot and knee control as well as the extension table, fits neatly into a compact red carrying case.

This beautifully engineered machine is a pleasure to test. It is expensive, and the sewer may be buying stitch patterns she will seldom use. But for the sewer who wants the options of the many stitches as well as the automatic operations this provides, she could hardly make a better choice. **Approximate Retail Price: $990.00**

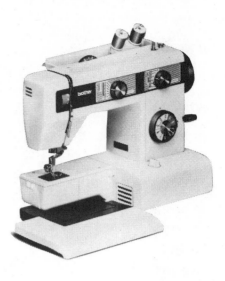

Brother Odyssey 8060

The Brother Odyssey 8060 is an off-white free arm machine with brown trim and multi-colored stitch symbols across the arm. It has a handle on top and a carrying case that fits over the machine. A permanently attached extension table is lifted from the left side, drops forward by means of a long front hinge and rests out of the way on the base when the free arm is needed. A light is mounted inside the hinged face plate with the switch in back.

This is a well-engineered machine that runs quietly and smoothly. Like other machines we have tested from the same manufacturer this one has highly visible controls which are placed for easy handling. Settings are color-coordinated in vivid hues on the stitch pattern selector as well as on the controls which regulate stitch length and width so we didn't have to waste time thumbing through pages in the manual each time we wanted to sew with a different pattern.

The all-over design of the machine is not streamlined but we

found it to be very functional. To convert the model into a free arm unit all we had to do was lift the sturdy, permanently mounted extension table slightly from the left and let it swing toward the front and down where it lay flat on the base. When this extension was in place, it provided ample additional work space both in front and to the left to support the garment we were stitching. We also admired the face plate which slanted back toward the needle bar so the needle area was in full view. We found it a simple task to change a needle or presser foot. Lighting is excellent, too. Coming from the left it illuminates the right side very well, due in part to this pared back design of the face plate.

The bobbin is wound on top of the arm and shuts off automatically when it is full. It is threaded into the bobbin case and mounted vertically in the shuttle area under the needle plate. The machine utilizes open eyelets and guides for one-motion top threading.

The spindle platform, which can hold two spools, folds over the arm when the carrying case is slipped over the machine. It rests at a forward angle and is flipped back for sewing. The spool of thread is seated securely and does not jump up and down on the spindle.

The Odyssey performed very

well in straight and zigzag stitching when we tested on organdy, cire, polyester double knit, rayon tricot, denim and a heavy coating. When we sewed on sheer nylon there was a tendency to swerve under the needle unless we firmly guided it. Although we encountered no skipped stitches, we did change from a regular needle to the 'gold stretch stitch' needle which was included with the accessories and found that it didn't make very much difference in the stitch quality on our synthetics and knits.

The tension control was excellent, and we were able to produce a balanced stitch on straight sewing going from a lightweight organdy to a heavy melton coating without having to change the tension from a 4.5 setting. When we did any zigzag sewing, however, we did heed the manufacturer and loosen the upper thread tension slightly to achieve a balanced design.

Brother has not added many superfluous stitch patterns to the Odyssey, which is its most expensive machine. The selection is well chosen with emphasis on utility stitches all of which are stretchable. The two decorative patterns, a scallop and connecting ovals, are simple, attractive and usable.

The elastic blindstitch made a passable hem on cotton and a good one on rayon knit, but we liked it best as a decorative edging on linen napkins. The elastic stitch, a three-step multi-zigzag, was effective for attaching elastic on a waistband and mending a small rip in a child's shirt sleeve. We also discovered that it makes a very sturdy fagot stitch between two layers of fabric when they are held slightly apart. We have noticed that some straight stretch patterns are actually too heavy for medium weight knits, tending to shred them because of the concentration of stitches; some patterns are also not really stretchable. This is not the case with the straight stretch stitch on this machine which was delicate enough to be used on a rayon knit

and 'gave' with the fabric, too.

We made good tight bartack buttonholes automatically on cotton and a light wool flannel with no need to pivot the fabric. There was a definite rhythmical click in the cam system that was puzzling as we dialed the four positions in sequence on the pattern selector. The mechanism seemed to work perfectly, though, and the settings were all correct so we concluded that this sound must be normal. Both sides of our buttonholes were uniform in density with the buttonhole adjusting dial set at three. This dial is an innovative feature, according to the manaul, but the explanation of how to use it was not clear either on the page which explained the control or in the section on buttonhole making.

The presser foot used for making buttonholes is an interesting design and is actually two feet in one. When not used for making buttonholes, a stopper is removed from the back and the sliding track separates from an inner plastic foot which can then be used by itself for sewing on buttons.

The machine comes with six snap-on presser feet. They include: a zigzag foot, a straight stitch foot, a narrow hemming foot, a two-way zipper foot, a darning foot and a buttonhole/button attaching foot. Other accessories are: five metal bobbins, a straight needle plate, a seam guide, a seam ripper, assorted needles with a twin-needle and a "golden needle," a spare light bulb, two screw drivers and an oiler.

On the whole, the instruction book is extremely good with large diagrams and easy-to-follow directions with the exception of the buttonhole adjusting dial and the diagram for inserting the full bobbin into the case. The sketch does not show which way the bobbin should unwind when the sewer threads it in the case. We've had a similar complaint about the instruction books accompanying other Brother machines.

The foot control is large enough

to be comfortable and responded instantly when we pressed on it. We could detect no coasting after releasing the pedal even when we sewed at high speed. The machine does have a low speed setting for stitch by stitch sewing or for the novice who is not sure of her skill yet. She just has to flip a switch on the base at the right side.

The machine comes with a one-year limited warranty against defective materials and workmanship excluding light bulbs, needles, belts and pulleys. Head parts are warranted for an additional 24 years.

Special capabilities of the machine are: darning, monogramming, twin-needle sewing, button attaching, and free form embroidery.

The Odyssey 8060 is an excellent machine. As a top-of-the-line model it has many noteworthy features, comes complete with carrying case and is still in the lower medium price range. The economy-minded sewer who is looking for a machine with good capabilities and good value should consider this Brother model.
Approximate Retail Price: $350.00

Elna Elnita SP

The Elna Elnita SP is a free arm machine that eliminates the need for an extension. A carrying handle is permanently attached to the arm but folds back out of the way. The light is mounted behind the face plate illuminating the needle area from the left side. The light switch is on the right side under the hand wheel.

Elna's Elnita SP is a sleekly designed little compact weighing 11 pounds. A relatively quiet machine, it runs like a charm with no vibration. We found that its stitch quality was excellent throughout the testing.

Although the Swiss-built Elnita is not large, it is very sturdy handling all of the test fabrics with the ease of a standard head. We seamed on bulky coatings, layers

of heavyweight denim, acrylic backed fake fur, batiste, chiffon and nylon tricot with excellent results. We had only to guide the fabric under the needle without having to push, pull or worry about any swerving. The one adjustment necessary was to loosen the tension slightly for some of the lighter weight knits to attain a balanced stitch. Otherwise tension control was excellent on the universal setting of five.

The manufacturer calls this model a wide free arm because the base ends about three inches from the left side leaving that area elevated about a half inch from the table top. This area can be used for larger tubular stitching such as hemming pants or putting in a sleeve on an adult garment, but this free arm would certainly not accommodate anything as small as a child's sleeve. And without any kind of extension for added work surface, the sewing platform is limited to less than five inches from front to back with the left side extending only one and a half inches from the needle to the edge.

Built-in stitch capacity is not extensive, but the patterns are good utility designs that the sewer will use often. Besides the regular zigzag there is a special zigzag, or overcast, which makes three tiny stitches up each side of the zigzag. It was especially effective when we made a long seam on a wool ribbed knit because of its elasticity. Patching a pair of blue jeans was easy with use of this stitch which

completed the task in one operation, sewing from edge to edge. The multi-stitches within the zigzag make it stronger than the ordinary zigzag. Therefore we could also set the stitch width to its widest range and lengthen the stitch as much as we wanted with no worry about long looping threads that would soon snag.

The elastic blindstitch is made into a good looking edging pattern by widening the stitch to the limit of the range and dialing the stitch length to a setting on the short side. This gives the pattern a degree of density which makes an attractive edge. We decorated and hemmed a luncheon napkin edge in an agreeable manner. However, when we tried to blind hem with this pattern our efforts were less successful. The pattern is designed with not enough contrast between the small zigzag that runs along the inside of the hem itself and the longer stitch that must barely catch the body of the hem every third stitch. When we set the stitch width at its widest the smaller zigzag, of course, became wider, too. We did finally manage a fairly decent blindstitched hem by trial and error folding to accommodate the short sweep of the wide zag.

It should be remembered that the stitch width has to be moved back to the zero setting before the pattern selector wheel will move. Then the stitch width can be reset.

When we made our first buttonhole on muslin it looked very professional until we cut it apart. The sides were so close together that it was virtually impossible to make a clean center cut without severing some threads on a side. Our second attempt was somewhat better, but we still had to cut with a great deal of care. Although this buttonholer is semi-automatic and the stitch width is pre-set, we did have control of the density by setting the stitch length for satin stitching. It should be noted that when starting to make a buttonhole the needle must be located in the center of the needle plate as well as in the center of the marked area on the fabric. If the needle has

swung to the left when the setting is dialed, it will start stitching on the right side of the buttonhole instead of the left (where it should be), and the buttonhole will have one side row of stitching out of position.

The controls are neat and accessible with the two most often used — the stitch width and length regulator — having indented crossbars at the center instead of knobs to make them easy to handle. The safety dial on the right side seems to be particularly innovative. The machine's mechanism is locked completely when the dial is set at zero, and there is no way to start it accidentally. Another commendable safety feature is the ability to lock the hand wheel at the same time by turning it forward.

Presser feet must be changed by releasing a long screw which is very visible. Only three feet come with the machine, and we sorely missed not having that old standby, the zipper foot. According to the manual, it can be purchased separately along with other feet for different types of sewing such as a button foot, blind stitch foot and gathering foot. Other accessories included are: darning plate, three bobbins, assortment of extra needles, seam ripper, lint brush, small screw driver and oiler. We were happy to see that the presser foot lifter could be raised another fraction of an inch above the lock position so we could place thick fabrics under the foot more easily.

Upper threading is simple with all of the guides and grooves in plain sight. Bobbin winding is also a cinch when all we had to do was turn the safety dial to the right setting and position the bobbin on the arm. By designing the bobbin with two different ends, one solid and one with holes, the sewer can hardly make a mistake if she remembers that the hole side always is on top, for winding and for insertion in the horizontal case.

The lighting is good with the bulb mounted behind the face plate so it shines from the left side onto the needle area. The face plate does not open, and in order to change the bulb we had to press a lug in back which dropped the assembly enough to remove the bulb from its bayonet socket.

The foot control is comfortable, a good sized button with a foot rest beside it and mounted on a base that is quite stable. We liked the quick response when we pressed on the control and experienced no coasting when we released it.

By comparison with other machines in this price range, few accessories are included with the Elnita. These aids are stored in a grey plastic pouch with a similar one used for the foot control. While this machine is an ideal portable, the grey plastic cover offers no pocket or place to hold the accessory kit or foot control. We are forced to conclude that it is designed more for storage than for transport.

The instruction book is excellent, leading the sewer through all of the operations clearly and concisely with good photographs and illustrations.

Special capabilities of the machine are: darning, free-form embroidery and monogramming.

The Elnita SP is a beautifully engineered machine which should last for many years and is ideal for the sewer who is short on space. It has the same sewing capacity as its big sisters but not the space between the base and the upper arm which might pose a problem when stitching on very bulky clothes. The question is whether the sewer wants to pay the price for this model because it is not inexpensive.

Approximate Retail Price: $390.00

Elna Lotus T SP

The Elna Lotus T SP is a compact, convertible, extremely portable machine, weighing less than 14 pounds. With a head that

is smaller than any we have seen to date, the cleverly designed flaps which double as a case when attached to the arm, or as extended work surface around the free arm when dropped, are an interesting innovation. We preferred to remove them, especially the front one which extended seven inches and proved to be more of a hindrance than a help because it prevented us from getting as close to the needle as we felt was necessary. We did find that when the free arm wasn't needed it was very convenient to have the left panel attached in the slot at the end of the free arm for the added work surface it gave us for sewing on bulky garments.

Another compact feature we admired was the accessory box neatly built into the top of the machine under a cover with everything resting in its own niche. We appreciated not having to rummage through all of the accessories to find a zipper foot or seam ripper when we wanted it. The top cover on our accessory section did not open by gently pressing up on the latch as the manual suggested. Instead, we had to cautiously pry it open on the edge with the blunt end of a nail file. Hopefully, in time, the catch would be easier to open. With the machine threaded the thread cuts across the top from spindle to guide and it was a nuisance to have to move the thread aside when opening the cover on the accessory box, and we also had to be careful that the thread didn't catch under the cover before closing it.

The Lotus is not cluttered with a lot of dials and levers but has a few controls which are easy to read, and very accessible. The two most used ones, the stitch width and

length regulators, function for more than one operation. Even the safety dial on the right side can be seen by leaning sideways to check the positions. We would like to see all machines have some sort of a locking device. This one is particularly good because not only does it lock the mechanism when the dial is turned to zero, but the hand wheel can then be turned forward so it, too, is locked until the dial is reset.

The Lotus ran smoothly and was relatively quiet. It fed evenly with the fabric needing very little guidance. Stitch quality was excellent for both straight and zigzag stitching.

The universal tension setting of five gave us a good balanced stitch on most of the fabrics we tested. However, we did have to loosen the tension a bit to a setting of three to relieve puckering and get an acceptable short stitch on a sheer nylon.

When we placed heavyweight fabrics under the needle, it was necessary to raise the presser foot even higher with the lifter than the 'up' lock position. The feed dogs seem to be higher on the needle plate than many of the other machines making it difficult to position bulky fabric seams under the presser foot.

The machine has some interesting utility and stretch stitch patterns — one group identified as automatic and the other group as

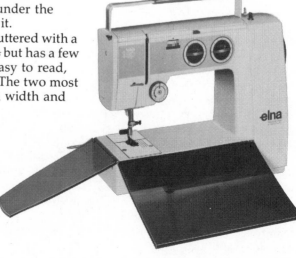

super automatic. The manual never tells us the difference, but from other testing we assume the designations have to do with the movement of the feed dogs. With automatic stitches, the action is only forward and with the super automatic, the action is both forward and reverse.

Some of the stitch patterns can be decorative as well as functional such as the tricot stitch which looks very much like a stretch smocking. It seemed to be a little heavy for a lightweight tricot that we used. Much more suitable for this fabric was the elastic blind hem with a width setting of two. The blind hem zigzag was not very successful in our attempts to hem with it because so little variety exists between the smaller zigs and larger zags. To make a true blindstitch on a hem, we had to make several adjustments in the fold of the hem and do a certain amount of juggling with the stitch width control to get an optimal swing of the larger zag.

We did accomplish an effective instant darn, closing a tear in a shirt by dialing the overcast or special zigzag in the automatic range. Actually, the pattern, called by many names in other brands, is really three short stitches up each side of the zig and zag. It is also remarkably good in joining two selvages together. For hemming on jersey, we tested the elastic edging stitch (a super automatic) with great success. It looked very good as a decorative pattern, also.

The bartack buttonholes we made were professional looking and strong, especially when we put embroidery cord under the satin stitches to make a raised effect. To get a good satin stitch for the sides of the buttonholes, the ideal stitch length setting on our machine was at one-half rather than between one-quarter and one-half. When we dialed closer to zero the stitches tended to pile up too much on the woven cotton. Buttonholing on the Lotus is a semi-automatic process and the sewer must pivot the garment at the end of the first side in order to make bartacks and the right side.

Upper threading was done quickly in one motion to the needle area with grooves instead of numerous eyelets. Bobbin winding was equally simple although we prefer systems which cut off automatically when the bobbin is full, which the Lotus does not. It is virtually impossible to go wrong either winding the bobbin or loading it. Designed with one end solid and the other with holes, the hole side of the bobbin is always up.

Lighting is excellent, shining down from the left under the face plate to illuminate the needle area. The bulb can be a little tricky to change, however. Because the face plate does not open we had to push a lug in back which dropped the light assembly enough for us to remove the bulb.

The foot control is comfortable with a button mounted on a base that is large enough to accommodate the upper part of the foot. The control was responsive to pressure, and there was no coasting.

Four presser feet come with the machine all of which mount around a set screw on the presser bar. The all-purpose and buttonhole/embroidery feet are hinged while the two-way zipper and darning foot are not. Other accessories include: darning plate, three bobbins, needle assortment, needle threader, seam ripper, small screw driver, lint brush and oiler.

The two instruction manuals included with the machine are both very informative, but we found it a little disconcerting to have instructions on how to operate all three Lotus models in both books. Elna could publish a guide for each model so the home-sewer wouldn't have to thumb through the book figuring out what applies to her machine.

The machine comes with a limited warranty to replace any part except needles plus a limited 19-year warranty on the electrical equipment.

Special capabilities of the machine are: darning, free-form embroidery and monogramming.

The T SP, Top Special of the three Lotus models is a beautifully precision-built machine. It is expensive and for that reason should offer more features than it does (i.e. an automatic buttonholer, a more versatile selection of stitch patterns and a drop feed control). The head is small but extremely sturdy, and for the sewer who wants a very fine portable to last for years, this may be a very good choice.
Approximate Retail Price: $620.00

Elna SU Air Electronics

This is a sophisticated, beautifully styled free arm machine with some fascinating new innovations. It will appeal to the adventurous sewer who wants a dependable machine with a host of stitch patterns, and who also has the expertise to operate complex controls. The controls are accessible, easy to handle and, with one exception, very visible. However, it takes time and patience to become accustomed to using them. One control, the stitch elongator wheel, juts out just enough to overshadow the setting dot on top of the stitch length regulator. Every time we moved the length control, it was necessary to bend to one side or tilt the machine back to make sure the setting was in the right place.

This convertible runs smoothly, feeds evenly and was the quietest machine CONSUMER GUIDE® tested. Since Elna's pressure control is set at the factory, we were interested in seeing how different weight fabrics would feed. We stitched long seams on both batiste and a heavy melton experiencing no swerving or slippage away from or under the needle. In fact, we hardly had to guide either piece.

The new electronic speed control allowed us to reduce speed from the maximum end of the slot to a minimum at any given interval while sewing. We topstitched a denim pocket rounding the corners slowly, stitch by stitch, and we also stitched an armhole with the lever at the halfway mark which was just the right speed to control the bulky fabric.

Tension control was excellent. A balanced stitch on a wide variety of fabrics was produced. We were pleased to see a tension that could self-adjust to such a range of fabrics. On other Elnas tested, the tension had to be loosened slightly for some of the knits.

The pneumatic foot control is an entirely new concept with a rubber button set on a large base that the sewer presses gently with the ball of her foot to activate the electronic motor. Although relatively small, it was not uncomfortable to use and had a non-skid bottom to keep it in place on the floor. Our foot control worked very well throughout the testing and then suddenly started to lose its efficiency. When depressed, the rubber button would not spring back. This was remedied by unplugging the control and then re-plugging it back into the machine. It seems like the control lost its air and needed a breather.

The Elna Electronic has six built-in stitches plus the capacity to accept over 50 cams, 18 of which are included with the machine.

The color system is extremely helpful as a guide for matching the right cams with proper settings on controls. By following the green guide marks we were able to dial any one of the built-in automatic stitches with ease. Set in the green areas, the elastic blind or edging stitch and the blindstitch patterns were more effective as edgings. However, the stitches were too dense for hemming. We dialed the stitch length control beyond the recommended green setting (which is between zero and one) for a more open stitch. All of the green settings for both the overcast and multi-stretch patterns made excellent stitches on the knits we tested.

Inserting one of the interchangeable cams was not difficult after we made sure both stitch width and length controls were set at zero. Once it was aligned with a red dot on the center post, each cam locked into place without the juggling we had to do on some other machines. With the three single Elna discs, we could still vary the stitch length as we did for blind hemming. This was not possible when we inserted a double Elna disc because the stitch length control has to be set in the red area and can only be moved slightly within that range. We were, however, able to elongate the automatic patterns by turning a special wheel. By doing this some patterns were altered so their appearance looked very different.

We discovered that the straight stretch stitch was delicate enough to be used effectively on a rayon knit. The tricot pattern on the same cam did not resemble the manual's illustration of this stitch at all. Among the most versatile of the many cams that overcast in one pattern or another was the double overlock which we used to join two pieces of denim together, seamed and overcast in one operation on a ribbed knit and affixed a patch on a pair of jeans.

The buttonholes we produced were strong and even, but in order to achieve a uniform look on both sides we had to make some adjustments within the blue range setting on the stitch length control. For the left side it was necessary to set the dial closer to the zero for greater stitch density. With this same setting the stitches piled up on the right side and were corrected by making the stitch less dense and turning the dial back to the middle of the blue setting. The buttonholes can be made automatically up to a certain point. When bartacking, we had to hold back the fabric so the stitches wouldn't feed beyond the end markings.

Elna has some excellent features that make sewing a simple task. One makes it possible to sustain a backstitch by dialing the stitch length control plus having an instant reverse lever on the base for quick backtacking. Another excellent feature is that the presser foot can be lifted high enough so bulk fabrics can be positioned under the needle without using a cumbersome see-saw motion.

After disengaging the needle mechanism by loosening the inner knob of the hand wheel, the bobbin is wound on top of the arm and when full, cuts off automatically. It is wound with the hole side up and inserted the same way in the horizontal bobbin case behind the needle plate. A special bobbin extractor, mounted on a spring, is pulled down from under the face plate and inserted into the bobbin hole when the bobbin is removed from the case. The upper thread comes from one of two retractable spindles through guides and open eyelets to the needle in a one-motion operation.

We have reservations about the Electronic's wide free arm. It is low and thinner than the traditional ones, but the extra work space given by the back extension piece doesn't add up to more than an inch. We also found it wasn't easy to place a bulky garment around the free arm for tubular sewing with the mobile support in front moved away from the free arm and the back extension removed. There was less than an inch of clearance between the base which remains attached in front and back and the free arm itself.

The safety switch is a good innovation. With a warning light as a reminder, it would be difficult to go away and leave the power on. The sewing light illuminates the needle area very well. It can be a problem to change the bulb, without a hinged face plate. A screw on top of the arm must be loosened so the bulb can drop far enough below the face plate to be changed.

The machine comes with five presser feet, all of which mount around a set screw on the presser bar. Included are a teflon coated all-purpose foot, embroidery foot, buttonhole foot, two-way zipper/cording foot and darning foot. Other aids are: five bobbins, needle assortment, needle threader, needle plate for darning or attaching buttons, seam guide, seam ripper, screw driver, lint brush and oiler.

The two instruction books which come with the machine are clearly illustrated. They are well organized and informative but only a few examples of what can be done with some of the good super automatic utility patterns are given.

The machine comes with a limited one-year warranty on any part other than needles, belts and light bulbs plus a limited 19-year warranty on parts except the ones mentioned above and the electrical equipment.

The Swiss-made Elna Electronic is beautifully engineered to give years of service and pleasure to the home-sewer. Truly a portable, it weighs less than 20 pounds with the wrap-around cover and has a full size head. It is an expensive machine and, though an outstanding one, we would like to see Elna design a larger foot control.

Approximate Retail Price: $1200.00

National 776

The National 776 is an off-white free arm machine with red trim that comes with its own carrying case. An extension table fits around the free arm by means of grooves and a pin. A support bracket on the left adds stability.

The light is mounted behind the hinged face plate illuminating the needle area from the left. The light switch is in back of the face plate. The pressure control, a ring with a pin inside it, sits on top of the face plate. The feed dog position is controlled with the stitch length control.

This machine has enough built-in utility and decorative stitch patterns to satisfy the most discerning sewer. You can pick and choose from any one of 28 patterns, many of them designed to create interesting motifs on clothes for embroidery or trimming. The utility patterns are equally impressive with some excellent stretch stitches to use on the many double knits, stretch terrys, ribbed jerseys and tricots or to strengthen seams on woven fabrics.

Although all of the pattern designs are different we didn't find a dramatic difference between the automatic and the super automatic stitches. Both contain some stretch and utility stitches as well as good decorative ones. We did note that when super automatic stitches were selected by dialing "S" on the buttonhole control we had the option of elongating or squeezing the pattern by turning the dial to a plus or minus side. We experimented further trying to alter the designs to appear in the same way by changing the setting on the stitch width and length controls but they retained their basic shapes better and developed more effective variations on the motifs when we used the "S" setting and its range. Any of these patterns could be stitched with a twin-needle within the limitations of the stitch width, of course.

When we tested on a knit with a tendency to fray, we selected the overcast stitch and guided the fabric so the extreme right of the stitch barely fell off the edge. The result was a neat seam which was finished so it could not unravel — all in one operation. And because it is a super automatic pattern we were able to expand the design slightly so it would adjust to the

added thickness and seam up a lightweight woolen basket weave in the same manner. We found another stitch pattern that functioned just as well for overcasting — the super automatic pine leaf.

To mend a three-cornered tear on a pillowcase, we selected the tricot stitch which helped us complete the task very successfully. It was also effective in reattaching eleastic to an undergarment as well as seaming on a rayon and cotton knit. Incidentally, National includes with the needle assortment a special scarfed needle identified by a blue top, which they recommend using for any stretch fabrics. We can only conclude that it must have done the trick because we had no problems with any of the stretchables.

Unlike others we have observed, the blindstitch pattern is well thought out with several straight stitches between wide zags. Instead of another presser foot, the manufacturers have devised a guide, a small thin piece of metal that fits down the center of the zigzag foot between its toes and is mounted onto the presser bar between the screw and the prongs of the other foot. With the guide's edge to direct the fold of the hem, we made a hem with only the vaguest hint of stitches on the front side of the fabric.

Setting the machine for basting meant that we had to remove the presser foot, lower the feed dogs (only by turning the hand wheel until they were at their lowest point), place a basting stitch guide over the needle plate, rethread the needle by wrapping the thread around its shaft once, replace the zigzag foot and stitch. The effort produced good, even half-inch stitches, but it would have been easier to use the longest stitch on the regulator. Instructions for the procedure were puzzling. First, we were told to set the zigzag width knob at a "BS" mark (between three and four); later, after we had attached the guide, rethreaded the needle and taken two small stitches to secure the beginning, we were told to reset the width knob to five.

Another good temporary stitch is the chain stitch. As this type goes, it's the best we have seen. We made a clean, single thread row of stitching with uniform loops on the back. Taking a short stitch at the beginning and end of the seam by manually turning the hand wheel we locked the line of stitching so it would not unravel until we wanted it to. To achieve the chain stitch it was necessary to rethread the machine using the chain stitch guide next to the take-up lever, and remove the bobbin to insert the chain stitch looper.

The bartack buttonholes we made automatically were first-rate after we had adjusted the stitch width to get the proper density of stitch. Curiously, when the buttonholer foot is in place there is less space between needle and foot than with any other presser foot. But the foot lifter can be raised manually above its lock position to place fabric of any thickness under the foot.

The stitch quality was uniformly excellent during most of our testing. On the machine we tested the upper tension setting for a balanced stitch was high, in the range between seven and eight for most fabrics. It had to be loosened a bit more when we stitched on a nylon knit. We could not, however, solve a puckering problem on sheer nylon by loosening the tension, resetting the pressure on the presser foot or

varying the length of stitch.

The bobbin is wound on the top of the machine arm and cuts off automatically when full. The winder can be adjusted should the bobbin wind unevenly. With a spool in back of the arm, the machine is threaded conventionally down through tension discs, up to the eye of the take-up lever and down through various guides to the needle. The guide marked "chain stitch" is threaded only for that operation.

The machine comes with six presser feet which are all mounted around a set screw on the presser bar. They include: a straight stitch foot, zigzag foot, buttonhole foot, button attaching foot, hemming foot and a two-way zipper foot with a quilting extension. Other accessories include: five bobbins, basting stitch guide, chain stitch looper, two quilting guides, fabric guide, assortment of needles including a twin and special scarfed needle, two felt spool pads, two screw drivers, a seam ripper, lint brush oiler and spare bulb.

The instruction book is thorough with diagrams illustrating points along with helpful hints in red type. Control settings for each operation are also conveniently boxed in red. There is no mention of the motor having two speeds, but we discovered a two-way stitch when inserting the power plug to the machine and, upon investigation, found a low and high setting which governed the motor speed. The manual does have specific details on maintenance, cleaning and oiling.

This machine is quiet and smooth running with good illumination around the needle area. The pattern selector on our model was stiff, but undoubtedly would become looser with constant usage. Although the general design is not sleek and streamlined, the most used controls are large, easy to read and very accessible.

The machine has a one-year warranty on the motor and a limited 25-year warranty on defective parts excluding needles,

belts, pulleys, and light bulbs.

Special capabilities of the machine are: darning, sewing on buttons, basting, chain stitching, and free-form embroidery.

Although the National 776 is not inexpensive, it does come with its own carrying case and is lower priced than the other two machines made by this manufacturer that we have reviewed. This fine machine is recommended for the more experienced sewer who can appreciate its potential.
Approximate Retail Price: $550.00

National 350

The National 350 is a handsome free arm machine with sleek, uncluttered lines. Navy with white trim, it has a decorative top cover that can be closed to conceal the controls (located across the upper arm) when the machine is not in use. The permanently mounted cover with back hinges has convenient diagrams inside reminding the sewer how to top thread the machine and wind the bobbin as well as a chart for the stitch identification patterns suggesting setting for stitch width and length. For storage and transporting, a carrying case must

be purchased separately.

National has designed a machine that not only looks terrific and has easy to read controls but has plenty of lighting where it is needed the most. One bulb illuminates the needle area from the face plate, and the other casts light down from the center of the arm onto the work area as well as shining in back of the stitch pattern window. Both bulbs light simultaneously when the power dial is switched on. According to the instruction book, however, when the power switch is off the machine is supposed to be inoperable, thus serving as a safety measure. This was not the case in the machine we tested; the foot control was not deactivated.

The machine runs quietly with little or no vibration and has many excellent features. The quality of stitching was first-rate and fed evenly needing no unnecessary pushing and pulling, only a guiding hand to keep the fabric straight. It sewed as well through four layers of heavy canvas as it did on two layers of polyester knit and a thin batiste. The upper tension setting had to be changed from five to just past six only when we stitched up a seam on nylon knit.

We especially liked the machine's ability to lock the thread at the beginning and end of a seam by merely flipping the reverse lever up to make a bartack of several small stitches. It is recommended that the seam be started one-quarter of an inch from the edge to make the beginning bartack. If the reverse lever is pushed down, it stitches backwards the same length as it does forward. The lever has to be held, though, limiting the amount of reverse stitching a sewer is likely to do.

Another plus feature is the presser foot regulator which allowed us to adjust the amount of pressure for the thickness of fabric. When we sewed on heavy coating, we increased the pressure to nine on the dial which helped control the bulk beautifully. When we stitched on chiffon, the ideal setting seemed to be two.

All of the 12 presser feet are a cinch to change; and we didn't have to waste time going from one operation to another. By the flick of a lever one foot comes off and another snaps into place when the presser foot lifter is lowered. The foot does have to be lined up exactly with the needle hole on the needle plate before it will snap on. The variety of feet covers just about every kind of sewing need; included are: a zigzag foot, sheer fabric foot, straight stitch foot, narrow hemming foot, overlock foot, blindstitch foot with adjustable seam guide, zipper/cording foot, button attaching foot, braiding foot, two buttonhole feet and a concealed zipper foot. We only wish the zipper foot was interchangeable so we could sew from either side when inserting a zipper instead of only from the right side. Happily, the accessories include another zipper foot made especially for attaching concealed plastic slide fasteners.

Other accessories and sewing aids include: six bobbins, a quilting guide, pads for the thread spindles, a thread stand, zigzag needle plate, straight stitch needle plate, two screw drivers, packet of regular needles, a twin-needle, a seam ripper and an oil can.

In the past National has been known for producing some good stretch stitches; this model has some particulary good ones including two excellent straight stretch stitches. The one pattern producing the coarser of the two was very effective when we stitched up a seam on helenca while the other pattern with a denser stitch seemed to have more strength than most lockstitches when it was used on the crotch seam of pants. Other utility stretch stitches such as the overlock, tricot/overcast and stretch blind hem worked well on our cotton and polyester knits.

Although this machine has fewer decorative stitches than former National models, they are all superior with the plus factor of being built-in. We were able to stitch a fine feather pattern, smock, scallop, and create a pattern they call the "bringing" stitch which effectively simulates a hem stitch. We were less than impressed with the flower motif, but at least it was interesting. Although some consumers may want more of a variety of decorative patterns, we felt these stitches filled the bill nicely, and of course they all can be twice as decorative for an interesting effect simply by using the twin-needle. Color coding the stitch patterns to the length of stitch is almost fool-proof insurance against making a mistake — even for the beginner.

The buttonholes tested were strong — certainly up to par with other bartack ones made on any machine in this price range. Dialing each of the three positions on the pattern selector (one for each side as well as one for bartacks) was simple enough; starting from the lower left side of the buttonhole, we did not need to turn the fabric — the machine took over. The nuisance was trying to figure out the buttonhole adjustor controlling the density of the stitch, which is situated on the back of the arm. The sewer has to get up and go around to the back to make whatever adjustment is needed. This was the only control that was not easy to read; the lettering was incredibly small. With some fiddling we did arrive at the optimal density of stitch but with little help from the instruction book.

As attractive as the open top cover is, it does have a tendency to get in the way when the sewer is threading the upper part of the machine. With the spool stand mounted on the right side of the back of the arm, it is necessary to bring the thread across the back, behind the cover, through a guide on the upper left side (still in back) and then trace the thread between the opened cover and the top of the machine to continue with the task. Once you get past this hurdle the rest of the threading is easy. It's not exactly one-motion threading but very nearly. The manufacturer has thoughtfully provided a white area behind the needle to make its eye more visible for threading.

The position of the thread stand also makes bobbin winding somewhat cumbersome. We had to approach this operation from the back in order to guide the bobbin thread through a tension disc (next to the spool stand), then to the right side of the machine, through a thread guide and down to the winder. After moving the winder into position, winding the bobbin was a breeze, and we didn't have to touch the balance wheel. (In many machines an inner knob on the balance wheel must be loosened before winding the bobbin.)

The bobbin case is a standard one which is inserted vertically into the shuttle; but it is difficult to change the bobbin when the extension plate is in place because of the way the bobbin cover opens. The navy blue extension plate stays in place well with the left side supported by a metal bracket. Certainly, it is handy to have spare bobbins, needles and presser feet at your fingertips in a compartment of the extension.

On the whole, the instruction book, is well thought out with good directions and diagrams, especially those dealing with the built-in stitch patterns. It is frustrating, however, that the artist does not make clear which way the thread should go around the bobbin tension disc prior to winding and which way it should go around the filled bobbin when inserting it in the case. We think it would also be helpful if, in their section on maintenance, National would show with arrows exactly where the sewer should apply the oil can, not just suggest she oil where moving parts work against one another.

A limited 25-year warranty comes with the machine. It covers any part that becomes defective by reason of faulty workmanship or materials. It does not cover electric equipment, including the motor (warranted for one year) or needles, belts, bobbins or bulbs.

This is a fine machine with performance and capacity to satisfy the needs of the experienced sewer as well as the inquisitive novice who wants more than just the basics in her machine. Although the motor has only one speed, the foot control is sensitive enough to allow the sewer to go as fast or as slow as desired depending on the amount of pressure applied to the control. Once the foot is removed from the control the machine stops instantly with no coasting. National has come a long way in the past few years putting the emphasis on clean styling along with worthwhile stitches that feature some excellent utility and stretch patterns rather than many seldom used decorative stitches.
Approximate Retail Price: $600.00

National EL 300

The National EL 300 is a dark brown free arm machine with a permanently mounted gold and white top cover, hinged to open from the front to reveal controls across the arm. On the inside cover are diagrams explaining how to thread the machine and a chart for built-in stitch pattern identification plus appropriate settings for stitch widths and lengths. A white extension table fits on either side of the free arm with the left side hinged and supported underneath with a bracket. The front opens for access to the shuttle area and also contains a niche to hold accessories and sewing aids. For illumination there are two lights, one under the face plate and the other under the arm. On the arm a switch, marked "electronic mode," controls both lights and power.

This handsomely designed machine has some outstanding features. The most notable of the innovations is the electronically

controlled needle height device which programs the needle to stop out of the fabric when the switch is turned to "up." After the sewer releases the foot control, the machines coasts for an instant; just enough to let the needle and take-up lever assume their highest positions and ready to resume stitching. With the control switched to "down" the needle remains in the fabric, and we observed that it was much more convenient to turn a right-angle corner because we could pivot the fabric with ease. The foot control was very responsive at high and low speeds.

We like the machine's ability to reverse stitch and backtack when the dual-lever is pressed up instead of down. This is a wonderful time-saver.

The quality of stitch was excellent with no skipped stitches and good tension control in all of our testing. We had to loosen upper tension a bit only when stitching on sheer nylon. Otherwise the setting of four seemed to be ideal for many types of fabrics. The special presser foot for sheers helped solve puckering problems on sheer nylon and chiffon.

The EL 300 comes equipped with just about every presser foot the sewer would ever need including a blindstitch foot for hemming that has an adjustable seam guide for different weights of

fabric. Another handy foot is the overlock with a thin strip of metal on one side to prevent curling when using one of the overcast patterns on a stretchy fabric. Another we haven't seen on many machines is the braiding foot designed to hold cord or woolen yarn when attaching it to the fabric with a zigzag stitch for dimensional embroidery or applique motifs.

The presser feet are easily removed from the common shank by merely pushing a lever in back of the presser bar. Some are not as easily snapped on to the shank's horizontal pin and required that we lift and lower the presser foot lifter several times.

In addition, the machine comes with the following: zigzag foot, sheer fabric foot, straight stitch foot, narrow hemming foot, zipper/cording foot, concealed zipper foot, button foot and two buttonhole feet. Other accessories include six bobbins, straight and zigzag needle plates, an assortment of needles including a twin-needle, spool pin felt pads, two screw drivers, a spare fuse and an oiler.

On machines which come with controls for adjusting the pressure on the presser foot, we have noticed that it has been necessary to use them more for good stitch quality on some models than others. The EL 300's pressure adjustor or its control design doesn't seem to be as super sensitive as we have seen. We did not have to change it with every different thickness of fabric; only when we stitched on a lightweight material such as nylon tricot and then changed to a wool flannel.

The built-in stitch patterns offer a good selection especially for stretch fabrics. We used the double overlock pattern on a knit that had a tendency to ravel, stitching a quarter-inch in from the edge and then trimmed to the stitch line. The result was an excellent seam. The stretch overlock on cotton jersey was equally impressive. We also approved of having two straight stretch patterns, one for a coarse,

thick stitch and the other for a denser one. It is not easy to rip out the denser stitch if the sewer has made a mistake, however.

Using the stretch blind hem to put up a hem meant that we had to readjust folds and both stitch width and length several times before we could get the long zag to catch a few threads of the outer layer without the shorter zig stitches following suit. The problem is in the design of the stitch pattern. There was not enough variation in the width of the short zigs and long zags.

According to the manual, it is possible to baste with stitches up to three-quarters of an inch long. Following the manual's directions carefully, we dialed the stitch length control to a setting marked only with a symbol of three triangles in a row. (Nowhere in the manual did it explain what the setting was for. When we got to the monogramming and darning section we realized the setting was a control to drop the feed dogs.) After some unsuccessful tries, we finally did get the hang of basting which is done by touching the foot control for an instant, releasing it so only one stitch is produced and, with the needle automatically stopped at its highest position, pulling the fabric back to create a long stitch and then touching the foot control again. This operation is repeated over and over to make a line of basting. Needless to say, it takes some practice to achieve uniform stitches. It seems far simpler just to use the longest stitch length which makes seven stitches per inch for moderately good basting.

Making a buttonhole on the EL 300 should be an easy task with the three positions set very plainly on the pattern selection panel. But the buttonhole adjustor dial in the back which controls the density of stitch was a stumbling block. The manual gives a description of what it is supposed to do but not how to accomplish it. After much experimentation we did make a good buttonhole. The adjustor dial still remains a mystery. With all of the other controls so accessible

and easy to read, it is too bad that the manufacturer placed this dial in such an awkward place on the back of the arm.

The extension table is easy to snap into place and conveniently has a front that folds back to uncover a niche for accessories and also allow access to the shuttle area. The table provides more than six inches of added working surface to the left of the needle area. The free arm is slender enough to allow stitching on almost any size of armhole or cuff.

The instruction book is very informative with the exceptions noted. Diagrams illustrate each operation with prescribed settings for each. Along with detailed information on cleaning and oiling there is also a brief but good check list to ensure better sewing.

The machine comes with a limited 25-year warranty to replace any parts which become defective because of faulty workmanship or materials with a one-year guarantee on electrical equipment and the motor.

Special capabilities of the machine are: darning, twin-needle sewing, attaching buttons, monogramming, free-form embroidery and basting.

The National EL 300 is an exceptionally good machine that the more sophisticated sewer should consider. It is not inexpensive, but it does have worthwhile innovations.
Approximate Retail Price: $700.00

Necchi Silvia Multimatic 584

The Necchi Silvia Multimatic 584 is a free arm machine with a carrying case that snaps on the machine base. An extension plate, with a detachable storage bin for accessories, and a front panel that opens with spindles for extra bobbins, fits around the free arm and is held securely by a long pin in the front. The light is from under the face plate and shines on the left side of the needle area.

Many of the machines we tested made automatic buttonholes by dialing five positions which usually consisted of two settings for bartacks, two for the sides and a fifth for finishing. But this five-step buttonhole procedure is an original. The first position made a bartack across the top, the second step made a satin or buttonhole stitch down the left side, but the third step simply produced a straight line of stitching in reverse back up to the original bartack. At this point we were sure something must be wrong either with the settings or the built-in mechanism. Upon rechecking the directions we set the indicator to the fourth position and were gratified to see it making perfect satin stitches down the right side over the straight stitch line. The fifth step made the finishing bartack. The result was one of the best buttonholes we have ever produced with even stitch density on both sides and bartacks strong enough to withstand wear and tear. The sliding buttonhole foot also made it possible for us to loop gimp on the knob in back and make a good looking corded buttonhole.

One of the very good additions on this model is the straight stretch stitch pattern. We found that it was light enough to use on a medium weight synthetic knit for making a curved seam and perfect to reinforce denim pants seams. It is also next to impossible to rip out if, by chance, the sewer happens to make a mistake and wants to remove the stitching.

Occupying the same setting on the selection panel with the straight stretch stitch is another fine pattern, the elastic overlock. Better designed than most we have come across, this one combines the zigzag with the straight stretch to make a very stretchable pattern. We tried it on a particularly spongy wool and a synthetic ribbed knit (which has a tendency to ravel) and were

pleased that it made the elastic seam with the overcast for the edges all in one operation. The same stitch made a pretty finishing touch when we shell stitched rayon knit edges.

After testing for a while, we became accustomed to setting the indicator to our choice on the pattern selection panel. The patterns with different color backgrounds are designed with symbols printed on the wide end for very good visibility. Unfortunately, the slot in which the indicator must travel is at the narrow end of this perspective and not very long so the settings are very close together. The color code for the straight stretch stitch is violet but this color area does not appear on the stitch length control, at least not on our test machine, even though the instruction book says there is one at four. It should be noted, too, that the blue area for the elastic overlock can hardly be seen on the stitch width control. Located at the widest point of the range, it must share the same setting with two other colors, but it has been partially concealed by the rim of the dial. We had to peer closely in order to detect it.

Necchi has a very good suggestion for the sewer who likes to add fine dressmaking touches to a blouse or create handmade effects on tableclothes. The elastic zigzag is used to fagot two fabric edges together. We were very impressed with the finished product, although it took some practice to hold the edges apart at an equal distance as we stitched. Because the pattern is made up of small stitches within each zigzag, the fagoting was very strong. We found this same stitch pattern to be a life-saver when applying a patch to the knee of a child's blue jeans, and by using the free arm, the operation was over in no time.

The quality of stitch was excellent in all of our testing. We achieved a balanced stitch with a tension setting of three when stitching on many weights of fabrics, but it was necessary to loosen the tension slightly to two

for sheer nylon. Even though we experienced no slippage from under the needle with the scarfed presser foot attached when sewing on the slippery cire, we changed to the smooth soled foot for seaming the sheer nylon and discovered that it did feed more smoothly. The pressure control was set at five throughout the testing, and since the stitch balance remained very good we saw no reason to change it. This is probably just as well because its location on the back of the face plate makes adjusting inconvenient.

One of the best innovations on the Multimatic is the design of the shuttle area. Not only is the case easy to insert with the transparent bobbin facing out, but it also sits at an angle in the shuttle for maximum visibility when the shuttle door is open. The sewer knows exactly how much thread she has on the bobbin before embarking on a long sewing operation.

The bobbin winder is located behind the hand wheel on the right side of the machine and takes some getting used to. When the empty bobbin is placed on the winder, the needle mechanism is disengaged, but there is no automatic cut-off when the bobbin is full. Once the bobbin is wound and in place, the machine is threaded in a one-motion operation.

The extension table is very sturdy, and gives ample work surface to the left and back of the needle but very little in front. We discovered it was hard to remove and appreciated the fact that the front could open for access to the shuttle without having to take it off unnecessarily. The table had to be removed, though, when we tested the drop feed control, which is on the back of the free arm.

The eye-catching deep olive color of this machine is attractive but it also absorbs much of the light. There is plenty of illumination on the left side of the needle but very little on the right. The foot control was wide and comfortable but not as responsive at either motor speed as we think it should be. We did not experience any coasting, though, when we released pressure from the pedal.

The eight snap-on presser feet are all mounted on a common shaft and are easily removed by flipping a lever. Included with the machine are: an all-purpose foot with a flat sole, an all-purpose foot with a scarfed sole, a transparent foot for embroidery, a hemming foot, buttonhole foot, adjustable blindstitch foot, one-way zipper foot, and a button attaching foot. Other accessories are: four spool retainers, sewing guide, four transparent bobbins, an assortment of needles including a twin-needle, threading hooks, a lint brush, seam ripper, oiler and two screw drivers, the larger with a magnetic base.

We think there should be a separate instruction book for the Multimatic instead of having only one for it and the 586, which obviously has features and presser feet the 584 does not. It is confusing to have to sort out the procedures which are not meant for this machine, especially when Necchi shows only the pattern selection panel for the 586, which has more patterns than the 584. The book is well organized and extensive, but some of the diagrams, such as the threading processess, could be larger and clearer.

The machine has a two-year warranty on all mechanical and electrical parts plus a limited 10-year warranty on the mechanical parts. Both warranties exclude light bulbs, needles and belts.

Special capabilities of the machine are: twin-needle sewing, darning, free-form embroidery and sewing on buttons.

The Necchi Silvia Multimatic 584, with its clean graceful lines, is a beautifully designed machine which performs very well, feeding evenly and having no vibration. It has many worthwhile features that many a sewer will find to her liking. The one we could do without is the automatic needle threader which is a nuisance.
Approximate Retail Price: $690.00

Necchi Silvia Maximatic 586

The Necchi Silvia Maximatic 586 is a free arm unit which comes with a white carrying case that snaps on the machine base. An extension plate, with detachable storage bin for accessories and a front panel that opens with spindles for extra bobbins, fits around the free arm and is held secure by a long pin. Light is from under the face plate and shines on the left side of the needle area. A power switch for the light and two-speed motor is on the motor housing in back of the free arm.

This machine looks much like its sister model, the Multimatic 584, with similar controls placed in the same positions and with the same elegant styling. Besides carrying a higher price tag, this top-of-the-line free arm machine offers seven additional stitch patterns plus interesting capabilities not found on the less expensive machine.

The selection of stitch patterns is first-rate. With this model there are four well chosen decorative patterns, which the creative minded sewer will surely want to use often, as well as two added stretch patterns. The stitch width and length controls are marked in numbers as well as color coded areas. The reverse control is a white lever that is pushed down for instant backtacking and held down for continuous reverse stitching.

We were especially intrigued with what we could accomplish by selecting the stitch pattern with the needle symbol on the panel. Exchanging the regular needle for a golden one (designed with the eye nearer the point and found in the needle assortment) we basted in half-inch stitches using the presser foot with a flat sole to help feed the cotton smoothly. Changing back to the ordinary needle, but with the same pattern selection, we hemmed on a wool and synthetic double knit with a perfect blindstitch without a blindstitch foot. The pattern is designed to create several small straight stitches between a wide zag that catches the fold. We were also able to produce a very good blanket stitch on heavy mohair by the same stitch pattern.

It should be noted that there is a very good blindstitch foot with an adjustable fold guide included in the accessories box. We made a fine hem on a rayon knit with this foot snapped on the shank using an elastic blindstitch, yet another stitching pattern.

Besides being able to baste, the Maximatic also has another capacity for temporary stitching which marks fabric, somewhat like tailor tacking. We attached the special marking foot, dialed the regular zigzag stitch, set the stitch width to four and with the paper pattern pieces still pinned to two layers of fabric, we sewed along the dart lines. Because of a vertical ridge down the foot's center the zigzag stitches were forced over the ridge to make loose loops. We carefully pulled the paper pattern away and separated the two layers of fabric slightly and snipped the thread loops, leaving small tufts of thread to mark the dart lines.

This model is supposed to come with quite an array of snap-on presser feet designed for specific sewing operations. We were disappointed to find that our accessory box didn't include all the feet shown in the instruction book. According to the page that lists the various feet, there were at least two missing we would like to have tested — the pintucking foot and the one for edge stitching. Unfortunately, it is almost impossible to identify all 11 presser feet by the diagrams shown in the accessory section unless they have distinctive shapes. Necchi has given us a descriptive list on the page opposite the diagrams with foot numbers, but even this identification does little good when the number is not printed on the foot itself. It wasn't even possible to tell if a foot was metal or made from transparent plastic. We did decide that a foot made of grey plastic with a smooth sole had to be the one with "low friction lower surface" for sewing on hard to slide fabrics. Whether we were right or not we found the foot helped feed a piece of split cowhide under the presser foot with no pushing or pulling.

The sewer who frequently works on knits and stretch fabrics will be pleased with the elastic stitches which have been included with this model. We seamed on lycra with the tricot pattern for an interesting effect which also allowed the proper amount of stretching. It doubled as a smocking stitch when we stitched over several rows of gathers. The super stretch stitch is probably the handiest pattern the home-sewer can have. We made seams on a boucle knit and a stretch terry using this marvelous pattern to join and finish the edges in a single operation with very good

results. The other stretch stitch patterns — elastic overlock, elastic blindstitch and the straight stretch — should cover about every kind of stitching required on stretch fabrics available in fabric stores.

In straight and zigzag sewing, we found the stitch quality to be uniformly excellent. The tension setting of three was ideal for most of our test fabrics such as organdy, Qiana, tricot, denim and melton. Sheer nylon puckered at this setting even after we had loosened it to two. We reset the pressure control, but it still didn't do the trick until we replaced the scarf-soled presser foot with a smooth sole. Actually the pressure control only had to be changed when we stitched on a spongy mohair which had a tendency to curl up in back of the presser bar when less pressure was exerted on the foot. This control is placed inconveniently behind the face plate and it is virtually impossible to change unless the sewer approaches it from the left side.

The buttonhole foot was missing from our machine, but we were able to borrow a similar foot from the 584. The Maximatic has the same unusual way of making automatic bartack buttonholes as we noted on the 584. After the upper bartack and left side are made, the machine stitches backward in a straight line when its third position is dialed; then it satin stitches down the right side over the straight line and makes the final bartack. The buttonhole we made was strong with good stitch density on both sides, but we had to hold back the fabric when bartacking so it would not progress further than we wanted. We could not drop the feed dogs easily for this step, either, because the control switch which governs that function is placed in back of the free arm and the extension table had to be removed.

We do commend Necchi for the bobbin design and for having transparent bobbins. After the bobbin is threaded into a case it isn't mounted on a vertical stud but rather rests at an angle with the bobbin facing up so the sewer

can instantly see the amount of thread remaining on the bobbin upon opening the shuttle cover. The bobbin and case are removed from the shuttle by using the magnetized end of the large screw driver found in the accessory box.

After testing two models by Necchi, we did become accustomed to the hand wheel location which is near the base on the right side rather than near the top. Once in a while, though, we still mistakenly reached for the selector knob (just above it) instead.

The bobbin did not cut off automatically which we thought a machine in this price range should feature. However, the top threading of the machine is a one-motion operation, quick and easy to do.

The extension table gives very little extra work surface in front, but it does provide enough on the left side and in the back. A very sturdy piece of metal, we had to give it a mighty pull in order to dislodge the large pin from its moorings in front which holds the table secure around the slender free arm.

The foot control, which is comfortable and wide, was responsive at both motor speeds, and we experienced no coasting when we released the control. The machine ran quietly and smoothly with only an occasional bit of bobbin chatter.

The eleven presser feet, all mounted on a common shaft, are easily removed by flipping a lever. Included with the machine are: a flat soled foot, scarfed sole foot, embroidery foot, marking foot, pintucking foot, edgestitching foot, hemming foot, buttonhole foot, adjustable blindstitch foot, one-way zipper foot, and a button attaching foot. Other accessories include: four spool retainers, sewing guide, quilting guide, rod for circular sewing, four transparent bobbins, assortment of needles including a twin-needle and the golden needle, threading hooks, lint brush, a seam ripper, oiler and two screw drivers, the larger with a magnetic base.

Even though the instruction book encompasses operations for both the 584 and the 586, we found it less confusing to use it this time because all of the information was pertinent to the more complex 586 while it wasn't with the 584. The instructions are specific with proper settings and presser feet given for each operation. Some of the diagrams are unclear, however.

The machine has a two-year warranty on all mechanical and electrical parts plus a limited 10-year warranty on the mechanical parts. Both warranties exclude light bulbs, needles and belts.

Special capabilities of the machine are: twin-needle sewing, darning, marking, free-form embroidery, basting and sewing on buttons.

Made in Italy, the Necchi Silvia Maximatic is a beautiful machine, well engineered and quite expensive. It should give many years of service to the sewer who wants a machine with good stitch performance that has, not an extensive, but excellent selection of built-in stitch patterns and can be transported readily with its own carrying case.

Approximate Retail Price: $800.00

Nelco
La Belle II 645F

A handsome machine, the Nelco La Belle II 645F has few dials or levers to clutter the design. It is a free arm unit with multi-colored stitch symbols against a black panel. A removable extension table has a hinged left side for storage. The niche is for accessories. A light is mounted behind the hinged face plate with the switch on the right side, above the switch for the motor speeds.

We found the large multi-colored stitch pattern symbols pleasing to the eye as well as being easy to read and handle. In the beginning we thought the stitch width lever might be inconvenient because of its location on top of the arm. This proved not to be the case; we quickly became accustomed to its placement.

A dial on the right side of the machine regulates the stitch length with markings representing stitches-per-inch; a color coded area for stitches made with a forward and reverse feed, an area for buttonhole settings and another marked "fine" for satin stitching. A center button is depressed to instantly reverse, and it must be held in to continuously backstitch.

The 645F's design is simple; however, some of its controls are inconvenient. For example: in order to change the feed dog setting, the sewer must open the shuttle door to move a lever beside the shuttle, and if the extension table is in place, she has to drop the hinged front section first. Another problem was adjusting the pressure control, a lever on the back, which was also stiff. In time, the sewer would undoubtedly get to know the settings by "feel" since there are only three positions, but before that time came she would surely have to stand up or approach the machine from the back to make the necessary changes.

The motor is moderately quiet and runs smoothly. We could regulate it to either of two speeds by changing a switch position on the right side of the machine. The motor would not run, however, unless the light switch was also turned on, a safety feature that is valuable.

Fabrics we tested fed evenly, and the stitch quality was consistently good in both straight and zigzag pattern sewing. We were able to sew on many types and layers of fabric without having to change the upper thread tension. We found a sheer nylon puckered at the same setting, and it was necessary to loosen the tension setting. We also tried changing the pressure control from two to one (a setting recommended by the manufacturer for lightweight fabrics), but the nylon swerved noticably under the needle, and we had to set the control back to two for even stitching. Actually, this setting seemed to be the proper one for most of our testing, with the exception of darning.

All of the built-in stitch patterns were excellent including some fine utility and stretch stitches with topnotch overcasting patterns. A well-designed overlock, a zigzag between two rows of straight stitching, seamed and finished the edges of a gauzy woven cotton satisfactorily as did a slant overlock, a stitch with more flexibility, on a ribbed knit. The straight stretch stitch was effective on a denim curved seam and quite good on medium weight synthetic knit, although it didn't have as much "give" as we would like to see.

The buttonhole we made on woven cotton was a disappointment. The bartack advanced so readily into the sides, we had to forcibly hold back the

fabric, and the sides were too close together no matter how carefully we tried to guide the material. There was no room down the center to slit the buttonhole opening without cutting through the side stitching. Stitch density was not uniform, either. Adjusting the satin stitch setting on the length control helped somewhat but not enough to make the sides even. Curiously, on the arm top is a location and marking for a stitch balance adjustor which we thought would cure the stitch density problem, but when we tried to change it, we found no control, only the markings. It was possible to make a better buttonhole on a light wool flannel, probably because the fabric is a little spongier, and it was easier to guide the stitch so the sides were not as close together. The stitch density remained uneven, however.

When lifted, the presser foot was high enough with ample space for the bulkiest fabric, which we appreciated when sewing on two layers of fleece. We could snap off a presser foot by the flick of a lever and mount a replacement by putting it under the shank and lowering the lifter.

A closed eyelet in the take-up lever does not allow upper threading in a one-motion operation. We think that Nelco should consider making an elongated groove as other manufacturers have done as a real convenience to the home-sewer when she is threading her machine.

The detachable extension table (called the Converto-table) fits snugly and firmly around the free arm. There was plenty of extra space in front and on the left side, which flips up for storage, but very little in the back. Having a niche under the front to hold accessories was very handy, and we were also pleased that the front part of the table could be opened for access to the shuttle area without having to remove the whole extension.

There are six presser feet included with the machine, five of which snap off and on a common shank. The two-way zipper foot, which we really like, is mounted around a set screw on the presser bar. Other feet include: a straight stitch foot, zigzag foot, buttonhole foot, stretch stitch foot and button attachment foot. Other sewing accessories are: quilting attachment, cloth guide, four metal bobbins, needle assortment including a twin-needle and one for sewing knits and two screw drivers.

The light is mounted to the left of the needle area, up behind the face plate. The screw-in bulb is simple to change.

The instruction book is excellent with clear and concise diagrams to illustrate procedures and charts to show proper settings for various stitching operations.

The machine has a 25-year warranty against imperfections in manufacture on all parts except needles, belts, light bulbs and electrical equipment.

Special capabilities of this machine are: darning, monogramming, twin-needle sewing, and button attachment.

The La Belle is a superior sewing machine in many ways. It is versatile without being overly complicated with excellent capabilities and should attract both the novice and experienced sewer. **Approximate Retail Price: $400.00**

New Home 910

The New Home 910 is an off-white free arm machine with a black front panel and carrying case. An extension table, stored on the carrying case top as part of the design, is molded plastic. It fits around the free arm and is held in place by a front pin. The light is mounted behind the hinged plate, illuminating the needle area from the left. Its switch is on the back of the face plate.

This machine is a very quiet, smooth-running model with the emphasis placed on visibility of controls rather than on simple design. With the exception of a pressure regulator on the arm top, the rest of the large white dials are prominently located within easy grasp and easily seen against a black background. We didn't have to reach around to the right side or fiddle with some lever behind the free arm to change a setting.

The combination stitch length-drop feed-reverse control functions in an efficient manner, but we had some difficulty determining the precise stitch length setting without leaning to the right when we dialed to the upper range past three because the setting mark is on the dial, not on the machine body.

The control that regulates the width of the zigzag has considerably more range than most machines. It made it possible to stitch patterns over a quarter-inch wide, at least 2mm wider than most zigzags we tested. This means that the adventurous sewer can have a field day creating different designs by dialing even more widths.

The choice of built-in stitch patterns is certainly extensive enough to please the most selective sewer. Out of the 28 possible utility and decorative patterns, we note that there isn't an arrowhead, dog or duck to be seen. There are many good patterns but there is also a great deal of similarity among the zigzag variations.

The machine feeds evenly and steadily. When we stitched on a long strip of polyester double knit, we only had to touch it occasionally for guidance and the fabric never swerved from under the needle. All of the fabrics we tested handled extremely well. With the upper tension set to five and the pressure control pin depressed half way, we were able to obtain a very well balanced straight stitch on a variety of fabrics, from sheer nylon to heavy melton coating. Neither control needed to be reset in spite of the vast difference in weight of the materials, not even when we stitched through four layers of heavy denim.

For manual zigzag sewing on muslin, we did loosen the upper thread tension a little as the manufacturer suggested so the upper thread appeared slightly on the underside. Our first attempt to zigzag led to a straight line of stitching because the instruction book had neglected to tell us that the needle position had to be changed to an "L" setting. Upon turning the page and reading directions for automatic zigzag stitching, we realized the error in setting and were able to produce a fine satin stitch using the marked range on the stitch length dial as well as a less dense pattern by setting it to a higher number.

The needle position is a vital setting for the many built-in patterns, but the manual does not stress this point. For example, in testing automatic stitches the initial instructions told us that the needle position should be set at L for any pattern. Yet, when we dialed the tricot stitch (a three-step zigzag) and the blindstitch, the machine again stitched in a straight line just as it had performed when we first attempted the manual zigzag. Both of these patterns do have initials above them (TS and BS) but there was no hint as to what the initials meant or that we should look for further directions. Eighteen pages later in the instruction book, we found a section explaining the tricot stitch

and discovered the needle position should have been set at R while the blindstitch setting was supposed to be M. The instruction book did tell us to set the stitch width regulator to zero before moving the pattern indicator to facilitate its movement.

One of the super automatic stitches we liked the most was the overlock stitch. With the needle position set at S (stretch) and the stitch width at the widest point of seven, we sewed a fine seam and finished the edges all in one operation on a spongy, loosely woven mohair and wool fabric. The width of the stitch made it especially good for this bulky fabric and the special presser foot allowed no curling of edges. When the machine was set for any super automatic stitch, we could stretch or elongate the pattern simply by dialing on either side of the S setting within the green range.

We loosened the upper tension to three, an important factor for good stitch quality when making automatic and super automatic patterns as well as for automatic buttonholes. By doing this, the buttonholes we made were excellent with equal stitch density on both sides and with strong bartacks. The presser foot had a cord spur on the back to carry gimp (cord) so we could also produce a first-rate raised or corded buttonhole.

The bobbin is wound on the top of the arm and the needle mechanism is disengaged when the bobbin is fitted onto the bobbin winder. The winding cuts off automatically when the bobbin is full, a feature we always like to see. The upper thread takes a conventional route from one of two spindles on the upper back, across the back and over the arm, threading through discs, eyelets and guides. An extra guide on the face plate, labeled "chain stitch" is only threaded when engaged in that operation.

The lighting was good with the needle area fairly well illuminated. The foot control was immediately responsive when pressed and did not coast after the pressure was

released, but was most uncomfortable. It is narrow and high so the sewer has no place to rest her heel unless she is wearing high heels.

The machine includes five snap-on presser feet that remove easily by flipping a lever in back of the presser foot. The feet are: an all-purpose foot, buttonhole foot, hemming foot, two-way zipper/cording foot, and button attaching foot. Other accessories are: the chain looper, five metal bobbins, blindstitch guide, two felt spindle pads, spare light bulb, needle assortment including a twin-needle and special scarfed needle, a seam ripper, lint brush, oiler and two screw drivers.

With the exception of the noticeable omissions, the manual is very informative with clear diagrams to illustrate the various operations. We think many sewers would find it helpful if more explicit uses of certain good utility automatic and super automatic stitch patterns were discussed and if a listing of the accessories and aids came after the machine parts were identified.

The machine comes with a full 90-day warranty against defects in material or workmanship and guarantees to repair or replace the head or any of its parts. It also has a limited 25-year warranty against defects in material and workmanship with the exception of electrical equipment which is warranted for a period of two years.

Special capabilities of the machine are: chain stitching, darning, twin-needle sewing, button attachment and free-form embroidery.

The New Home 910 performs very well and has many good features. The extension table provides plenty of work surface around the free arm, but it is lightweight and does not sit very securely around the arm. Unquestionably, the machine is expensive because of the numerous stitch patterns, and it is up to the sewer to determine whether they are worth the price.
Approximate Retail Price: $700.00

Penney 6520

This machine is an attractively designed flatbed unit with handle controls which are outlined in white against a black front panel. It would seem to offer the budget-minded sewer a great deal for her money with six built-in stitch patterns plus an automatic buttonholer, but in testing, the machine didn't measure up to its potential, and there were more problems than pleasure.

Much of the blame must be attributed directly to an inadequate instruction book. When we started to try out the various stitch patterns, we found that with the exception of a few, which were color coordinated, the suggested stitch length and width settings given were completely incomprehensible. Part of this is the fault of the marking system on the dials where graduated lines are used instead of numerals for a range gauge. The most experienced sewer would have difficulty interpreting the optimal settings with such inadequate directions. The book was organized in a peculiar way, too. For example, we were given directions for darning and embroidery before straight and zigzag sewing procedures were discussed.

The diagram for upper threading also was not very clear in the manual, showing open eyelets on the arm when, in fact, they were closed and hard to thread. The last guide before the approach to the needle bar was so recessed that we had to open the face plate to pass the thread behind it. However, the bobbin loaded through a cover plate that lifts from the front and was easier to seat in the shuttle race than most of the flat bed models we have tested.

The quality of stitches produced with no tension adjustment were quite good. We could go from sewing sheer nylon to a heavy coating with the tension set at four plus. The needle stayed in a left-hand position throughout all of our straight stitching, which was a bit disconcerting when we are used to having it in the center of the presser foot.

The pressure control or darner seemed to function best for regular and straight stitching on all fabrics used when the inner pin was almost completely down to the ring, even when we sewed on heavy melton. Experimenting, we decreased the pressure to sew a seam on acrylic backed fleece, as the manual directed, but the machine did not feed properly, resulting in small irregular stitches which started to pile upon one another until we increased pressure on the presser foot again.

Irregular bobbin stitches appeared occasionally at the beginning of a seam, but this condition corrected itself after several stitches. At first we thought we hadn't left enough thread behind the presser foot before starting to sew. But after leaving a good six inches in back and carefully rechecking all threading, we were never able to solve this problem.

In spite of uncertain settings, we admire the selection of stitch patterns which is a well-rounded collection of good utility ones, some stretchable, and two fine decorative designs. If Penney's is going to have a separate row of symbols on the arm especially for double needle stitching, it should also include this type of needle in the assortment that comes with the machine.

With no color coordination to guide us for optimal settings when blindstitching or making a multiple zigzag, we had no choice but to experiment again. We set both the stitch length and zigzag control below the halfway mark and produced a reasonably good blind hem on cotton. To join two layers of lycra we used the multiple zigzag for its reliable stretchability setting the stitch length close to the fine end of the range and leaving the zigzag at the halfway point.

We had less difficulty selecting settings for the straight stretch stitch because the zigzag control was color coded. Remembering that all other straight stretches we had tested were made with a long stitch, we dialed the control to its maximum length and made a commendable, though heavy, stitch which was better suited for reinforcing pockets and curved seams on heavy woven materials than for knits. With the pattern selector in the same position, we set the zigzag dial to a yellow setting (at the widest part of the range) for an excellent overlock stitch on boucle. Even though this was one of the color-coordinated patterns, the manual neglected to inform us to set it at the yellow range, an omission which is unacceptable.

The automatic buttonholer was well-marked in green on all of the necessary controls. The buttonholes we produced on woven cotton were not first-rate and both sides were not equal in stitch density. Although we adjusted the stitch length for a less dense satin stitch, they still had a tendency to pile up. After several attempts we finally did achieve a passable buttonhole, but only by pushing and pulling the fabric so the stitches were more or less even and the feed was consistent.

The two cords attached to the foot control and leading from the machine to a socket were not marked to indicate the one for motor and the one for light. We mixed connections and as we were plugging the foot control cord into the wall socket, the machine started stitching by itself with no fabric under the needle. Of course, it was a simple matter to interchange the two cords, but it would also be simple to designate by a mark which cord controlled which power source.

The machine comes with a full two-year warranty against defective materials or workmanship and a limited 20-year warranty on mechanical parts.

Special capabilities of the machine are: darning,

monogramming, twin-needle sewing and button attaching.

The 6520 is not particularly quiet running; there was some bobbin chatter as we stitched. Although the foot pedal was supplied by the manufacturer for this testing, the purchaser will have to buy a carrying case separately or console with foot control or knee pedal to activate the motor of the machine. The extra cost must be considered along with the initial price of the machine.

Approximate Retail Price: $200.00

Penney 6905

The Penney 6905 is a handsome machine designed along pure, uncluttered lines with only a few controls to master. This model functioned with precision and was extremely quiet and smooth running with only the slightest bit of vibration when used at top speed.

Several operations are combined into one control. One such control is the stitch pattern knob that can dial settings for an automatic buttonholer, for straight or zigzag stitching and for many of the seven built-in stitch patterns. The markings on the machine's arm are clear with right-angled lines drawn from pattern symbols across the arm top to various positions around the control. Although the selector knob on our test machine was a trifle stiff, we had no problem dialing the different settings for straight and pattern sewing. The knob turned smoothly, and we could stop it at any point when testing widths in the regular zigzag range. Switching from one built-in pattern setting to another, we could hear a new cam click automatically into place.

We did run into difficulties with the settings on the selector when

we attempted to make a buttonhole. The first side is stitched in reverse, and we were prepared for it by starting at the lower right side of the marked position on the fabric. We turned the knob to the line indicating the first buttonhole position and were alarmed to discover that the stitches were piling on top of each other making a knotted lump. Undaunted, we fiddled with the buttonhole setting on the stitch length regulator thinking that we could solve the problem by lengthening the pitch of the stitch. However, our attempt to solve the problem failed. We then decided to try the second buttonhole setting (marked for bartacking) and discovered the machine buttonhole stitching in reverse. Upon studying the buttonhole settings very carefully, we realized that the white lines on the arm did not coincide with the indicator on the knob. During the first attempt when we thought we had dialed the first position, the machine was, in reality, out of gear. Of course the line on the arm that seemed to be for the second setting (or bartack) was the proper setting for the first side. These line markings on the arm for the buttonholer are confusing for the unwary and should be corrected.

After unlocking the secret of the settings, we are happy to report that we made excellent, strong buttonholes on cotton and polyester double knit. No pivoting was necessary nor was there any need to change the stitch balance from the center point of the control because stitch density was equal on both sides.

The machine has the ability to rewind a bobbin from the spool while the machine is still threaded. We simply brought the thread up from the needle through the front top thread guide and inserted a thread end through the hole in the empty bobbin, which was placed on the bobbin spindle. After disengaging the needle mechanism with the stop motion knob on the hand wheel, we proceeded to wind the bobbin in the same manner as we did when

starting to sew with a brand new color of thread.

After inserting the bobbin into its case and drawing the thread to the outside and under the tension spring, it must also be threaded into a small guide on the case. We have seen several bobbin cases designed to be threaded the same way, but this one is the easiest to thread that we have seen.

The materials used to test the 6905 were sheer nylon, organdy, cire, rayon tricot, woven cotton, polyester double knit, denim, wool flannel, heavy coating and an acrylic backed fleece. The tension control on the machine produced the best stitch quality in the middle range of the normal setting for straight stitching. We loosened the tension slightly when producing stitch patterns and buttonholes.

The pressure adjustment seemed to be only moderately critical on the 6905. We did use the same settings suggested by the manufacturer with good results.

The selection of stitch patterns is first-rate, offering the sewer excellent utility patterns, some of which can be used for decorative trims, with stretch patterns for knits. There are two patterns designed to seam and overcast at the same time. We used the overlock, a combination of zigzag between two rows of straight stitching, to complete a seam on a basket weave cotton so any further raveling would be prevented. On a stretch terry cloth we chose the slant overlock, a serging pattern, that was more effective because of elasticity on the knit. The rick rack and straight stretch stitch are both dense and heavy, not suited for lighter fabrics. We thought that the straight stretch stitch was more appropriate when we used it for reinforcing curved seams on denim and a heavier gabardine.

Upper threading just misses being a one-motion operation from spindle to needle area if it weren't for the closed eyelet on the take-up lever. We wish the manufacturer would have made it an open slot because it was not easy to thread the take-up lever. We had to turn the hand wheel in order to position the lever about a half-inch down from its upper most position so it would extend far enough away from the face plate so we could insert the thread through the eye. What a bother!

Lighting was good although it would cast even more illumination on the needle area if the bulb were mounted lower behind the face plate. The built-in drawer for accessories on the lower right side is an exceptionally good idea. It is out of the way yet the sewer always has ready access to the presser feet and other aids she needs. The extension table is firm with no supporting legs on the left side so the home-sewer can use it for tubular sewing of a wider nature for hemming trouser pants or children's waistbands. The table on our test model was not easy to mount, however, and we had to be sure the two pins, fore and aft, were aligned exactly with the holes in the base of the machine, which was not always easy. When we did get it in place, though, it remained stable.

The machine comes with seven presser feet that all mount around a set screw on a common presser bar. They include: a zigzag foot, a straight stitch foot, a stretch stitch foot, hemming foot, two-way zipper foot, buttonhole foot, and button attaching foot. Other accessories are: four metal bobbins, an assortment of needles including a special one for stretch fabrics and a twin-needle, two felt pads for spool pins, a seam guide, quilting attachment, two screw

drivers, a spare light bulb, seam ripper and oiler.

By comparison with the other Penney model tested, the instruction book accompanying this one is exceptional. It is informative and complete with good diagrams, settings and sewing tips. We were intrigued with the suggestion for making a thread chain that beats some of the chain stitching procedures with attachments we have encountered. All we did was to stitch off the edge of a fabric piece and continue stitching until we obtained the length of chain we wanted. By placing the fabric back under the presser foot, we finished off the chain taking several stitches to secure the end, and we had a belt loop. Miraculously the machine didn't jam while we were stitching without any material under the foot.

The machine comes with a full two-year warranty against defective materials or workmanship and a 20-year warranty on all mechanical parts.

Special capabilities of the machine are: darning, monogramming, twin-needle sewing and button attaching.

Complete with its own soft vinyl carrying case, the Penney 6905 is a fine machine which gives a good performance. The comfortable foot control was responsive instantly, and we detected no coasting when it was released. The sewer who wants excellent value should definitely consider this machine. **Approximate Retail Price: $300.00**

Pfaff 209

The Pfaff 209 is a free arm machine accompanied by a rigid plastic case which locks to the base with two clasps. A molded plastic extension table fits around the slender free arm to give more work surface. The light is mounted behind the hinged face plate,

illuminating the needle area from the left side. A light switch is on the left side of the face plate.

In many ways the Pfaff 209 is an outstanding unit with a relatively quiet motor and no vibration at any speed. We found that the built-in stitch selection was small but select with the emphasis on utility stitch patterns rather than decorative ones. The capacity for stretch stitching is lacking, however. The only pattern that could be considered stretchable is the multi-stitch zigzag. Although this model is in the moderate price range, it is to be commended for having an automatic buttonholer; a feature we see on more expensive machines but seldom at this price.

The controls are designed for high visibility with markings in white against a black background. And, in case the sewer has any doubt about settings, Pfaff has repeated the symbols or numbers next to the control on the body of the machine. Only one — the black reverse lever — is not very discernible against the panel of the same color.

Stitch quality was very good in both straight and zigzag stitching on all of our test fabrics. Adjustments did have to be made in the upper tension within the range that the manufacturer considers normal, between three and five on the dial. For hemming

a pair of heavy denim jeans (which is actually sewing through three layers of cloth) we found the best setting for a balanced stitch to be five. When we tested on rayon tricot, lighter cotton, polyester double knit and wool flannel, we needed to loosen the dial to four; and for best results on sheer nylon and cire the ideal setting was at three. We appreciated not having to fiddle around with other controls besides the upper tension (such as a pressure regulator and drop feed control) to obtain good stitch quality. It would be even more satisfactory to adjust the tension even less.

The machine fed evenly with no swerving under the needle even when we tested on a slippery nylon knit. The feed dog teeth were sharp, but they did not snag our fabric and there was no problem removing a spongy mohair from the needle area. We were also pleased to see enough space between the needle and the raised presser foot to position a bulky coating fabric without undue squeezing.

The bobbin is wound on the top of the arm and a slot in the bobbin must be fit onto a spindle pin. The top of the machine is threaded from spindle to needle in a one-motion operation.

The foot control would not always respond instantly when pressed, and as we tried to find the right spot to activate it (which seemed to be on the right side) it would suddenly respond with a sharp burst of speed. The control is a large rectangle which we first used in a longitude position, thiking it was meant to accommodate most of the foot. Realizing our mistake, we turned it in the correct horizontal position, but after depressing it with the ball of the foot, we concluded that it responded best when the upper part of the foot was used.

The automatic no-turn buttonholer produced very professional looking bartack buttonholes with good stitch density on both sides. Both strong bartacks were made without

stitches piling up and without the necessity of holding back the fabric so it wouldn't advance.

Testing the multi-stitch zigzag on cotton jersey and wool ribbed knit at the suggested settings gave us an excellent stitch which was as flexible as the fabric. We did not have the same experience with the blindstitch pattern. Following the manual's directions, we set the stitch length at four, the width at three, and produced a pattern that was much too large for hemming. By reducing the stitch length setting to 2.5 the result was much more suitable for this purpose.

The stitch length control was awkward to dial because of the design. This kind of a vertical wheel with only the rim as a dial is acceptable when the control is seldom used, as in a stitch positioner or an elongator for automatic stitches but not as a control that must be turned frequently.

Four presser feet come with the machine which mount around a set screw on the presser bar. They include: an all-purpose foot, hemming foot, buttonhole foot and a button attaching foot. Other accessories included are: four plastic bobbins, an assortment of needles, an oiler and unidentified clamps and screws.

The instruction book is confusing and printed in very small type. Not only does it cover several Pfaff models, but the limited text appears in 14 languages, English being second on the list. We never realized how much we relied on printed directions and helpful suggestions until we were confronted with practically none in this manual. Controls and various parts of the machine are identified (along with parts which belonged to other models,) and there is a paragraph on how to regulate tension controls. That is the extent of printed instructions. The rest of the manual is devoted entirely to step-by-step diagrams for each operation. These drawings are explicit, but there should be some procedure identification. In this manual the diagrams are

numbered consecutively throughout, but the sewer never knows when one function is completed and another begins. A novice would be hard pressed to follow these drawings. A series of sketches showed us how to thread the needle, but in spite of arrows and overlays it was impossible to tell whether the thread should go from front to back or the reverse. We correctly threaded from front to back because that is the way most machines are threaded. The setting and procedure for an automatic buttonholer, which is a built-in feature of the 209, were explained toward the end of the instructions. The instruction manual depicted how to make a buttonhole with the basic zigzag method of positioning the needle and adjusting stitch length and width; even after 23 diagrams we were not shown when to pivot the fabric. The sewer would also find it difficult to know where to oil. Although an oiler is included with the accessories, the only diagrams for maintenance deal with cleaning the shuttle area.

The machine comes with a two-year warranty against defective materials and workmanship plus a 25-year warranty covering mechanical parts only.

Special capabilities of the machine are: darning, free-form embroidery and button attaching.

Made in West Germany, the Pfaff 209 is a handsomely styled free arm unit that performs well. With its accompanying case, the machine is light enough in weight to be portable. Many of the features are well done, but we would like to see another stretch stitch pattern built in. At this moderate price, we think the manufacturer could include a zipper/cording presser foot in with the basic accessories. Above all, we would like to see Pfaff put out an instruction book in English for this model alone and in print large enough to be easily read with the printed directions and fabric suggestions to go with the various operations.

Approximate Retail Price: $400.00

Pfaff 1222E

The Pfaff 1222E is a free arm electronic machine. The carrying case top opens to provide storage space for accessories and spools of thread. A flat extension table fits around the free arm by means of two pins to secure it. A bulb, under the face plate, sheds light from the left of the needle area. A master switch on the base turns on the current for both light and motor.

The 1222E has remarkable push button selection for all of the built-in stitch patterns. It is convenient having pertinent information shown on each button which includes proper needle position and stitch length range along with the stitch symbol. We could make the right settings in an instant without bothering to refer to the instruction book. Highly visible (white on black), the buttons can also be concealed when not in use by lowering a hinged cover that blends with the symmetry of the arm.

We have to admire the number of excellent designs which can be created by only ten basic buttons — five utility and five decorative. The selection is impressive enough when each pattern is made by itself, but consider how many other designs can be created when two or more of the buttons are pushed simultaneously to combine the stitch patterns. The instruction book has an illustrated chart with combinations as well as settings for 52 patterns, enough to satisfy the most decoration conscious sewer.

An excellent feature is the Stopmatic control of the presser foot lifter which, when engaged at its lowest point, picks up the bobbin thread. We also found it very handy to flick to the top position to disengage the needle mechanism when winding the bobbin. Once we became accustomed to the pivotal lever (different from any we have tested) and the four positions it can assume, we realized the advantages of the design. It was no longer necessary to turn the hand wheel to raise the needle high or untwist it for bobbin winding. But the lever on our test machine did not perform one function it was supposed to according to the instructions. When the lever is parallel, the needle should stay in the fabric while the presser foot is raised so the fabric can be pivoted easily. The needle failed to stay in our fabric. We felt that the control's functions should have been explained sooner in the manual. Twice it is referred to as a critical part of an operation — when bobbin winding and when employing the automatic needle threader — and both times we found ourselves flipping pages to learn how to use it.

Less noteworthy was the automatic needle threader. Following directions explicitly, we tried many times before we could make it work and, after one success, failed to make the thread loop through the needle in our very next try. With upper threading basically a one-motion operation from spindle to needle, we did not feel that hand threading the needle was that tedious a task. One of the best ways Pfaff could facilitate this operation would be to place a white area on the presser foot shank behind the needle for better visibility.

We connected the Matchmaker (an even-feed device) to the all-purpose presser foot and stitched a long seam on horizontally striped knit without basting. Both layers of fabric fed so evenly that the stripes were perfectly matched. This control is also extremely helpful when we basted using the longest stitch (six per inch) length. There are instructions to speed-baste also, that call for raising the needle to its highest point, then pulling the material as far as desired, lowering the needle and repeating the operation for each additional stitch. We found the process to be awkward and time consuming.

The Pfaff Electronic ran quietly and smoothly. Having found good tension control in the other Pfaff reviewed, we were surprised to run into difficulty with this model. Upper tension adjustment didn't do the trick, so we finally resorted to loosening the bobbin tension slightly. We were pleasantly surprised to find this no chore at all; we did it with a fingernail which makes us wonder if it could have been jarred loose in the process of shipping. This adjustment solved the tension dilemma, and we were able to achieve a balanced stitch on polyester double knit, batiste, cotton, wool coating and acrylic backed fleece with upper tension set at four. The ideal setting was nearer three for sheer nylon and cire, both of which had a tendency to swerve from under the needle and needed careful guiding.

The buttonhole we produced was excellent and strong with an even density of stitch on both sides. When making our sample on muslin, we found it necessary to adjust the stitch length setting on the Ultra-matic dial to the plus side of the range in order to space out the satin stitch. We moved it back to the center of the range when we made buttonholes on a lightweight batiste.

The metal bobbin is wound on a magnet on the tip of the arm and shuts off automatically when full. The bobbin is threaded into a case that fits vertically on a stud in the shuttle under the needle plate. With a spool on one of the two spindles in back, the thread is drawn around the upper left side into the tension discs and then threaded in front through guides and open eyelets to the needle in a one-motion operation.

The electronic foot control responded instantly to the touch. Depending on how much pressure we applied to the control, we were able to stitch as fast as we wanted. We could go slowly, stitch by stitch, when sewing through several thicknesses of fabric, even though this is only a one-speed motor.

Eight presser feet come with the machine, all of which fit around a set screw on the presser bar. They include: an all-purpose foot, blindstitch foot, darning foot, felling foot, one-way zipper foot, cording foot, clear-view foot and buttonhole foot. Other accessories are: a needle assortment, spool retainer, seam ripper, five plastic bobbins, quilt guide, screw driver, lint brush and oiler.

The instruction book is well organized and clearly describes all operations by photograph and diagrams. We think it would be of value to the sewer to have a listing of all the accessories and certainly to identify the numerous presser feet. Although a drawing of the proper foot is shown at the beginning of each new sewing process, the diagrams are small and it is sometimes hard to figure out which one is being used.

The machine comes with a two-year warranty against defective materials and workmanship plus a 25-year limited warranty covering mechanical parts.

Special capabilities of the machine are: darning, and free-form embroidery.

The Pfaff 1222E is a well-engineered machine which performs beautifully. It has clean, handsome lines and a case that doubles as a cover and storage area. For a machine in this bracket, (it is expensive), we would like to see Pfaff design a better presser foot; one that would slip off and on more easily. Above all, we would like to see an adjustable zipper foot which could be used from both sides. Its innovations are worth the money with the exception of the automatic needle threader which seems little more than a gimmick. For the adventurous and creative home-sewer who wants both utility and decorative stitch patterns and has the expertise to enjoy a complex piece of machinery, the Pfaff would be an excellent choice.

Approximate Retail Price: $998.00

Riccar 806

The Riccar 806 is a free arm machine with a carrying case that slides over the machine head and clamps under the base. An extension table fits around the free arm with two pins. It has a hinged left side that pushes up vertically when stored, plus niches with top covers front and back for storing accessories. The light shines from under the hinged face plate illuminating the needle area from the left side.

This machine earned high marks for its sewing performance. It fed evenly and was smooth running with a relatively quiet motor. With a minimum of controls on the arm, the design remains uncluttered, clean and simple. We found it inconvenient, however, to have the pressure control tucked behind the face plate even if the cover was hinged. The home-sewer can easily forget it exists while she is likely to keep an eye on other necessary settings which are in plain sight.

Stitch quality throughout our testing was first-rate. The pressure regulator did not seem to be a critical component for stitching on different weight fabrics as it has been on other machines. For example, we set it at three, a range for medium weight fabrics, when we started testing on woven cotton and polyester knit. Forgetting about the control we continued to sew on many other types and weights of fabric, still producing the same excellent stitches. It wasn't until we tested on an acrylic backed fleece that it became apparent the fabric wasn't feeding properly. We remembered the hidden control and were able to correct the feed by increasing the pressure to a four setting. Continuing with the experiment, we retested the cire and batiste with a lighter pressure setting of two but, the stitches were less than perfect.

While the tension wheel is available and highly visible, we never found it necessary to change from the setting of four. The tension accommodated itself equally to sheer nylon, polyester double knit and heavy melton without showing any alteration in quality of stitch.

With a minimum of dialing and fuss, we made one of the best bartack buttonholes in all our testing. We set the stitch length to the center of the green area (between zero and one), and the stitch density was uniform on both sides, the bartack tight and strong with no need for further reinforcement. We made an equally successful corded buttonhole by looping gimp around the catch at the back of the foot and drawing the two sides forward and parallel to satin stitch over the cord.

On the stitch length control the outer rim of the dial has a range of zero to four with color coded areas marked for settings to correspond with colors on the panel. Inside the dial is a button which is pushed for instant backtacking or held to sustain reverse stiching. At the right side of the machine base is a small knob which raises or lowers the feed dogs.

Although the Riccar 806 may not have as many built-in stitch patterns as other models, we like the selection's emphasis on utility and stretch capacity as well as potential for decoration. We found it relatively simple to blindstitch a

straight hem mostly because of the presser foot design. As we have seen on many other machines, the foot has a ridge down the center which helps control the hem fold. But this one is unique because the ridge can be moved sideways to adjust to bulkier fabrics. Using the blindstitch, we also made an attractive border of shell tucking on rayon tricot, and with the stretch blindstitch pattern we shortened the stitch length to produce a handsome edge around a linen place mat.

We were pleased with the overcasting stitch patterns which seam and finish an edge at the same time. A pattern resembling cross stitching was effective when we tried it on a ravel-prone boucle knit as was a serging stitch on rayon knit. The instruction book recommends that the elastic straight stitch, a triple lock that makes two stitches forward and one stitch in reverse, be used primarily for reinforcing seams subject to strain, but we found it was also decorative as topstitching on woven fabrics and on medium to heavy weight knits.

This Riccar has a "walking foot," a cumbersome gadget that prevents slippery fabrics from swerving from under the needle. It also even-feeds two layers of fabric so stripes and plaids can be stitched to match accurately without pin-basting.

The presser feet can be changed in an instant. The one in place is removed with a flick of a lever and a new one snapped on by lining the foot pin up with the shaft and lowering the presser lifter. Not so with the walking foot, however. It has to be mounted on the presser bar with prongs around a set screw after the shaft (the basis for the other presser feet) has been removed. This design is used by many manufacturers but here the screw is small and shallow, and a screw driver is needed to loosen it. Following directions, we removed shaft and screw which was a mistake. When we proceeded to put on the walking foot it required considerable effort plus a lot of bending to the left side to get the

screw back in place and around the prongs of the walking foot. It was possible to remove a component from the presser bar by simply loosening the screw enough to slip the prongs of the shaft or walking foot away from it and remount the other in the same way.

The white areas on the shaft and walking foot were pasted on and fell off during our testing, making it a little harder to see the eye of the needle for threading. Paint would be a help here.

In order to wind the bobbin, the sewer must lean over the machine or approach it from the back, tracing the thread from the spindle to the left back guide, downwards to a thread plate on the lower right back and then around the right side to below the hand wheel where the empty bobbin is placed on the winder. Unfortunately, the bobbin does not cut off automatically when full.

The machine utilizes the one-motion threading concept. From one of the two spindles in the back, the thread is traced over the arm, through springs and open eyelets, from right to left in one motion to the needle area.

Lighting is adequate and the one-speed motor is activated by the foot control which is very responsive. It is also very comfortable, accommodating a large portion of the foot.

All 10 presser feet included with the machine are snap-on with the exception of the walking foot. They included: zigzag foot, cording foot, hemming foot, satin stitch foot, buttonhole foot, button attaching foot, two-way zipper foot, blind hem foot; embroidering and walking foot. Other accessories include: needle assortment including a twin-needle, needle plate for straight stitching, quilter, four metal bobbins, two screw drivers, seam ripper, lint brush and oiler.

The instruction book was very informative with large, explicit drawings showing settings and accessories to be used with an operation.

The machine has a two-year

warranty on all electrical and mechanical parts with a limited 20-year warranty on mechanical parts. Both warranties exclude needles, pulleys, belts and light bulbs.

Special capabilities of the machine are: darning, free-form embroidery, twin-needle sewing, even feeding, sewing on buttons.

The Riccar 806 is well engineered and performs superbly. The sewer who wants quality along with a good selection of utility stitches will find that this machine has many attractions. **Approximate Retail Price: $550.00**

Riccar 808 E

The Riccar 808 E is a free arm machine with a carrying case that slides over the machine and clamps under the base. The extension table has niches for storing accessories. The light shines from under the hinged face plate illuminating the needle area on the left side. The switch is on the right side.

The electronically controlled Riccar 808 E is quiet and has a large selection of built-in stitch patterns.

The speed regulator provided instant response from the foot control at all times even when we barely touched it, and we experienced no coasting once the control was released. Whether we sewed at maximum speed or slowed down to a stitch-by-stitch action on five layers of heavy denim, the needle power remained constant and the stitches did not vary.

Another feature which we found especially handy was the needle stop control. By pushing this lever up when we reached the end of a seam, an electronic device raised the needle so the fabric could be removed from under the needle easily. With the lever pressed down, the needle was lowered into the fabric to allow for pivoting. Care must be taken, however, to use this control only when the machine is not running; it snaps back into a neutral position as soon as it is released. We also noted that the needle was raised, but the take-up lever was not necessarily all the way up.

When sewing on sheer nylon, tricot, cotton polyester double knit and a heavy melton, we found the tension control was excellent and we never needed to change it from a setting of four. The only adjustment we made was to shorten the stitch length for lighter fabrics so they wouldn't have a tendency to pucker. The pressure control, tucked in an awkward place behind the face plate, seemed to be superfluous. The setting at three (to handle medium weight fabrics), was ideal for batiste and melton as well. When we tested on a bulky acrylic backed fleece, we did change the setting to four, increasing the pressure on the presser foot, but when we examined the results in comparison to a sample with the control set at three, there was very little difference in the quality of the stitch.

The stitch width control is a dial marked with a zero to five range, with color coded areas to match the pattern selection. The outer rim of the dial is the stitch length control and has a range of zero to four. Inside the dial is a button that is pushed for instant backtacking or held to sustain reverse stitching. At the right of the machine is a knob that raises and lowers the feed dogs.

Among all of the various built-in buttonhole mechanisms available, this is one of the best. The five-step procedure does not require that feed dogs be dropped or fabric held back. The sewer marks the buttonhole range, snaps on the sliding buttonhole foot and dials the numbered settings. We made strong, professional looking bartack buttonholes with the density of the satin stitch consistent on both sides. To achieve a raised effect, we attached a loop of gimp around a

knob on the foot's back, drawing the ends forward under the foot and slipping them into a clip on the foot's front. This held the gimp secure allowing us to zigzag over the cording without having to worry about its parallel position.

Testing on a wide variety of fabrics, including some hard-to-manage materials such as nylon cire and heavy boucle, we found stitch quality to be very good, even and with no skipped stitches.

There are enough built-in stitch patterns to please the most imaginative sewer as well as many utility and stretch stitches for practical use. All are color coded to correspond with settings on other controls, a feature we found very helpful and time saving.

All of the patterns we tried were balanced, especially the many stretch stitches that can be used on knits. When using the red-coded superautomatic patterns, we could also change the looks of the design by using the elongator on top of the arm to telescope or stretch the pattern. Using the elongator was an annoyance, however, because a coin or screw driver has to be inserted in the groove to turn it and even then we were never really sure whether we were condensing or lengthening the design without much experimentation. Our only criticism concerning the pattern selection has to do with the similarity between the designs. For instance, we could overcast with any number of patterns and could blindstitch a hem using at least three others. Are they all necessary?

The presser feet snap on and off a common shank easily enough by flipping a lever to line up and remove the foot pin and by lowering the presser lifter to replace the foot pin. A white area on the shank front allowed us more visibility when threading the needle, which is always appreciated. This shank must be removed to mount a walking foot on the presser bar and this can be awkward to do. The trick is not to remove the set screw entirely (as

the instruction book suggests) because it is short and difficult to place again. Rather, unscrew it just enough so the shank prongs can be released.

The walking foot may be hard to mount, but it is well worth the trouble when sewing slippery fabrics or those plaids and stripes that have to be matched. This device acts as a feed mechanism for the top layer of fabric thereby making sure it feeds at the same rate as the bottom layer. Unfortunately, with this foot in place the space between the foot and feed dogs diminishes, making it difficult to position heavier fabrics under the needle.

Bobbin winding was inconvenient because the thread must take a zigzag route across the back before being placed on the winder, below the hand wheel. After some practice we could trace the thread in back without getting up from our chair, but it was necessary to lean far over to the right to make sure the empty bobbin was placed properly on the winder and had engaged the mechanism. It was necessary to watch the bobbin fill so the machine could be stopped at the right time. From either of two spindles in the back of the arm, the thread is traced over the arm, through springs and open eyelets from right to left in one motion to the needle.

The well-designed extension table fits snugly around the slender free arm with plenty of work space on the left side of the needle. We were able to approach the shuttle under the needle without removing the table by flipping back the front side. The back also has a top cover and under both are storage compartments for accessories and other sewing aids which we liked.

Twelve presser feet are included with the machine, all snap on with the exception of the walking foot. These include a zigzag foot, satin stitch foot, cording foot, hemming foot, buttonhole foot, button attaching foot, two-way zipper foot, overcast foot, blind hem foot, concealed zipper foot, embroidery and walking foot. Other accessories are: needle assortment including a twin-needle, needle plate for straight sewing, quilter, four metal bobbins, two screw drivers, a seam ripper, lint brush and oiler.

The extensive instruction manual has large, clear diagrams showing settings and explaining sewing operations with occasional red overlays to emphasize coded areas or threading directions. Although much space is devoted to how to make pin tucks, blindstitch hems, smock, cord, overcast, sew with the stretch stitches and applique, the capabilities of many other stitch patterns are ignored. We were pleased to see that this book, unlike one which accompanied another Riccar machine, tells how often to oil the machine. The section on maintenance is very thorough.

The machine has a two-year warranty on all electrical and mechanical parts with a limited 20-year warranty on mechanical parts. Both warranties exclude needles, pulleys, belts and light bulbs.

Special capabilities of this machine are: darning, free-form embroidery, twin-needle sewing, even feeding, sewing on buttons.

The Riccar 808 E is a first-rate machine. It runs smoothly, feeds evenly and we never detected any bobbin chatter or vibration. The novice will probably want a less complicated model, but the experienced sewer who wants plenty of stitch capability and has the know-how to use the various controls will find this free arm a pleasure to own.

Approximate Retail Price: $770.00

Sears Kenmore 1525

The Sears Kenmore 1525 is a smoke-colored free arm machine with a removable extension table that has a retractable support leg. The light is located behind the face plate, and a switch operates both light and power so the machine cannot be accidentally started if the switch is off.

It has much to offer in the way of a moderate but good selection of utility and stretch stitch patterns, yet it is in a lower price range. It runs very quietly with no vibration.

The design of this free arm model is uncluttered with large, accessible and easy to read controls. The extension table, which fits around the free arm, is somewhat different from the run-of-the-mill that we have seen. The front slants slightly away from the free arm, and because of the slight incline we didn't have to bend over as much when guiding fabric under the presser foot. This slanted front is easily removed by releasing a button on the left side, giving free access to the shuttle area to change a bobbin or push the control to drop the feed dogs — all without taking off the whole table. Sears doesn't give much added work space on the left with this extension, however, there is only about an inch from the end of the arm. There is a retractable leg for support of the left side, but it seemed superfluous because the table was very stable in its mounting.

The six stretch stitch patterns are surely adequate for the sewing and mending demands of the average sewer. The straight stretch stitch made a good elastic seam on cotton jersey and on a wool knit.

We did find it imperative to use the straight stitch foot and needle plate for this operation especially when we tested on nylon tricot. Otherwise the fabric puckered. The upper tension had to be loosened to below two from a normal three for the tricot and the pressure control lowered almost to its maximum position. When sewing a curved seam on denim, we also used the straight stretch for added strength without having to loosen the tension or change the needle plate.

The sewer who likes to make toddlers' dresses will enjoy the smocking stretch stitch because it is so easy to do. Placing a strip of fabric under a line of gathering, we stitched over the gathers and produced some remarkably good smocking. The overcast stretch stitch seamed and finished the edges on helenca adequately, and the elastic stretch stitch refastened some elastic that had come unsewn on a pair of panties. This same stitch, however, was not all that stretchable when we tried it on lycra.

The stitch quality was found to be very good after necessary adjustments were made to accommodate differences in various fabrics. Our machine didn't falter when we stitched five layers of muslin, and the ability to raise the presser foot an extra quarter inch above the lock position when the lifter was up helped place the bulk of added thickness under the needle.

The necessary adjustments were the pressure on the presser foot and upper thread tension.

Pressure had to be increased with lightweight fabrics and decreased with bulkier materials. The upper tension had to be loosened when we sewed on cire, Qiana and nylon tricot. At no time was it necessary to make an adjustment on the bobbin tension because a slight turn on the upper tension disc always brought the stitch back into balance.

After a clutch on the hand wheel has been released the bobbin is wound on top of the arm. An automatic cut-off stops the winding process when the bobbin is filled. The top threading follows a conventional path, down between the tension discs, up through a groove in the take-up lever, down through several guides to the needle.

The buttonholes we turned out were professional looking but not on the first try. The operation is only automatic to a degree. A plastic buttonhole guide must be placed under the pressure foot so the back edge of the foot is against the rear of the guide and the upper thread must also be between the presser foot and the guide. With the guide in place the garment, marked with the positions of buttonholes, is positioned under the guide and the presser foot lowered. Stitch width is set between one and one-and-a-half and stitch length at 12 (not in the satin stitch zone, however). By turning the special stitch modifier to its F setting the left side is made. Now comes the tricky part — making the rounded end. The modifier control must be turned to setting R to make the right side, but in the turning, the sewer is also making the rounded end and how fast the control is turned determines the number of stitches formed in this crucial area. Since there is approximately one inch on the dial between settings it takes some practice to negotiate this maneuver at the right speed for the uniform amount of stitches. We would hope that Sears will eventually design a better buttonholer which will automatically control the density of stitches on the ends as well as

on the sides. The buttonhole with rounded ends can look very much like a well done hand-worked one if one gets the hang of it, but a bartack buttonhole on a machine is easier.

The satin stitch, which was first-rate, requires a special presser foot with a channel running down the center on the underside. The presser feet are the kind that have prongs which fit around a screw which must then be tightened. With the exception of the zipper foot all are hinged to "walk" over pins or bulk. The zipper foot is adjustable so it can be used on either side of the needle or with the needle sewing through a center hole when the sewer is inserting an invisible zipper.

Presser feet included with the machine are: a zigzag foot, straight stitch foot, satin stitch foot, and a two-way zipper foot with the capacity to stitch close to an invisible zipper. Other accessories are: five bobbins, straight and zigzag needle plates, a buttonhole guide, needle threader, extra needles, two screw drivers and a seam ripper.

The idea of the numbers on the stitch length control relating to the actual stitches-per-inch is a good one; it gives the sewer a frame of reference rather than some meaningless range from one to four. We are curious, though, why the numbers go only to 12 when finer adjustments can be made before reaching the red area for satin stitching. There is plenty of room on the dial.

Lighting is good on the 1525, shining down from behind the face plate so the needle area is well illuminated. The narrow high foot control is uncomfortable to use for any length of time, and because it is light in weight it also has a tendency to slide on a bare floor despite two rubber tips in front.

The instruction book is well-written, informative, and diagrams proper settings for each operation. We noted many good suggestions on how to correct certain operational problems which might occur, and often do. One section is even devoted to all

of the parts which can be ordered from a Sears service center.

The machine is heavy. A carrying case can be purchased separately for storage or transport, but one could hardly term this model a true portable.

Sears gives a full 90-day warranty on all parts and mechanical adjustments plus a two-year warranty on electrical equipment and a 25-year warranty on the machine head.

Special capabilities of the machine are: darning, free-form embroidery and sewing on buttons.

The sewer who wants more than the basics but doesn't want to be overwhelmed by a lot of decorative stitch patterns she won't use often will find the Kenmore 1525 a very attractive machine. The novice may find the controls out of her league in the beginning, but they are not so complicated that she couldn't master them given instructions and time.

Approximate Retail Price: $240.00

Sears
Kenmore 1780

The Sears Kenmore 1780 is an outstanding machine in many ways. Certainly it has all the stitch patterns that the most demanding sewer could want for utility, stretch or decorative sewing. The machine has a capacity of 12 built-in stitch patterns and the option of 30 other designs with cams which come in their own accessories box. An extension back of the free arm can be removed completely for tubular sewing or released and swung up to the back on a pivot pin for a flatbed. The left side of the extension also has a plate which covers a pinion gear and guide pin used for making buttonholes. A light is mounted behind the hinged face plate. On the right side of the base is a switch that controls the electric current for both the light and motor. If a carrying case is desired it must be purchased separately. The design of this model is low-keyed; accessible controls have settings which are clear and distinct.

Another commendable feature is the drop-in bobbin which rests horizontally in the shuttle without need of a separate case. With a small window on the shuttle cover, we could readily check to see how much thread was left in the bobbin. For further visibility, three of the bobbins are sensibly made of lightweight plastic; the other five have the same cutout design on either side that we have seen on other Kenmore models in the lower priced field.

Upper threading is practically a one-motion operation to the needle area. Although the two spool spindles are located in the back of the machine (not the most convenient place), we didn't find it all that difficult to bring the thread through the visible guides on the upper back of the arm to the front. Both spools can be held securely in place with spool pin tops that also help to keep the thread from feeding improperly. The spool pin tops prevent accidental winding around the spindle under the spools.

The extension behind the free arm adds some work space, but when we were sewing on a bulky corduroy jacket we could have wished for more flat surface in front of and to the left side to support the weight of the garment. We did appreciate the simplicity of swinging the extension back out of the way when we wanted to blindstitch a hem on a sleeve.

Another feature we liked was the ease with which presser feet can be changed by flicking a lever on the presser bar instead of having to mount prongs around a screw. This model has a good selection of feet including a white plastic one for blind hemming. By placing the fold of a hem against the center upright piece on the foot, we made a nearly invisible blindstitched hem. Besides seven other utility presser feet, the

adjustable zipper foot is extremely handy not only for putting in regular and invisible zippers but also for making cording for clothes, draperies or slipcovers.

Other accessories include: five metal and three transparent bobbins, two spool spindles and spool pin tops, straight and zigzag needle plates, a darning plate, needle threader, buttonhole guide with three templates, a seam ripper, extra needles with a twin-needle, three screw drivers and a special "Q" stitching set.

Sears provides a special needle and foot in the "Q" set which is for synthetic knits and other difficult stretch fabrics. We suspect the needle is another version of a ball point; we turned out first-rate stitches on nylon tricot, stretch terry and cire without a skipped stitch.

The tension control was excellent, and we only had to loosen it slightly when we sewed on nylon tricot and cire. In almost all of the testing stitch quality was excellent, and the machine ran smoothly and quietly. We did have to watch the pressure on the presser foot. This was invariably the first control we checked when fabric puckered or didn't feed properly, and usually it was because we had forgotten to adjust the control to the different weight of fabric. On a polyester chiffon it was necessary to push the inner pin all the way down for maximum pressure to get the kind of stitch we considered acceptable. Certain knits, such as a polyester and cotton, swerved when we fed them under the presser foot unless we manually guided them.

The buttonhole attachment is complicated and not all that easy to assemble. The instruction book is informative up to a certain point, but it fails to show exactly how to mount the guideplate onto the pinion gear after it is uncovered on the extension. Once the sewer gets the darning plate in place over the needle plate and the template of her choice into the guideplate, she must then draw the bobbin thread up through the darning plate slot. When we

finally started stitching, the process was completely automatic, and we were able to make eight different sizes of regular buttonholes and four sizes with a keyhole at the end. On a medium weight cotton with a light interfacing inbetween the stitch was not as dense as we would have liked it, and because we had no control over the stitch length (which was set at zero for this operation), we could not remedy the situation. On light wool flannel using a buttonhole twist, the results were more satisfactory with a keyhole buttonhole.

Besides all of the 12 built-in stitch patterns the creative sewer can have a heyday with 30 drop-in cams that make decorative and stretch stitches. Designs run the gamut from tulips and trees to fish and arrowheads. All 10 of the decorative patterns and the five stretch ones tested were of excellent quality. In the section of the instruction book which told us about sewing with cams it was not made clear what the difference in colors meant since 20 of the cams are green and 10 are orange. It came as a surprise when we started stitching in reverse. After searching the entire book, we finally found the answer in the section which had to do with replacements of accessories. It clarified the situation by telling us that the orange pattern cams (basic decorative designs) only, go forward but the green ones are reverse cams which can also go backward depending on the pattern. Since our overedge was basically a one-directional pattern, it went backwards. Instructions for

starting a pattern at the beginning of the design completely defeated us. We could detect the cam follower in the holder which the instructions referred to, but we failed to see any engraved dot on any cam.

Illumination on the 1780 model is excellent, shedding light directly on the needle area from behind a hinged face plate. With the needle bar set toward the back, needle changing was a slight problem because of the face plate overhang. After several changes involving the use of the "Q" needle, we did find it easier.

The one-speed motor is regulated with a wide foot control that accommodates the front half of the foot. It is of much better design than the foot control on the other Sears machine tested.

A great deal of work has obviously gone into the graphics and contents of the instruction book, and yet it is not all that good. The spiral binding at the top sometimes jammed pages as we flipped them back and forth to check on other sections of the manual for various operations. Sections are graduated at the bottom so the sewer can see at a glance where each operation or general category is discussed; but we question the organization of the book. It would seem far better to show the function of each control in an initial section so the sewer has a clear picture of how the machine as a whole operates and then approach each operation in detail. In this book each operation is taken as a whole, and sometimes the function of controls gets lost in the shuffle; they are simply not explained completely. As noted earlier, the section on cam designs left out information about color significance. The information in this book was frustratingly vague when it came to explaining the lengthening and shortening of the modifier. Along with an excellent section on performance problems and how to correct them, the instructions devote four pages to the care and maintenance of the machine.

The machine comes with a 90-day warranty on all parts and mechanical adjustments, a two-year warranty on electrical equipment and a limited 25-year warranty on the machine head.

Special capabilities of the machine are: darning, free-form embroidery, monogramming, twin-needle sewing and sewing on buttons.

The Sears Kenmore 1780 is an excellent machine despite some of the negative aspects we have discussed. The home-sewer who wants a free arm machine near the top of the line with a sensible price tag and many decorative stitches will find this a good value.
Approximate Retail Price: $430.00

Singer Fashion Mate 248

The Singer Fashion Mate 248 is a flatbed machine. A lid on top covers the bobbin winder and cam holder which, when open, contains a chart of stitch patterns created by cams. The light is mounted in the center back of the arm with a switch on the shield over it. A carrying case must be purchased separately.

The Singer 248 has a clean, mint-fresh look about it. The most frequently used controls are well-marked, easy to read and placed so the sewer has them at her fingertips. We found that most were easy to handle with the exception of the pressure control located on the arm top which was almost impossible to move. The control was so stiff we had to stand and apply pressure with both thumbs before we could make it budge. This condition could be factory stiffness that would disappear with use.

The plastic lid that covers the bobbin winder and cam holder was sprung when the test machine was received, and although we couldn't open or close the cover entirely, it was possible to wind the bobbin and use the cam holder. We thought the top of the lid was an odd place to locate the spindle for a spool or reel of thread. When winding the bobbin it was imperative that we leave the cover open to use the bobbin winder which meant that we couldn't see how much thread remained on the spool because it was out of sight in the back. The spindle is in a horizontal position though, and a spool holder keeps it firmly in place so thread can feed evenly from it, and the spool will not fly off the spindle.

We discovered that it was a simple operation to remove and replace cams. By pulling up the pattern disc releaser, a kind of pin in the center of the mechanism, the cam popped up, and we lifted it off the spindle. To put another in place, we fit the disc over the positioning key on the disc holder and then pressed down firmly. Before making the change, it was essential that the zigzag lever was pushed to the straight stitch mark so the cam would be positioned correctly. Once we forgot to use the lever and found the cam was not in operation. Consequently we were straight stitching instead of blindstitching.

With the exception of the straight stitch, there are no built-in patterns. One of 15 cams which accompany the machine must be inserted to produce every stitch from a basic zigzag to complicated decorative patterns. Many of these cams (11 in all) produce purely decorative stitches which we think is shortsighted of Singer since most manufacturers have taken into account all of the new fabrics available today. We have emphasized the utility and stretch patterns to make sewing easier for the home-sewer. We hope the makers of this machine will offer optional cams which are more useful to the purchaser than solid scallops, solid pyramids and solid diamonds.

Most of the bobbins on flatbed machines we have tested are difficult to insert into the shuttle area. It was a relief not to worry about broken fingernails when we positioned this front loading bobbin. It simply drops into a horizontal position just under and in front of the face plate, and doesn't have to be threaded into a separate case. We also appreciated the transparent bobbin that allowed us to quickly check the amount of thread left on it. A home-sewer doesn't want to rewind a bobbin in the midst of a complicated sewing operation.

On the whole, stitch quality was consistently good in both straight and pattern stitching. We did encounter some uneven stitches sewing on a wool and synthetic double knit, but we were able to balance the stitch by increasing the pressure on the presser foot. Stitching on a sheer nylon, we found it was necessary to decrease the pressure to achieve an acceptable stitch. We sewed on woven cotton, cire, ribbed knit, sheer nylon, tricot, double knit, heavy coating and an acrylic backed fleece without having to change tension from a setting of five. We did notice some swerving under the needle when sewing on lighter knits and had to guide them firmly to sew a straight seam.

A very good hem was taken up on a muslin skirt by using the blindstitch pattern, but we thought this design was even better as an overcasting stitch. Outside of possibly the multi-zigzag, the regular zigzag and a fagoting pattern, the blindstitch is the only pattern that could be used to finish a seam and prevent raveling. The multi-zigzag, always a good versatile pattern for mending and for sewing on lycra and helenca,

was very effective when we used it to apply new binding on a blanket. Another stitch pattern which has great potential is the fagoting design which could be used on stretch fabrics but is not mentioned in the manual.

The bartack buttonhole we produced on woven cotton was strong with a uniform stitch density on both sides after we had adjusted the stitch balance, accomplished by turning the reverse button to plus or minus (an ingenious double control). Unhappily, the two sides were too far apart in the center, and when we cut a slit there was still enough fabric inside to ravel unless it was cut away. Since the buttonholer is completely automatic and the positions are a part of the stitch length control, there was no way we could adjust the satin stitch to make it wider so the sides would be closer together. The buttonhole we made on a light wool flannel was more successful, partially due to the thickness of the fabric, but even then we noted that the interfacing was apparent and unraveling from the inside when we used the seam ripper to slit the opening.

Of the six presser feet included with the machine all snap onto a common shank except the button attachment foot. They include: a general purpose foot, straight stitch foot, buttonhole foot, two-way zipper foot, special purpose foot and a button attaching foot. Besides the 15 cams for stitch patterns other aids include: extra spindle for twin-needle stitching, three transparent bobbins, an assortment of needles including a twin-needle and yellow band needle for sewing on synthetic knit and stretch fabrics, a straight stitch needle plate, a darning needle plate and oiler.

The spiral bound instruction book is practically a whole sewing book, illustrating not only how to operate the machine and make the most of its potential, but also how to make darts, flat fell seams, cording and a myriad of other sewing hints. It does not discuss

the decorative stitch patterns except to name them and show a chart. We think the sewer would benefit with guidance on how to use some of the 11 decorative patterns, and she could be advised about possible optimal settings. Singer devotes 14 pages to the care and maintenance of the machine explaining the importance of regular cleaning and oiling.

The machine ran smoothly but was not particularly quiet; we heard bobbin chatter most of the time. This model's head is rather heavy but even though it wasn't mounted in a console there was no vibration. We would not recommend that the purchaser buy a carrying case for this machine because it is not of portable weight. Unlike most foot controls which plug into a socket on the machine's side, this one is permanently attached with another cord for the electrical connection in the wall. The foot control is wide and comfortable to use, although it did not always respond instantly when pressed. We detected no coasting when the pedal was released.

Lighting on the machine is not good. With the bulb mounted on the center back of the arm, it's not surprising that little illumination is directed to the front and left where the needle area is and where we need it the most. We found it necessary to have another light source from our left to see adequately while sewing.

The machine has a full 30-year warranty on the machine head against defective parts other than those listed below. There is also a full two-year warranty on the motor, light assembly, wiring, switches, speed control. A 90-day warranty is given on minor adjustments, belts, rings, bulbs and attachments.

Special capabilites of the machine are: twin-needle sewing, darning, free-form embroidery and button attaching.

The Fashion Mate 248 is a very good machine with some interesting capabilities and features, especially in this low price range. We would like to see

more utility and stretch stitches included in the pattern selections. Better yet, Singer might concentrate on building in a few good stitch patterns and get rid of the cam system entirely.

Approximate Retail Price: $150.00

Singer Athena 2000

Although the Athena 2000 with solid-state electronic controls has been designed for easy operation it is a machine for the experienced home-sewer who wants greater stitch capacity and more versatility. The complex free arm is programmed to make proper settings with the touch of a button. However, adjustments do have to be made manually on occasion to achieve the desired quality of stitch.

The stitch selection panel is in white against a black background. As part of the electronic controls, patterns are programmed to start automatically at the beginning of each design. Early in the testing it was discovered that when the dials of either or both stitch length or width controls were turned to observe the effect on the stitch, and then returned to the zero setting, we had to reset the pattern button. If we didn't, the machine would turn on when we pressed the foot control, but the needle wasn't sewing; it was merely going up and down.

The reverse stitch setting, also on the panel, has no red light; the button is held for the duration of the reverse sewing. Be advised that when this setting is used the needle takes one stitch forward before going in the reverse direction.

For straight stitching on most fabrics, we approved of the stitch length the electronic controls selected; except when sewing on heavy wool coating. We preferred a longer stitch and manually dialed the regulator to three.

When testing on the many other stitch patterns, the automatic settings were fine except for some patterns, such as the arrowhead and bead stitches based on a satin stitch. To get the effect we wanted it was necessary to increase the density by setting the dial to 0.5.

With a setting between four and five, the tension stayed constant as we stitched seams on sheer nylon, polyester knit, cire, batiste, denim and heavy wool. However, we had to change the pressure regulator for the presser foot by increasing it to between normal and maximum for the lighter weight synthetics, and decreasing it toward the darning symbol for the heavyweight cloth.

Making a bartack buttonhole may be a one-step procedure as far as the setting on the selector panel is concerned, but requires another step or two to complete the job. After snapping on the buttonhole foot, with or without the underplate, the sewer must also pull down a lever beside the needle bar. The satin stitching on buttonholes we made (on light cotton and denim) was not dense enough. When we tried to go around a second time to increase the strength, we had to reset the buttonhole button on the panel because the pattern repeat setting was activated. As the instruction book indicates this feature let us sew one unit of a pattern at a time. To correct the density of the satin stitch so we could make a strong buttonhole going around only once, we set the manual stitch length control to 0.5 which took care of the left side; to close up the stitch on the right side we dialed the reverse stitch-balance to the right. After our machine was adjusted, we made a good corded buttonhole. All of this seemed like a lot of fiddling with controls for a simple automatic buttonhole. We do admire the design of the buttonhole foot which guarantees the proper size buttonhole when the button is merely placed in the back foot on a carrier.

The quality of all stitches was excellent. Among the Flexi-Stitch patterns are some very good

stretch stitches. A maxi-stretch stitch, which is straight, made a very durable seam on the crotch of a pair of denim jeans. We also liked the feather stitch on helenca. The overedge stretch stitch joined and finished a seam on nylon tricot in one operation and with no curling because the presser foot made for this pattern has a tiny rod on the right side.

The elastic stretch stitch functions in somewhat the same way as the overedge stretch, but it has even more stretch. We made quite a professional looking seam on a ribbed knit for a sweater top.

The machine's capacity for temporary stitching is a time saver for the earnest sewer. According to the instruction book, it is possible to speed-baste with stitches up to one inch, but the longest we could make by following directions carefully was one-half inch. Speed-basting requires nothing more than adjusting the tension and pressing a button on the selection panel. On the other hand, chain stitching, another temporary stitch, was not as successful in our test. The results of stitching a quick temporary tuck on fabric were better than the thread chain we made on paper for a belt loop. This operation seems to be a matter of setting the tension at the right degree. One wonders if it is worth the bother to chain stitch when the bobbin has to be removed, a bobbin case insert fitted in place, and the needle plate changed when speed basting requires only one setting and no aids.

Along with the one-step buttonhole presser foot, another, equally fascinating is the even-feed foot which is recommended for fabrics that tend to stick, stretch or slip. With a composition material that resembles feed dogs on the foot, it feeds top and bottom fabric layers together so they start and end evenly. After we had pin-basted two layers of a large plaid so the cross-bars matched, we were delighted that the cross-bars matched perfectly after completing

the seam. We used this foot on a bonded polyester and a fake fur with the same positive results. The seams needed no extra coaxing to come out even at the end.

It was difficult mounting all five of the presser feet, which are supposed to snap onto the shaft by lowering the presser foot lifter and pressing the presser-foot screw down until the foot snaps into place. We concluded that it might be because the test machine seemed stiff in some respects.

Stiffness was also noted when we had to move the bobbin latch to a "wind" position. But this condition disappeared, and the latch became easier to move after we had filled several bobbins. Winding the bobbin in place from the top thread is an interesting feature along with the transparency of the bobbin. The see-through window on top of the slide plate is equally helpful to the sewer so she can see at a glance when her bobbin thread is low.

Nine presser feet come with the machine; five that snap on and four that have their own shafts. Accessories included with the machine are: a zigzag foot and needle plate, straight stitch foot and needle plate, chain stitch fittings, one-step buttonhole foot and underplate, two-way zipper foot, button foot, special purpose foot, overedge foot, darning and embroidery foot, even-feed foot, seam guide, blindstitch hem guide, secondary spool pin, four

transparent bobbins, small and large spool holder, cover plate for darning, buttonhole gauge, extra needles and twin-needle, seam ripper and lint brush.

The Athena is designed along futuristic lines with a forward slanting arm which is meant to give more visibility to the work area. The manufacturer has taken a new approach for added work surface when the free arm is not being used. Instead of an extension or slide-on table, Singer has a permanently mounted panel in back of the free arm which can be flipped up into place or dropped for tubular sewing. The free arm, incidentally, is wider than most we have seen.

Lighting could be better. The bulb located under the center of the arm directs illumination too far to the right of the needle area leaving it shadowy.

The machine comes with a two-speed motor which is regulated by the power/light switch. When it is turned off the machine cannot be turned on accidentally, a well conceived feature. A broad foot control regulates the speed within the motor range selected.

Our machine was reasonably quiet with no vibration or coasting. The two sewing manuals, The Operator's Guide and Sewing Applications, are excellent. In some instances, though, it seemed there was undue referral to the other booklet when it would have been helpful to have the information at hand.

There is a limited 30-year warranty on electronic pattern control and selection components plus a full two-year warranty on the motor, light assembly, wiring, switches and speed control.

Special capabilities of the machine are: darning, speed basting, chain stitching, free-form embroidery, twin-needle sewing and attaching buttons. Other special features are a magnetic needle plate, a soft feed dog, and a safety circuit breaker to prevent damage from momentary overloads. The machine features a permanently lubricated

mechanism requiring no periodic oiling, just lint and dust removal.

The Athena is an innovative machine. The customer should definitely take advantage of courses offered by the dealer to become well acquainted with the controls and use them effectively. This is an expensive machine with interesting features, but we wonder how many times the average home-sewer will use all of those stitch patterns.

Approximate Retail Price: $950.00

Universal/ Standard 7000

The Universal/Standard 7000 is an off-white free arm unit trimmed in dark brown with a permanently mounted carrying handle on top. Accompanying the machine is a rigid plastic cover that fits over the machine needing no clamps at the base. An extension plate unfolds from the base to create added work surface in front of the free arm and is braced underneath for complete steadiness. The light shines on the needle area from behind the hinged face plate; the switch is located in back of the face plate.

This machine is designed along sleek, clean-cut lines with a minimum of well-placed controls that are easy to read. Even the upper tension dial has been recessed at the top of the arm but with large white numbers against a black background for good visibility. Adjusted to a setting of four, it was ideal for all of the fabrics tested and gave a good balanced stitch on an acrylic backed knit as well as a nylon Qiana. The lower part of the face plate tapers conveniently back to give a clear view of the well-lighted needle area.

For best stitch quality we did have to change the pressure control on the presser foot to get an even feed for various weights of fabric. It was particularly critical when we were stitching on sheer nylon and batiste to increase the pressure by pressing the inner pin almost completely down to the outer ring so there were no skipped stitches. We also decreased the length of stitch to a one setting on the sheers — especially the nylon — to eliminate the puckering. When sewing a seam on a wool rib knit or coating, we released the pressure and only lowered the inner pin slightly. No amount of adjustment on the pressure, tension or stitch length, however, would remedy the slight swerving we experienced when stitching long strips of rayon and polyester knits.

Our test machine obviously needed some sort of factory adjustment. From the beginning it was apparent that either the inside belt which powers the hand wheel was slipping or the stop-motion-knob on the hand wheel was malfunctioning. We had no trouble winding the bobbin with the use of this knob; yet, when we tightened it to connect the needle mechanism and prepared to stitch by pressing on the foot control, the motor would respond but the needle would not budge for several seconds on many attempts. At other times, the response was immediate.

There were mechanical difficulties when testing the built-in stitch patterns. Almost every time we dialed a new selection the first few stitches were those of the previous pattern we had tested; then the selected pattern would start to appear. There was a definite lag before the many cams sorted themselves out. The one position which never failed us was the manual setting for straight and ordinary zigzag stitching.

In spite of all these malfunctions, we were able to stitch up good samples of the patterns. The two stretch stitches, both at the same position on the selector dial, were of good quality. We set the stitch length control to the green stretch symbol and found the straight stretch effective on both woven and knitted fabrics. It was not just a reinforcing stitch

with no give, the kind used so often on blue jeans, but one that actually stretched with the material. This is not, however, one to be used on lightweight fabrics, because it is too heavy. The sewer would also do well not to make a mistake with this stitch — it is difficult to rip out without tearing the fabric. Universal calls the other stretch stitch a 'single overlock.' This, too, proved first-rate for seaming and finishing a synthetic knit with a tendency to ravel all in one operation and without undue waviness.

Other patterns proved equally good — the blindstitch, ribbon stitch and one they refer to as 'elastic stitch,' an excellent pattern seen on many machines that makes several small stitches with each zig and zag. With both stitch width and length set at two, we found this pattern made a very good stretch seam on tricot, and we could press the seam flat with no difficulty.

The reason we couldn't make any kind of automatic buttonhole was due to the fact that the positions are dialed on the pattern selector. No matter how we tried to compensate for the lag, we couldn't overcome the problem enough to complete the operation. Every position was out of synchronization with the exception of the left (first side stitched in reverse) which acted as it should. It was a disappointing failure in what appears to be a very good system.

A most approvable feature is the presser foot lifter that locks up in two positions. Although we could not manually lift it above the upper lock, we were able to slide bulky layers of fabric under the foot with no difficulty, partially because the feed dogs are fine and do not protrude extensively above the needle plate. With a good drop feed control, we wonder why Universal doesn't simply label the two possible positions 'up' and 'down' rather than with triangles and bars which could lead to confusion for the sewer.

By turning the stop-motion knob on the hand wheel the

needle mechanism is disconnected to allow bobbin winding on the top of the free arm. A full bobbin is automatically cut off and is inserted into a bobbin case which is inserted vertically into the shuttle under the needle plate. With the spool on one of two retractable spindles on the arm, threading is a one-motion operation with grooves and slots and guides to the needle area.

The machine comes with five presser feet all of which snap on with the exception of the two-way zipper/cording foot. The presser feet are: an all-purpose foot, straight stitch foot, buttonhole and button foot and the zipper foot. Other accessories are: four bobbins, a pack of all-purpose needles plus a twin-needle, two washers for the spindles, a quilting guide, a seam ripper, two screw drivers and an oiler.

The extension for the free arm is unique, folding flat onto the base or swinging up and snapping into place for added work surface in front of the free arm. It would be handy to have more space to the left of the needle, but many other portable machines aren't designed for this, either. We thought it was a slight nuisance to have to fold down the extension for access to the shuttle when a bobbin needed changing.

The carrying case makes sense. Of rigid plastic it slides down over the machine with a slot on top to accommodate the built-in handle. There are no clamps or hooks to wrestle with on the base. When the sewer lifts the portable she is

actually lifting the machine itself, not just the case, and doesn't have to worry about dropping the insides.

The instruction book could be better. The manufacturer prefers to explain how to operate the controls and what their settings mean as we get into each operation instead of devoting an explanatory section in the beginning. It's not until after we have started sewing and turning a corner that we learn about the pressure control or how to change the presser feet. And the buttonhole instructions would be much clearer visually if diagrams were shown of the needle area with the presser foot in place making a buttonhole. It is also confusing the way the bartack position is numbered (one and three) when there is only one position on the dial.

The machine has a limited one-year warranty on any parts except needles, belts and light bulbs; limited 19-year warranty on any part except the ones mentioned above and the electrical equipment.

Special capabilities of the machine are: darning, twin-needle sewing, attaching buttons and free-form embroidery.

This machine was hard to evaluate because of the mechanical problems which were present during the testing. We admire the design and many of the features; the stitch pattern selection is good although hardly extensive. However, the Universal 7000 is not inexpensive, and the home-sewer may want more for the money if she can afford this price range.
Approximate Retail Price: $470.00

~~~~~~~~~~~~~~~~~~~~~~

Addendum Universal 7000

Because of the obvious malfunctions in the original test model, another Universal 7000 machine was tested with none of the problems that plagued us before — no slipping belt, no lag in placement of cams when we dialed different stitch patterns and no jammed buttonhole mechanism.

Response from the foot control was instantaneous with no coasting when we released the pedal.

We were able to produce a buttonhole on this machine, but the results were only fair. On woven cotton our buttonhole stitch tended to pile up; when we reset the stitch length to make the stitch less dense, it became too open. After experimenting with five buttonholes, we did finally make a relatively good one but only by adjusting the satin stitch setting beyond the buttonhole marking on the stitch length control.

The retest machine performed very well with the above exception. It has attractive features and is certainly pleasing to the eye. A small but good selection of utility and stretch stitch patterns will appeal to many sewers.

Viking 5710

One of the most compact portables we have seen is the Viking 5710 which stores an extension table, foot control and accessories drawer around the free arm like a jigsaw puzzle. With the rigid slip-on case in place, the machine weighs less than 20 pounds.

Handsomely designed, this machine has crisp, clean lines. The controls most frequently used are placed conveniently across the arm with very readable markings. Each of the three dials moved easily, and we were able to master them in no time. It was unusual, though, to have the upper tension control so prominently displayed. But we did appreciate the very clear marking where the tension should be set when making a buttonhole. A white dot also indicated the tension setting Viking considers normal for most fabrics — between five and six. Testing on a wide range of fabrics from sheer nylon and cire to heavy weight melton, we found that the recommended setting did produce

a well balanced stitch. Only when we sewed a seam on rayon tricot was it necessary to loosen the tension to 3.5.

White stitch pattern symbols for the controls stood out against the russet panel on the arm. We especially liked the use of the symbols on the stitch length control between the numbers, leaving no doubt where the dial should be set for optimal range when making buttonholes, blindstitching or using stretch stitches. The button for reverse stitching on the stitch length dial is slightly awkward to use. We found it necessary to push the button gently with a thumb while placing the rest of the hand on top of the arm. The machine would tilt a bit if we pushed the button firmly with only a forefinger.

With interesting economy, one dial governs three operations with settings for width of zigzag, built-in stitch patterns and automatic buttonholing. Like many of these multi-purpose controls we have seen, there are definite settings for stitch widths and straight stitching. When we attempted to stitch with the dial set inbetween markings to see if graduated widths were possible, the machine appeared to be out of gear. The sewer has a choice of three zigzag widths only.

Testing on the Viking was a pleasure. Stitch quality was excellent both in straight and pattern stitching. A number of snap-on presser feet were available to help us stitch satisfactorily on different kinds of

fabrics. A smooth soled foot made it easier to sew on organdy and voile, but we experienced puckering when we tried to use it on sheer nylon. The roller presser foot effectively controlled boucle and a strip of imitation leather. The rollers offered better traction against the fabric.

The zipper foot, which can be used on either side of the needle, is the most interesting one we have ever come across. Resembling a sled runner, there are notches for the needle to pass by on both front and back, but there are also two horizontal pins used for mounting inbetween. Depending on which side the sewer wants to sew, she snaps on the pin just behind that groove. The blindstitch foot was a great help when we sewed on several thicknesses of fabric. By turning a tiny wheel on the foot, we could move the guide line in or out.

Snap-on presser feet are certainly much more convenient than the ones that mount around a set screw on the presser bar. The Viking feet all fit on a common shank or ankle, but they snap off and on differently than other machines we have seen. Instead of a lever releasing the foot, we simply pulled it down and forward, and it dropped off. To insert another foot we slid the new one into a space with a spring on the bottom of the ankle and, pressing it back and down, it slid into place. We were happy to see another time saver — the white area painted on the ankle to give us more visibility when threading the needle.

The pivotal lever which lifts the presser bar is handy once the sewer gets used to it, but since the lever is positioned to the right, we wonder if a left-handed sewer could use it as dexterously. According to the manual, the lifter has a higher position to give more space between foot and feed dogs so thicker fabrics can be inserted more readily under the needle. The lifter on our test machine was either jammed or broken and would not budge above the lock position.

The selection of built-in stitch patterns is not extensive, but there is an emphasis on the utility and stretch designs that every sewer will find useful. We were able to make an almost invisible hem on woven cotton by using the straight blindstitch. The elastic blindstitch was equally effective for a hem on a boucle blend. When we reduced the stitch length this pattern also made a very pretty trim on a collar. The three-step zigzag overcast seams on stretch terry very well, and we also liked its stretchability in several directions when sewing on lycra. For seaming and overcasting in one operation, the elastic knit or overlock was just right when we sewed on nylon knit. It stretched with the fabric and without breaking the thread. The elastic straight stitch was fine enough to be used on a rayon tricot and yet was strong enough to reinforce a curved denim seam.

The buttonholes we produced on cotton as well as lightweight wool flannel were very professional looking with stitches on either side uniform in density. Fine stitch adjustment can be made by turning the reverse button, but it was unnecessary for our buttonholes. We did try the control, however, and found it was not easy to make this adjustment. A knob on the back of the buttonhole foot served as a carrier for gimp, and we made excellent corded buttonholes, also.

Viking has a unique but simple bobbin winding system. By threading the machine first except for the needle, we could easily wrap the thread around the bobbin and wind away. We are surprised, however, that a machine of this calibre has not designed a bobbin to automatically stop when it is full. The bobbin, incidentally, does not hold as much thread as many others we have encountered, but Viking provides the sewer with eight bobbins so she won't have to wind one color of thread on top another.

The electronic foot control is the largest we have seen on any machine. It supported our whole foot comfortably with room to spare. Even when we pressed the motor lightly, it responded instantly and with no coasting.

The extension table, which is scored lightly in small squares to form a nonslippery surface, offers quite a bit of extra work space around the free arm.

Illumination was adequate around the needle area, and we could change the bulb with no difficulty by pushing the bulb up and turining it to the left. Maintenance is simple; since the machine is permanently lubricated, no oiling is necessary, and all the sewer must do is clean away fluff and loose threads that accumulate around the feed dogs and shuttle.

The instruction book is excellent with clear, well-illustrated drawings that show how to go about each procedure. Our only suggestion is to put the section dealing with contents of the accessory box up front with the machine parts instead of in the back.

The machine carries a 25-year warranty against defective material or workmanship with the exception of the electric motor and foot control which are so warranted for five years from purchase date.

Special capabilities of the machine are: darning, free-form embroidery, twin-needle sewing.

Swedish-built Viking 5710 is a fairly quiet machine, which runs smoothly and feeds evenly. It is superbly engineered. It is not inexpensive, but we suggest that the serious sewer who wants a high quality, lasting product should consider this model.
Approximate Retail Price: $500.00

Viking 6460

The Viking 6460 sewing machine comes with a rigid case. The multi-colored panel across the arm represents stitch patterns. A removable accessory drawer fits under the free arm, and an extension table, with a scored, non-skid surface, fits around it. The light is mounted under the arm in a pull-down bracket and is protected by a grid. The switch is on the bracket.

Color coding on the Viking 6460 is an important feature. Many other machines we tested use different tints to coordinate control settings with stitch patterns, but none relies upon color in the same way as this free arm unit. With each of the eight insertable cams (called 'stitch programmers' by Viking) we had a choice of four patterns by matching the same color behind the stitch symbol shown on the panel with settings marked on the stitch selector and dials regulating width and length of stitch.

These controls are well located and easy to handle, but the bases around the dials should be wider so the color bands could be made more prominent, especially on the stitch length control where three tones are crowded together in narrow strips to make a rainbow in one range. They are simple enough to change, but they must be inserted on the back of the arm which is a nuisance. After changing them several times, we realized that one could be placed from the front by feel, and we no longer had to stand and lean over the machine to make sure it was in the right position. The sewer will have to check the back to see which programmer is in place when she starts each new sewing session.

According to the manual, we could straight stitch and make buttonholes regardless of which programmer was in the machine. Not wishing to be so completely dependent on cams, we experimented without a programmer in place and discovered that it was possible to sew straight, do a simple zigzag and make buttonholes. The instructions should tell the sewer that this can be done.

Although tension control is very good we had to adjust it for a wider range of fabrics than we did on the 5710 model. When sewing

on sheer nylon, rayon tricot and double knit blend, we found the best tension was a looser setting of three and a slight increase in pressure on the foot to prevent these fabrics from swerving under the needle. We were able to achieve a balanced stitch on spongy mohair — wool, bonded knit, cire, woven cotton, melton and eight layers of denim with tension and pressure control on the red dots, settings that Viking considers normal for regular sewing.

The pressure on the presser foot is controlled by a dial on the side of the face plate. It has symbols for increasing and decreasing the pressure and for the darning setting. A red dot marks the setting for regular stitching. The feed dogs are controlled by a button below the stitch width dial, which is pushed in to lower the feed dogs below the needle plate for darning or embroidery.

We were impressed with the remarkably long stitches (five to the inch) that we could produce merely by dialing the control to its longest setting. Without changing presser feet or rethreading the machine, we basted a seam quickly after loosening the tension a bit, and we were able to make interesting topstitching on a suede jacket. We also tailor-tacked quickly, transferring paper pattern markings to two layers of fabric, but this operation required the use of a special marker presser foot designed with a slender metal ridge down its center. After setting the stitch width to three for lightweight cotton and loosening tension to the buttonhole symbol (around three), we stitched through the pattern tissue watching the thread make loops over the center ridge. It was then a matter of unpinning the pattern piece and gently pulling apart the two layers of fabric just enough so we could snip the loops of thread to leave small tufts on either layer. Of course, it would be necessary to set the stitch width to a wider zigzag for heavier fabric.

As we noted on the other model reviewed, the presser feet are

mounted on a common ankle or shaft in a different manner than we have seen before. The foot is held by a spring on the ankle bottom, and all we had to do was pull the foot down for removal and push another in place between bracket and spring for the next operation.

Other interesting feet, besides the special marker foot, accompany the machine. A roller foot, adding extra friction, made it easier to control stretchy knits and plastic coated materials; a special darning foot allowed for yarn insertion, and with the use of the raised seam foot with grooves underneath to carry gimp, we made parallel raised seams after inserting the twin-needle and another spool of thread. The unique zipper foot which resembles a sled runner let us approach a zipper or cording from either side. Button attaching was accomplished without any foot on the ankle, but we were fascinated by the button redd, a plastic U-shaped instrument that was inserted under the button so a stem or shank of thread was created as we guided the needle between the holes.

We produced the same fine professional looking bartack buttonholes on the 6460 that we were able to make on the 5710. Again, although there is a ring around the reverse button to make

fine adjustment in the satin stitch, we found no reason to use it for buttonholes on cotton and polyester double knit. Stitch density was uniform on both sides and first-rate.

Stitch quality was excellent on almost all of our test fabrics in both straight and pattern stitching. The motor was relatively quiet and the machine ran very smoothly, feeding evenly. The motor responded instantly when we pressed on a comfortable foot control, and we could go slowly, stitch by stitch, with full power at slow speed.

We found nearly all stitch patterns (32 in all, not counting straight and zigzag stitching) to be satisfactory. There are very good utility designs, some excellent stretch patterns and enough decorative ones to make the most demanding creative sewer happy. We also noted that some patterns bore striking resemblances to other designs, a situation that often occurs when the manufacturer includes so many.

We wound the bobbin both ways suggested by the manual, first from the back, which was somewhat awkward, routing the thread through a back guide and then to the right side where the winder is located. Then we wound it taking the thread directly from the needle and stretching it across the front to the winder. The latter way was much easier because we could see what we were doing. It was necessary, however, to run the machine at a moderate speed while winding to prevent the needle from bending out of shape.

The upper thread goes from spindle to needle, through open eyelets and grooves in a one-motion operation.

Lighting was quite good though it tended to shed more light on the right side of the sewing area from its mounting under the arm. Illumination was even better when we took the advice offered in the manual and lowered the bulb bracket slightly. The extension table gave us plenty of work space around the free arm, and is designed with a transparent panel

directly over the shuttle so we could see well enough to change the bobbin without removing the table.

Directions and illustrations in the instruction book were very good with maintenance hints and an operational guide chart in back to guide us. A second book, the Viking Sewing Manual, provided additional ideas to make the most of the machine's features.

The machine comes with a 25-year warranty against defective materials or workmanship with the exception of the electric motor and foot control which are warranted for five years from date of purchase.

Special capabilities of the machine are: darning, free-form embroidery, twin-needle sewing, tailor tacking and basting.

The Viking 6460 is a very fine machine with superb design and precision engineering. It is hardly a machine for the beginner, however, with the many complex controls. It is also expensive and the sewer is paying a price for the wide selection of stitch patterns. She will however, have a sewing machine that will last for years.
Approximate Retail Price: $870.00

White 710

The White 710 is a free arm machine with permanently mounted extension flaps, in front and back, which mold around the arm, for tubular stitching. The front flap can also be raised to gain access to the shuttle area. A top cover conceals many of the controls. Inside the cover is a handy reference chart explaining how to thread the machine and a chart for built-in stitch length and width. A light is mounted behind the hinged face plate to illuminate the needle area. The switch for two motor speeds and the light is located on the right side, under the hand wheel. When off, the electric circuits for the light and motor cannot accidentally be turned on.

A handsomely designed machine, the White 710 is quiet and smooth running. Although there are many controls, all are accessible including the pressure regulator for the presser foot, which is hidden behind the face plate, presumably for the sake of good styling. This control is not as sensitive to minor changes in fabric weight and bulk as some others. But when it became necessary to make an adjustment, the hinged face plate was easily swung open, and we only had to press the bottom lever or push down the top plate for the appropriate position. Testing on a variety of fabrics, we had to change the control from regular to heavy only when we stitched on heavy coating and through four thicknesses of canvas. For repairing a worn spot in a sheet, we released it entirely to the darn setting so we could guide the fabric ourselves.

An upper tension setting of four produced a good balanced stitch on almost every fabric we tried with the exception of rayon knit and sheer nylon. On these materials the tension was too tight and had to be loosened to three.

The feed dog control is a dial on the base of the machine which is set up for regular sewing and down for darning or free-form embroidery. A lever above and to the right of the stitch length dial is pushed down for backstitching and held for the desired number of stitches.

There are 26 built-in stitch patterns, and the specific categories can be identified quickly by color. Stitch quality was very good in all of the patterns, and we had no problems with skipped stitches, uneven feed or variation of stitch length. We discovered several good stretch stitches in the regular category, namely the multiple stitch zigzag, the stretch blind hem and the interlock stitch. All stretch stitches were effective on our knits.

We feel there is a certain similarity between some of the patterns. For example: why should it be necessary to have a blind hem, reverse blind hem and stretch blind hem? Or two overlock patterns plus an overcast, all of which stretch when the fine interlock for seaming tricot and jersey is in the regular group? No duplication occurs, however, in the decorative section, and the sewer who likes to be creative, trimming clothes with interesting stitch patterns, will have a marvelous time sewing with the six patterns offered.

The pattern selector seems unnecessarily complicated, though. In order to turn the dial that moves the selector in the window, the sewer has to press on a release button. We also feel that the stitch pattern symbols would be more visible in the window if they were lit from behind even though they are set against a white background.

The one-step automatic buttonholer would appear to be a very good feature, especially because the home-sewer can dial the size of buttonhole she wants and be assured that she'll have the same dimension for as many buttonholes as needed. Unfortunately, the buttonholer on our test machine was not working properly, undoubtedly due to something that happened during shipping. We were able to use the stitch density dial to balance the satin stitch and make a good turn-around buttonhole by manually adjusting the width for the sides and bartacking the ends. White recommends dropping the feed dogs when making the bartacks, an excellent suggestion, because the stitches were formed in one area for greater strength and we didn't have to hold the fabric back to keep it from advancing while bartacking. Using the same procedure we made very professional looking gimp buttonholes by hooking cording around the point in back of the buttonhole foot and bringing it forward under the foot so the zigzag stitch covered the cord on either side.

In the instruction book we discovered a very good way to make buttonholes on knits that are also elastic and give with the fabric. To make them we used the overlock pattern in the group of stretch stitches, again using the manual pivoting rather than the automatic buttonholer.

More machines should have two lock positions on the presser foot lifter when it is up and be able to raise the lifter even a fraction of an inch higher than the top position for really bulky fabrics, as the 710 has.

The inner knob of the hand wheel is pulled out to disengage the needle mechanism for bobbin winding which takes place on top of the arm. A full bobbin will cut off winding automatically.

The bobbin case is different from the standard ones we have seen. After drawing the thread under the tension spring, it goes through a guide which resembles a hook on top of the case. The sewer has to be certain when she inserts the bobbin case into the rotary hook that the thread remains around the guide, especially after the thread is drawn up through the needle plate by the upper thread. We think the bobbin threading should be simplified.

The machine comes with six presser feet that all snap on a common shank. They include: an all-purpose foot, embroidery foot, buttonhole foot, straight stitch foot and a zipper/cording foot. Other accessories are: four bobbins, an assortment of needles plus a twin-needle, straight stitch needle plate, two felt spool washers, quilting guide, cloth guide and screw, a seam ripper and tubed oiler.

The permanently mounted extension table gives added work space, front and back and is nicely rounded so a garment can be handled comfortably. However, the extension table does not allow any added space on the left side to support the garment. Pressed down, the extension flaps mold snugly around a slender free arm when the home-sewer stitches in tubular areas.

For a machine in this price range — and it is expensive — we were surprised to find lighting as poor as it is. Set behind the face plate on the left of the lever that controls the pressure on the foot, the lighting barely illuminates the needle area enough to sew by. Either the light should be relocated or the bulb should be stronger. A good safety feature is the switch that controls the power as well as the light so the machine cannot be accidentally started by pressing on the foot control when the switch is off.

The foot control, relatively comfortable to use, responded immediately, and we experienced no coasting at either speed. A portable top that latches onto the base is an attractive pale blue. The machine is not particularly lightweight, weighing over 30 pounds.

The instruction book which comes with the machine is excellent, well organized and informative, with many clear diagrams to illustrate techniques and operations. It also shows how to clean and oil various points and how to change the light bulb.

The machine has a limited one-year warranty on any parts except needles and belts. There is also a 20-year warranty on electrical equipment.

Special capabilities of the machine are: darning, free-form embroidery, button and twin-needle stitching.

The White 710 performs very well. Some of the controls seem unnecessarily complicated (such as the pattern selector), but the experienced sewer will find its stitch capacity and other capabilities very appealing.
Approximate Retail Price: $800.00

Glossary of Sewing Terms and Techniques

Alteration Line: The line drawn on a pattern at the point where alterations will be made.

Armscye: The armhole opening for a sleeve.

Backstitch: Machine stitch in reverse used to reinforce the beginnings and endings of seams.

Backtack: Same as backstitch.

Bartack: Short sections of satin stitch used to reinforce corners of pockets and ends of the fly zipper opening.

Basic Ease: The extra amount added to body measurements when designing a pattern, to allow for breathing room and body movement.

Baste: Fairly long, temporary stitches used to hold layers of fabric together.

Blind Hem: An invisibly sewn hem by hand or machine.

Blind Tucks: A series of tucks constructed so the fold of one tuck meets the stitching line of the next tuck.

Blindstitch: A hand stitch used for hemming which is invisible on the right side of a garment.

Bodice: The portion of a garment that is above the waist.

Casing: A folded-over edge of a garment, or tunneled section, through which elastic or cording is threaded.

Clean Finish: Any method used to finish the raw edges of a garment piece.

Clip: Short snip made by the scissors point into the selvage or seam edge.

Continuous Thread Dart: The dart technique used on sheer fabrics which eliminates the need for a knot at the dart point.

Cut-In-One: Two or more pattern pieces cut in one piece — such as a bodice front and front facing.

Dart: A stitching technique used to build shape into a garment. It can have a single or double point, be straight or curved.

Designer Ease: The extra amount added by a designer to the basic ease to give a particular style.

Directional Stitching: Stitching seams in the proper direction to preserve the grain and prevent stretching.

Double Welt Seam: A seam with both seam allowances pressed to one side and topstitched with two rows of stitching approximately ¼ inch (6mm) apart.

Ease: The difference between the measurements of two garment pieces to be sewn together.

Easestitch: A stitching technique used to control ease around a sleeve cap, at shoulder back and elbows or waistlines.

Edgestitch: Machine stitching close to the finished or folded edge of a garment piece.

Enclosed Seam: A seam along a faced edge that is enclosed between two layers of fabric.

Facing: A second, shaped piece of fabric used to finish garment edges.

Fitting Shell: A trial garment, usually made of muslin or gingham, made from a basic pattern to be used during the fitting process.

Flat Fell Seam: A strong,

double-stitched, decorative seam used mainly on sportswear.

Fly: Flap or fold of fabric used to conceal a zipper or button opening.

French Seam: A narrow, enclosed self-finished seam that is used on sheer fabrics.

Fusible Interfacing: Interfacing fabric with a fusible material on one side — to be bonded to garment pieces.

Gather: To pull fabric along two lines of stitching into a series of even puckers.

Gimp: Thin cording used in corded buttonholes.

Grade: To trim all seam allowances within an enclosed seam to different widths.

Grain: The lengthwise and crosswise direction of threads in woven and knitted fabrics.

Grainline: The heavy arrow on a pattern that indicates the fabric grain.

Guide Sheet: The sheet of instructions included with a pattern.

Hand Prick Stitch: The stitch used to hand finish a zipper application — similar to a small backstitch.

Hemming Stitch: A simple running hand stitch used to secure hems.

Hong Kong Finish: A narrow binding of fabric edges generally used as a seam finish.

Interfacing: Special fabric used to support garment edges and detail areas.

Intersecting Seams: Seams that cross each other — should be trimmed and pressed before stitching.

Lapped Seam: A topstitched seam finish where one layer of fabric laps over the other.

Layout Diagram: Diagram found on guide sheet showing the position of pattern pieces on the fabric.

Markings: The construction marks on a pattern such as notches, dots and squares to be transferred to garment pieces.

Master Pattern: Large, multi-size pattern designed to be traced off rather than used for cutting.

Miter: The diagonal seam at a corner.

Multi-Size Pattern: A pattern printed in more than one size on the same sheet of paper.

Muslin Shell: A basic garment made from muslin to be used during the fitting process.

Nap: The textured surface of a fabric with the fibers all lying in one direction.

Notch: Construction symbol on patterns; cutting wedges of fabric from a seam edge.

Notions: Tools and small items other than fabric which are used to complete a garment.

Open Dart: A wide dart without a center foldline; stitched like a seam.

Overcast Seam: A seam finish done by hand with an overcasting stitch or by machine with a zigzag stitch.

Pin Tucks: Very narrow tucks.

Pleats: Folds of fabric stitched in place to control fullness.

Pre-Shrink: Washing or steaming fabric to remove fiber shrinkage prior to cutting.

Seam Allowance: The width of fabric between the seamline and fabric edge.

Seam Finish: A technique used to handle the raw edge of a seam.

Seam Guide: A device attached to the bed of the machine or lines engraved on the throat plate used to measure seam widths.

Selvage: The finished lengthwise edge of woven fabrics.

Shank: A link between the button and fabric which allows room for the overlapping layer of fabric, made from thread or can be part of the button.

Slash: A straight cut into the fabric, longer than a clip.

Sleeve Cap: The upper, curved portion of a set-in sleeve.

Slip Baste: The basting together of two fabric layers using the slipstitch.

Slipstitch: A nearly invisible hand stitch used to hold two folded edges together or one folded edge to a flat layer of fabric.

Spaced Tucks: Narrow or wide tucks with wide spaces inbetween.

Standard Body Measurements: The measurements issued by the Bureau of Standards for the pattern industry.

Staystitch: Stitching used to support garment edges and prevent distortion during construction.

Stitch-In-The-Ditch: The technique of stitching in the seam well on the right side of the garment.

Tack: Layering two fabric layers together with a loose stitch.

Tailor Tacks: Thread loops used to transfer construction marks to fabric.

Thread Tracing: The technique of transferring fold or stitching lines to fabric with a long running stitch.

Topstitching: A decorative line of machine stitching.

Trim: The cutting away of excess fabric.

Underlining: A separate layer of fabric stitched into the garment seams for added support or thickness.

Under Collar: The underneath collar section or collar facing.

Understitch: A line of stitching along a faced edge which holds the facing in place.

Upper Collar: The top part of the collar that shows on the finished garment.

Welt Seam: A plain seam with both seam allowances pressed to one side and then held in place with one row of topstitching.

With Nap: A pattern layout with the tops of pieces all facing the same direction; to be used with napped fabrics.

Without Nap: Pattern layout with the tops of pattern pieces placed in both directions; to be used for fabrics without a nap.

Directory of Sources and Manufacturers

A

Allied National Inc.
13270 Capital Ave.
Oak Park, MI 48237

Allyn International
1244 Broadway
Denver, CO 80203

American Thread Co.
High Ridge Park
Stamford, CT 06905

Angel Aids
Box 162
El Toro, CA 92630

Authentic Patterns
P.O. Box 4560
Fort Worth, TX 76106

B

Belding Lily Co.
P.O. Box 88
Shelby, NC 28150

B. Blumenthal & Co.
140 Kero Rd.
Carlstadt, NJ 07072

Bo Sew Accents
P.O. Box 426
Woodland Hills, CA 91364

Boye Needle Co.
916 S. Arcade
Freeport, IL 61032

Brewer Sewing Supplies Co.
847 W. Jackson Blvd.
Chicago, IL 60607

Britex Fabrics
146 Geary St.
San Francisco, CA 94022

Brother International Corp.
8 Corporate Place
Piscataway, NJ 08854

Burda Patterns
2750 South Cobb Industrial Blvd.
Smyrna, GA 30080

Butterick Fashion Mktg.
161 Sixth Ave.
New York, NY 10013

C

C-Thru Ruler Co.
6 Britton Dr.
Bloomfield, CT 06002

Coats & Clark Sales Corp.
72 Cummings Point Rd.
Stamford, CT 06902

Conso Products — Div. of the Graber
   Co.
261 Fifth Ave.
New York, NY 10016

D

Dennison Mfg.
77 Ford Ave.
Framingham, MA 01701

Donahue Sales/Talon
41 E. 51st St.
New York, NY 10022

Donner Designs
P.O. Box 6747
Reno, NV 89513

E

Elizabeth Mohr Jones, Ph. D
122 Ulen Blvd.
Lebanon, IN 46052

Elna Sewing Machines - *see* White Co.

Henry A. Enrich & Co., Inc.
350 5th Ave.
New York, NY 10001

E-Z Buckle, Inc.
545 N. Arlington Ave.
East Orange, NJ 07017

F

Fabrics in Vogue, Ltd.
Suite 303 East
200 Park Avenue
New York, NY 10017

Fantastic Fit Products
1200 Mt. Diablo Blvd.
Walnut Creek, CA 94596

Fashion Services, Inc.
600 First Ave. North
Minneapolis, MN 55403

Fashionetics, Inc.
P.O. Box 146
Armonk, NY 10504

Folkwear
P.O. Box 98
Forrestville, CA 95436

G

General Electric, Small Appliances
   Div.
1285 Boston Ave.
Bridgeport, CT 06602

Gem Fabric Centers
5806 Burnet Rd.
Austin, TX 78756

Gingher, Inc.
P.O. Box 8865
Greensboro, NC 27410

Herbert Gladson, Ltd.
45 West 45th St.
New York, NY 10036

Greist Division, MITE Corp.
44 Blake St.
New Haven, CT 06515

J

Jacobson Products Co., Inc.
15537 Cabrito Rd.
Van Nuys, CA 91406

J. C. Penny Co.
1301 Avenue of the Americas
New York, NY 10019

Jean Hardy Pattern Co.
2151 La Cuesta Dr.
Santa Ana, CA 92705

JHB Imports, Inc.
1955 S. Quince
Denver, CO 80231

June Tailer, Inc.
P.O. Box 208
Richfield, WI 53076

K

Kingshead Corp.
P.O. Box 821
Hackensack, NJ 07602

Kwik Sew Pattern Co., Inc.
300 6th Avenue North
Minneapolis, MN 55401

L

Left Bank Fabric Co.
8354 West 3rd
Los Angeles, CA 90048

Leiter's
P.O. Box 978
Kansas City, MO 64141

Little Miss Muffet, Inc.
6709 Glenbrook Dr.
Knoxville, TN 31919

M

3M Minnesota Mining & Mfg. Co.
3M Center
St. Paul, MN 55101

Marks International
60 Wells Ave.
Newton, MA 02159

Maxant Corp.
117 S. Morgan
Chicago, IL 60617

Maxine Fabrics
417 Fifth Avenue
New York, NY 10016

McCall Pattern Co.
230 Park Ave.
New York, NY 10017

Mobilite, Inc.
100 Engineer's Rd.
Hauppauge, NY 11787

Molnlycke, Inc.
1415 Toulumne St.
Fresno, CA 93706

N

Natural Fiber Fabric Club
Dept. 521 Fifth Ave.
New York, NY 10017

Necchi - *see* Allied National, Inc.

Nelco Sewing Machine Co., Inc.
164 West 25th St.
New York, NY 10001

The New Home Sewing Machine Co.
171 Commerce Rd.
Carlstadt, NJ 07072

Normark Corp.
1710 East 78th St.
Minneapolis, MN 55423

O

Osrow Products Co.
303 Winding Rd.
Old Bethpage, NY 11804

P

Pellon Corp.
119 West 40th St.
New York, NY 10018

Penn Products Co.
963 Newark Ave.
Elizabeth, NJ 07207

Pfaff American Sales Corp.
610 Winters Ave.
Paramus, NJ 07652

R

Rex Cutlery
Subsidiary of Cole Consumer
   Products, Inc.
50 Inip Dr.
Inwood, L.I., NY 11696

Riccar America Co.
3184 Pullman St.
Costa Mesa, CA 92626

Risdon Mfg. Co., The
2100 S. Main St.
Waterbury, CT 06706

S

Save Time Enterprises
4302 Senisa Way
Irvine, CA 92715

Sawyer Brook
P.O. Box 194
Orford, NH 03777

Ferd. Schmetz Needle Corp.
240 Grand Ave.
Leonia, NJ 07605

Scovill Mfg. Co.
Sewing Notions Div.
P.O. Box 5028
Spartanburg, SC 29304

Sears, Roebuck and Co.
Sears Tower
Chicago, IL 60684

Sew Easy Lingerie, Inc.
1625 Hennepin Ave.
Minneapolis, MN 55403

The Sewing Corner
1313 S. Killian Dr.
Lake Park, FL 33403

Simplicity Pattern Co.
200 Madison Ave.
New York, NY 10016

The Singer Co.
30 Rockefeller Plaza
New York, NY 10020

Singer Sewing Machine Co.
321 First St.
Elizabeth, NJ 07207

Spadea
2 Bridge St.
Milford, NJ 08848

Stacy Fabrics Corp.
469 Seventh Ave.
New York, NY 10018

Standard Sewing Equipment Corp.
11740 Berea Rd.
Cleveland, OH 44111

Staple Sewing Aids Corp.
141 Lanza Ave.
Garfield, NJ 07026

SureFit Patterns
65 Oak St.
Norwood, NJ 07648

Swiss-Bernina, Inc.
534 W. Chestnut St.
Hinsdale, IL 60521

T

Talon - *see* Donahue Sales

Thai Silks
393 Main
Los Altos, CA 94022

Travco Plastics Co., Inc.
4718 Farragut Rd.
Brooklyn, NY 11203

U

United Cutlery & Hardware Products
   Co.
108 E. 16th St.
New York, NY 10003

Universal Sewing Notions, Inc.
2523 Andros Lane
Ft. Lauderdale, FL 33312

V

Viking Sewing Machine Co., Inc.
2300 Louisiana Ave. North
Minneapolis, MN 55427

W

White Sewing Machine Co.
11750 Berea Rd.
Cleveland, OH 44111

William E. Wright Co.
South St.
West Warren, MA 01092

Hugh H. Wilson Co.
Div. of Wilson Mfg. Co.
P.O. Box 247
Sunbury, PA 17801

Wiss - The Cooper Group
P.O. Box 728
Apex, NC 27502

Y

YKK U.S.A., Inc.
1251 Valley Brook Ave.
Linghurst, NJ 07071

Index

G

Garment repair, buyer's guide, 257-258
Gathered sleeve, 148
Gathers, 95-96
Girl's body measurements
   English, 15
   metric, 13
Girl's figure type, 9-10
Glossary of sewing terms, 311-312
Glue stick application, 82, 110, 151
Grading of seams, 84
Grainline, 55, 58, 226-227
Grain perfect fabric, 226-227
Grain, straightening of, 226-227
Greige goods, 226
Guide, seam, 78
Guide sheet, pattern, 57

H

Half-size figure type, 9-10
Half-size body measurements
   English, 14
   metric, 13
Hand needles, buyer's guide, 235-236
Hand sewing tools, buyer's guide, 243-244
Hand stitches
   catchstitch, 199
   hemming stitch, 199
   overcast, 197
   prickstitch, 160
   slip baste, 208
   slipstitch, 199
Hand overcast, 197
Hem finishes
   bound, 197
   Hong Kong, 198
   lace, 217
   overcast, 197
   pinked, 196
   turned and stitched, 196
Hemming tools, buyer's guide, 246-247
Hem techniques
   across pleats, 93
   double stitched, 200

fused, 201
hand stitched, 199-200
preparation, 196
pressing, 198
topstitched, 201
widths, 195
Hong Kong finish
   hems, 198
   seams, 79
Hooks and eyes, 159, 190-191

I

Inside hem technique, 200
Interfacing
   application of, 72-74, 97-98, 105, 114-115, 137, 163, 167, 179-180, 212, 220, 223, 227
   purpose of, 71
   selection of, 71, 212, 220, 223, 227
   types of, 71
Interlock knit fabric, 222
Intersecting seams, 77
Inverted pleat, 91
Invisible zippers
   with facing finish, 162
   without facing finish, 160-161
Iron, 66
Ironing board, 66
Iron-on (fusible) interfacing, 71-74

J

Junior body measurements
   English, 14
   metric, 13
Junior figure type, 9-10
Junior petite body measurements
   English, 14
   metric, 13
Junior petite figure type, 9-10

K

Keyhole buttonhole, 179
Knife pleat, 91
Knit fabrics
   cutting, 223

interfacing, 223
marking, 223
pattern layout, 223
pre-care, 222
pressing, 224
seam techniques, 80, 224
understanding, 222

L

Lace fabric
   hems, 217
   layout, 216
   marking, 216
   seam techniques, 216
   underlining, 215-216
Lapped seam, 82
Lapped zipper
   with facing finish, 157-159
   without facing finish, 156
Layering of seam allowances, 84
Layout, pattern
   border prints, 211
   diagonals, 210
   knits, 223
   lace, 216
   napped fabric, 219-220
   plaids, 204-207
   sheers, 212
   stripes, 209-210
Length adjustments, pattern, 21-22, 46
Lined patch pocket, 107-108
Linen, 225
Lining fabrics, 227
Loops, button, 212

M

Machine basting, 83
Machine buttonholes, 177-179
Machine hems, 201
Machine needles, buyer's guide, 236-237
Manmade fibers, 225-226
Marking techniques
   chalk pencil, 64
   pins, marking with, 64
   tailor's tacks, 65
   thread tracing, 65
   tracing paper and wheel, 63

R

Rayon, 225
Reading the pattern, 55-57
Reading the pattern envelope, 15-17
Reinforcing patterns, 18
Reinforcing pocket corners, 111
Relocating buttonholes, 175-177
Rolled collar
  one-piece, 119-121
  two-piece, 118-119

S

Satin weave, 226
Seam binding
  for hems, 197
  to extend seam allowance, 150
Seam bulk, reducing, 84
Seam finishes, 78-79
Seam guides, 78
Seam roll, 67, 70
Seamline, pattern, 56
Seams
  basic, 76
  double welt, 81
  knit, 80
  flat-felled, 81
  French, 82
  lapped, 82
  welt, 81
Seams for special fabrics
  knits, 80, 224
  lace, 216
  napped fabrics, 220
  plaids and stripes, 207-208
  sheers, 213
Seam techniques
  backstitching, 76
  clipping and notching, 84
  curved seams, 84
  enclosed seam, 84
  finishes, 78-79
  intersecting seams, 76
  knit, 80
  pressing, 77
  trimming and grading, 84-85

understitching, 85
  with ease, 86
Self-fastening tape, 193
Self-lined patch pocket, 108-109
Selvage, 58, 211, 219
Set-in sleeve application, 144-145
Sewing area, 5
Sewing boxes, buyer's guide, 247-248
Sewing machine needles, buyer's guide, 236-237
Sewing tapes, buyer's guide, 246
Shank buttons, 187, 189
Shankless buttons, 187, 188-189
Shaped facings, 98-100
Shaping bias, 102
Sheer fabrics
  cutting, 213
  dart techniques, 90, 214
  facings, 214
  hems, 212
  marking, 213
  pattern layout, 212
  stitching, 213
Shell, muslin fitting, 19, 31, 45, 50
Shirt collar, 123-126
Shirt sleeve application, 145-146
Shoulder adjustments, 24-26, 31-33
Silk, 225
Single knit fabric, 222
Size selection of patterns, 11-15
Skirt adjustments, 41-43
Sleeve board, 68
Sleeve cap
  alteration of, 142-143
  controlling ease, 144
Sleeves
  adjustment of pattern, 30-31, 142-143
  controlling of ease, 144
  gathered sleeve, 148
  modified shirt sleeve, 147
  set-in sleeve application, 144-145
  shirt sleeve application, 145-146
Sleeve vents
  bound, 132-133
  patch, 130-132
  tailored placket, 134-136
Slip basting, 208
Slipstitch, 199
Slot zipper
  with facing finish, 153-155
  without facing finish, 152-153

Snaps, 192-194
Snap tape, 194
Spaced tucks, 93
Spandex, 225
Special fabrics
  border prints, 211
  diagonals, 210
  knits, 221-224
  lace, 215-218
  napped, 218-221
  plaids, 202-208
  sheers, 212-214
  stripes, 208-210
Standard body measurement chart
  English, 14-15
  metric, 12-13
Standing collar
  one-piece, 121-122
  two-piece, 122-123
Staystitching, 76
Stitching-in-the-ditch, 101, 174, 186
Storage and sewing boxes, buyer's guide, 247-248
Stretch stitch, 80
Stripe fabric
  balanced stripes, 209
  layout, 209-210
  unbalanced stripes, 209
Suggested fabrics, 7, 17
Synthetic fibers, 225-226

T

Tailored placket sleeve vent, 134-136
Tailor's ham, 67, 70, 89, 119, 121
Tailor's tacks, 65, 213, 216, 220, 223
Taped seams, knits, 224
Tapes and trims, buyer's guide, 249-251
Teenage boy figure type, 9-10
Thread, buyer's guide, 248-249
Thread tracing, 65
Toddler's figure type, 9-10
Topstitched hem, 201
Topstitched seam, 80
Topstitching, 83
Tracing paper, marking with, 65
Tri-acetate, 225
Tricot knit, 226
Trimming seams, 84-85